Revolutionary Princeton 1774 - 1783:

The Biography of an American Town in the Heart of a Civil War

Other Books by William L. (Larry) Kidder

The Pleasant Valley School Story: A Story of Education and Community in Rural New Jersey (2012)
(Winner of the 2013 Scholarship and Artistry Award presented by the Country School Association of America)

A People Harassed and Exhausted: The Story of a New Jersey Militia Regiment in the American Revolution (2013)

Farming Pleasant Valley: 250 Years of Life in Rural Hopewell Township, New Jersey (2014)

Crossroads of the Revolution: Trenton, 1774-1783 (2017)

Ten Crucial Days: Washington's Vision for Victory Unfolds (2019)

Edited by William L. Kidder

Meet Your Revolutionary Neighbors (2015)

Book chapters by William L. Kidder

Revolutionary Princeton 1774 - 1783:

The Biography of an American Town in the Heart of a Civil War

by

William L. Kidder

A KNOX PRESS BOOK
ISBN: 978-1-68261-939-1
ISBN (eBook): 978-1-68261-940-7

Revolutionary Princeton 1774–1783:
The Biography of an American Town in the Heart of a Civil War

Cover Design by Ann Weinstock, A Tall Glass of Color

The scene on the cover is from "The Death of General Mercer at the Battle of Princeton, January 3, 1777" by John Trumbull, American, 1756–1843, Trumbull Colllection, Yale University Art Gallery, New Haven, CT. The center of the image focuses on Nassau Hall, at the colonial College of New Jersey, now Princeton University.

Permuted Press
New York • Nashville
permutedpress.com

Published in the United States of America

Acknowledgements

Friends in the local historical community in Mercer and surrounding counties have provided inspiration and support in many ways through their many discussions, inquiries, and offers of help. I would especially note members of the Princeton Battlefield Society and the staff of the Historical Society of Princeton, especially Paul Davis, who were very enthusiastic about this project and always offered support. I very much appeciate the guidance of Elizabeth Allen at the Morven Museum and Garden in dealing with the myths associated with the house and its occupants. As always, Richard Patterson, Executive Director of the Old Barracks Museum and members of his staff provided support and encouragement. Will Krakower, Historical Educator at the Princeton Battlefield State Park was also both helpful and encouraging. In many ways this book began from conversations with Will about the Thomas Clarke house and farm and how it should be highlighted in interpretations of the battlefield.

Librarian Kathie Ludwig, and her husband David, once again not only provided help with the resources of the David Library of the American Revolution, but also many conversations that kept me thinking about how to present the story. This is the fourth book I have written that relied heavily on the resources of the David Library as well as the comradery and encouragement received from staff, volunteers, and fellow researchers. The move of the David Library to Philadelphia feels much like the loss of a good friend even though the resources will continue to be available.

Once again, the New Jersey State Archives provided a vast array of important documents and the staff always made visits there productive and pleasant.

The Princeton University Library Special Collections staff made available a number of manuscripts and made using them an enjoyable experience.

Fellow historians and writers who gave of their time to read early versions of the manuscript and offer advice or point out errors include: John Beakes, John Lawrence Brasher, Paul Davis, Rick Herrera, Kimberly McCarty, and David Price.

I am greatly indebted to my publisher, Roger S. Williams, for his continuous enthusiasm and support for this project. As always, it has been a joy to work with him.

As always, I must thank my wife, Jane, for putting up with my concentration on this project that must have seemed an all-consuming obsession at times. And, I cannot omit acknowledging the continuing contributions of my cat, Izzy, who so enjoys being with me when I work that she literally tells me to get to work each day. As usual, she is with me as I write this.

I must acknowledge the people who have attended my many talks over the past several years about subjects related to New Jersey in the Revolution. Their wide variety of questions have made me think and look at things in different ways. The continuous thinking stimulated by those questions played an important role in the development of this story.

While all these people, and no doubt others I have failed to mention, helped me develop and improve this work, any errors are solely my responsibility and I welcome having them pointed out to me.

Author's Note

While some readers enjoy dealing with the characteristics of 18th century documents, I have generally modernized spelling and punctuation in quotations. This is done so that readers can more easily focus on the ideas and information expressed without distraction.

Maps have been created and included to help the reader visualize the geography, settlement patterns, and evets mentioned in the text. To make the maps readable, while they do have an accurate distance scale, the exact location and scale of structures has not been possible to achieve and not all buildings have been included. The maps show details to the best knowledge of the author based on his best interpretation of the resources available to him. Our understanding of the past is always a developing subject and it is author's hope that the maps, as well as the text, will encourage further research.

Contents

Maps

Illustrations

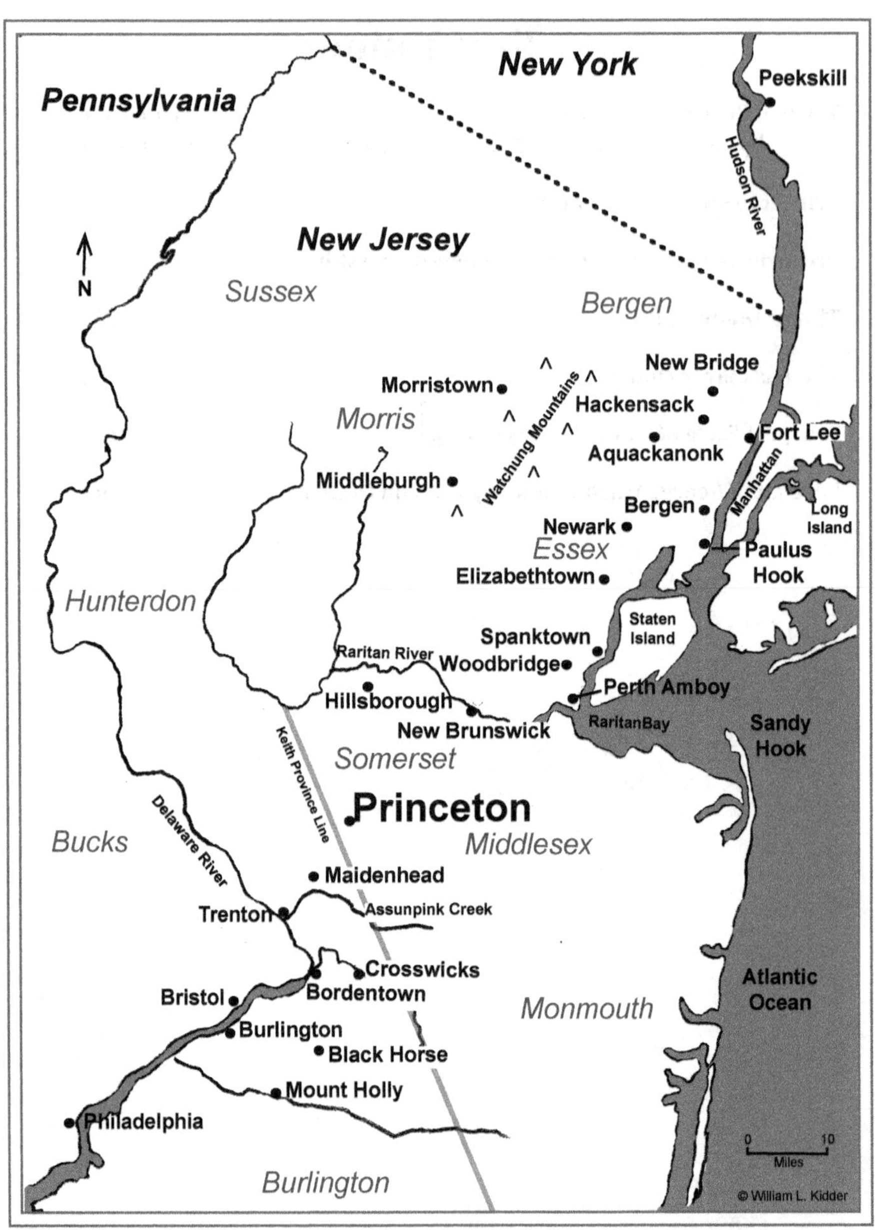

Map 1: Central and Northern New Jersey - 1774 - 1783

Two proprietary colonies, East Jersey and West Jersey, were united in 1704 into the one royal colony of New Jersey. The line dividing them was drawn several times and one is still evident today as part of civic boundaries and roads. During the War for Independence, New Jersey had two capitals, Burlington, and Perth Amboy.

Introduction

Around 9:00 a.m. on the bitterly cold Friday, January 3, 1777, the terrifying sounds of musket and cannon fire made by several thousand soldiers finally diminished and became more distant. Thirty-four-year-old farmer Thomas Clarke and his twenty-four-year-old sister Sarah, their twenty-eight-year-old enslaved woman Susannah, and nineteen-year-old French Huguenot farmhand David de la Force, cowering in the shelter of their farmhouse in the Stony Brook community just south of the village of Princeton, New Jersey, all felt tremendous relief. Following their farmer's routine, they had awakened early to start the farm chores that bitterly cold morning when they unexpectedly heard and then saw a long column of American Continental soldiers and militiamen marching up the little-used dirt road that passed the front of their house. As they watched, several hundred soldiers turned left from the column and marched across crop stubble and winter wheat shoots on their frozen farm fields and the adjacent icy cropland and bare orchard of their forty-one-year-old brother, William. In horror, these peaceful Quakers watched an intense battle flare up when those American troops ran into about five hundred British troops coming toward them from the Post Road connecting Princeton and Trenton. The resulting combat ended in less than an hour, but the fighting had been very heavy near their houses, with an occasional British bullet peppering a wall while they cowered inside. As the sounds of battle became more distant, Thomas and Sarah's great relief suddenly changed to shocked sadness when several American soldiers came to their door carrying wounded, heavily bleeding men, including one identified as a high-ranking officer. The peaceful Quaker siblings accommodated these injured men in their home, knowing there must be more wounded and dead outside lying on their fields.

This short battle was just one event in a decade-long conflict experienced by the people of Princeton that brought them and their fellow Americans freedom from the acts of a distant Parliament as citizens of a new nation. Stories of battles like the one at Princeton on January 3, 1777, provide exciting reading, but the often-overlooked stories of local people who experienced the events leading up to, during, and following those battles are also compelling and profoundly human. The War for Independence was much more than just a series of clashes between opposing military forces. The American army that was ultimately victorious and provided the conditions for fruitful peace negotiations required the support of the general population. That army was a continual experiment in military structure, use, and support. Many people contributed to or were affected by the efforts to create and support the military, even though they did not participate in even one battle. Looking back, it is easy for us to pick out those who made the "correct" decisions, but at the time when those decisions were being made, no one knew what their effect would be. As a fact of life, we human beings live immersed in situations and events that we have little or no control over and must decide how to mold our lives in ways we hope will allow us to survive as comfortably as possible and be honored by history. The chapters that follow explore stories of the people of Princeton between the years 1774 and 1783 to help us understand how the American Revolution affected people of that time, including those whose names, like most people's, don't have a prominent place in surviving history. We can imagine ourselves in their situation, or in similar circumstances today, and thereby learn a little more about what it means to be a human being.

This story is a case study of life during the Revolution, and the author hopes it will inspire others to develop the stories of other groups of people in different locations. As we will see here, the nature of its citizens and its geographic location greatly influenced the story of Princeton. The cultures, beliefs, practices, and histories of those we live among influence our lives today and the geographic position of our homes put us in direct or indirect contact with significant events beyond our control. The purpose of this book is to raise questions in the minds of its readers about their own lives as much as it is to tell a true, fascinating story, seemingly with only local interest, about the Revolution.

The Settlement and Development of the Princeton Area

Just a hundred years before our story begins, travelers described the area of west-central New Jersey as a wilderness through which a Native American trail ran connecting the Raritan and Delaware Rivers. Europeans began to settle the territory that became Princeton in the late 1600s. James, Duke of York, brother of King Charles II, granted the land that would become

New Jersey to Sir George Carteret and Lord John Berkeley, in 1664 after the British victory in the First Anglo-Dutch War. Already home to Dutch families, the northeastern portion of that land quickly began receiving new settlers, including New England Puritans, Baptists, and Quakers, who never fully recognized the claims of proprietors Carteret and Berkeley. When his stressful dealings with these settlers bankrupted him, Berkeley sold his portion in 1674 to a group of Quaker investors, including William Penn, who developed the colony of West Jersey, leaving Carteret with East Jersey, which he later sold to Scottish investors. The two proprietary colonies united as one royal colony in 1702. However, the proprietors of East and West Jersey retained significant power, the province maintained two capitals, Perth Amboy in the East and Burlington in the West, and the two regions developed distinctive cultures. East Jersey settlers looked culturally and economically to New York, while Philadelphia influenced West Jersey settlers, both economically and religiously, as home to the Philadelphia Yearly Meeting that oversaw the West Jersey Quakers.[1] The fertile soil of William Penn's land on the western edge of East Jersey attracted Quakers seeking a place to practice their religion without the fear-inspiring prejudice they had experienced in Anglican England and then Puritan New England. Because the boundary between East and West Jersey was unclear for many years and disputes over land deeds arose, Surveyor-General George Keith surveyed and established a Province Line between the two provinces in 1686–87 to help settle those disputes.[2]

The area that became Princeton developed on the east side of Keith's Province Line, and settlement began in the early 1680s with the arrival of Henry Greenland and then his son-in-law Daniel Brinson from Burlington, who purchased 424 acres near today's Kingston in 1686. John Horner followed in 1695, purchasing five hundred acres located between today's Washington and Harrison Streets. In 1696, John Houghton purchased land, and Richard Stockton (ancestor of the signer of the Declaration of Independence) purchased some property from Brinson. The same year, Benjamin Clarke, a native of Scotland living in Piscataway, New Jersey, purchased twelve hundred acres on the western side of today's Princeton, and William Olden of Piscataway bought four hundred acres from him. Joseph Worth acquired two hundred acres from Benjamin Clarke in 1697, most if not all on the south side of Stony Brook in the vicinity of the mills that bear his name. The same year, another early settler, Benjamin FitzRandolph, came from Piscataway, where he had been a neighbor of Benjamin Clarke and purchased 316 acres between today's Alexander Street and Washington Road from John Horner and Richard Stockton.[3]

The region became known as Stony Brook[4] and was a frontier region located between two waves of population advance. One stream flowed west from the area of the Raritan and Millstone Rivers near Piscataway in East Jersey. The other flowed east along the tributaries of the Delaware River, where Quakers had landed at Burlington in 1677/1678 and began settling Trenton, Nottingham, and Chesterfield in West Jersey. The developing Stony Brook/Princeton community drawing settlers from East Jersey was advantageously located about halfway between New Brunswick at the head of navigation on the Raritan River, and Trenton at the head of navigation on the Delaware River, and therefore midway between the growing seaports of New York and Philadelphia. The main thoroughfare, an old Indian trail, which developed between New Brunswick and Trenton, bisected the Stony Brook land. This road connected with others leading north to New York and the New England colonies and south to Philadelphia and the Southern provinces, providing easy access to markets for farmers' produce and bringing them items required to support their daily lifestyle. The road became known by several names, including the Upper Road, the Post Road, or the King's Highway.

The settlement grew as families divided the land between their members, sold property to newcomers, and began to build businesses. The Stony Brook settlement soon stretched east from the Keith Line to today's Harrison Street in Princeton and centered on Worth's Mill. In 1712, Thomas Potts, a miller from Pennsylvania, received rights to dig a mill-pond and raceway leading from it, and two years later, Joseph Worth sold six and one-quarter acres to Potts, who then built two grist mills and a bolting mill under one roof. In 1715, Potts sold one-fourth of this mill to Joseph Worth and one-fourth to carpenter Joseph Chapman, who sold the remaining one-half to Joseph Worth in 1716. Also, in 1716, Joseph Chapman purchased from Samuel Stockton fifteen acres adjacent to the mill lot and sold it, for one-fourth share in the mill complex, to Joseph Worth in 1721. The grist mills provided a source of animal feed and flour for the early settlers in the area. The mill pond was "a beautiful sheet of water, shaded by tall trees on either side of it," located a "considerable distance above" the mill that local people "resorted to for the amusements of fishing, boating, bathing, and skating."[5] After 1721, someone added a cooper's shop. Matthew Clarke added a tannery and shoe shop in the 1760s, and by 1767, William Clarke constructed a blacksmith shop. As the community developed, the Clarke, Worth, and Olden families continued to form a close community of in-laws, siblings, and cousins. The name Stony Brook referred to the complete area of settlement until the village of Princeton received its name in 1724.

According to the journal of early settler Nathaniel FitzRandolph, the name Princetown came into use when the first house was raised there by James Leonard in 1724. The name worked well with the small nearby villages established at Kingstown (now Kingston), Queenstown, and Princessville. These names reflected the loyalty to the British crown that was strong in the area until the mid-1770s.[6] The Stony Brook name then referred only to the southern portion of the development. In the late 1730s, the first bridge was built over the Stony Brook at Worth's Mill, about the same time that a stage wagon began to run twice a week between Trenton and New Brunswick in response to the growing importance of this thoroughfare.

The Stony Brook and Princeton lands straddled two counties dating back to the 1680s. The division line between Somerset County on the northwest side of the line and Middlesex County on the southeast side ran basically down the middle of the main street of Princeton village and, with some variation, for several miles on the same road toward New Brunswick and Trenton as far as the Keith Province Line. Residents residing on land on the north side of the county line lived in Montgomery Township and looked to the village of Somerville, eighteen miles distant, for county court concerns. Residents on the south side of the line belonged to West Windsor Township and looked to New Brunswick, sixteen miles distant, as their county seat. This division made life a bit awkward for residents when dealing with county political matters, such as taxes, business licenses, and militia formation. However, it provided Princeton the opportunity, if not always the reality, to have more representatives in the colonial Assembly than towns existing within a single county.

The Stony Brook Quakers, also known as Friends, organized a local meeting to gather at least once a week for services, and their growing community needed a house of worship. In 1709 Benjamin Clarke conveyed about nine and three-fifths acres to Richard Stockton and others to build a meetinghouse and establish a burial ground. After many years of holding meetings at Joseph Worth's home, they constructed a meetinghouse in 1724, and by 1730 there was also a schoolhouse on the lot. When the meetinghouse burned down in 1760, the men immediately rebuilt it. The Stony Brook Preparatory Meeting was part of the Chesterfield Monthly Meeting held at Crosswicks, where members recorded births, deaths, marriages, new members, and member dismissals. The Friends traveled to Crosswicks in Burlington County to attend monthly meetings, and the road that developed to connect the Stony Brook Meetinghouse with the Chesterfield Meetinghouse at Crosswicks became known as the Quaker Road.

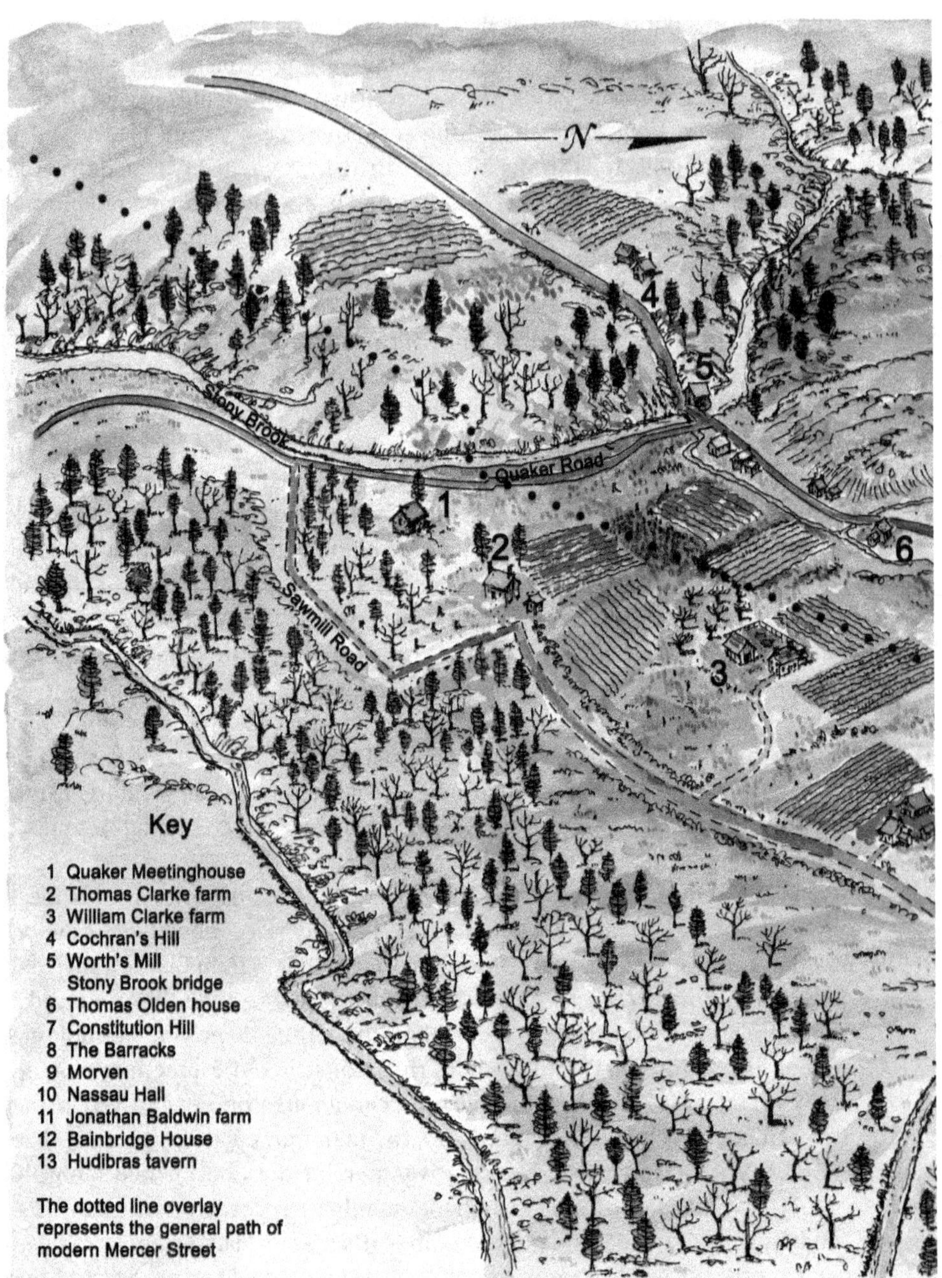

Map 2: Princeton and Stony Brook about 1774

An artist's impression by John R. Wright

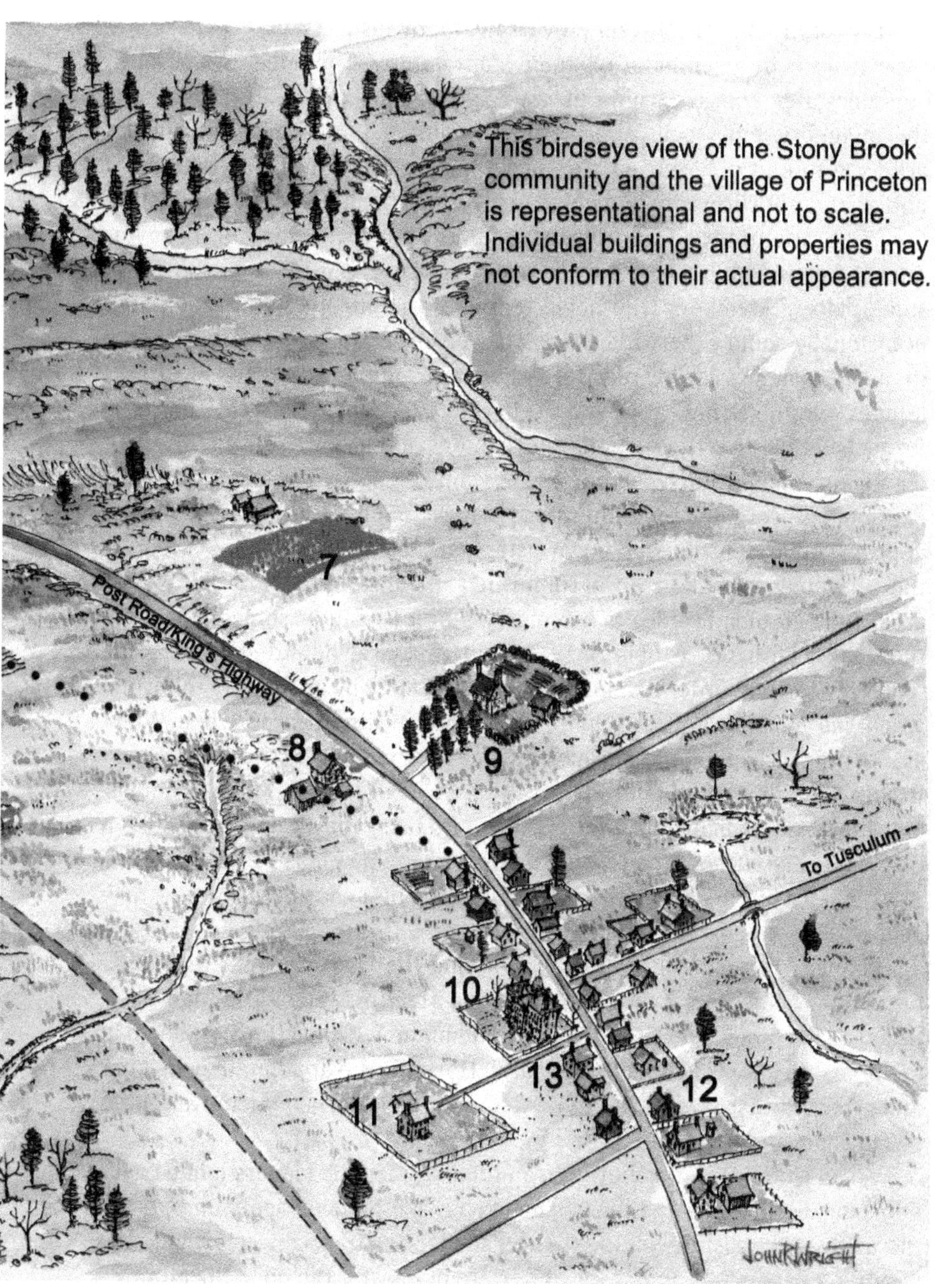
This birdseye view of the Stony Brook community and the village of Princeton is representational and not to scale. Individual buildings and properties may not conform to their actual appearance.
7
Post Road/King's Highway
8
9
To Tusculum
10
13
12
11
JOHN R WRIGHT

The Stony Brook Quakers oversaw many aspects of everyday life experienced by members of their community. The Meeting minutes contain statements regarding how well "love and unity subsists" among the members, how "evil reports" are discouraged, and that "endeavours are used to end differences." Not attending meetings brought community notice, and not surprisingly, week-day meetings had the lowest attendance. Constant attention effectively reduced any "indecencies" in behavior during meetings, but leaders noted that "drowsiness" was "too prevalent in some places." Members who neglected attending meeting more than very occasionally could expect to have to answer for it. Members were expected to avoid playing cards, making wagers, drinking excessive spirituous liquors, administering oaths, and the like. In 1774 it was noted by the Stony Brook Meeting that "the customs and fashions of the world prevail too much among us, moderation & temperance is wanting tho' care is taken."

Couples presented their intentions to marry and submitted to having the appropriateness of their union investigated, and then witnesses attended the ceremony to make sure it conformed to Quaker standards. Problems arose when a member desired to marry a first cousin or someone outside the Quaker faith. On October 5, 1769, Hannah Clarke admitted to marrying "contrary to good order to a man not of our society by an hireling minister" when she married Robert White.[7] The problem disappeared when White successfully asked to join the Quakers and became quite active in the Stony Brook Meeting. Hannah and Robert lived adjacent to her siblings Thomas, Matthew, and William Clarke, on a lot bordering the Post Road. William Clarke and his wife, Ann, had found themselves condemned in 1772 for "being married by a hireling priest, and likewise being first cousins." However, they achieved forgiveness and remained in the Stony Brook Meeting.[8]

People expressing an interest in joining the Quakers went through a process to be accepted. From Stony Brook Meeting, Widow Hannah Clark requested in January 1774 that her granddaughter, Rachel Hunt, be taken in membership. Catherine Olden and Sarah Horner were appointed to visit her and reported that she proved to be "a tender spirit." The Meeting accepted her in February.[9]

When charging a member with an offense, meeting leaders made every effort to investigate "in the spirit of meekness," without partiality, and to seek the truth as the test in judging them. The Meeting took care to provide the poor with necessities. In one effort to raise money for the poor, the Monthly Meeting designated Isaac Clark of Stony Brook to be one of the collectors. If a local meeting came under discussion because of some irregularity in its doings, a member from another meeting might be assigned to help it get back on track. The Monthly Meeting chose several members to attend the Quarterly Meeting, where problems at lower levels could be adjusted. Maintaining harmony within the community was a significant concern. Over the years, Stony Brook Meeting members Joseph Horner and Benjamin Clarke often attended the Quarterly Meeting representing the Chesterfield Monthly Meeting. Samuel Worth was assigned to be one of the men to look into the issue of a man accused of having relations with another man's wife and that man assaulting him on the highway.[10]

The Quarterly Meeting reported to the Philadelphia Yearly Meeting that worked to maintain consistency among all the preparatory meetings, like Stony Brook.[11] Like all Quaker meetings, Stony Brook received warnings from the Yearly Meeting "to watch for evidence of superfluity of dress, furnishings, and houses. Young women were warned to avoid 'Broidered Hair or Gold or Pearls or Costly Array,' and young men 'needless furniture' for their horses. Friends must also guard against 'being vainly exalted or puffed up,' drinking to excess, keeping unseasonable company, falling into debt, going to court to settle disputes, and selling inferior wares."[12] These Quaker farmers and craftsmen were prosperous but not interested in making a show of wealth or of seeking high office. They lived comfortably but did not display magnificent homes, expensive furniture, or other signs of wealth.

Like other people at that time throughout the British colonies, Quakers often employed indentured servants and owned enslaved persons, even though they were leading the movement to treat slaves as human beings and to emancipate them.[13] Concerns among Quakers in West Jersey about the ethics of slavery first appeared in 1688 when the Germantown, Pennsylvania Quakers wrote up an anti-slavery petition. From that time until the years of the Revolution, Quakers debated how they could enslave individuals of African descent while firmly believing in the spiritual equality of all humans. The debate led to increasing abolitionist expressions, protests, and actions, including among the Princeton-area Quakers.[14] Quakers manumitted many slaves, including ones at Princeton, during the 1770s.[15]

While early Stony Brook residents were primarily Quakers, Presbyterianism became prevalent throughout the area as the population grew. The Presbyterians were not strongly anti-slavery at this point, and some Quakers may have converted to escape criticism for owning slaves. Commenting on the enslaved people around Princeton, Presbyterian Reverend John Witherspoon, president of the college in Princeton, a slave owner himself, noted rather casually, if not defensively, that "Negroes are exceedingly well used, being fed and clothed as well as any free persons who live by daily labour."[16]

Some Congregationalist New England families converted to Presbyterianism and relocated to Long Island and then to New Jersey. By the 1750s, members of the Stockton family and some other early Quaker settlers had converted to Presbyterianism, while others had not. The increased Presbyterian settlement in the Princeton area took place at the height of Scotch-Irish immigration from North Ireland, during which about one-third of its population sailed to America between 1731 and 1768, with many settling in New Jersey.[17]

Crops grown by the Quaker and Presbyterian farmers in the rich clay loam covering red sandstone on the farms around Princeton and Stony Brook included wheat, rye, barley, Indian corn, buckwheat, flax, and hemp. Farmers also grew small amounts of tobacco for their own and their slaves' use. Economically, Rev. John Witherspoon, believed, "The productions of New Jersey, and the source of its wealth, are grain of every kind.... Horses, cattle, salted beef and pork, and poultry. In times of peace, great quantities of all these are sent to the West Indies, and flax-seed to Europe." Never entirely self-sufficient, New Jersey imported tea, sugar, wine, spirits, and all types of cloth.[18] Although an agricultural revolution had begun in England about 1750, it had not spread very profoundly into the British colonies by the 1770s. One New Jersey farmer who was experimenting and looking for agricultural improvement judged that New Jersey farmers refused "to leave the beaten road of their ancestors" and were "averse to running any risque at all." A treatise on animal husbandry published in England in 1775 stated that "The American planters and farmers are in general the greatest slovens in Christendom." In general, they reportedly did little to restore overworked soil by using manure, crop rotation, root crops, and legumes.[19]

Several residents of the village and Stony Brook area provided services to the farmers as millers, artisans, and merchants, or provided services to travelers as well as the local population as doctors, lawyers, or innkeepers. While Princeton was primarily an agricultural community, its farmers and artisans represented a range of wealth, and the village—with its college, established in 1756—attracted wealthier people interested in education and a sophisticated social environment.[20]

Influenced by the Great Awakening, Presbyterianism had split into "Old Light" traditionalists and "New Light" reformers who focused on the need for having a profound spiritual experience, a new birth, to ensure salvation. The Princeton area drew mostly "New Light" Presbyterians. "New Light" Presbyterians organized the Presbytery of New Brunswick in 1738, breaking from the "Old Light" Philadelphia Presbytery. While Quakers and

Presbyterians got along very well, Quakers tended to characterize the Stony Brook area and Presbyterians the village.

Presbyterianism played a vital role in the development of the College of New Jersey at Princeton. First chartered in 1746 by the New York Presbytery, the college first met at Elizabethtown in the home of its first president, Jonathan Dickinson. When Reverend Aaron Burr became its second president, it moved to his parsonage in Newark. When Jonathan Belcher became governor of New Jersey in 1748, he took an interest in the college and granted it a permanent charter. In 1752, the trustees of the college meeting at Newark voted to relocate the college because they wanted to find a less populated location nearer to the center of the province and "more sequestered from the various temptations attending a promiscuous converse with the world, that theatre of folly and dissipation." The trustees considered both New Brunswick and Princeton, but the people of Princeton complied with certain conditions first. These included providing £1000 proclamation money,[21] ten acres of cleared land contiguous to the proposed college buildings, and two hundred acres of woodland within three miles of town.

Princeton residents who helped bring the college to their village were John Stockton (father of Richard Stockton the signer), Thomas Leonard (a trustee of the college), John Horner, and Nathaniel FitzRandolph, all large landowners from families that had helped create the settlement over several generations. Each man contributed to the required sum of money and solicited contributions from others. Stockton and Leonard gave two hundred acres of woodland a mile or so north of the village, and Horner gave seven acres of cleared land nearby. The trustees voted on January 24, 1753, to accept Princeton as soon as "Mr. [Fitz]Randolph has given a deed for a certain tract of land four hundred feet front and thirty poles [495 feet] depth, in lines at right angles with the broad street where it is proposed that the College shall be built." The next day, Nathaniel FitzRandolph and his wife Rebeckah presented the trustees with a deed for "a certain plot of land bounded Northward by the King's Highway, and containing about four acres and a half," for the college building and a president's house.[22]

In addition to seeking a Presbyterian college for their town, the residents of Princeton in 1755 obtained permission from the Presbytery of New Brunswick to build a church. However, a delay in construction meant the college chapel served as a Presbyterian church, without an ordained pastor and ruling elders until about 1766 when the church building, on land purchased from the college, became functional.[23]

Colonial Governor Jonathan Belcher backed the college's move to Princeton and was always remembered gratefully for it. The trustees named the primary college building, Nassau Hall, in honor of King William III, Count of Nassau, at the suggestion of Belcher when he declined to allow the building to bear his name. Groundbreaking for Nassau Hall took place in 1753, and workers completed its construction in 1756. The Presbyterian schism was a factor in the calling of John Witherspoon to head the college. In Scotland, he had become well known for his "New Side" beliefs and ability to work with people. After he accepted the college presidency and took charge in 1768, one of his first contributions to his new home was to help bring the two factions together. No longer fighting so much with each other, Presbyterians would be free to focus their attention on the problems just beginning to create animosity between the colonies and the British government.[24]

Those problems started with differences that arose during and after the French and Indian War. In 1758, Princeton citizens petitioned to have a military barracks built to reduce the use of private homes for lodging soldiers, and the petition was signed by Quaker John Clarke, father of Thomas and William and their siblings, along with members of the Worth and Olden families of Stony Brook. While the colonial government did not construct a barracks in Princeton, a stone house that became known as "the barracks" on today's Edgehill Street may have served that purpose at some point in the eighteenth century.

By 1774 when our story begins, New Jersey's population was approaching one hundred and thirty thousand. It was one of the smaller British North American colonies; only four of the other twelve had fewer inhabitants. Neighboring Hunterdon County with 15,500 people was the most populous New Jersey county, while Middlesex had about 11,500. For the most part, the Quaker farmers did not get involved in the political discussions and activities that were becoming more and more heated. People were generally content because the province was prosperous. As a predominantly rural society, New Jersey was home to people who were more concerned with what was happening on their farms than with political discussions. Their Royal Governor, William Franklin, was a colonial, the son of Benjamin Franklin, and generally respected for his actions in office. The focus of the colonial Assembly had been more on local concerns than matters of the more extensive empire.[25] However, several Presbyterians of the village were among the leaders in New Jersey of the rising protests against acts of Parliament that affected all the colonies.[26]

The very diverse, relatively peaceful farming and college settlement at Princeton was poised, along with the thirteen British North American colonies in general, to become immersed in the earth-shattering events that took place during the decade that began in 1774.

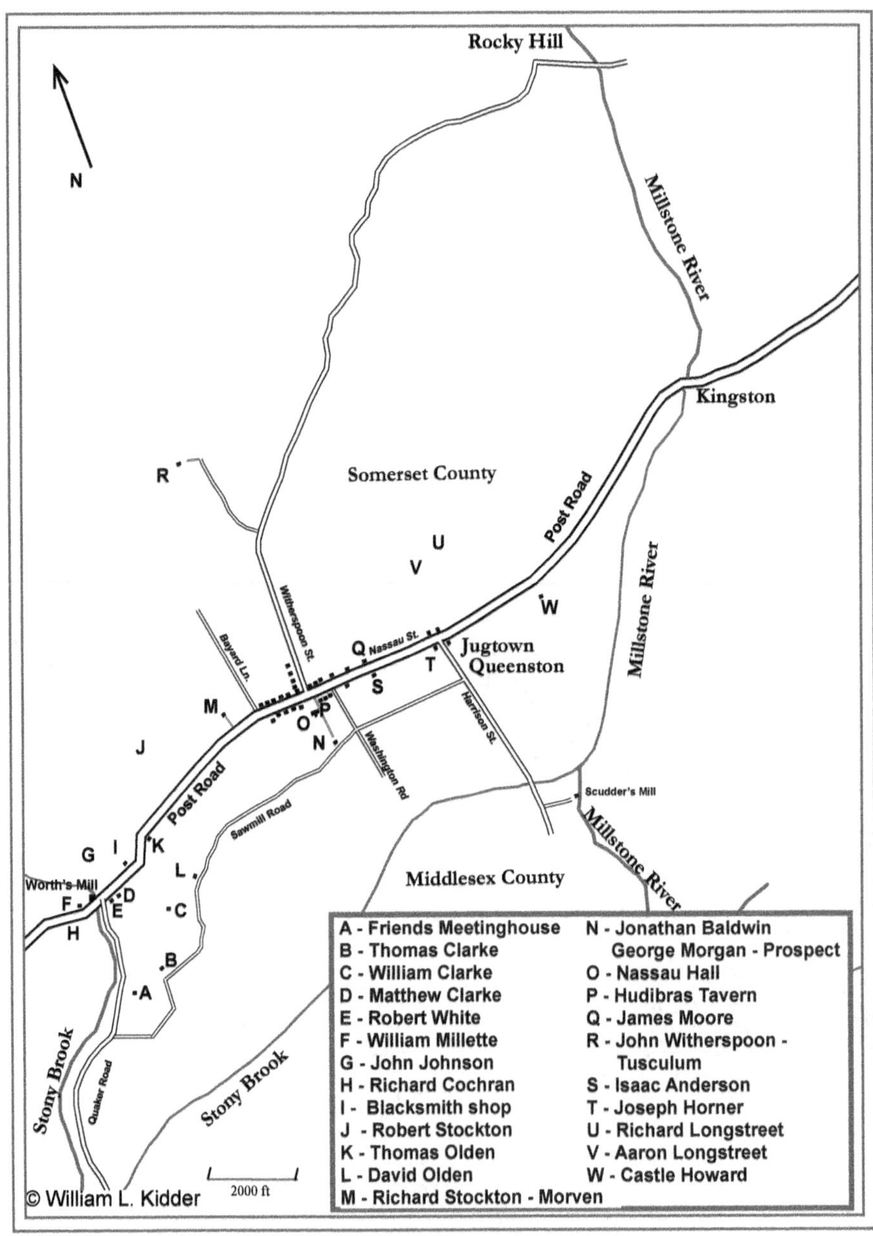

Map 3: Greater Princeton - 1774 1783

Chapter 1

1774

Over the prior decade, many residents of Princeton, like many people in the thirteen British North American colonies, had become increasingly concerned about acts passed by the distant British Parliament that affected their lives. The resultant protest actions, however, came more under the heading of news than something in which people were actively involved. The rising tide of protests against these acts reached flood level on December 13, 1773, when protestors acted out their disgust with a small tax on tea and destroyed a shipment of it in Boston Harbor. Parliament reacted by passing increasingly objectionable laws that accelerated cooperation among the people of the thirteen North American colonies to resist them. New Jersey had not been an active leader in the early protests, but this was about to change, and Princeton residents would make life-changing decisions when forced to pick a side to support.

Protests in Princeton

One night in late January, a few days after Paul Revere rode through Princeton spreading the news about the destruction of tea in Boston Harbor,[1] College of New Jersey students held their own protest against the tax of imported tea. Several boys broke into the college steward's storeroom, took out the winter supply of tea, and then went from room to room, removing all privately owned tea. They destroyed the tea in a bonfire built in the yard in front of Nassau Hall while tolling the school bell and making "many spirited resolves." Other students enthusiastically burned effigies of Massachusetts Governor Thomas Hutchinson, "amidst the repeated acclamations of a large crowd of spectators." Not everyone in the village agreed with the boys' actions, and tempers flared on both sides. Innkeeper William Hick, whose inn stood across the street from the college, drew negative attention to himself by making pro-government remarks that others in the assembled crowd found obnoxious.[2] College senior Samuel Leake became so emotionally caught up that he somehow insulted a college trustee, possibly local lawyer Richard Stockton, who came by and calmly tried to break up the "riotous proceedings."[3] Afterward, *The Pennsylvania Gazette* reported that "we hear from Princeton, in New Jersey, that the officers and students of the college, have unanimously agreed to drink no more TEA." This protest differed from the one in Boston in that the tea destroyed was already purchased and, therefore, not subject to the new tax.[4]

Heated debates continued over the following months, and at least some people began to advocate for separation from England through the united action of the thirteen colonies, even though they had little idea of what kind of government would develop in the independent country. Each man's first loyalty was to his province as a part of the British Empire, but any concept of a central governmental structure for the thirteen colonies was vague at best.[5] Everyone faced the question, was it better to be a citizen of the greatest nation and empire of its time that they knew, or break away only with the hope that they could develop something even better?

New Jersey had been slow to engage in the increasingly contentious protests. However, by 1774, many men serving in New Jersey's colonial Assembly found themselves in a delicate position. They were attempting to provide good government for their citizens while at the same time wanting to cooperate with the multi-colony movement protesting questionable acts of Parliament. At the Assembly's February 8 meeting at Burlington, regular legislative business included the presentation of a petition from "divers Freeholders of the Western Precinct of the County of Somerset, praying to be relieved from the burden of maintaining" the bridge over Stony Brook at Worth's Mill just south of Princeton. The same day, in reaction to the multi-colony tea protest, the Assembly agreed unanimously to participate in "mutual Correspondence and Intercourse with our Sister Colonies." It appointed a ten-man Standing Committee of Correspondence and Inquiry to "obtain the most early and authentic intelligence of all Acts and Resolutions of the Parliament of Great Britain, or the Proceedings of Administration that may have any relation to, or may affect the liberties and privileges of His Majesty's Subjects in the British Colonies in America." This committee would work with similar ones in the other colonies to address common issues relating to the collective rights and liberties of the colonies.[6]

Royal Governor William Franklin came to Princeton often because of his work with the college trustees, and between April 19 and 21, he attended the first two days of a trustee meeting at Nassau Hall. The Board appointed local trustee, lawyer, and graduate of the college Richard Stockton to examine the school's property deeds to determine the eastern line of the college land so he could direct the college steward where and how far to construct a fence toward the street. Then, in a sign of the times, the trustees examined the case of student Samuel Leake, the student who had recently insulted a trustee at the students' tea protest, and revoked his previously designated honor as class salutatorian at the upcoming commencement.[7]

The trustees raised their concern that the college kitchen was not suited to serve as the dwelling for the steward. The Board wanted the steward, who provided food and other services to the students, to live there and authorized spending up to thirty pounds proclamation money for modifications. They recommended removing the chimney, constructing two new stacks (one at each end of the building with fireplaces on both the ground and upper floors), dividing the first floor into two rooms and the second floor into four, and adding a door between the kitchen and bakehouse. They ordered Steward Elias Woodruff, who had come from Elizabethtown and lived across the street from the college with his wife and six children, to undertake this work.[8] The trustees had appointed Woodruff on September 23, 1773, to replace Princeton resident Jonathan Baldwin, who had resigned on April 21.

Baldwin was born about 1731 in Newark and had graduated from the college in 1755. He received a Master of Arts degree in 1757. Taking up residence in Princeton, he served as steward from 1759 until his resignation. About 1760, Baldwin married Sarah Sergeant, born about 1736, daughter of Jonathan Sergeant and sister of Jonathan Dickinson Sergeant, and by 1774 they had two daughters and a son.[9] Baldwin lived on his farm, located behind the college. His farmhouse stood where Prospect House is today. As steward, Baldwin was to maintain the physical condition of the college and its students. Like anyone trying to satisfy the food preferences of college students, he had not always received high evaluations from them.

Just before his resignation, when some students grew tired of receiving butter they judged to be inedible, student William Smith wrote that "some of the students to be up with him made his image of butter and hung it up by the neck in the dining room." When Baldwin came in, Smith carried "it over to him and let him see it, which I believe does not sit very easy upon his stomach."[10] The butter incident was just one rather mild complaint Baldwin dealt with during his tenure. At the other extreme, an arsonist had set fire to and destroyed his barn in 1772.[11] When resigning, Baldwin said he wanted to devote more time to his farm and also participate more actively in the rising political protests.

Paul Revere rode through town again in mid-May, carrying news about the Boston Port Act from the Boston Committee of Correspondence to Philadelphia. He also distributed copies of a broadside printed on black-bordered paper decorated with a skull and crossbones and a liberty cap. This broadside proclaimed the Boston Committee's call for a ban on all British imports in response to Parliament forbidding ships to load or unload in Boston harbor until the colony paid for the destroyed tea. The New Jersey committee wrote to Boston expressing solidarity with its people, while declining, like Pennsylvania and New York, to participate in an embargo on trade with Great Britain.[12]

Meetings of county freeholders and inhabitants followed. One occurred at Somerset County Courthouse on July 4. The Presbyterian Church in New Brunswick hosted another on July 15, because too many people showed up to fit in the Middlesex County Courthouse. Both groups expressed their "firm and unshaken" loyalty to the King and that they were "entirely averse from breaking their connection with the Island of Great Britain." However, they rejected the fundamental idea that Parliament had power over them because it was "contrary to the spirit of the British constitution, and so inconsistent with Liberty, that we look upon it as our duty to oppose it by every lawful mean, and suffer the last extremity rather than submit to it."

They decried Parliament's cruel acts of oppression against the people of Boston and established a subscription for their relief. The inhabitants affirmed their support for a "Congress of Deputies from the several Colonies," a Continental Congress, to meet and "present a dutiful address to his Majesty, praying for a general redress" of their grievances. They supported the idea of a "general Non-Importation Agreement" and a "general Non-Consumption Agreement" to be drawn up by the Congress, as "the only possible measure, to preserve the liberties of this country, at present in such imminent danger of being annihilated." Finally, each county appointed a committee to meet when necessary, to correspond with other county committees, and join in electing delegates to the proposed Congress. The Somerset committee included Princeton residents College President Dr. John Witherspoon, lawyer Jonathan Dickinson Sergeant, and merchant Enos Kelsey. The Middlesex meeting appointed Princeton residents John Johnson, John Combs, Jr., Jonathan Baldwin, and Rune Runyon to be on its Standing Committee of Correspondence. Former college steward Baldwin was increasingly active politically and also served on the Committee of Observation and Inspection for Windsor Township.[13] The freeholder meetings charged their committees to meet with similar ones from other counties at New Brunswick on July 21.[14]

At that July 21 meeting, Jonathan Dickinson Sergeant served as secretary, or clerk, for the seventy-two attendees. This meeting reiterated the ideas expressed in the county resolutions and chose James Kinsey, William Livingston, John Dehart, Stephen Crane, and Richard Smith to attend the Continental Congress called to meet on September 5 in Philadelphia. The committee also set up a system of voluntary subscriptions to aid the people of Boston.[15] These meetings of freeholders and residents, and the committees they formed, provided opportunities for a broad spectrum of people to participate in the unfolding events and feel a part of them, thus strengthening the protest movement. However, it could not bring everyone into agreement and support. A portion of the population believed boycotts to be an ineffective measure and saw this particular one as a threat to their liberty by exposing them to potential retaliation by people in their community with whom they disagreed on other matters. Adding to the concerns was fear that, should the colonies leave the British Empire, there would be nothing left to unite them, and their significant differences and suspicions about each other would lead to all manner of conflicts and disunity.[16]

John Adams Comes to Princeton

On the oppressively warm Saturday morning of August 27, several days before the Continental Congress was scheduled to meet, thirty-nine-year-old John Adams set out from New Brunswick in a carriage smartly drawn by four horses. Squeezed into the vehicle with him were his older cousin Samuel Adams, Thomas Cushing, and Robert Treat Paine, the Massachusetts delegates to the upcoming Continental Congress, and also their four servants. After a jarring, dusty ride of about fifteen miles over the uneven dirt Post Road—sometimes called the King's Highway or the Upper Road—connecting New York and Philadelphia, they entered the pretty village of Princeton at about noon.

Their driver stopped the carriage in front of the tavern owned by thirty-eight-year-old Jacob Hyer, which proudly displayed an image of the literary character Hudibras on its sign. This tavern stood quite near massive Nassau Hall, housing the College of New Jersey, constructed with the light brown, locally quarried sandstone. Presbyterians had brought the college to town in 1757, and Hyer had humorously named his tavern after the title character in Samuel Butler's 1663 mock-heroic poem satirizing religious dissenters, such as "New Light" Presbyterians. The innkeeper greeted the delegates and ordered his staff to help the servants bring in their luggage and move the carriage and horses to the inn's stable area to receive care. Hyer was proud to provide excellent service for both man and horse.

Princeton street scene and Nassau Hall c1780 by Gillette G. Griffin

Courtesy of Historical Society of Princeton

Hyer had begun operating the Hudibras, "a long L-shaped building of stone, with wide porches," in 1768, after leaving another Princeton tavern, the King's Arms.[17] However, the observant Adams may have noted that the building was less than a year old. A fire had ignited in the original building in January 1773 when an enslaved woman staff member went to bed and left a candle burning that fell unnoticed to the floor. The flame ignited the floorboards, burned a hole through them, and ignited the laths between the floor and the ceiling below. Cries of "Fire!" heard sometime between 3:00 and 4:00 a.m. woke up one Princeton resident who immediately arose, dressed, and dashed outside. Learning the Hudibras was burning, he ran there and "found the north-east corner in flames without, also the garret within." Boys from the nearby college pulled their fire engine out from its shelter between the college and the college kitchen near the east end of Nassau Hall. Other students carried out two ladders and over one hundred numbered leather buckets, marked "N.H." for Nassau Hall, and set up a bucket brigade. Unable to save the tavern and its winter provisions, beds, and other furniture, they did preserve the detached tavern kitchen, shop, and other buildings by tearing down the covered passageway to the kitchen.[18] The rebuilt tavern had reopened for business the in November 1774, so the structure was only about ten months old when the Adams party arrived.[19]

Hyer also earned income as a hatter and farmer. He and his wife Elizabeth Dildine Hyer had six children between the ages of four and fourteen. Hyer touted his inn as located halfway between New York and Philadelphia, where stage-wagons from both those cities spent the night, and he was able "to entertain travelers and others in the best manner." He could also forward for customers any "goods or parcels" destined for places along the stage route.[20] Coaches arrived from New York and Philadelphia on Monday, Tuesday, Thursday, and Friday evenings. Passengers paid a premium to ride inside the coach rather than on it. Each was allowed a fourteen-pound bag or paid two pence per pound over that limit. The passengers spent the night at the Hudibras, and the next morning, having exchanged passengers, each coach returned to its city of origin.[21]

Adams Discovers Princeton

After consuming an early afternoon Hudibras dinner, Adams sought out John Pigeon, an eighteen-year-old Nassau Hall student from Massachusetts. Adams had a letter for Pigeon from his father, a prosperous Watertown, Massachusetts merchant. In gratitude, Pigeon took his home-state visitors for a walk of the small village.[22] Adams did not leave a description of it, but Silas Deane, a Connecticut delegate to the upcoming Congress, was rather unimpressed, or perhaps merely travel-weary when he arrived. He wrote to his wife on another sweltering day "without the least breath of air stirring" that "Princeton is a new town and, though the best situated to command a good air, has no good farm-houses and settlements. The college is an elegant building of stone, well calculated, and to appearance well provided. The Tutors waited on us, but tutors and scholars are the same everywhere, so need not enlarge... The people are neat, and there is elegant entertainment for strangers at the taverns."[23] Shortly after the Revolution, Rev. Manasseh Cutler described Princeton as "a small town—or, rather, has but a small number of houses in the most compact part—but it is most delightfully situated on the summit of a very broad hill, which descends every way with a long easy slope, and commands a most extensive prospect in every direction. Few of the buildings are large, none very elegant."[24]

Although not readily visible to these casual visitors, Princeton was a growing and ever-changing community, hence its appearance as a new town. A year before Adams arrived, graduating student William Richmond Smith wrote to a friend who had graduated the year before and described recent changes in the village. He noted that Mrs. Field had built "a very brilliant house" between the houses of Gilbert Gaa and Mr. Plum, and hoped "travelers may not mistake it for the college." William Mountier had "built himself a little tower nearly opposite to the Hudibras," possibly to rival it. Smith

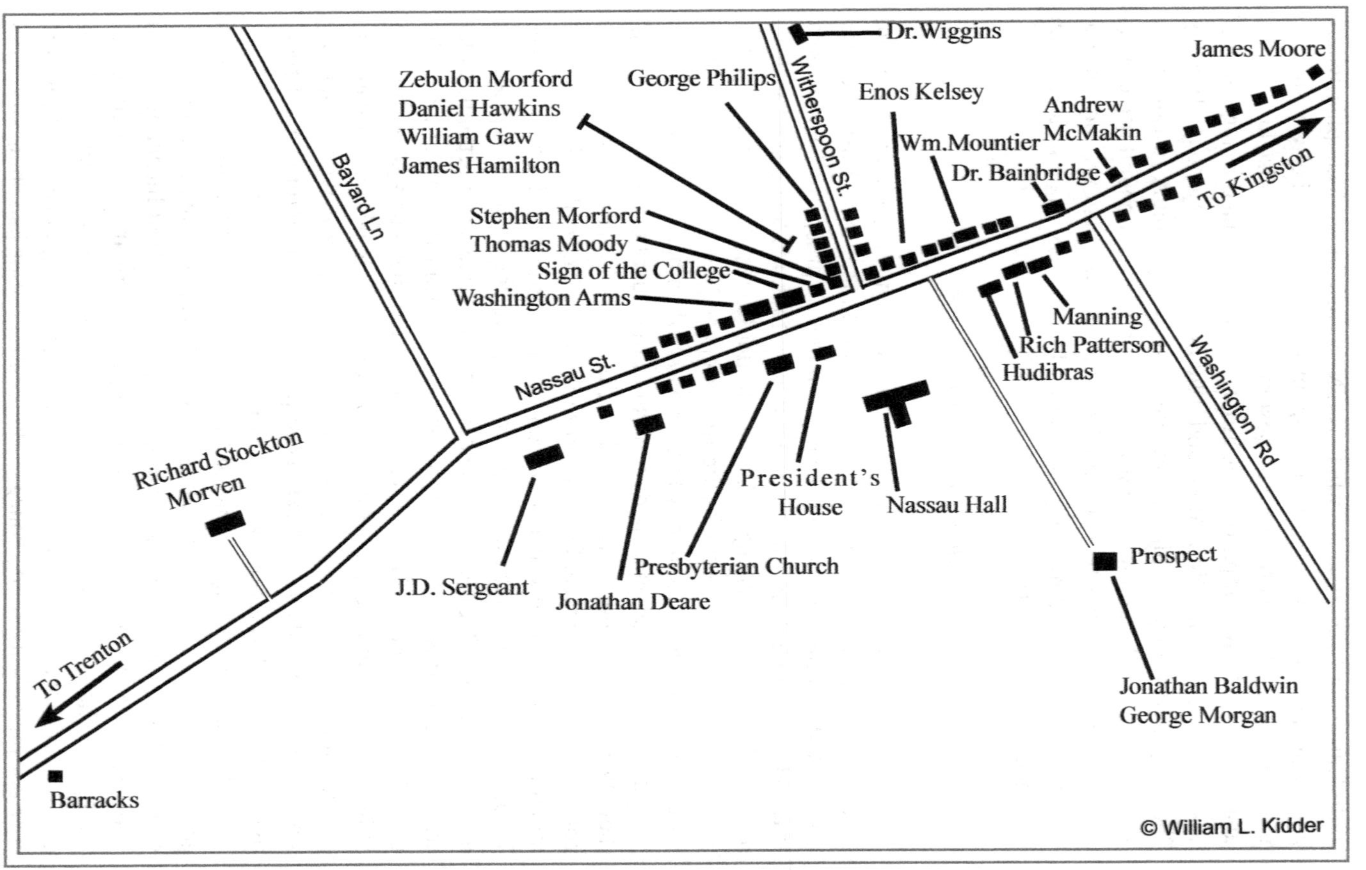

Map 4: Princeton Village 1774-1783

commented that Mountier's slaughterhouse now sheltered horses. Mr. Plum had installed new siding on the front of his house and painted it "so that if your eyes are not uncommonly strong when you come to Princeton you may chance to lose them." Richard Paterson had completed a "considerable addition to his house." During the 1773 Hudibras fire, the college boys saved his home and shop by using their fire engine to put out burning embers on its roof. Paterson's next-door neighbor, Mr. Manning, had repaired his old house and built a new one. A little further down the main street stood a newly built home and another recently painted so that now "it cuts a flaming dash," and Mr. Potter "has made considerable amendments on his castle."[25]

Across the street stood the Georgian brick-front house rented from Robert Stockton, Richard Stockton's brother, by thirty-one-year-old Dr. Absalom Bainbridge, a 1762 graduate of the college who had then studied medicine under an established doctor. Originally from a large and prominent family living just down the road in Maidenhead, he still owned property there. Dr. Bainbridge had only recently opened his practice in Princeton, where he and his wife, Mary, were the proud parents of their first child, a three-month-old baby boy named William, born on May 7.[26]

Leaving the Hudibras and walking south on the main street, Adams and his group passed in front of Nassau Hall. Looking directly across the street, they saw the Sign of the College tavern, owned by Richard Stockton and leased to William Whitehead. He had taken over its operation from William Hick the previous April 1.[27] Hick was an Englishman who settled in Princeton in 1763 and began running the tavern in 1767. He made a very successful life in Princeton and acquired a large amount of property that he rented out to various people. However, his comfortable and promising life began to fall apart when his "principles & inclination" caused him to stand up in loyalty to the British government as the protest debates intensified. After drawing frightful negative attention during the January tea party incident, Hick moved to Perth Amboy, where he ran the King's Arms tavern. Once the war began, he suffered significantly as a Loyalist.

Opinions about whether or not to protest the actions of Parliament could be very contentious. Even people who agreed that Parliament's actions were improper could still disagree about how to deal with them. To replace Hick, Stockton put a notice in the Philadelphia papers announcing the Sign of the College tavern's availability for lease beginning April 1, and describing it as "large and commodious, with the addition of a handsome wing on the west end, lately finished, for the entertainment of company on public occasions." Large stables, a coach house, and other buildings were other recent improvements made by Hick, before realizing the trouble he would soon face.

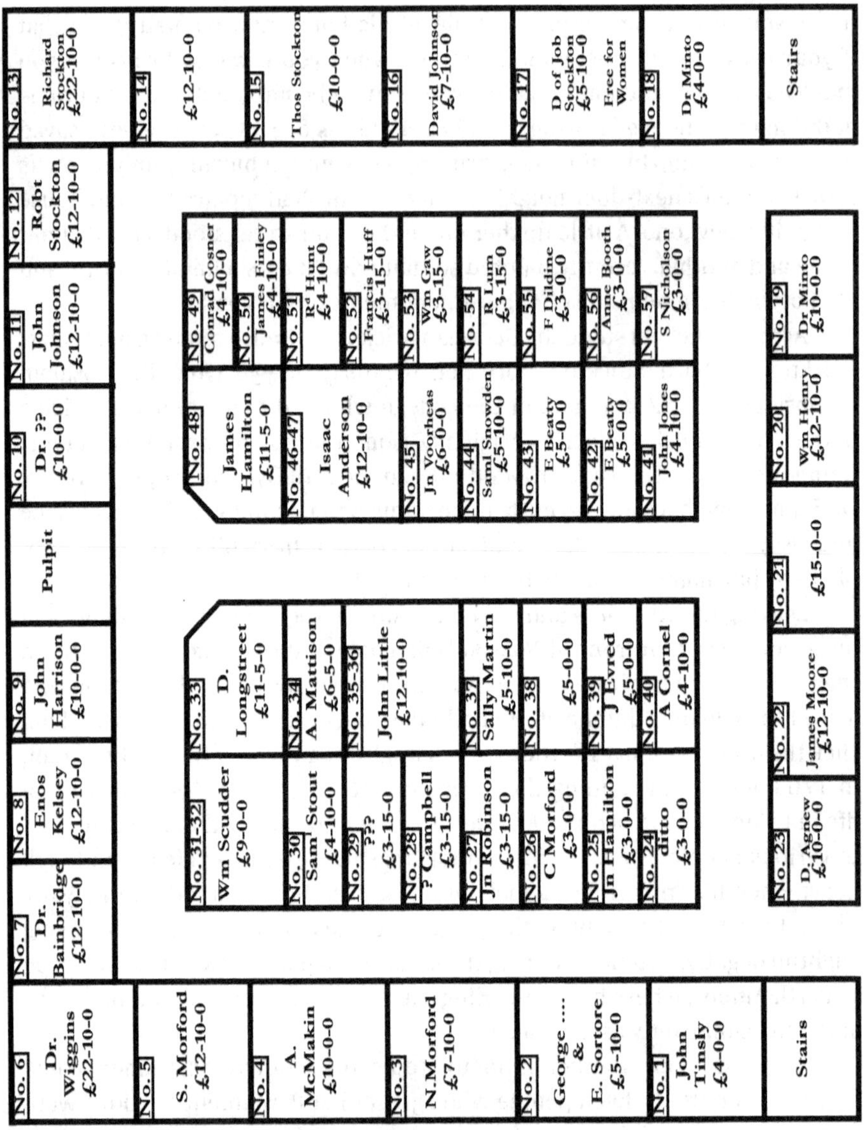

No. 1 John Tinsly £4-0-0
No. 2 George .... & E. Sortore £5-10-0
No. 3 N.Morford £7-10-0
No. 4 A. McMakin £10-0-0
No. 5 S. Morford £12-10-0
No. 6 Dr. Wiggins £22-10-0
No. 7 Dr. Bainbridge £12-10-0
No. 8 Enos Kelsey £12-10-0
No. 9 John Harrison £10-0-0
Pulpit
No. 10 Dr. ?? £10-0-0
No. 11 John Johnson £12-10-0
No. 12 Robt Stockton £12-10-0
No. 13 Richard Stockton £22-10-0
No. 14 £12-10-0
No. 15 Thos Stockton £10-0-0
No. 16 David Johnson £7-10-0
No. 17 D of Job Stockton £5-10-0 Free for Women
No. 18 Dr Minto £4-0-0
Stairs
No. 19 Dr Minto £10-0-0
No. 20 Wm Henry £12-10-0
No. 21 £15-0-0
No. 22 James Moore £12-10-0
No. 23 D. Agnew £10-0-0
No. 24 ditto £3-0-0
No. 25 Jn Hamilton £3-0-0
No. 26 C Morford £3-0-0
No. 27 Jn Robinson £3-15-0
No. 28 ? Campbell £3-15-0
No. 29 ??? £3-15-0
No. 30 Saml Stout £4-10-0
No. 31-32 Wm Scudder £9-0-0
No. 33 D. Longstreet £11-5-0
No. 34 A. Mattison £6-5-0
No. 35-36 John Little £12-10-0
No. 37 Sally Martin £5-10-0
No. 38 £5-0-0
No. 39 J Evred £5-0-0
No. 40 A Cornel £4-10-0
No. 41 John Jones £4-10-0
No. 42 E Beatty £5-0-0
No. 43 E Beatty £5-0-0
No. 44 Saml Snowden £5-10-0
No. 45 Jn Voorheas £6-0-0
No. 46-47 Isaac Anderson £12-10-0
No. 48 James Hamilton £11-5-0
No. 49 Conrad Cosner £4-10-0
No. 50 James Finley £4-10-0
No. 51 Rd Hunt £4-10-0
No. 52 Francis Huff £3-15-0
No. 53 Wm Gaw £3-15-0
No. 54 R Lum £3-15-0
No. 55 F Dildine £3-0-0
No. 56 Anne Booth £3-0-0
No. 57 S Nicholson £3-0-0
Stairs

Undated Pew Ownership Plan of the Presbyterian Church of Princeton c1770s

Adapted from illustration in Hageman, *History of Princeton and Its Institutions.*

The adjoining garden and lot contained more than an acre and were "well manured."[28] Not long after taking over the inn, Whitehead purchased many items from Princeton merchant Thomas Patterson including two dozen china cups, two dozen wine glasses, and several cream pots and sugar bowls.[29]

Continuing on the south side of the street, the visitors passed the rectangular, two-story, brick college president's house with its gable roof, built simultaneously with Nassau Hall. A one-story bay extended out on the west side near the rear corner. The windows on the front had flat, stone, winged arches topped by keystones. The front door, surmounted by a triangular pediment, was topped by a small semicircular window, or fanlight.[30] It was very similar to Dr. Bainbridge's house, built about the same time and designed by the same architect.

Just beyond the president's house, they passed the brick Presbyterian Church, where the present church stands today, but with its right side wall facing the street. Two entrances on the outer wall facing Nassau Hall led into the sanctuary, with the pulpit against the opposite wall, and the space between filled with pews owned by members of the congregation. A gallery running around three sides accommodated students. Situated on college land, the church also served as a college chapel, and the school had free use of the building during the three days of commencement exercises each year. The college president and tutors filled the roles of pastor and preachers.[31]

Pigeon's tour then walked the Adams group just beyond the main village to view the home and estate of forty-three-year-old lawyer Richard Stockton and his thirty-eight-year-old wife, Annis Boudinot Stockton. Richard served as a member of the Royal Governor's Council, and the past February 28, Governor Franklin had appointed him to the New Jersey Supreme Court.[32] Richard's grandfather headed one of the families that settled the area in the 1690s and purchased a large quantity of land in the heart of present-day Princeton. Today's Nassau Street was its northern boundary, Washington Road the eastern border, and then it extended west beyond the present Edgehill Street and south to Stony Brook. In 1701, Richard purchased from William Penn fifty-five hundred acres stretching northward from Stony Brook to Rocky Hill and westward from the Millstone River to the Keith Province Line. He began construction on a new house, and the family is reputed to have built and lived for a few years in a part of the stone house now known as "The Barracks" located on Edgehill Street.

The family prospered, converted to Presbyterianism in the second generation, and Richard graduated from the college in 1748, before it relocated to Princeton, and became a highly successful lawyer. Annis came to Princeton with her family about 1756, and her father, Elias Boudinot, Sr., operated a tavern and served as postmaster for the town. She married Richard Stockton in about 1757 or 1758. Their beautiful native brick Georgian style house, set back from the main road and probably built in the 1760s to replace an earlier one that burned down on Christmas in 1758, was probably three bays wide and stood one and a half or two stories high. A spacious center hall divided the house on the first floor with doors at each end and two rooms on each side of the hall.[33]

The grounds of the Stockton's estate displayed numerous beautiful trees and flower gardens, supervised by Annis. She named their home "Morven," after the mythical castle of King Fingal in the 1762 Poems of Ossian claiming to recount a traditional Scottish epic. She was proud of the avenue of "stately Elms! And lofty Cedars!" leading to the house from the street.[34] Richard had visited England in 1766, where he attended the celebration of the Queen's birthday at court, presented the King with an address from the college trustees, and met with various officials. He also went to Scotland to meet with Rev. John Witherspoon to help convince him to come to Princeton and head the college as its president. Richard also loved gardens and wrote to Annis that "I had rather ramble with you along the rivulets of Morven or Redhill, and see the rural sports of the chaste little frogs, than again be at a birth-night ball."

Richard contributed to the gardens by collecting and sending her "a charming collection of bulbous roots" and other items from England. The plantings long with their Georgian house became the source of personal identity for Richard and Annis. The estate announced their wealth and culture while revealing Annis's creative talents.[35]

The Stocktons were personal friends of Royal Governor William Franklin, and Richard was among the majority of New Jersey protestors who still hoped for reconciliation with the British government. New Jersey was a colony regarded as lacking revolutionary zeal.[36] Richard's involvement in the protests against the acts of Parliament grew from his early belief that colonists should elect members to it. Although an official in the royal colonial government, he strongly condemned the Stamp Act in 1765 and aggressively called for support of the Stamp Act Congress in New York, believing the only recourse the colonists had was to petition the King for redress. Because the colonists had no representatives in Parliament, Stockton rejected the idea that Parliament held authority over the colonies.[37] The Adams party did not meet with Stockton, although he was perhaps home at Morven setting up legal cases for the coming month in his judicial role and helping to make preparations for the September college commencement.[38]

John Adams Discovers Nassau Hall

While heading back toward the Hudibras to complete their tour, the Massachusetts delegates stopped at Nassau Hall, described in a contemporary account as "spacious, built of stone, and stands on the highest ground in the town. It fronts to the north, and toward the street, and has before it a very large yard, walled in with stone and lime. The ground descends considerably from the college to the street, which gives it a lofty appearance."[39] Two feet of soil graded away at the base of the building made the basement floor just about level with the ground, making the building appear to be four stories tall. Adams described Nassau Hall as being "about as large as" the college building in New York and "commands a prospect of the country." It measured 176 feet long and 54 feet wide, with a front central projection of about four feet and a two-story, 32-by-40-foot prayer hall extending out on the back. A modest cupola occupied the center of the hip roof. There were three entrances on the front, one in the center and the other two near the ends, each reached by a set of wooden steps without balustrades. The basement had sixteen rooms, used primarily for recitation, while on the main floor, seven or eight feet above the ground, were the dining room (refectory), library, Rittenhouse orrery (planetarium), and the prayer hall. The student quarters on the second and third floors could accommodate 147 students living three to a room. Each student room had individual studies for two students, each with a window and a third window between them for added light. A ten-foot-wide corridor extended the length of each floor. In 1770, the campus yard between the building and the street was enclosed by a brick wall with pilasters at regular intervals, and a paled fence on a stone foundation bordered the front on the village street. Buttonwood trees were planted in the "college yard" in 1765.[40]

The college also operated a well-respected grammar school known for "its liveliness" and Dr. Witherspoon's prize competitions instituted in 1771, in which "accuracy and mental alertness were the winning qualities." Drill and exercise occurred so regularly that fluency, such as in the use of Latin, "was in the end almost inevitable." Witherspoon had made improvements to the college since becoming president in 1768, and it was in the best condition it had ever been in, with good prospects for continued development. He achieved this even with a smaller teaching staff than he would have employed if the inadequate endowment, which he had so far doubled, had been more prosperous.[41]

At Nassau Hall, the Adams group accepted an invitation to visit the chambers of Professor of Mathematics and Natural Philosophy, twenty-eight-year-old William Churchill Houston. Houston grew up on the North Carolina frontier in a family from Scotland that achieved modest prosperity, and he benefitted from the energetic efforts of the community to provide a quality education for its children. Some of his tutors were College of New Jersey graduates who steered him toward it. Houston graduated with high honors the same year that John Witherspoon took office as president, and immediately joined the teaching staff. His first post was master of the grammar school and then senior tutor in the college. Finally, he assumed the newly established position of Professor of Mathematics and Natural Philosophy in September 1771. Houston enthusiastically supported the many changes Witherspoon brought to the college. An acquaintance graciously described him as "tall and slender, dignified and graceful, extremely intelligent, grave, serious and uniform. His style of speaking was clear, calm, free from excitement, like a gentle flowing stream without a ripple or tumult, and yet by its simplicity, truth and earnestness, seldom failed to produce conviction."[42]

Houston first accompanied the group to the library, which Adams found, "not large, but has some good books." He then took them to the "Apparatus," where, according to Adams, they "saw a most beautiful machine, an orrery, or planetarium, constructed by Mr. Rittenhouse of Philadelphia. It exhibits almost every motion in the astronomical world. The motions of the Sun and all the planets with all their satellites. The eclipses of the Sun and Moon &c." The first components of the orrery had arrived on campus in April 1771, a few months before Houston became a professor. The wonders continued as "he showed us another orrery, which exhibits the true inclination of the orbit of each of the planets to the plane of the ecliptic. He then showed us the electrical apparatus, which is the most complete and elegant that I have seen. He charged the bottle and attempted an experiment, but the state of the air was not favorable."[43]

As they finished examining these famous, state-of-the-art scientific teaching devices, the college bell rang, signifying the time for prayers. Houston walked them to the prayer hall, with its gallery and a platform surmounted by a high pulpit. On the walls hung portraits of King George II and former Royal Governor Belcher. Forty-year-old College President Rev. John Witherspoon entered the room and led the prayer service in his broad Scottish accent. Student and later faculty member Ashbel Green later described him as "of the middle size...fleshy with some tendency to corpulence." His eyes radiated his intelligence and "his eyebrows were large, hanging down at the ends next his temples; occasioned, probably, by a habit he had contracted of pulling them, when he was under excitement." His dress always avoided the "extremes of slovenliness and foppery." On all occasions, he appeared "graceful and venerable," and people felt his presence, which over his lifespan Green found was exceeded only by that of Washington.[44] During the service, it amused Adams to hear that "the scholars sing as badly as the Presbyterians at New York." After prayers, Houston and Witherspoon escorted the delegates up to the balcony where they had a view "of an horizon of about 80 miles diameter."

John Adams Talks Politics

The group walked next door to Witherspoon's house for a glass of wine. The front door opened into a hall extending through the house with a staircase at its rear, against the left wall. The library, fully paneled on the fireplace wall, stood to the left of the hall, and to the right was the parlor and behind it the dining room. During their conversation, Adams approvingly found Witherspoon to be "as high a Son of Liberty, as any man in America."[45] Witherspoon had established his reputation as a convincing proponent of the cause with his writings, such as his June 29, 1773, pastoral letter to all congregations in the Philadelphia Synod.[46]

New Jersey citizens held a spectrum of opinions about how to deal with the current political situation. Some were ready to advocate for independence, while many others held out hope for reconciliation. Everyone faced the challenge of deciding what course of action to support and risked confrontation when expressing their beliefs during social discourse (recall tavern keeper William Hick). Many people remained neutral or silent, unwilling to take a public stand on the issues. Whether favoring independence or reconciliation, a foundational belief was the need to reestablish a proper power relationship between the King and Parliament. That effort involved challenging Parliament's right to govern the colonies. The colonies were far-removed from Great Britain and did not elect representatives to it. Additionally, the King historically had granted certain rights to the colonists in their charters that should continue to define the relationship between the colonies and the British government.[47]

Witherspoon undoubtedly expressed to Adams his strong beliefs about the acts of Parliament. He considered the upcoming Congress to be "representative of the great body of the people of North America," distinct from the colonial assemblies and created for an entirely different purpose. It justifiably created "an interruption or suspension of the usual forms, and an appeal to the great law of reason, the first principles of the social union, and the multitude collectively, for whose benefit all the particular laws and customs of a constituted state, are supposed to have been originally established." He believed the "great object of the approaching Congress should be to unite the colonies, and make them as one body in any measure of self-defense, to assure the people of Great Britain that we will not submit voluntarily, and convince them that it would be either impossible or unprofitable for them to compel us by open violence." But the colonies could only succeed if they united for action. Witherspoon cautioned that no colony should act independently to resolve its problems but always support a union that allowed the colonies to "correspond and ascertain how they shall effectually cooperate in such measures as shall be necessary to their common defense."

However, Witherspoon was not yet advocating for independence and was adamant that the Congress should profess "loyalty to the King, and our backwardness to break our connection with Great Britain, if we are not forced by their unjust impositions." As for Parliament, he declared, "we are firmly determined never to submit to it, and do deliberately prefer war with all its horrors, and even extermination itself, to slavery riveted on us and our posterity." To get Britain's attention, he believed a non-importation agreement "should be entered into immediately." Measures must be taken to promote local manufacturing, and the militia of every colony should be "put upon the best footing." An address should be prepared to let the British army and navy know "the reproach which they will bring upon themselves, and the danger to which they will be exposed, if they allow themselves to be in the instruments of enslaving their country."

Witherspoon creatively recommended that every colony should "form a Society for the Encouragement of Protestant Emigrants from the 3 Kingdoms." Also, the "Congress should raise money and employ a number of writers in the newspapers in England, to explain to the public the American plea, and remove the prejudices of Britons" toward the colonists' actions. He had worked with newly appointed Congressional delegate William Livingston, the future governor of independent New Jersey, to "procure an instruction that the tea [destroyed in Boston] should not be paid for" by the colonies. Witherspoon described Livingston as "very sincere and very able in the public cause, but a bad speaker, though a good writer."[48] Livingston, like Witherspoon, continued to work toward reconciliation rather than independence. Like many others, he feared the consequences arising from a dissolution of the social structure and the political chaos that could result from removing the monarchy. But he ardently supported the challenge to the authority of Parliament.[49]

After their glass of wine over political discussions, Witherspoon accompanied the New England delegates back to their lodgings at the Hudibras, "took a dish of coffee" with them, and told Adams that all his students were "Sons of Liberty." As early as the summer of 1770, students had assembled in their black gowns on the lawn, the college yard, in front of Nassau Hall and, while the college bell tolled, they burned, at the hands of the public hangman, a letter about New York merchants breaking the non-importation agreement.[50] Witherspoon believed in preparing his students to be community leaders, so his lectures on moral philosophy contained references to government, law, politics, religion, ethics, and history. Almost half of his lecture content concerned political, governmental, and legal concepts and advocated for natural rights, mixed government, civil liberty, and the right to resist tyranny.[51]

Back at the Hudibras, they met two "cordial friends to American Liberty." A Mr. Hood from New Brunswick and twenty-eight-year-old Princeton lawyer Jonathan Dickinson Sergeant, Jonathan Baldwin's brother-in-law. Sergeant was an enthusiastic supporter of the colonial efforts to resist Parliament's actions who had served as clerk of the committee that selected the New Jersey delegates to the Continental Congress. A graduate of the college in 1762, he studied law with Richard Stockton in Princeton.

During the evening of this long day, twenty-year-old student Samuel Whitwell, another Massachusetts native whose father had sent a letter for him with Adams, met them at the Hudibras, usually off-limits to students.[52] Adams found that, like Pigeon, Whitwell loyally portrayed the college administration as "very strict, and the scholars study very hard."

All students lived in Nassau Hall, and each possessed a print copy of the strict code of student behavior dating back to 1760. Students were required to attend all classes, prayers twice each day, and church on Sundays. Card and dice games, frequenting taverns, making boisterous noises, keeping horses, blowing horns, building bonfires, and holding student meetings or leaving town without the permission of the president were forbidden. First-year students, usually about fourteen to sixteen years old, and sometimes younger, had to run errands demanded by upperclassmen, and all students had to tip their hats when approaching within ten rods of the president and five rods of tutors. The day started at 5:00 a.m., except in the winter when it was 6:00 a.m. Trumpets sounding in the corridors awoke students because the college bell had proven useless. Morning devotions in the unheated prayer hall began the day, followed by an hour for study, then a breakfast of bread and butter with milk or cider at 7:30 a.m., a more substantial hot dinner at noon, and later supper, much like breakfast.[53]

Adams Hears Witherspoon Preach

After the long afternoon and evening touring the village and discussing politics with local people, the next morning, Sunday, August 28, Adams penned a letter to his wife, Abigail. He apologized for not writing earlier during his trip because he had found only one opportunity to write and would have needed to send it by "the Post," but did not want to do that "for fear of foul play." He said he hoped to find a trusted person in Philadelphia to convey this letter to her. John briefly described their journey from Boston as being "upon the whole an agreeable jaunt," providing "opportunities to see the world, and to form acquaintances with the most eminent and famous men, in the several colonies we have passed through." His party had agreeably met with nothing but "unbounded civility, complaisance, and respect." Adams mentioned his pleasant visit to Nassau Hall and that he would be hearing Dr. Witherspoon preach that day. He looked forward to beginning work in a day or two, having judged, perhaps a bit too optimistically, that the people he had met along the way "universally consider our Cause as their own, and express the firmest resolution, to abide the determination of the Congress."[54]

After sealing his letter, Adams walked over to Nassau Hall, where he listened to "Dr. Witherspoon all day." Fortunately, he found Witherspoon to be "a clear, sensible, preacher." Ashbel Green reported that Witherspoon never took notes into the pulpit, but "memorized what he wanted to convey, [yet] not so as to prevent the extemporaneous expression of any thought which occurred as pertinent, while delivering his discourse."[55] Manasseh Cutler, hearing him deliver a sermon a few years later, noted that Witherspoon "is an intolerably homely old Scotchman, and speaks the true dialect of his country, except that his brogue borders on the Irish. He is a bad speaker, has no oratory, and had no notes before him." Still, Cutler believed he was very much worth listening to with attention. This was because, even though the subject might be dry and his delivery required the closest attention to catch his message, "the correctness of his style, the arrangement of his matter, and the many new ideas that he suggested, rendered his sermon very entertaining. The attention of the congregation strongly marked their regard for good sense and clear reasoning, rather than the mere show of oratory and declamation."[56]

After the service, the delegates resumed their enlightening conversation with Jonathan Dickinson Sergeant and took dinner and coffee with him before spending the evening talking about public issues. Sergeant's son remembered his father as having "a cheerful, and, at times, even playful disposition" while still having "the highest professional eminence" and being a "public-spirited citizen."[57] The New Englanders found Sergeant to be very likable and knowledgeable about the delegates from New York and Virginia, as well as some of the principal lawyers in the middle colonies. For example, Sergeant described Melancton Smith as "the oracle of New York for Chamber

Council." He described John Morin Scott as an admirable speaker who was like an old man he had known who could "set up all night at his bottle," yet in the morning could "argue to admiration." Describing another New Yorker, he said James Duane had "a plodding body, but has a very effeminate, feeble voice." Of the Virginians, Sergeant warned, they "speak in raptures about Richard Henry Lee and Patrick Henry—one the Cicero and the other the Demosthenes of the Age."[58] Unlike Stockton and Witherspoon, but like Adams, Sergeant was one of those men already convinced that independence was the only answer to their concerns.

Adams Continues on to Philadelphia

After a second night at the Hudibras, Hyer's servants helped the servants of the Massachusetts delegates bring out their carriage, clean, harness, and hitch their horses so they could set off early in the morning for a hot, jarring trip to Trenton. Concerning the roads, Witherspoon noted, "there are statutes for the wideness of the public roads; also for repairing, though it is generally poorly done—yet from the climate and the level position of the country, the roads are excellent in summer."[59] "Excellent" was a relative term and did not imply that traveling was comfortable, but merely that the roads had fewer problems and dangers than in other seasons. As they departed the village, the delegates passed Morven on their right and then saw to their left the old stone house known as The Barracks that had been the original Stockton home before Morven. This house was ninety by twenty-five feet and two stories. The first floor had five rooms with fireplaces on the first floor and six rooms on the second floor, in addition to rooms for servants. It was not a pretentious home, but very utilitarian. The property also had a kitchen garden, a Dutch-style barn forty by forty feet, a stable for cattle, a wagon house, a cider house, and other outbuildings.[60] Continuing south, they entered that part of the community, known as Stony Brook, which had begun as a Quaker settlement and was still home to some extensive Quaker families interspersed with several Presbyterian families.

Witherspoon once described the road to Trenton as a "continued and gradual" descent from Princeton to the Delaware River. Other travelers noted the land was mostly level, but with some long hills and "some parts were covered with trees, but far the greater part of the country was without woods," and there were "very extensive" fields of grain "on both sides of the road." Traveler Peter Kalm noted that around Princeton, "the woods were likewise more cut away, and the country more cultivated, so that one might have imagined himself to be in Europe."[61] Trees throughout the Princeton area included oaks, ash, maple, birch, chestnut, walnut, pine, and locust, along with numerous fruit trees on the farms, especially apples, pears, cherries, and peaches. At several points, the horses and the carriage splashed through fords in streams running through shallow ravines that crossed the path of the road.

Just beyond Morven, they passed the house and farm of Robert Stockton, Richard's brother, and near a bend in the Post Road on the left sat the small house of Thomas Olden, a relative of William Olden, who came to Stony Brook from Piscataway in 1696 and purchased four hundred acres from Benjamin Clarke. Originally Quakers, over time, several Olden family members switched to the Presbyterian or Episcopalian churches. The house of David Olden sat further from the road, also on the left.

Next, on the left, they passed the farms of William and then Thomas Clarke, brothers descended from Benjamin Clarke. In 1695–96, Benjamin had purchased twelve hundred acres from Thomas Warne and became the second-largest landowner in Stony Brook after Richard Stockton. His grandson, William, inherited his father's land in 1768 and, in 1772, sold 199¾ acres to his younger brother Thomas so that the brothers possessed adjoining farms of roughly the same acreage. While William married Susannah Attmore, known as Ann, and raised a large family, Thomas never married and shared his house with his unmarried sister Sarah, ten years his junior. Over time, the brothers' farms varied in size between 150 and 180 acres of improved land, in addition to woodlands and uncultivated acres. Each farm usually kept between three and five horses, about half a dozen cattle, three to nine hogs, and unknown numbers of sheep. Crops included hay, grains, and flax. The growing grain Adams saw from the road could have been corn and perhaps rye or oats, and the stubble of the recently harvested winter wheat. These farmers also employed the usual mix of period farming utensils, including plows and wagons.[62]

In a separate household along the Post Road, on land adjoining Thomas Clarke's farm, lived their sister Hannah and her husband, Robert White. They had no children or other people residing with them.[63] Although all were Quakers, siblings William, John, Thomas, Matthew, Ezekiel, and Sarah Clarke, along with their brother-in-law Robert White, jointly owned an enslaved woman, Susannah. Susannah may have lived with one of her owner families or rotated among them as needed. Quakers at this time were attempting to end the practice of slavery, but several, including members of the Clarke family, still owned a few. Across the road from the Clarke farms, the Adams carriage passed the farm of John Johnson, a Presbyterian Church elder who lived with his family and slave on a 300-acre farm, where he also did some distilling.

When the Adams party reached Stony Brook, they passed the mills and shops of Samuel Worth, grandson of Joseph Worth, who came to Stony Brook in 1696 from Woodbridge, East Jersey. Other nearby shops included the tannery and shoe shop of another Clarke brother, Matthew. They passed another large farm as they ascended the hill just across the Stony Brook. This farm belonged to William Millette, a tall, good looking, almost sixty-year-old Presbyterian gentleman who always displayed courtly manners.[64] He and his wife Charity had five children, a fourteen-year-old boy, a thirteen-year-old boy, and three daughters between the ages of twelve and ten. Across from him was the farm of about forty-year-old Richard Cochran, who came to America from his native Scotland about 1750, and in 1765 purchased his 234½ acre farm at Stony Brook, previously the land of Samuel Stockton. In addition to farming, Cochran occasionally imported goods to sell but did not keep a store. He married Mary Antill in 1767, and they had three young children: a daughter and two sons.

The property and house were in bad shape when Cochran made his purchase. He made many improvements so that Witherspoon could describe him as living like a gentleman in good repute, raising abundant crops of wheat, Indian corn, rye, and others and having many horses, cattle, sheep, and hogs. To help him with the farm work, he owned seven enslaved persons. As a learned gentleman, Cochran also had an extensive library containing more than three hundred valuable books. In addition to this farm, he owned four houses that he rented out in the village. He served as a judge of the Inferior Court of Common Pleas for Somerset County, having been appointed by Governor Franklin in 1772.[65]

After ascending Cochran's Hill (also known as Millette's Hill), the Massachusetts delegates soon crossed the Province Line into Maidenhead, Hunterdon County, then arrived at Trenton, crossed the Delaware River, and finally reached Philadelphia just in time for the opening of the Congress.

After the New England delegates left town, life continued as usual, and the college became engrossed in preparations for the annual commencement scheduled for September 26–28. While Princeton prepared, the Continental Congress met in Philadelphia beginning September 5. Paul Revere once again rode through Princeton a week or so later carrying the Suffolk Resolves passed in Massachusetts on September 9 that outlined recommendations for how the colonies should respond to the Coercive Acts passed by Parliament to punish Boston for the tea destruction.

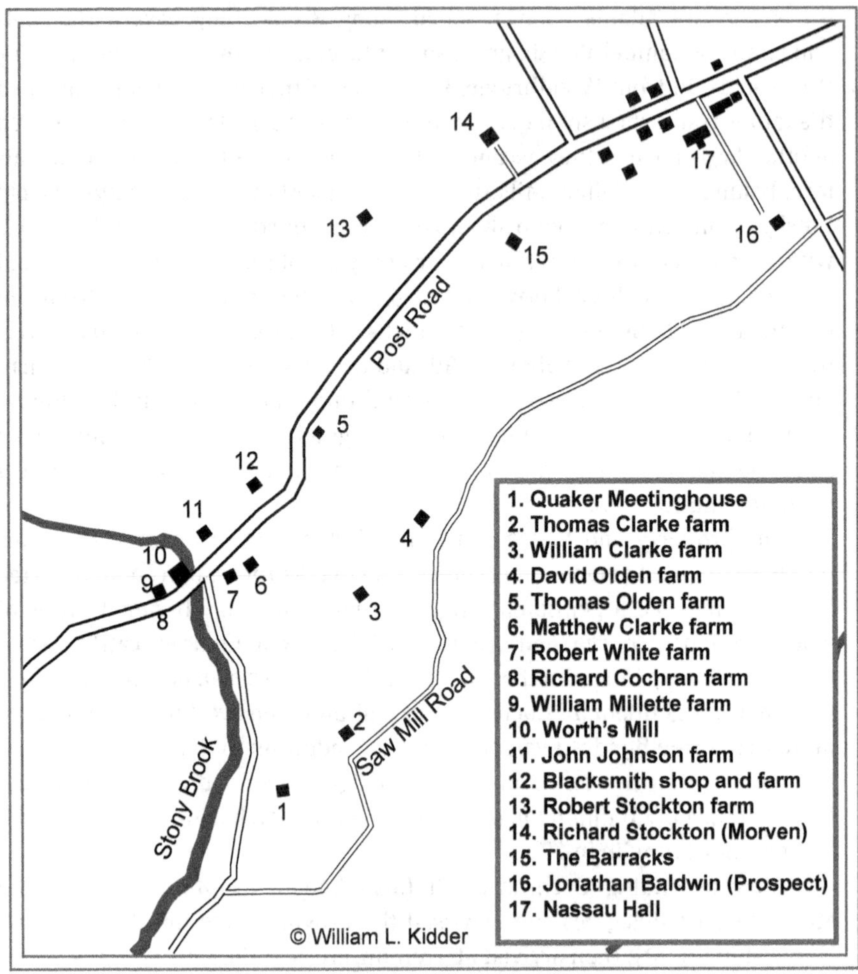

Map 5: Princeton - Stony Brook - 1774 - 1783

The College of New Jersey Commencement

The highly popular college commencement annually attracted more than just the families of graduates, drawing people from near and far. Taking advantage of that populous audience, Alexander MacWhorter, secretary of the New Jersey Society for the Relief of the Widows and Children of Deceased Presbyterian Ministers, announced the next meeting of that society at Princeton on September 27 at 9:00 a.m. In some of the ads, he noted that the college commencement would follow the next day when Dr. Witherspoon would preach a sermon, and "there will be a collection made for the purposes of this charitable institution."[66]

Commencement ceremonies began on September 26 when the president and officers of the college and "other gentlemen of literature" examined the grammar school students, and every class gave "specimens of the proficiency according to their standing." Several of the students, including ten-year-old Richard Stockton of Princeton, entertained the assemblage in the evening with Latin and English orations. On Tuesday the 27th, the college undergraduates gave a series of voluntary competitions in Latin and English. The college trustees also met, and the committee that had examined candidates for degrees on August 16 and 18 recommended the full class for degrees, except for two who needed to study and be re-examined just before commencement.

Those authorized the Bachelor of Arts degree included Henry Brockholst Livingston (son of William Livingston), Samuel Whitwell (who had met with John Adams in August), and David Witherspoon (son of College President Rev. John Witherspoon). David had come to America with his family in the summer of 1768, enrolled in the college's grammar school, and entered the college freshman class in 1770. He earned no individual honors, and although graduating at age fourteen was a bit immature for his age.[67] When the committee appointed to provide a dinner for the trustees and their friends reported the cost was £11.15, the surprised and frugal board ordered "that for the future there be no public dinners at the expense of this Board."[68]

The main commencement events took place throughout the day on Wednesday the 28th, including the Latin Salutatory Oration and forensic debates in English and Latin. The graduating seniors received their diplomas, and the college awarded honorary degrees. Ceremonies ended with a prescient Valedictory Oration on "the Horrors of War." Throughout the day, "a very numerous assembly of gentlemen and ladies; some of them from the most distant provinces of the continent" were in attendance.[69] Given the heated atmosphere of the times, the ceremonies could not avoid political messages. However, they were significantly toned down from those that had recently become controversial and caused the trustees to crack down in 1772. Political statements had been heard frequently at previous college commencements under Rev. Witherspoon, and some attendees had charged him with teaching his students to be disloyal to the British government. A "Friend to Impartiality" who attended the 1772 commencement said he felt more like he was observing "a circle of vociferous politicians" in a coffee-house than in the "calm shades of academic retirement." Another anonymous observer, "Causidicus," objected that an education that made a boy's "judgment early biased, and impressions, perhaps injurious to our happy Constitution, made on their minds, before they are able to distinguish what is right, from what is wrong, in such matters is improper in the highest degree, and utterly inconsistent with the business of a college." The 1774 orations demonstrated the consequences of the Trustee restrictions to freedom of speech, a casualty of the political debates of the time, and addressed less incendiary topics such as "Agriculture" and "Courage."[70]

If this year's commencement was politically subdued, this did not mean that the students avoided involvement in public issues. By June, the students had formed their own independent militia company, complete with green, yellow, and white uniforms but lacking sufficient muskets for more than about half of them. Student Charles Beatty praised his brother for his willingness "to fight and die in defense of your Liberties, and the Liberty of your country."[71] On this commencement day, the Continental Congress rejected Joseph Galloway's Plan of Union for the colonies, and about three weeks after commencement, the Continental Congress adopted the Continental Association, containing rules that directly affected the people of Princeton. They must cease to import products from Britain and stop the slave trade beginning December 1. Non-consumption of British products and foreign luxuries would start on March 1, 1775. On September 1, 1775, an embargo of all exports to Britain, Ireland, and the West Indies would commence. Each county, town, and city would elect a committee to enforce these restraints and punish violators through publicity and boycott, intense peer pressure that could get ugly. By April 1775, the Association had been adopted by the twelve colonies with delegates in Congress, and Georgia passed a modified version in January 1775. The Congress adjourned on October 26, 1774 and resolved to meet again in May 1775 if grievances still existed.

Several days after commencement, Witherspoon paid off the accounts with merchant Thomas Patterson established by about ten student graduates, including Samuel Whitwell. The boys had primarily purchased clothing.[72]

Slavery in Princeton

The subject of liberty was continually in the air, even though the very people arguing for it held other human beings in bondage. While it is difficult to document the full extent of slave ownership in Princeton, advertisements for runaways, tax records, probate records, and manumissions can give us a clue. Regarding runaways, Constant, the twenty-six-year-old enslaved man owned by John Williams Sanders, a man from the West Indies, ran off in the fall. The newspaper notice described him as well-built and a sensible and active fellow who was "accustomed to attend a gentleman." He was learning to play the fiddle and was very fond of it. He ran off with several sets of clothing, boots, and shoes. Sanders felt Constant might carry a forged pass to get him to New York or Philadelphia, where he could try to procure passage on a ship headed for his original home in the West Indies. Sanders offered a reward of eight dollars for securing him to any "of his Majesty's gaols," and identified men in Philadelphia, New York, and Elizabethtown who could pay the reward, in addition to himself.[73] On November 8, Aaron Longstreet, Jr., offered a four-dollar reward for the return of his runaway enslaved man Peet. He ran on September 19, was about twenty-seven years old and had "a large scar on one side of his neck, and another on his head, occasioned by a cut with a knife." Could that scar be evidence of fights with other slaves or even his master?[74]

Merchant account books also mention enslaved persons who may not be mentioned in other sources. Slaves often went out to make purchases for their masters, generally for textiles, thread, or small items. In Thomas Patterson's account book, we find Robert Stockton's "Negro" purchasing two yards of lace in August and Dr. Bainbridge's enslaved man Prime purchasing thread in August. The next year we find additional purchases by Prime and also by Bainbridge's "wench." Other slaves who made purchases include Dr. Thomas Wiggins's "wench," Jonathan Sergeant's "Negro," and Richard Cochran's "Negro." John Witherspoon seems to have had several slaves, including a "Negro," a "wench," and a "Negro Fortune" and/or "Fanna." Others might include William Whitehead's "Sally" and Elias Woodruff's "Amos." White women were typically given as Mrs. or Miss or just given as the man's "Lady," and Woodruff had no sons named Amos.[75]

The New Jersey Medical Society held its "half-yearly meeting" at the Hudibras on Tuesday, November 8, and its proceedings included a medical dissertation delivered by the president before dinner. Both the outgoing and new presidents, Absalom Bainbridge and Wiggins, respectively, were Princeton residents. Bainbridge was probably the speaker unless Wiggins was already acting as president.[76] Both doctors were slave owners.

Two young black men, Bristol Yamma and John Quamine, sailed from Newport, Rhode Island, in November, and arrived at Princeton late in the year to be privately tutored by Witherspoon. Both men had come to the colonies on a slave ship from what is now Ghana and been enslaved at Newport. Newport ministers Samuel Hopkins and Ezra Stiles developed an African missionary plan and began looking for free black candidates for training as missionaries to return to Africa. They began to focus on Yamma and Quamine, who, through a series of events, including winning a lottery, purchased their freedom in 1773. Hopkins and Stiles selected them to be the first missionaries under their plan and arranged for their education in Princeton. Quamine's wife stayed behind because she was enslaved to a College of New Jersey graduate living in Rhode Island and was not allowed to travel.[77] Witherspoon owned slaves and had even written advice to slaveholders, but agreed to tutor these two men although he was getting very involved in the Revolutionary activity that cut into his college work.

Richard Stockton's Hopes for a Settlement

Toward the end of the year, on December 12, Richard Stockton sat down at his desk at Morven. Taking up his pen, he wrote a proposal to Lord Dartmouth, Secretary of State for America, entitled *An Expedient for the Settlement of the American Disputes humbly submitted to the consideration of his Majesty's Ministers by an American*. It began, "The State of American Affairs is so truly alarming at this time, that every real friend to the British Empire ought to suggest every probable expedient that occurs to him for the accommodation of the unhappy disputes between Great Britain and the Colonies." As background, he stated the North American colonies could raise five hundred thousand militiamen, equally as fit as English Militia and many having seen actual service in the French and Indian War. Even to the "astonishment of many Colonists themselves," the people were "perfectly united in a determinate opposition" to the British Parliament having authority for internal taxation. There was no doubt that if the British government persisted in implementing the acts against Boston or any other laws involving the absolute power of Parliament over the colonies by force, the American people "would unite in attempting to repel force by force." If war consequently broke out, "the certain consequences of this unnatural war will be dreadful to both Great Britain and America: and the probable effects thereof may be fatal to the whole British Empire."

To prevent a war, Stockton recommended that the King require his colonial governors in North America to recommend to their Assemblies to pass acts appointing commissioners to go to England to confer with the King's Ministers, or commissioners appointed by Parliament. They would meet "respecting the grand points in dispute between Great Britain and America; and finally to determine thereupon." To prevent future disputes, these American commissioners would also have the power to negotiate with government commissioners to establish "one general system of government for all the colonies on the continent, similar to the British," or make "some material alterations in the present mode of provincial government." Americans themselves should be able to support the American government adequately. When it came to Americans paying for the cost of military actions taken by the British Government to defend them, the American government(s) must agree to the method of payment. He closed by recommending that the King advise Parliament to suspend the Boston Port Act until the proposed Commissioners could determine how to proceed.

Stockton expressed his humility in offering these recommendations, but insisted that "some expedient must be immediately fallen upon, or we shall be involved in a civil war the most obstinate awful and tremendous that perhaps ever occurred since the creation of the world." He would "esteem it a signal blessing of divine providence, conferred upon him, if any one idea he hath suggested may be of any use at this dreadful crisis." However, even if no recommendations are accepted, "he will at least be able to comfort himself with the uprightness of his intentions in this feeble attempt; and with the assurance that it can do no harm either to himself, or any other person."[78] Two days after Stockton wrote this letter, Annis placed an order with Thomas Patterson for a variety of textiles, including broadcloth, Buckram, silk, and Holland, as well as thread and a teapot.[79]

In northeast New Jersey, twenty-year-old Jemima Condict wrote in her diary on October 1 that "It seems we have troublesome times a coming for there is great disturbance a broad in the earth & they say it is tea that caused it. So then if they will quarrel about such a trifling thing as that what must we expect but war & I think or at least fear it will be so."[80] These feelings were probably shared by many people living in Princeton. However, by the end of the year, Charles Beatty, who had earlier praised his fellow college students for preparing to fight and die, said of the students, "you expect each one is preparing for an expected war—believe me we are not such patriots here as you imagine, we care not what Great Britain is going to do. We are not anxious to instruct ourselves in the military art—we hope we shall never have occasion to be conversant in military affairs." At this point, war with Great Britain seemed less likely, and militia drilling had become more playful than genuine.[81]

In general, people hoped that faithful adherence to the Association created by the Continental Congress would bring the British government to its senses, that economic consequences would bring pressure on Parliament from Englishmen. How long would this hope last? How would England respond to Stockton's "humble" recommendations? Would Jonathan Dickinson Sergeant come to accept the reasoning of his older, more experienced mentors, Stockton and Witherspoon? How enthusiastically and consistently would the residents of Princeton conform to the demands of the Continental Association?

Chapter 2

1775

As the New Year began, the people of Princeton continued to debate about how to deal with the actions of Parliament, and many felt it all might lead to war. The swirling vortex of events erupting beyond their control forced all Princeton residents to decide which position to support on the continuum of choices. They could eagerly or reluctantly, wholeheartedly or partially, throw in their lot with those hopeful people remaining loyal to Great Britain, in the expectation that they could peacefully resolve the issues by working with a government they knew and had long respected. Or, they could eagerly or reluctantly, wholeheartedly or partially, support the radical insurgents hoping to create a better type of government to guarantee their freedoms. But that new government might adopt one of several complex political structures, inviting further controversy. Each person's decision would dramatically affect the core nature of their daily life experiences, continued ownership of property, family safety, and future family happiness. They made their decisions as much for reasons of family survival as for belief in political theory. Whichever choice they made, there was no guarantee they were supporting the ultimately winning side. So, it should not be surprising that many people tried to stay neutral or only tentatively backed whichever side currently seemed to be winning during the long conflict just beginning. In the meantime, the restrictions of the Continental Association started to influence their lives.

Colonial Government vs. Extralegal Committees

Princeton's Richard Stockton served in the royal colonial government as a member of His Majesty's Council for the Province of New Jersey and also as the Third Justice of the New Jersey Supreme Court. William Franklin, the illegitimate son of Benjamin, had been governor since 1763 and had generally proven himself to be patient, understanding, and reasonable in handling such issues as the Stamp Act and the quartering of Royal troops. New Jersey, unlike several other colonies, had not experienced divisive local events involving its current Royal Governor that served as warnings of more significant confrontations to come. Neither hating nor loving him, New Jersey citizens generally respected Franklin.[1] Governor Franklin delivered a speech of hope to open the legislature on January 18. Afterward, Richard Stockton sat on a committee of three to prepare and bring in a draft response. The legislature approved that statement in which the Council clearly stated its loyalty to the Crown and its desire to help resolve the growing political difficulties and reunite the people.[2]

Leaders of the protest against Parliament began organizing committees outside of the government to bring about change. A gathering of Middlesex Freeholders met at New Brunswick on January 3. They agreed that every city, township, and district in the county, following "the eleventh Article of the Association of the Continental Congress," should meet and choose a Committee of Observation and Inspection to enforce compliance with the rules of the Association restricting economic activity with England.

Those committees would gather at New Brunswick on January 16 to select a Committee of Correspondence for Middlesex County. The Freeholders chose Princeton's Jonathan Baldwin to serve on the Committee of Observation and Inspection for Windsor Township and also on the Committee of Correspondence for Middlesex County, created to exist only until the meeting of the next Continental Congress. They saw the Continental Congress as a tool to help negotiate a resolution with England, rather than as a separate government. Therefore, the committeemen expected the colonial Assembly to nominate delegates to the upcoming Continental Congress. However, if they did not, then the County Committees of Correspondence would select them. The Freeholders confirmed their approval of the actions taken by the recent Continental Congress and resolved "to contribute all in our power towards carrying into practice the measures which they have recommended." In short, they would enforce the requirements of the Association.

The Freeholders adopted several resolutions. The fifth expressed the depth of hard feelings developing between those who held different opinions on the current situation. It stated, "We think it our duty publicly to declare our contempt and detestation of those insidious scribblers, who, with the vilest views, enlist themselves in the cause of the Ministry and by the vilest means endeavor to effect a disunion among the good people of the Colonies, that they may become a prey to the oppression against which they are so laudably and unanimously struggling." The Freeholders especially condemned those printers who "labor to circulate their pestilent compositions through the land, under the show of friendship and a regard to the public good; who, with the most unexampled effrontery against the sense of every man of the least information and impartiality, will persist in retailing the rotten, exploded, and ten thousand times confuted doctrines of a passive acquiescence in the measures of Government, however distempered and tyrannical."[3] In other words, they decried those who blasted out emotional diatribes rather than present factual information accurately and clearly. This failing could be ascribed to both sides, as can be seen throughout human history. Life became more difficult for those who disagreed with the protest actions, including those people who opposed the requirements of the Association because it granted unheard of powers to local people charged with enforcing a policy developed outside of the legitimate government.[4]

Loyalists often blamed Presbyterians for inciting opposition to the British government. However, John Witherspoon, as chairman of a committee of the Presbyterian synod, sent a letter to all the churches of New Jersey in May. He disclaimed any desire to inflame the people to seek independence, but also warned that if the British continued to enforce their actions by violence, "a lasting and bloody conflict must ensue."[5]

Jonathan Dickinson Sergeant served as the clerk for the Princeton Committee of Correspondence. He signed a letter in late April advocating for the convening of a Provincial Congress, a formal statewide organization, in response to the "very alarming intelligence lately received" about the April 19 incidents at Lexington and Concord. This letter went to the Committee at Woodbridge and then to Perth Amboy, where those attending a meeting of the inhabitants of Perth Amboy on April 28 heard it read. The idea caught fire, and on May 2, the New Jersey Committee of Correspondence called for a Provincial Congress to meet at Trenton on May 23.[6]

While New Jersey was creating a Provincial Congress, the Second Continental Congress began meeting on May 10, as scheduled. The Massachusetts and Connecticut delegates departed their homes on Monday morning, May 7, making the same trip John Adams and his party had made the year before. On May 12, Connecticut delegate Silas Deane wrote to his wife from Philadelphia. He told her about his journey through relatively peaceful New Jersey. He wrote that, after lodging one night at New Brunswick, "early the next morning, the militia mustered and guarded us to Princetown, where we were received by a Company under arms, the president and students, &c.

hence we rode to Trenton, and dined: thence to Bristol, and lodged, with a guard."[7] No casual tours of Princeton village and college took place this time.

Also, on May 12, a meeting of the Somerset County Committee of Correspondence at the Somerset Courthouse appointed Princeton merchant Enos Kelsey and Jonathan Dickinson Sergeant to be deputies to the Provincial Congress. At about the same time, Middlesex County chose Princeton residents Jonathan Sergeant, the father of Jonathan Dickinson Sergeant, and Jonathan Baldwin as delegates to the Provincial Congress.[8] Although several men serving in the Royal colonial government also served in the extralegal Provincial Congress, voters did not choose Stockton this year.[9] The committee instructed the deputies to help write up a plan for the militia of New Jersey, presumably similar to, but separate from, the longstanding civilian home guard established several decades earlier by the colonial government.[10] At the May 24 meeting, delegates elected Hendrick Fisher from Somerset County, living about fifteen miles from Princeton, to be president and Jonathan Dickinson Sergeant to be secretary. However, Sergeant resigned on May 30, replaced by William Paterson of Raritan, the son of Princeton merchant Richard Paterson.[11]

The work of the colonial Assembly, despite Royal Governor Franklin's efforts, shifted more and more to complement that of the extralegal Continental and Provincial Congresses. The Assemblymen increased their support for the resolutions of the Continental Congress while interest in making a separate effort at reconciliation with Great Britain declined. Leaders agreed that the use of violence should be a last resort. They did not want to drive away those not yet fully committed to the cause. Local committees, however, continued working to organize their militia companies. Widespread disagreement on how to resolve the conflict still existed. Many people were troubled by visions of the possibly disastrous consequences that could develop from the internal differences among the thirteen colonies with the shattering of their shared loyalty to Great Britain.[12]

On June 3, the Provincial Congress named Jonathan Baldwin to its elite Committee of Correspondence, a body given the power to convene the Congress.[13] On July 28, the Freeholders of Somerset County met at Somerset Courthouse and elected a Committee of Correspondence that included John Witherspoon and Princeton innkeeper Jacob Bergen.[14] Bergen was a prominent citizen who paid taxes as a householder in 1780, owning two horses, three cows, and a riding chair.[15] He would be politically active throughout the developing conflict.

While Princeton men became involved with the county and state committees in various ways, in Philadelphia the Continental Congress converted the militia troops besieging Boston into a Continental Army on June 14 and named George Washington its commander in chief on June 15. These military actions were not efforts to win independence but rather to achieve reconciliation with Great Britain on Congress's terms. Americans, including many in Princeton, generally hoped to establish a confederation under the King, independent of the authority of Parliament. As yet, only a minority hoped for complete independence from Great Britain. Full warfare commenced with the military engagements at and near Boston, the creation of the Continental Army, and the invasion of Quebec. However, the military objective remained reconciliation.[16]

Beginning on August 5, the Provincial Congress included Princeton's Jonathan Baldwin and Jonathan Sergeant from Middlesex County and Jonathan Dickinson Sergeant from Somerset County. The Provincial Congress told local committees to submit at its next meeting the names of all people who refused to sign the Association or had refused to pay "their respective apportionments"—that is, taxes—to support the cause.[17]

The Provincial Congress believed its accountability to the electorate was essential, so on August 12, the delegates called for an election on September 21 to choose representatives to sit in the next Provincial Congress scheduled to meet October 3. They wanted this election because it was evident that "this Province is likely to be involved in all the horrors of a civil war." Therefore, it would become "absolutely necessary to increase the burthen of taxes already laid upon the good people of this Colony for the just defense of their invaluable rights and privileges." Therefore, citizens "should have frequent opportunities of renewing their choice and approbation of the Representatives in Provincial Congress." This action demonstrated that they not only believed in "no taxation without representation" but also supported frequent elections to keep their representatives accountable.

Future elections would occur annually on the third Thursday in September as long as the troubles persisted. Annual elections would be held the same day to choose freeholders of each county for the County Committees of Observation and Correspondence with power to "superintend and direct the necessary business of the County, and to carry into execution the Resolutions and Orders of the Continental and Provincial Congresses." Also, each year on the second Tuesday in March, townships would elect their Committees of Observation and Correspondence with the power to carry out the acts of the Continental and Provincial Congresses and county committees.[18]

On August 17, the Provincial Congress appointed Jonathan Dickinson Sergeant to be the Provincial Treasurer and a member of the Committee of

Safety that functioned during Congress's recess.[19] The New Jersey Committee of Safety met at Princeton in August and September 1775 and requested that the various township committees send it a list of their militia officers, along with certification of their election according to the directions of the Provincial Congress, so that it could produce their commissions.[20] On August 31, it directed the minutemen to adopt hunting frocks for their uniform, "as near as may be similar to those of the riflemen now in the Continental service."[21]

Merchant Enos Kelsey was appointed on September 14 to serve on the Committee of Safety meeting at Princeton and on a committee to employ printer Isaac Collins of Bordentown to print the Provincial Congress Minutes and Committee of Safety proceedings "as to them may appear necessary." Neither Jonathan Sergeant, Jonathan Baldwin, nor Jonathan Dickinson Sergeant attended the October session of the Provincial Congress held at Trenton. While these extralegal groups developed, the colonial government continued to operate in parallel. His Majesty's Council for the Province of New Jersey met in Burlington on November 15, with Richard Stockton still a member, and continued through November 24. Stockton also continued to serve as Chief Justice.[22]

The Continental Congress resolved to drive the British from Quebec to prevent an attack on New York via the Lake Champlain/Hudson River corridor. In July, it gave its newly established Continental Army orders to invade Quebec with two forces. One under General Benedict Arnold would approach the city of Quebec by way of the Maine woods, and the other under General Richard Montgomery would advance along the Hudson River/Lake Champlain route. By mid-October, things were not going as planned, and Congress felt the need for additional Continental troops to make the slowly progressing Canadian campaign a success and to prepare for an anticipated British attack on New York City.

New Jersey had not yet raised any troops for the Continental Army, but on October 9, Congress asked it to raise two regiments. Four days later, the Provincial Congress considered that request but took no immediate action on it. The law required Princeton men to join the part-time militia, but now they would have the alternative to join the Continental Army as full-time soldiers removed from everyday family and town life. The Continental Congress ruled that, because resources were tight, recruits must arm themselves, and instead of receiving bounty money, each would get only a felt hat, a pair of yarn stockings, and a pair of shoes. The pay would be five dollars per month during their one-year enlistment, but if the war ended sooner, they could be discharged with an extra month's pay.[23] Before the end of the month, potential recruits living in Princeton read in Philadelphia papers such as *Dunlap's*

Pennsylvania Packet about the need for men to enlist in these regiments.[24] On October 28, while General Montgomery was preparing to attack Fort St. Jean on the Richelieu River in Quebec, the Provincial Congress commissioned William Maxwell as colonel of the 2nd New Jersey Regiment. Recruiting for the New Jersey regiments began. Because the only domestic source of recruits was the militia, any local man enlisting or obtaining a commission became a loss to his militia regiment.[25]

The Continental Army finally succeeded in taking Fort St. Jean on November 2, just a week after the New Jersey regiments received authorization to begin recruiting. Montreal was defeated with little resistance on November 11, leaving only the capture of the city of Quebec to finish the job. The New Jersey regiments busily recruited men to join the siege of Quebec, if they could get there in time. On November 27, the Continental Congress ordered the still incomplete New Jersey regiments to be placed in barracks as near to New York as possible. It also requested the Convention of New York to supply them with "as many arms as they can spare," since not every man who joined the Continentals could provide his weapons.[26] Frustrated by the slowness in filling the New Jersey regiments, the Continental Congress kept pushing the State to get them moving. On December 8, the Continental Congress again ordered the New Jersey regiments to march to New York City as soon as "barrack necessaries and arms" were provided.[27] Although raising the Continental regiments was going slowly, the process still put a strain on the New Jersey militia. It made it even more difficult for militiamen to obtain weapons and accouterments because items purchased by the government were given to the Continentals as a priority, with the militia getting whatever was left, if anything.[28]

Militia

New Jersey's history as a proprietary and then a royal colony produced a culture rich in protest, especially involving land deeds from the proprietors. Membership in a local militia company had been required in New Jersey from its beginning, making the militia formed by the Provincial Congress just a new manifestation of a longstanding, though poorly enforced, element of life in colonial times. In some ways, it was a throwback to volunteer militias called out to assist abused and imprisoned landholders in the 1730s and '40s.[29] However, for Princeton families, as for all New Jersey families, militia duty during the Revolution became radically different in its effects on daily life in comparison to the colonial period.

The news of Lexington and Concord produced widespread concerns throughout the colonies. In Princeton, fear of armed confrontation rose to new levels, and militia organizations took on new importance. The college students took a renewed interest in the military exercises of their makeshift militia company that had become something of a joke the past few months. Charles Beatty now wrote, "All around is war and bloodshed. You need not speak here without it is about Liberty—every man handles his musket and hastens in his preparations for war."[30]

The Provincial Congress passed its first Militia Law on June 3, ordering each township to form one or more companies of about eighty men between the ages of sixteen and fifty capable of bearing arms. Each company must elect a captain, two lieutenants, and an ensign, who would then appoint sergeants, corporals, and drummers. The companies grouped into regiments, and the company officers elected the field officers—including a colonel, lieutenant colonel, major, and adjutant—for each regiment. Captains were to maintain muster rolls. Men enlisted were to meet at least once a month for drill, at times and places determined by their officers. Each man was to equip himself as the regimental field offices ordered. The law required the men's obedience to their officers and their attention to learning military exercises, neither one a given. Informal companies already created could continue, provided they conformed to this militia ordinance. Militia duty was voluntary at this point and would involve the same men who were part of the mostly dormant colonial government militia.[31] But this law now required every white, free man in Princeton aged sixteen to fifty to decide how actively he would become involved, and then explain that to family and neighbors.

The militia law unsurprisingly proved defective, so on August 16, the Provincial Congress passed a revised version. Henceforth, the Provincial Congress would appoint the field officers of regiments. It also established between one and four regiments for each county, calling for two regiments in Middlesex and two in Somerset. Because the militia companies consisted of family members and neighbors with previously established authority relationships, Congress felt it necessary to remind junior officers to obey their superiors. It also created a procedure for dealing with those who didn't, set fines for those not enrolling or bearing arms, and for neglecting training, weapons, and equipment requirements for private soldiers.

Militia duty was no longer voluntary, so every man in Princeton, and his family, had to deal with it. Captains could use the money collected in fines to help arm men unable to procure equipment. All militia officers had to sign the Association and resign any commission they held from the Royal Governor of the Province. In imitation of the New England colonies, the

Provincial Congress called for creating volunteer minute-man companies. Middlesex should raise six companies, each containing sixty-four men and officers, to make up one battalion, and Somerset five companies to make up one battalion. The minute-men would be senior to the regular militia and serve a term of four months. Congress appointed two brigadier generals for the militia regiments and put an end to men raising independent, volunteer, light infantry companies because they interfered with organizing the militia.[32] It would take some time for the militia to become fully formed and for men to know just where they fit in. Companies were not being regularly called out for active duty yet, except for some policing actions in support of the Provincial Congress. Princeton tanner James Moore served in the militia company of Captain Peter Gordon in Colonel Nathaniel Heard's regiment beginning in December for one month, more or less, and went to Long Island to disarm some Loyalists.[33]

Community Life

During this volatile year, the Quakers of Stony Brook tried to carry on life as usual when they were not involved in the political debates. In June, the Chesterfield Monthly Meeting asked Robert White to inform Susannah Field of her rights of appeal against charges that she had not been attending meetings and had a child outside of marriage.[34] The Meeting asked Joseph Horner and Samuel Worth to acquaint John Clark (not the father of Thomas and siblings) with a complaint that he was "guilty of fornication with a woman he hath married and hath married his first cousin and had unchaste freedom with her before marriage and neglects making satisfaction." Clark made no effort to reconcile things, so the Meeting appointed James Olden and Joseph Horner to prepare a testimony against him. Thomas Olden and Matthew Clarke also came under complaint for marrying "contrary to the rules of our society." The Society of Friends disowned them until they "come to a sense of their misconduct and condemn the same to the satisfaction of the meeting." After the militia acts of June and August, Quaker men began to be accused of training with or bearing arms in the militia. On a positive note, Benjamin Clarke became the receiver of money for the poor.[35]

Friends visited with those who neglected to attend religious meetings or were "subject to a drowsy spirit therein," and the offenders gave "encouragement to hope for more diligence and circumspection in future." The belief against oaths proved challenging for some, and they noted that "the few friends who violate our Testimony respecting oaths incline to justify their conduct," rather than correct it. The Quakers had been making efforts to end the practice of enslaving people and had convinced a number to accept the idea of freeing their slaves. But even with so many ideas of freedom floating around, those considering manumissions were "discouraged from the apprehension of encumbrance which it might occasion to their outward estates." That is, former owners were financially responsible for the needs of the freed people so they would not become wards of the government. No members had imported or bought "Negroes," but "we think a more Christian care towards those amongst us needful."[36]

Like all communities, Princeton experienced changes in its population every year. Early in the year, village merchant Richard Paterson put several houses and lots up for sale, including his residence, which also contained his store, near the Hudibras. The stone building stood two stories high, fifty-three feet in length and thirty feet in breadth. The first floor contained five rooms, each with a fireplace, with one eighteen-by-thirty-foot room outfitted as the store. The second floor had six bedrooms, with fireplaces in three, and the garret above all. A cellar ran under most of the house. A detached kitchen, twenty-two feet long and sixteen feet wide; a "negro house"; a combined barn, stable, and carriage house fifty feet long and twenty feet wide, on fixed stone pedestals, with roof and siding covered with cedar; a well; a garden; and a yard all greatly enhanced the property. He noted that the house, standing less than a hundred yards from the college, could accommodate boarders in its several apartments. He also advertised another two-story brick house, with a cellar kitchen, on one acre of land. Finally, he offered forty-eight acres of good, well-improved land adjoining the town containing a convenient, continuously flowing stream of water and a small frame house with a good well and garden.

Merchant Paterson also used this newspaper ad to point out that he had "an assortment of dry goods, which he will dispose of at a low rate for cash, country produce, or short credit." He also advertised an enslaved man and two boys for sale. Everything had to go because Paterson was quitting his business and closing out his affairs. Paterson also asked everyone who owed him money to pay him so that he could pay his debts. His creditors did not wait, however, and to avoid legal issues, his lawyer son William took out a mortgage on his father's property. The situation did not end quickly or smoothly, and William ended up representing his father in more cases than he did for all his other clients combined.[37] At least one historian has concluded that elements of the affair left "an unpleasant air" about it, even if it was not actually "fraudulent." However, William had a solid reputation and eventually overcame his original middling status to rise high in State politics.[38]

A portion of Princeton residents did not own property, and there were several properties available for rent. Richard Stockton advertised the rental of his property known as Mount Lucas beginning April 1. He described it as being about one and a half miles from Princeton on the public road leading to Rocky Hill. The house was modest, one and a half stories tall with four rooms on the lower floor and bedchambers above, with a cellar and a kitchen. There were small amounts of meadow, arable, and pasture lands along with a garden producing various vegetables and berries. The orchard had both apple and peach trees. He summed up saying, "The whole is exceedingly well fitted for a gentleman retiring from business, or may suit a neat farmer."[39]

The eighteenth century was a time when most activities required vast amounts of human labor. Everyone needed some kind of human labor assistance, in addition to mechanical and animal power. Labor needs could be satisfied through a combination of free labor, indentured servitude, and human enslavement. Princeton craftsmen and merchants often employed indentured servants, a form of temporary slavery that could be equally unpleasant while it lasted. Jonathan Baldwin's indentured servant, Peter Murphy, ran away on June 17, 1774. He was an Irishman who spoke "respectful English" and described as about five feet ten inches tall, with brown, curly hair and a reddish complexion, wearing a brown coat, white breeches, and a rough beaver hat. Baldwin offered a thirty shilling reward for his return if secured within the province, and six dollars if out of it.[40]

Toward the end of May, college student Charles Beatty reported that people in Princeton put aside and forgot "the sad state of affairs" in Massachusetts involving the events at Lexington and Concord to join enthusiastically in celebrating the May 28 wedding of Anne Witherspoon, John Witherspoon's daughter, to Rev. Samuel Stanhope Smith.[41] Several months earlier, on March 14, twenty-nine-year-old Jonathan Dickinson Sergeant had married sixteen-year-old Margaret Spencer, daughter of influential Presbyterian Rev. Elihu and Joanna Spencer of Trenton.[42] While some couples joined in matrimony, others sought it.

In August, thirty-year-old Dr. Benjamin Rush of Philadelphia made one of his occasional trips to Princeton and stayed with his good friends Richard and Annis Stockton at Morven. Rush had studied medicine in Scotland and had helped Richard Stockton convince John Witherspoon to accept the job of president of the College of New Jersey. He now had a thriving medical practice in Philadelphia and had been thinking about marriage and starting a family. Just a year or so before, he had almost married, but his prospective bride tragically died of a sudden, brief illness not long before the planned wedding day. Visiting the Stocktons also meant visiting the six Stockton children, ranging in age from two to sixteen, and the family's staff of slaves and servants, including ten-year-old Marcus Marsh, whom Annis had nursed after his enslaved mother died not long after his birth in 1765.[43]

During this visit, Rush recalled he was struck by "a young lady between 16 and 17 years of age, [who] soon attracted my attention. She was engaging in her manners and correct in her conversation." He admired her "brown hair, dark eyes, a complexion composed of red and white, a countenance at the same time soft and animated, a voice mild and musical and a pronunciation accompanied with a little lisp." This charmer was the Stockton's eldest daughter, Julia. Rush and Julia had first met twelve years before when he came to Princeton and accompanied his friends Richard and Annis to commencement exercises at Nassau Hall. Then four-year-old Julia grew tired, and on the walk back to Morven, eighteen-year-old medical student Rush carried her in his arms. Now, Julia further impressed Rush with her opinion of Rev. Witherspoon after hearing him deliver a sermon. She declared that "He was the best preacher she had ever heard." Rush felt, "Such a declaration I was sure could only proceed from a soundness of judgment and correctness of taste seldom to be met with in a person of her age." He felt the best thing about Witherspoon's sermons was "their uncommon good sense and simplicity of style." Rush had been smitten and decided, "from this moment I determined to offer her my hand."

Rush visited Morven several times over the next few months, and by October 25, he and Julia became engaged. During the following two months, he visited Julia several times and wrote her letters two or three times each week, sending them by stagecoach to Princeton. These letters focused on his love for her. But the increasing violence going on around them raised his fear of an uncertain future, and he wrote, "Many of our future joys, and sorrows will flow I dare say from the good & evil which befall our country." More joyously, he explained the ways that she had already made him a better man and doctor through her love. In her letters, she expressed fear that her youth might prevent her from being a satisfactory wife to a busy doctor and public man. So he told her, "the eyes of men—angels—& of heaven itself will be fixed upon you, and you will at once be employed in sowing those seeds of benevolence which will yield you a full harvest of honor & happiness both here & hereafter." Although Rush was a very kind man who worked throughout his life for the causes of "blacks, women, criminals, orphans, and the insane," he could be very quarrelsome with some of his colleagues. Julia would prove to be a moderating influence, and he acknowledged this later when he wrote, "To me she was always a sincere and honest friend.

Had I yielded to her advice upon many occasions, I should have known less distress from various causes in my journey thro' life."

However, it took until a December visit for them to set a wedding date, and Rush held his bachelor party on December 27. The courtship had developed steadily even though her father and her fiancé held opposing views on the subject of independence. Annis's brother, Elias Boudinot, another frequent visitor to Morven, was more politically in line with Rush than with Richard. The members of these extended families displayed part of the range of ideas with which the people protesting were struggling at the time.[44]

The New Jersey Medical Society met at Princeton at William Whitehead's The Sign of the College tavern on November 14 at 11:00 a.m.[45] The previous August, Princeton's Dr. Thomas Wiggins, a member of the Society, had a brownish bay horse, fourteen hands high and about eleven years old, stolen from his pasture.[46]

Bristol Yamma and John Quamine, the two free black men from Rhode Island, had settled into their studies well. By February 27, 1775, Witherspoon reported that "Bristol Yamma has secured the money you lent him. He & his companion behave very well[, and] they are become pretty good in reading & writing & likewise have a pretty good notion of the principles of the Christian Faith." However, their money ran out by the end of the winter and they had to return to Rhode Island. The disruptions caused by the rising tide of war forced them to leave Princeton before completing their education. The missionary project did not work out, and neither man returned to Africa, primarily due to the war. John Quamine died while serving on a privateer during the war.[47]

The College of New Jersey

The college trustees met on September 27, commencement day, and recommended all twenty-seven members of the senior class for their degrees—except Thomas Craighead who was absent but would get his degree after paying his dues to the steward. Professor William Churchill Houston resigned his collateral office as "inspector of the rooms," but offered to pay five pounds per year out of his salary to the person appointed by the board to fulfill that duty.[48] The commencement ceremony once again contained orations with strong political content after a two-year hiatus, with titles such as "Civil Liberty Promotes Virtue and Happiness," "The Pernicious Effects of Arbitrary Power," and "The Growth and Decline of Empires."[49] The large audience expressed "great satisfaction with the performances of the young gentlemen who were admitted to the honours of the college." Among those receiving degrees was John Pigeon, who had given John Adams his tour the year before.[50]

While the courtship of Benjamin Rush and Julia Stockton progressed toward marriage, political events continued to escalate the colonial conflict. By the end of the year, the desire for independence still did not predominate among people in New Jersey. The debate continued between those believing reconciliation was either unlikely or unacceptable. The increasing militarization imposed on the people by the extralegal Provincial Congress made many people fearful and feeling exhausted. Governor Franklin did all he could in November to convince the Assembly to retake control of the government from the Provincial Congress. However, although Franklin was one of only four royal governors still in office in the thirteen colonies, he could not achieve this.[51] In the distant war outside New Jersey, the year closed with an assault against Quebec on December 31 that resulted in a disastrous defeat for the Americans with the death of General Montgomery and wounding of General Benedict Arnold. The New Jersey troops had not yet arrived there.

Despite the efforts carried out under the Association to bring England to its knees, England seemed to be hardening its position, and the colonists' military activities did not seem to be working. New Jersey Continental troops were still trying to get themselves ready to join the invasion of Canada, and people hoped the military action would cease before it involved any of the New Jersey militia, including Princeton's. The colonial government, although technically still existing, by all practical considerations, had been replaced by the Provincial Congress.

Chapter 3

January–November 1776

As 1776 dawned, many people in New Jersey wondered just what path the Continental Congress would lead them down. Would the colonies remain part of the British Empire or declare their independence? Would Congress march the colonies to a short term military but long term peaceful reconciliation, or to an even more intense war for independence? Leaders on both sides of the issue believed a majority of the people supported their actions, and only a small splinter group opposed them. Given the communication technologies of the time—print, voice, travel at horse speed—an incomplete, sometimes confused understanding of where things were heading was unavoidable. It was no wonder that so many people attempted to maintain neutrality or tended to change their minds, either in light of new information about events or from reacting to persuasive ideas delivered in written documents or oral exchanges. Throughout the year, people felt the effects of the acts of the Continental Congress, the resolutions of the Provincial Congress, and the changing nature of those government entities.

On January 1, New Jersey was one of thirteen colonies working together striving for reconciliation with Britain, and life in Princeton continued to function in a relatively typical fashion while complicated by the requirements of the Continental Association. But by December 31, the colonies were fighting a war for independence, and Princeton had been devastated by a storm of events beyond the control of its residents.

Life in Princeton Under the Association

As an extralegal document, individuals could sign the Association as they were pressured to do, or not, and risk the consequences. Enforcement was primarily by peer pressure working through the committees of observation, and the intensity of that pressure varied depending on a variety of factors. Altering one's lifestyle or even income source to adhere to Association requirements could be accomplished gradually in some cases but not at all in others. In February, after the Provincial Congress elected Jonathan Dickinson Sergeant to represent New Jersey in the Continental Congress, he received a pleading letter from three of his Princeton neighbors: Alexander McDonald, George Gillespie, and J. W. Sanders. All three men were originally from the West Indies, where they owned property, in addition to lands they held in Great Britain. They asked for relief from the provisions of the Association because their core business transactions involving trade with the West Indies, hitherto valued by the community, had become anathema, and put the lives of their families in danger as perceived criminals. They informed Sergeant that they had come to live in Princeton "for various reasons, but without the least idea of taking, or being forced to take any part in the present unhappy dispute betwixt Great Britain & these colonies." However, despite their "constant wish & endeavor to avoid giving offense to any persons whatever," they had been "summoned before the Township Committee [of Safety] to sign the Association, or give our reasons for declining it." They felt they should not be required to sign because "the Congress could not mean the Association to extend to persons in our circumstances."

No part of the Association provided them protection, and "on the contrary [they] might be exposed to forfeiture if [they] did sign it, or take any part in the matter." While the township committee seemed satisfied with their explanation, it claimed to have no power to excuse them and referred the matter to the County Committee, which might then pass it on to the Provincial Congress. While the three men expected the Provincial Congress would provide them relief, attending a session personally at New Brunswick was not only "troublesome & vexatious in itself, but it empresses the minds of the people with unfriendly ideas of our principles." Their situation was common knowledge, and one of their servants, sent to "buy some necessary for the family," was turned away by the merchant who declared, "your master's a Torrie." They worried that because "the minds of the people are getting daily more and more inflamed, it is not improbable but they may in time refuse to supply us with all the necessarys of life, or even deprive us of what we have under the notion of our being enemy's to the Libertys of America."

The three men asked Sergeant to bring their concerns to Congress and have it "publish such Resolves" spelling out "the line of conduct expected to be observed to and from us, & all peaceable West Indians now residing in the Continent of America." Like others in their situation, they could have returned to the Indies. However, they felt "the connections we have formed in this Country has endeared it to us, and made us very unwilling to tear the tender partners of our hearts from their families and friends, unless forced to it by dire necessity: the denial of safety and protection." If Congress could not comply with their wishes, they requested "a reasonable time to settle our affairs, hire a vessel to carry us off, & grant us a safe pass from their ships of war & privateers."[1] It is unclear what the immediate effects of this letter were. However, one or more of the three men may have departed the colonies for a time. A year later, John Witherspoon wrote to his son that "Mr. McDonald is come back & taken the Oaths to the State of New Jersey & behaves well." He subsequently appears on the Somerset County tax lists in 1779 and 1780, but the other two men do not.[2]

Other Princeton citizens who did not submit to the rebel congresses and committees also experienced unpleasant actions at the hands of their neighbors. Richard Cochran, living on the Post Road near Worth's Mill, was frequently called upon during 1775 and 1776 to join the American cause and take up arms as a militiaman. He consistently refused, and several times found it necessary to conceal himself in the woods. He never took any oath or subscribed to any agreement, such as the Association, so he was frequently threatened with jail. However, while very much oppressed and persecuted by the rebels, he was allowed to remain in his house.[3]

The embargo under the Association significantly increased the need for local production, and the Somerset County Committee of Observation and Correspondence met at Hillsborough on February 14 to consider ways to promote local manufacturers. Knowing Somerset County occupied an attractive location for trade, they solicited reports from various people regarding efforts to produce a variety of products. The committee concluded that they must do "what it was their duty and in their power to do, to continue and improve the disposition now so generally prevailing." Therefore, they decided that whatever would "make it easy for every person old or young, rich or poor, to do a little, and immediately to turn that little to their own advantage as well as throw it into the public service, must have the most immediate and powerful influence." The committee determined to establish market places for manufactured products in general and linen and wool in particular.

These market places would accommodate goods "in every stage of their progress" and include "wool, woolen yarn, cloth, fine and coarse wool cards; and for flax rough and dressed, linen yarn in any quantity, cloth green and whitened, also reeds and mounting for looms, wheels, reels, etc." On market days, people with unspun wool or flax could give it to less fortunate people who could then spend many hours spinning it into thread. This plan would encourage people to buy what they could "turn to account" and sell "what they have to spare." The committee believed that, when provided with raw materials and other help, "many poor people (old and young) would spin a little if they knew where to turn it into ready money at the end of a week or a month." In general, production would increase as everyone found raw materials more available and there was a market for their completed work. The proposed system provided a low expense and risk-free opportunity "for everyone to turn his own or families industry to his own immediate and greatest gain." This system would offer reciprocal advantages to both large producers and the country folk by attracting purchasers from a distance to an abundance and variety of products.

Writing on behalf of the committee, Rev. Witherspoon expressed the hope in a newspaper notice "that public spirited persons, will have encouragement to this plan, at first, particularly by bringing to sale, whatever they can spare, because it is supposed there will be many more buyers and sellers in the present state of things. After it is begun there is little doubt, that common interest will keep it up, and perhaps invite others to imitate it." Princeton would hold the market day for the western precinct of Somerset County beginning the first Tuesday of March and subsequently on the first Tuesday of each month. Every week, with only a few exceptions, some location in the county would hold a market.[4] Although not stated, the Princeton market would also benefit the Middlesex County areas near the village.

While dealing with the changes wrought by the Association, life continued in many standard ways with its usual difficulties. The June Quaker Monthly Meeting accused Mary Anderson of Stony Brook of marrying a non-Quaker and neglecting to attend meetings. Since she did not seem to be concerned about this, the Meeting disowned her until she came to a sense of her errors and condemned them.[5] Enslaved man John Longstreet escaped from Princeton sometime in 1776 and claimed freedom in New York City.[6]

Princeton and the War in Canada

At its January 13 meeting, the Committee of Safety ordered the president of the Provincial Congress to inform the Continental Congress that the Provincial Congress would meet at New Brunswick on January 31, to work on raising a third regiment for the Continental Army. Things were going slowly because of efforts to structure lines of authority among the extralegal committees. The Committee of Safety had not authorized officers to begin recruiting, because they felt the full Provincial Congress should choose those officers rather than just the Committee.[7] At some point before August 21, Dr. Thomas Wiggins became chairman of the Princeton Committee of Safety.[8]

While the debates over independence became a part of everyday life, the war in Canada brought troops through Princeton for various reasons. Alexander Graydon received a captain's commission in the 3rd Pennsylvania Regiment on January 5 and recruited men for his company. Toward the end of May, he received orders to "carry a sum of money in specie to General Schuyler at Lake George, for the purpose of promoting the operations in Canada." Accompanied by Ensign Herman Stout, he set out "in a chair, that being thought the most convenient mode of carrying the money, which was enclosed in two or three sealed bags." A chair was a small, two-wheeled, horse-drawn carriage designed to carry one or two individuals in a chair mounted on it and with space, or a container, for a small amount of luggage. It was something like the sports car of its time. Their escort consisted of just one mounted soldier, and they carried orders "for obtaining fresh horses as often as they might be necessary." While Graydon looked forward to enjoying the country on his route, which he had never seen before, he noted: "we did not so well like the responsibility of our charge." He felt very vulnerable to having the £1662 1s 3d stolen from him and his small escort, so they tried to conceal "the treasure, so far as might consist with the requisite vigilance."

On the second day of their journey, they stopped at Princeton and stayed at a tavern where they dined and had their bags brought to their room while the tavern servants took care of the chair and their horses. They found "the innkeeper, like the generality of his profession, was loquacious and inquisitive; and being an extremely good Whig into the bargain, took the liberty of sounding us respecting the contents of our bags, of which he had formed a very shrewd guess." Graydon did not try to conceal either the money or their mission from the innkeeper, both of which "he was equally desirous of knowing." Upon learning they were heading to Canada, "he entered into a dissertation upon our affairs that quarter, telling us, among other things, that the Prussian General, the Baron Woedkie, had been a few days before at his house, on his way to that country." The innkeeper had not been impressed by the baron and entertained Graydon with his impression of the baron "in very hard terms, repeatedly exclaiming, with a most significant emphasis, that he was no general." A primary reason the innkeeper gave for this evaluation was that the baron "had made his servant grease with a feather a certain part, to which he gave its very coarsest appellation, that had suffered from the friction of riding." Graydon naturally wondered, "whether our host had become acquainted with this circumstance by looking through a key-hole, or by what other means, we were not informed, but its unlucky effect upon him convinced me of the justness of the observation, that no man is a hero to his valet de chamber."

Graydon later commented that "the same baron it was, who, finding liberty one day the impassioned theme of some members of congress, and others, exclaimed—Ah! Liberdy is a fine ding; I likes liberdy; der Koenig von Prusse is a great man for liberdy! And so no doubt he was, for his own liberty or importance as a member of the Germanic body; and it might puzzle many a flaming demagogue to show a better title to the character." Graydon later found that "although The Prussian General made a great noise upon his first appearance [in America], the public mind in respect to him, whether correct or not, pretty well accorded with that of our host."

Upon departing the tavern, Graydon said the friendly innkeeper "expressed much anxiety for our safety, and that of our charge, recommending to us in future, not to take our bags out of the chair, where we breakfasted and dined. The propriety of this advice we were aware of, and observed it where practicable; that is, where the treasure was sufficiently under our eyes without removal." After completing his mission to the north, Graydon returned to Philadelphia carrying dispatches, rejoined his regiment, and marched to New York, again passing through Princeton. We do not know if he had an opportunity to visit the innkeeper to let him know of his successful mission.[9]

The Independence Debate

The debate over using tactics such as the Association to bring England to its senses or declaring independence as the only way to fix their problems continued with increasing intensity. The debates were not always about doing just one thing or the other. Short of independence, what actions would achieve the desired results, and how much pressure should be put on individuals to support them? For independence, should it remain as a goal if nothing else solved the problems, or should it be proclaimed immediately? Differences among family members and friends in the debates were often a matter of degree rather than of kind.[10]

One Princeton resident, Robert Lawrence, stated his position on the independence debate rather bluntly when he compared the colonists and British subjects living in England to brothers of the same parent. He reflected, "They allege that they are our parent kingdom, and we are derived from them and therefore we ought to do even to them as an obedient child ought to its parent." In Lawrence's opinion, the colonists only expected equality with the citizens of England by having representatives in the legislature that passed laws that affected them. However, he questioned, "Was ever such an unnatural parent heard of when a child desires no more than to be equal with his other brethren, to declare him illegitimate and therefore has no right to their birthright." Such a child would naturally be convinced "that he is disowned by his parent[,] made a bastard and thereby he is fully discharged from his filial duty by his unnatural parent."

The child then should have the right to "break off all connections with his lordly brothers and set up for himself as we have done, and [we] should be very well contented if they would permit us to enjoy the like privilege that generally bastards have[,] that is to shift for themselves and to be independent of all the family that we are said to belong too. But they will not allow us neither a lawful childs right nor a bastards independence[.] What kind of progeny they would have us to be I know not." Lawrence could not come up with a word for what Britain wanted and ended his comment with, "What mungrel relation they would have us to be I cannot find out[,] for I know of no word or term in the English language to distinguish it by."[11]

The new year had begun with the publication of Thomas Paine's *Common Sense* on January 9, the same day that Dr. Benjamin Rush set out from Philadelphia for Princeton to marry Julia Stockton on January 11, with their friend Rev. Witherspoon officiating.[12] Also, on January 9, the New Jersey Committee of Safety began meeting in Princeton. It ordered a man and horse to be kept ready, no doubt at a tavern, by the local committees of Newark, Elizabethtown, Woodbridge, New Brunswick, Princeton, and Trenton to forward expresses to and from the Continental Congress.[13]

By April, the people of Princeton began hearing that British peace commissioners, the brothers General William Howe and Admiral Richard Howe, were on their way to New York. This information impacted individual beliefs about reconciliation or independence. An anonymous writer in the Pennsylvania newspapers, under the name Cato, published a series of letters, the second of which gave strong arguments for entering into negotiations rather than seeking independence.[14] He referred to the longstanding and recent statements of the extralegal committees and government bodies that, whatever their grievances with the ministry or Parliament, they were steadfastly loyal to the King and proud to be part of Great Britain. Jonathan Dickinson Sergeant, having returned from Congress to Princeton "in a very indifferent state of health," could not have been more opposed to that idea and had to decide whether he would be more useful to the cause of independence at home or in Congress. In a letter to John Adams on April 6, he acknowledged that forty-six thousand British soldiers, hardly peace commissioners, accompanied the commissioners mentioned in Cato's published letter.

Sergeant told Adams that the long debates in the colonies had given the British government the time needed to get this force ready to destroy their cause. He declared, "O for the just vengeance of Heaven on the heads of those who have labored so assiduously to fetter our hands these six months past! If we fall I must ascribe it to our fatal mismanagement. We have backened the zeal of our people, discouraged our warmest friends, strengthened the hands of our enemies open & concealed, consumed our time, wasted our strength; but I hope we shall yet awake & at least not fall unrevenged."

Sergeant did not want the report of these approaching British forces to intimidate the colonists. He believed, "We can if we are in earnest cope with all this power & with the assistance of Heaven may defeat them." Downplaying or hiding the correct information would be worse for the people. Instead, Sergeant believed, "They should be solemnly appealed to, they should be called upon to make the last effort of their strength and I trust we may yet be delivered." He regretted the people "had never been lulled into a sort of security" before hearing about the Howes and their strong expeditionary force. He confessed, "You see I am rather in the dumps; but you must ascribe part of it to my disorder & part to a reflection which has some time haunted me, that there is a tide in these matters which I fear we have suffered to ebb." When the commissioners and their troops should finally arrive, Sergeant believed, "We have resources if we have the virtue to use them. The Crown lands, the quit-rents, the Tories...Could not we bid as high for Hessians & Hanoverians in the article of lands & estates as our enemies? My head aches & my heart aches. I tremble for the timidity of our counsels. Adieu!"[15]

Sergeant wrote Adams again on April 11, telling him, "The Jersey-Delegates (will you believe it) are not in the sweetest disposition with one another." William Livingston was absent, and John DeHart had gone home to declare himself a candidate for the Provincial Congress, where he could "control the mad fellows who now compose that body" and do more good. Richard Smith's health prevented his consistent attendance. Sergeant told Adams he would return to Congress if called on by the other New Jersey delegates, so the colony would not be unrepresented, even though "I fear it will be misrepresented if we attend."

Sergeant was conflicted about returning to Congress, concerned that "some very pious people are circulating a rumor that I have left Congress in disgust at the Doctrines of Independency which are there advanced." At times he felt he could do more by serving in the Provincial Congress rather than the Continental Congress, where the other New Jersey delegates did not agree with him about the need for independence, so his voice would be small there. He knew that in the Provincial Congress, "the old leven of unrighteousness will strive hard to poison that body by pushing in every creature that can lisp against Independence, which in other words, in my opinion, is every creature who would wish to give up the quarrel." He felt he could do little in the Continental Congress as a lone voice in the New Jersey delegation. However, he proclaimed that in the Provincial Congress, "I can & will preach up the necessity of a new government." He asked Adams for his speedy opinion because "by Sunday I must determine one way or the other if possible." Rather than be ignored in the Continental Congress, he could help persuade the Provincial Congress to send it enough delegates who supported independence.

Sergeant told Adams that Benjamin Rush had sent him a copy of the *Pennsylvania Evening Post* containing an essay on government written by a man he highly respected.[16] Rush also had informed him that the Pennsylvania Assembly had resolved to maintain opposition to "any propositions... that may cause, or lead to, a separation from our Mother Country, or a change of the form of this Government."[17]

Regarding the independence debate, Sergeant believed, "the grand difficulty here is that people seem to expect Congress should take the first step by declaring Independence, as they phrase it." However, this worried him because he believed, "there is a tide in human things & I fear if we miss the present occasion we may have it turn upon us." Sergeant was sure that Congress would not declare independence any time soon. In reality, he felt the colonies were already independent because every act of the Continental Congress "is that of Independence and all we have to do is to establish order & government in each colony that we may support them in it." This focus on the colonies rather than the Congress led him to challenge, "could not this idea be substituted in the place of Independence in the controversy, which, as it is treated, is no determinate object, brings nothing to an issue." The way things now stood, Sergeant told Adams, "the Catos (Cato you know is the common name of a Negro slave in modern times) will keep us in play talking about it & about it 'till the spirit of the people will evaporate or these blessed [peace] Commissioners will have time to play their pranks. God bless us. I wish Quebec was taken! What think you of all this?"[18] Sergeant returned to the Continental Congress by April 23.[19]

Rev. Witherspoon immersed himself in public affairs during the spring and summer, becoming a leading advocate for independence, which he now believed was necessary. On May 13, his letter appeared in the *Pennsylvania Packet*, signed "Aristides," defending Thomas Paine's call for independence, as argued in *Common Sense*.[20] On May 17, the day appointed by Congress as a fast day, he delivered a politically laced sermon on "The Dominion of Providence over the passions of men," dedicated to John Hancock as President of the Continental Congress. He announced, "I willingly embrace the opportunity of declaring my opinion without any hesitation, that the cause in which America is now in arms, is the cause of justice, of liberty, and of human nature. So far as we have hitherto proceeded, I am satisfied that the confederacy of the colonies has not been the effect of pride, resentment, or sedition, but of a deep and general conviction that our civil and religious liberties, and consequently in a great measure the temporal and eternal happiness of us and our posterity, depended on the issue."

Referring to the British government authorities, he judged, "Many of their actions have probably been worse than their intentions." He also believed these officials were no worse than any group of humans, and their mistakes had occurred "because they are men, and therefore liable to all the selfish bias inseparable from human nature." Politically, he rejected the claim of Parliament to the right "of making laws to bind us in all cases whatsoever, because they are separated from us, independent of us, and have an interest in opposing us." He proposed that separation was "the true and proper hinge of the controversy between Great Britain and America." Britain's distance from its colonies made it impossible for them to administer colonial affairs wisely and prudently, and "the management of the war itself on their part would furnish new proof of this, if any were needful... If, on account of their distance and ignorance of our situation, they could not conduct their own quarrel with propriety for one year, how can they give direction and vigor to every department of our civil constitutions, from age to age?"[21]

It was an emotional sermon that future student and colleague Ashbel Green felt "must, at the time it was preached and published, have been powerfully felt, and have contributed not a little to promote that sense of dependence on God, and earnest looking to him for protection and aid, which distinguished the pious and patriotic fathers of American liberty and independence." Witherspoon strongly advocated for independence and took every opportunity to do so.[22]

By mid-May, the Canadian expedition was in shambles, with the Continental Army in full retreat from Quebec. When word of this reached Jonathan Dickinson Sergeant in Princeton on May 20, he wrote to John Adams that "the many studied embarrassments thrown in the way of the Canada-Expedition have at last in a great measure answered the purpose for which I fear they were all along intended." Sergeant continued to have little respect for the work of the Continental Congress, telling Adams, "Ever since I have seen the inside of the Congress I have trembled." He felt that change could only come through bolstering the "Councils of our Middle Colonies" to get on board with independence and better policies for conducting the war.

The New Jersey election was a week away, and Sergeant hoped to win a seat in the Provincial Congress, believing he had a better chance in the county of his birth rather than where he now resided. Born on his father's farm in Somerset County, he now lived in a house he recently built for his young family on the Middlesex County side of the Post Road running through town. He was well known politically in Somerset, where he had served on patriot committees in 1774 and 1775. In Middlesex, he would have to compete with a core of political veterans known to those voters. Sergeant wanted very much to leave the Continental Congress. He told Adams, I "am determined that I will not continue to attend along with my present colleagues any longer than I cannot avoid," and "at present several little circumstances will form an excuse for my being absent." One of those "little circumstances" was no doubt four-month-old son William and his young wife, Margaret, while a related excuse may have been work on completing his new house in Princeton.

Sergeant feared that the upcoming campaign against the weighty British forces "will be a most awful one." He would feel more confident about it "if we were possessed of more unanimity & vigor. I wish people knew their men [in Congress] better & the steps they are taking; but alas! I fear they are betrayed without knowing it." If the colonies did not achieve more unification and adopt policies that made sense to him, he told Adams, "I will try to get a commission in the army that I may get knocked on the head betimes. This I think would be more eligible than to live to be a spectator of our country reduced to submission."[23]

Washington marched his army to New York after the British evacuation of Boston in March and began making preparations to defend it against the expected British expeditionary force. At about the same time Sergeant was writing to Adams, Congress called General Washington to Philadelphia from New York to discuss the Canadian campaign debacle and the upcoming campaign in general. Washington departed New York on May 21 and spent the night in Newark. On May 22, he had breakfast at Woodbridge, crossed over to Staten Island to inspect progress on defensive works construction, and then crossed back to continue on to Philadelphia. He apparently spent the night in Princeton at Jacob Hyer's Hudibras tavern and perhaps had an opportunity to talk with local leaders. He arrived in Philadelphia on the afternoon of May 23.[24] Washington remained in Philadelphia throughout the month before requesting leave to return to New York on June 3. During that time, part of his conversations concerned the New Jersey militia and its role in helping defend New York as well as their own province. He left Philadelphia on June 4 and took dinner at the Hudibras before continuing to New Brunswick, where he spent the night.[25]

Sergeant did win a seat from Middlesex in the Provincial Congress, while Witherspoon represented Somerset County. When enough members were present at Burlington, after an opening prayer offered by Witherspoon, the Provincial Congress began work on June 11. Four days later, Witherspoon and Sergeant voted yes on the resolution declaring Governor William Franklin an "enemy to the liberties of this country; and that measures ought to be immediately taken for securing" him. Franklin should be offered parole and permitted to choose to reside at Bordentown, Princeton, or his farm at Rancocas. However, if he refused parole, he should be secured under a militia guard.[26] Passing this resolution, the day after denouncing Governor Franklin's call "in the name the King" for a meeting of the Assembly on June 20, prompted Sergeant to write to John Adams quoting Julius Caesar at a turning point in his life, "Jacta est Alea. We are passing the Rubicon & our Delegates in Congress on the first of July will vote plump."[27]

On June 22, the Provincial Congress accepted Sergeant's resignation as a delegate to the Continental Congress because of his conviction that "it is better that I stay in the Colony for the present."[28] Then the Congress elected Richard Stockton, Abraham Clark, John Hart, Francis Hopkinson, and Witherspoon to represent New Jersey in the Continental Congress for one year. It also gave them instructions to, if they judged "it necessary and expedient," join in declaring independence and create a confederation for union and collective defense.[29] Although Congress was moving in the direction he supported, Sergeant explained to Samuel Adams, "I have declined being appointed anew to the Continental Congress for reasons which I have not room to explain (this being the only white piece of paper in Bristol). However you will have a sound delegation & they were instructed to vote right." He reminded Adams that, although previous delegates had kept people in the dark about their opinions, the new ones should be more open. But if Adams found any of them to be wavering or subverted, Sergeant would hope to be confidentially informed.[30]

When Witherspoon departed Princeton to attend Congress, he left William Churchill Houston, with two tutors, in charge of the college.[31] Witherspoon wound up serving in Congress for the next six years, wearing his clerical clothing, taking very little time off, and enriching the debates with his wisdom and experience, resulting in great confidence and admiration from his fellow delegates. He could have easily taken more time off because only two delegates from each state were required to be in attendance at any one time, and most delegations rotated among themselves to keep two delegates present.[32]

Witherspoon normally avoided prematurely speaking on important occasions, such as the debates about independence going on in Congress when he arrived. But, in this situation, he had no question about the legality of separating from England and believed that a statement of independence was needed immediately. He rejected the argument put forth to delay a vote on it, because there were new members in Congress, and stressed that the entire country had thoroughly debated the subject for some time and no one needed clarification concerning the arguments for and against independence.[33]

While the Continental Congress debated independence, back in New Jersey, the Provincial Congress appointed Jonathan Dickinson Sergeant to a committee assigned to write a constitution for the new state. By tradition, the committee composed at least some of it at the home of Robert Stockton on his farm next to Richard Stockton's, and his property became known as Constitution Hill. The committee produced this document within forty-eight hours, and it would serve until 1844.[34] However, as far as things had gone toward agreement on independence, this constitution still contained a statement reflecting the continuing hope among many for reconciliation. The last clause stated that, if the Americans and Great Britain resolved the issues separating them, this constitution would become null and void.

The College of New Jersey

Many American troops passed through Princeton during the first half of the year, with some temporarily taking quarters in parts of Nassau Hall and other locations, adding to the sources of confusion in the area. Witherspoon did not think his college boys should get involved militarily. However, Nathaniel Macon of North Carolina, class of 1778, later wrote that "while at Princeton New Jersey in 1776 I served a short tour of militia duty."[35] He was surely not the only one. In May, a company of student volunteers marched away to Elizabethtown intending to enlist in the Continental Army. Not all of them stayed with the army long, and some seniors came back at commencement to receive their degrees. Professor William Churchill Houston, having accepted a captaincy in the militia, had to divide his time between college and militia duties.[36] Senior John Pintard, in early 1776 made a habit of rising before dawn to help with militia units before attending morning prayers at Nassau Hall. Then, against the wishes of his family, he volunteered for the militia company commanded by his professor, Captain Houston, and served for about six weeks in the city of New York and vicinity. He did guard duty and served as his company cook at Elizabethtown, but saw no combat.[37]

When the college board of trustees met on September 25, on what was supposed to be commencement day, they did not have a quorum "on account of the difficulty of public affairs." Those in attendance agreed to recommend to the next meeting of the board that it should grant the degrees and that the resignation of Elias Woodruff as steward be accepted, and Aaron Mattison be appointed his successor. Commencement became a private affair, with no audience and no account of it published. The board scheduled a follow-up meeting for November 3 at Princeton because they believed a fall meeting was "of great importance." The minutes note that this meeting never took place because "the incursions of the enemy into the state & the depredations by the armies prevented this meeting, & indeed prevented all regular business in the college for two or three years."[38]

Senior William H. Vernon of Rhode Island wrote to his "Honor'd Papa" on September 26 and told him about the modified commencement. His letter is the only surviving evidence of just what happened in those troubled times. He reported, "two days before we met, and considering the public disturbances, and the back preparation we ourselves had made, one half of the class being unprepared and absent, in expectation of a private Commencement, having deliberately and maturely considered these on the one side and the disappointment of the people on the other, we determined on a private one." They ceased preparing for the usual commencement orations. However, on the appointed day, Dr. Witherspoon asked that as many of the class as were prepared "to speak that the people might not be entirely disappointed." Only seven students were willing to speak, and Vernon was not one of them. He had not practiced his scheduled oration on heroism but was persuaded by some of his fellow students to participate anyway and do a speech on standing armies, repeating one he had done the previous winter. The lack of trustees attending meant graduates could not receive their degrees, but Witherspoon informed the audience that the seniors had earned them. After the audience left, Witherspoon told the students that the trustees would meet the first Wednesday in November and would send their degrees to students not able to be present.[39]

In October, Witherspoon placed a notice in the paper that the college vacation would end, and college business begin on Monday, November 4. All returning and new students should be aware that student rooms would be assigned on Wednesday the 6th, and those not yet in attendance would forfeit any claim to a formerly occupied room unless they had previously arranged a leave of absence. The grammar school, where boys "are taught the Languages, Writing and Arithmetic with the utmost care," would open the same day.[40]

Regular Militia Service January to June

At a meeting on February 28, the Provincial Congress named officers for the 2nd Regiment of Foot Militia in Somerset County commanded by Colonel Abraham Quick. These officers included men from Princeton, such as Captain William Churchill Houston, First Lieutenant Aaron Longstreet, Second Lieutenant Zebulon Barton, and Ensign James Stockton.[41]

On June 15, the Provincial Congress ordered Middlesex County militia Colonel Nathaniel Heard to arrest Governor Franklin and described how Heard should act with "delicacy and tenderness." He should offer Franklin the opportunity to sign his parole, allowing him to stay at his location of choice: Princeton, Bordentown, or his farm at Rancocas. If he refused to sign his parole, Heard should place Franklin under a strong guard until further orders from the Congress, now known as the Convention.[42] When Heard confronted the governor, Franklin refused parole, so Heard gathered up sixty militiamen at the Perth Amboy barracks, marched to the governor's mansion, and surrounded it. Heard reported his action to the Convention, which then ordered him to bring Franklin to it at Burlington. The route chosen by Heard took Franklin from Perth Amboy to New Brunswick, where they spent a night, and the next morning they came through Princeton and other towns on the Post Road, where people saw the disgraced Loyalist governor surrounded by an armed guard of militiamen. At Burlington, the Convention questioned him, and Witherspoon found himself frustrated by Franklin's attitude. According to Ashbel Green, Franklin "treated the Congress with marked indignity." This incensed Witherspoon, who could not contain himself and blurted out "a copious stream of irony and sarcasm, reflecting on the Governor's want of proper early training in liberal knowledge, and alluding to an infirmity in his pedigree."[43] On Monday, June 24, the Convention ordered the governor transported to Connecticut, and on Wednesday morning, a guard of twenty-three light horse troopers set out with Franklin in a closed coach for New Brunswick, by way of Princeton, the first leg of his journey to Connecticut and exile.[44]

The Five-Month Levies

On June 21, the Provincial Congress appointed Princeton student Benjamin Brearley Stockton, son of Thomas Stockton of Princeton, to be a surgeon's mate in a combined battalion of Middlesex and Monmouth County Militia in now General Nathaniel Heard's Brigade of the five-month levies.

Stockton had left school before graduation to study medicine but had not yet finished his training. He was in that battalion at the Battle of Long Island (also known as the Battle of Brooklyn Heights), the first of the string of battles in which the British gained control of New York. In December, he joined the Hospital Department of the Continental Army.[45]

The troops of Heard's Brigade were volunteers who agreed to serve full-time for five months to help defend New York. Just how many Princeton-area men joined this force is not known. The five-month levies required so many men that the regular New Jersey militia was supposed to be freed from duty defending their state. Washington planned to defend New Jersey against British incursions from Staten Island by using militia troops from Pennsylvania and Maryland in his Flying Camp.

However, that plan did not work well, and beginning in July it became necessary to call out New Jersey militiamen to defend their state. This put an enormous strain on the men whose regiments and companies were reorganized for this duty. One half of each regiment and each company would be called out one month, and then the other half called out the following month. That rotation would continue as long as needed. Two regiments would combine, with the colonels of the two regiments alternating command each month and their officers and men serving every other month. For the common soldier, this meant sometimes serving under officers he did not know and not always the same officers.

This system completely upset the county organization the men understood. When the five-month levy enlistments expired at the end of November, the men had to return to their county militia regiments. As the calendar moved into December, New Jersey militiamen, both officers and privates, did not know just how to reconstruct their original companies and regiments. For example, some officers now had conflicting ranks. A private in the regular militia might have served as an officer in the levies and now was back to being a private—or was he? Officers who left the regular militia to join the levies had been replaced in their regular militia units. When their five-month service ended, did they return to their old militia rank and position or not? How about the men who replaced them? Did they simply revert to previous rank and duty? This confusion, combined with the British chasing Washington through New Jersey, made it very difficult for the New Jersey militia to coalesce and truly assist Washington in December.[46]

Independence

Princeton's Witherspoon and Stockton voted for independence on July 2 in Philadelphia. Pennsylvania had chosen Richard Stockton's son-in-law, Benjamin Rush, to represent Pennsylvania in Congress, just in time for him to vote for and sign the Declaration of Independence. The vote was for the freedom of the thirteen colonies, not necessarily for the formation of a new nation. As interpreted by historian of colonial New Jersey John E. Pomfret, "Each colony accepted the Declaration as an individual community, with its hopes, to a degree at least, distinct from the common aspirations that bound them all together."[47] John Adams explained the significance and difficulty of the feat to Hezekiah Niles, noting that "The colonies had grown up under constitutions of government, so different, there was so great a variety of religions, they were composed of so many different nations, their customs, manners and habits had so little resemblance, and their intercourse had been so rare and their knowledge of each other so imperfect, that to unite them in the same principles in theory and the same system of action was certainly a very difficult enterprise." He exclaimed, "The complete accomplishment of it, in so short a time and by such simple means, was perhaps a singular example in the history of mankind. Thirteen clocks were made to strike together; a perfection of mechanism which no artist had ever before effected."[48]

After the delegates to the Continental Congress finally accepted the wording for a Declaration of Independence on July 4 and copies were printed for distribution, a crowd assembled in front of Nassau Hall the evening of July 9 and heard it read. An observer noted that the college building "was grandly illuminated, and INDEPENDANCY proclaimed under a triple volley of musketry, and universal acclamation for the prosperity of the UNITED STATES. The ceremony was conducted with the greatest decorum."[49] Jonathan Dickinson Sergeant, with Margaret and little William, undoubtedly attended and cheered heartily with the crowd.

This joyous celebration contrasted sharply with the rapidly growing fear resulting from the enormous British expeditionary force landing on and occupying Staten Island and threatening New Jersey as well as New York. Washington had organized a military force he called the Flying Camp to reinforce his Continentals around New York and protect New Jersey. General Hugh Mercer, commanding this Flying Camp, ordered all Pennsylvania militia to march to Woodbridge. They would pass through Princeton, and Commissary Carpenter Wharton, at Trenton, noted on July 15 that two thousand Pennsylvania militiamen arrived there. A battalion had marched for Woodbridge to join troops stationed there to protect New Jersey from British forays from Staten Island. Wharton supplied them with provisions for one day at Trenton, expecting that when they arrived at Princeton, they would receive food for two days to get them to Woodbridge. Wharton appointed two men to serve as commissaries for the Flying-Camp units passing through Princeton. Wharton, therefore, would only provide troops with supplies to get them as far as Princeton, when those two men would take over.

Supplying these troops required large quantities of food, and Wharton had just received at Trenton 150 oxen, 500 sheep, and 1,500 barrels of flour, but that was only enough to last a short time in supplying the troops passing through, even if the men kept moving. He promised to submit returns to account for the money he received from Congress, but he currently needed $15,000 to supply the Maryland and Pennsylvania troops as they passed through Trenton. Finally, Wharton agreed to accept the appointment as Commissary of Stores for the Flying Camp if he was relieved from supplying the Pennsylvania militia.[50]

Now that New Jersey had declared itself an independent state, on July 15, an ordinance establishing regulations for the election of the first New Jersey State government passed the Provincial Convention. This legislation created safeguards, including loyalty oaths, to limit officeholders to those men supporting the Declaration of Independence and the new State Constitution. It also directed that the new General Assembly and Legislative Council initially convene at Princeton on August 27.[51]

Regular Militia Service After Independence

Maintaining the college routine while dealing with the recurrent calls for men to join the army was proving difficult. With the militia called out in large numbers, the Continental Congress resolved on August 14 that the tutors at the college in Princeton should be exempt from duty and directed to continue their teaching functions.[52] Several days later, on August 17, the Convention received a resignation letter from militia captain William Churchill Houston. He stated that, "from his connexion with the college in the absence of Dr. Witherspoon," he could not pay due attention to his company and begged leave to resign his commission. The Convention accepted his resignation.[53]

The division of the town between Somerset and Middlesex County put the men living in and around Princeton in a complicated situation concerning the county-oriented militia system. Princeton men living south of the Post Road, which separated the counties, belonged to the 3rd Middlesex Regiment of Colonel John Duychink. On August 9, William Scudder received his commission as First Major of that regiment.[54]

The approaching warfare led to a notice appearing in *The Pennsylvania Gazette* on July 16, asking the people of Pennsylvania and New Jersey to send "all the old sheets and other old linen they can possibly spare" for use by the military hospital in New Jersey. The notice encouraged people to follow up on this request with the words, "none will refuse complying with this request when they consider that the lint and bandages to be made of this linen may be used in dressing and curing the wounds of their own fathers, husbands, brethren or sons." The notice listed Princeton's Dr. Absalom Bainbridge as one of five New Jersey doctors accepting the donations.[55]

Loyalists After Independence

Captain Ibbetson Hamar of the British 7th Regiment of Foot came with his regiment to Canada in 1773, and during the American expedition against Fort Chambly in 1775 he was taken prisoner along with others of his regiment at the fall of the Fort in October. Congress sent the prisoners, along with their wives and children, to Trenton, where they arrived in November. The officers signed paroles and resided at various places about Trenton while the enlisted men quartered at the Trenton Barracks.

On January 17, Hamar requested and received permission to take quarters with Mrs. Hamar at Loyalist George Stainforth's home, near Strawberry Hill close to Princeton.[56] Six months later, on July 9, he submitted a second petition asking to be allowed to stay in the Trenton/Princeton area and not be removed to interior Pennsylvania with the other captive officers at Trenton.[57] It appears that his wife had died sometime before and that he was developing a budding romance with a local widow.

Several relatives of Richard Stockton acted on their loyalist beliefs. On August 3, Richard Witham Stockton accepted a captain's commission in a regiment of Loyalist Brigadier General Cortlandt Skinner's New Jersey Volunteers.[58] On August 10, the Convention ordered Joseph Stockton of Hillsborough committed to the common jail of Somerset until further order of the Convention or future legislature of the State. He soon after appeared before the Convention and took the necessary oath of loyalty specified in the election ordinance, so the Convention ordered his bond canceled, and on August 19, he was released from confinement and considered a proper subject of the State.[59] However, he soon revealed his true convictions and joined a Loyalist regiment in November.[60]

Life in Princeton after Independence

While life in Princeton after Independence may not have materially changed, people's sense of identity certainly did. Some of the changes were simple or symbolic on the surface. Like many clergymen, after the colonies declared independence, Witherspoon abandoned the "full-bottomed wig" and "wore his own natural hair which covered the whole scalp, and at its lower extremity, was confined in an artificial curl, or buckle."[61] While serving in Congress, Witherspoon kept in contact with his family through letters. On July 29, he wrote to his youngest son, David, then a teacher at Hampden-Sydney Academy in Virginia. He gave David news of David's brother James, who was developing some frontier land at Ryegate, in today's Vermont. James, along with several men, "went over through the woods for intelligence & when they came to St. Johns found it in the enemy's hands, were in great danger of being taken & obliged to return through the woods with but one biscuit apiece to maintain them for two or three days." David's brother, John, was at New York working in the military hospital and "well pleased with his situation." Any expectations or plans to see family members were full of "uncertainty on account of the Congress."[62]

By August, Witherspoon told David that John in New York expected a British attack any day and that James expected to be back in Princeton soon. While explaining to David about the difficulty in raising quality troops to oppose the British, Witherspoon noted, "The Philadelphia Associators, who went to the camp, have many of them behaved very badly. They were mutinous and disorderly; many went away without leave, and I believe they are now mostly dismissed." They had been ordered to New Jersey to relieve its overused militia but had been more trouble than help.[63]

The Quaker Quarterly Meeting had to report in August that some members could not resist the consumption of spirituous liquors, but others were careful about it. In general, members were respecting the need to stay clear of military training and services, except for a few who were under care about it. Members continued to refrain from buying or importing slaves, except for two people they put on notice. However, too many slave owners were neglecting the education of their slaves.[64]

In about the middle of August 1776, while people worried about the war and the upcoming initial meeting of the new State government, deadly illness struck the Princeton area. A series of disorders began with the bloody flux, taking the lives of many people. In the fall, after the bloody flux (fever, intestinal bleeding, and diarrhea), pleurisy and other fevers continued to cause suffering into the spring of 1777. One victim of the bloody flux was Benjamin Olden, the son of Joseph and Anne Olden, who lived near the Stony Brook Friends Meetinghouse, although they were apparently now Presbyterian. He attended the college for several years as a member of the class of 1776 but died in September at the age of 16. Smallpox also broke out, affecting both civilians and soldiers. In one case near Princeton, authorities quarantined fourteen sick soldiers in one house, where seven of them died. Several families and many soldiers received inoculations, and among that group, only one child died.[65]

New State Government

On August 27, New Jersey's five-month levies fought in the Battle of Long Island, or Brooklyn Heights, while the new State legislature met in Princeton, unaware of the fighting. The newly elected General Assembly lacked a quorum until Thursday, August 29, when the delegates unanimously chose John Hart to be Speaker and Princeton's Jonathan Deare, an English gentleman and lawyer, to be Clerk of the Assembly. Termed "Esquire" in tax records, Deare had a small twenty-acre farm and paid taxes for just one horse and one cow in September 1779.[66] On October 2, a paper from the Librarian of the College of New Jersey was read offering, by order of the faculty, the college library for the use of the Assembly. This offer was accepted with thanks. The Assembly appointed Princeton resident David Olden to be Sergeant at Arms and Robert Hamilton to be Doorkeeper.[67]

The first Joint Meeting of the Legislative Council and the General Assembly took place on August 30 in the college library. The delegates chose John Stevens chairman of the meeting, and he immediately proposed that the first order of business should be to select the governor. The vote resulted in a tie between William Livingston and Richard Stockton. Procedures had not been clear, and the next day, the Joint Meeting chose a new chairman, Nathaniel Scudder, and held a second vote for governor under the new ruling that the chairman could not vote except to break a tie. In the voting that followed, the delegates elected William Livingston governor and Richard Stockton Chief Justice of the State. The Joint Meeting then adjourned to resume on Monday, when the legislators learned that members had notified Stockton of his election as Chief Justice and that he would respond shortly. On September 3, Stockton declined the office of Chief Justice, feeling he could do more by retaining his seat in the Continental Congress and perhaps upset about the election. The next day, the Joint Meeting elected a group of judicial officials and Jonathan Dickinson Sergeant as clerk of the Supreme Court; however, two days later, he declined to serve.[68]

On September 12, the Assembly and Council formed a joint committee to settle the accounts of four men who had served as treasurer of the State. The committee met at the Hudibras.[69] On September 13, the Joint Meeting elected tavern keeper Jacob Bergen to be a justice for Somerset County, and on September 19, chose Jonathan Baldwin to be a Justice of the Peace for Middlesex County.[70]

On October 8, the Assembly held a final meeting in Princeton before relocating to the Old Meetinghouse in Burlington and continuing sessions there beginning in mid-November.[71] While at Princeton, the new State government had organized itself and established State and county civil officeholders, militia field officers, court justices, justices of the peace, and other officials.

Supplying the New Jersey Continental Troops with Clothing

The new State government quickly began efforts to purchase clothing in New Jersey for use by the army. On October 1, the Assembly appointed William Churchill Houston and Jonathan Baldwin to receive $30,000 from Congress for that purpose.[72] In Philadelphia, Richard Stockton served on a Congressional committee, consisting of one representative from each state, appointed to "devise ways and means for furnishing the army with clothing, &c." and notified the legislature, sitting at Princeton, that it should appoint persons in each county to acquire clothing.

Stockton went to Saratoga, New York, to investigate army conditions for Congress. He noted that New Jersey's Colonel Elias Dayton and Major Francis Barber of the new 3rd New Jersey Regiment had arrived the previous evening, "and the regiment is now within a few miles of this place, marching with cheerfulness, but great part of the men barefooted and barelegged." Barber had been born in Princeton in 1750 and commissioned as Major in the 3rd New Jersey on January 1, 1776. The lack of sufficient clothing for the troops was painfully obvious, and Stockton found, "My heart melts with compassion for my brave countrymen who are thus venturing their lives in the public service, and yet are so distressed. There is not a single shoe or stocking to be had in this part of the world, or I would ride a hundred miles through the woods and purchase them with my own money; for you'll consider that the weather here must be very different from that in New-Jersey: it is very cold now I assure you." Writing to Abraham Clark, he begged, "For God's sake, my dear sir, upon the receipt of this, collect all the shoes and stockings you can, and send them off for Albany in light wagons; a couple of two-horse wagons will bring a great many, which may be distributed among our several regiments who will be all together at Ticonderoga in a few days. If any breaches and waistcoats be ready, send them along; but do not wait for them if the shoes and stockings are ready and the others not."

The troops at Ticonderoga expected to be attacked hourly by a British fleet and soldiers, veterans of several engagements around Lake Champlain during Benedict Arnold's well-executed retreat from Canada to prevent the British from reaching Ticonderoga before the end of the fighting season. Stockton felt the defensive works at the fort were very strong, and the boom "thrown across the water from Ticonderoga to Mount Independence" would prevent the British fleet from passing the fort to attack from multiple directions. "Therefore, I trust, with the blessing of Almighty God, that we shall disappoint their wicked and sanguinary purposes." Still, Stockton worried about the troops and asked, "but shall the brave troops from New-Jersey stand in the lines half-leg deep in snow, without shoes or stockings? God forbid! I shall empty my portmanteau of the stockings I have for my own use on this journey, excepting a pair to take me home; but this is a drop of water in the ocean."[73]

In a letter from Princeton to General Horatio Gates on October 30, Witherspoon mentioned Gates's son, Robert, a student at the college grammar school. Witherspoon told him that "it is not long since I heard from Mrs. Gates & your son who went home the beginning of vacation. I expect her here with him in about 10 days when the college session begins. I have the pleasure of assuring you that he has in all respects behaved in the most unexceptionable manner & acquitted himself well at examination for admission into college so that I hope you will have much pleasure in him." Regarding his own family, Witherspoon reported that his son James "finds he can do nothing in the present situation of affairs upon his farm & therefore is desirous of going into the army," and Witherspoon knew James wanted to serve with Gates. Rather than obtain a commission in a New Jersey regiment, in late October, James carried letters from his father to General Philip Schuyler, commander in Northern New York, and General Gates, seeking an appointment as an aide-de-camp or similar position. Witherspoon felt, "I think it could be a happy introduction and as he is young, vigorous & active I hope he would acquit himself with fidelity & credit in that service." Although Witherspoon had given James a letter to newly promoted General Maxwell, he still depended "on your friendship & advice to him which he will certainly follow." On November 16, James received a commission as the Major of Brigade in Brigadier General William Maxwell's New Jersey Brigade.[74]

Witherspoon had heard about the destruction of Benedict Arnold's fleet on Lake Champlain but hoped for more success in that area. With that in mind, he wrote: "I have given all the attention in my power to the supply & interest of the Northern Army & shall continue to do so."[75]

In early November, the Continental Congress gave Witherspoon "leave to take with him to Princeton, Archibald Gardiner, James Henderson, Peter Jack, and Hugh Ross, four of the prisoners lately sent to Philadelphia, and there to keep them till the farther orders of Congress."[76] This may have been the first of several efforts by Witherspoon to arrange for British prisoners of war to be brought to Princeton to work for people in various ways. If so, they would not be in Princeton very long this time.

On November 17, Witherspoon wrote to son-in-law Benjamin Rush that his son John had informed him in detail about the treatment for the sick in the army. He expressed the belief that "D[octor] M[organ] seems very unfit for his charge & seems set upon nothing but making money." Dr. John Morgan, under whom young John Witherspoon studied medicine, headed the hospital system and had received heavy criticism for how he was running things. A proud father promoting his son, Witherspoon asked Rush, "If John wants a set of instruments please to direct & assist him. I am glad to find by all accounts from different hands that he has been pretty active." Witherspoon had been in Princeton on college business, but "as soon after the trustees meeting as the business of the college will permit I propose to return [to Congress] being anxious for the public cause."[77]

November 17 was the day that British forces on Manhattan captured the garrison of Fort Washington. Within days they would cross the Hudson, which Washington had already crossed over, and capture Fort Lee, directly across the river from Fort Washington. Thus began the pursuit of Washington across the State of New Jersey toward Philadelphia by way of central New Jersey towns such as Princeton.

Washington's Retreat Across New Jersey—Threat to Princeton

During Washington's retreat across the State, each express rider that galloped past Nassau Hall carrying military dispatches from Washington to Congress brought fresh bad news. Knowing that British soldiers were approaching their homes, the people of Princeton had every reason to fear their arrival. The town had played a central role in establishing the New Jersey Provincial Congress as early as April 1775. In August and September 1775, the Committee of Safety, acting for the extralegal Provincial Congress, headquartered at Princeton and then again beginning in January 1776. In August, the new State government organization took place, the first State legislature met in Nassau Hall and inaugurated William Livingston as the first

State governor in September. The Great Seal of the State, the earliest American State Seal, had been adopted there in October. The town was home to three delegates to the Continental Congress, and two had signed the Declaration of Independence. American troops had quartered in Princeton in September, and no doubt had been passing through town all summer and fall.[78] If any New Jersey town represented the enemy to the British, it was Princeton, and the British reputation for plunder was growing daily.

On November 21, while Washington's army was retreating across New Jersey near the Passaic River, John Witherspoon was still at Princeton and concerned about the sick soldiers passing through town. He wrote to Richard Stockton in Philadelphia that "there was sent to me this day the enclosed list of medicines ordered for tending the sick which if they are furnished it seems Dr. Bainbridge whom I did not see has offered his assistance. You may do in this as you think best but nursing & attendance & shelter to them are absolutely necessary." The twenty-seven items on the list included opium, emetic tartar, cream of tartar, and gum camphor. He noted that "I spoke to John Hill two days ago who promised to take care of them provided some money was sent up for the necessary expenses." Witherspoon recommended providing Princeton merchant Enos Kelsey with money to use to supply John Hill as needed. He suggested it might be better immediately to appoint a deputy quartermaster to serve at Princeton. Kelsey also served as a Somerset County justice of the peace and a judge in common pleas court. In May, he won election to the New Jersey Provincial Congress and also helped to raise supplies for the Continental Army. Witherspoon hoped to get to Philadelphia for a day or two the next week to check on some affairs but was not sure if he would be able to.[79]

On November 22, the Continental Congress sent John Witherspoon, George Ross, and William Paca to consult with General Washington at his headquarters, wherever in the State it might then be, about how the army could be enlarged and stabilized. The vanguard of his retreating army got to Newark late on the afternoon of November 22, and Washington arrived with the rest of the troops the next day. The delegates found Washington at Elizabethtown after passing through the many sick and wounded soldiers moving wearily in advance of what remained of the main army.

George Ross wrote from Princeton on November 28 that "the distress of our soldiers who I have met almost naked and hardly able to walk or rather wade through the mud has given infinite pain." Even worse, he found that "they fall dead on the road with their packs on their backs or are found accidentally perishing in hay lofts." In his opinion, there was "too much inattention to the sick. Pray God forgive the negligence wherever it may be." The committee had already taken the step of gaining the approval of Congress for their appointment of "an assistant quarter master and commissary, to provide for a number of sick, and to take care of stores sent to Princeton." They had also paid Jacob Hyer to maintain an express horse at the Hudibras to expedite communications.[80] While looking to the future, they were shocked by the condition of the troops in the rapidly disintegrating army and must have wondered whether anyone could save the cause.

Closing the College

After meeting with Washington at Elizabethtown and seeing enough of the retreating army to be greatly alarmed, John Witherspoon returned to Princeton, sadly knowing that he must close the college and fearfully aware that he could not protect his students.[81] He wrote to Governor Livingston on November 29 from Princeton to provide him with the devastating information learned at Headquarters so Livingston could communicate it to the General Assembly. Washington felt his forces were "altogether insufficient to face the enemy" and complained of massive desertion. Also, many men just left when their enlistments expired, even though they were badly needed. The British seemed destined to head through New Jersey for Philadelphia, and Washington planned to remove all military stores to Pennsylvania and hoped to enlarge his forces with militiamen to prevent its capture. Washington wanted to make a stand, perhaps at New Brunswick, but could only risk it if he obtained more men.[82]

Joseph Clark, one of Witherspoon's students, recorded in his journal that "on the 29th of November, 1776, New Jersey College, long the peaceful seat of science and haunt of the Muses, was visited with the melancholy tidings of the approach of the enemy" to New Brunswick. Their next stop would be Princeton, and not knowing that General Howe would order General Lord Cornwallis to halt at New Brunswick, at least for a short time, people believed the enemy troops would get to Princeton within a few days.

The twenty-three-year-old Clark was born near Elizabethtown, already in British hands, where he had been apprenticed to a carpenter when seventeen years old, but prepared himself for college and was able to enter the College of New Jersey. For Clark, the news of the British approach "alarmed our fears" and worries that "we must soon bid adieu to our peaceful departments and break off in the midst of our delightful studies." The full impact of the news hit home for Clark when Witherspoon gathered the students together, entered the meeting hall, "and in a very affecting manner informed us of the improbability of continuing there longer in peace." He gave the students instructions and "much good advice" before "very affectionately" bidding them farewell. Looking around him, Clark saw that "solemnity and distress appeared almost in every countenance."

Students from great distances now had to search for a way to get home with or without their belongings. Many would leave things behind "through the impossibility of getting a carriage at so confused a time." Returning home from college was not easy for the boys at Princeton, who typically arranged transportation months ahead of time. With New Jersey in a state of panic, farmers hid their horses and other livestock, and those people departing town in fear used their horses themselves. Princeton farmer and distiller John Johnson, who strongly favored the Revolution, lived on a large, productive farm near Worth's Mill and had earlier asked Clark about teaching his young son. So, Clark quickly settled his business at the college, brought his trunk and desk to Johnson's house, and "agreed to stay with him until spring."[83] He could not go home to British-occupied Elizabethtown, but staying with Johnson put him directly in the path of the British advance.

As the war became more intense during the fall, some students had joined the army, and others did so now. William Barber of Princeton, younger brother of Major Francis Barber, had taken a commission as ensign in the 3rd New Jersey the month before on October 19, perhaps emulating his big brother. Samuel Reading Hackett accepted a commission as ensign in the 4th company of the 3rd New Jersey Regiment on November 29. Adam Hoops, Jr. of Carlisle, Pennsylvania, would take a commission as 2nd Lieutenant in Colonel Moses Hazen's 2nd Canadian Regiment on December 9. Local student Ebenezer Stockton, son of Robert Stockton, had entered the college in 1774 and no doubt walked the mile or so home, but whether he remained there or departed to get further away from the approaching enemy is not known. Aaron Dickinson Woodruff, class of 1779, son of former college steward Elias Woodruff, was already home. John Armstrong, Jr., of Carlisle, Pennsylvania, joined the army and became an aid to General Mercer. He would return to Princeton with Mercer in about a month.[84]

Decisions to Stay or Evacuate Princeton

Residents of Princeton had to decide quickly whether or not to leave town and how to protect their belongings if they could. The retreating American army approaching Princeton had been through four months of bitter fighting during which they experienced repeated defeat and retreat. The men with Washington were the surviving remnants of a much larger force depleted by battlefield casualties, illness, and desertion. The British soldiers following them and pushing their retreat across New Jersey had also experienced the tough campaign for control of the city of New York and surrounding areas and were looking for a closing victory. On their march through New Jersey, the British and Hessian soldiers, along with their wives, had become feared for plundering and physically abusing both supporters and opponents of the Revolution. Both the American and British armies would pass through Princeton, neither one pleased to be there. Both would need large amounts of food, wood, and shelter from the local people. The town of Princeton symbolized the rebellion to the British military. The British would not be inclined to treat the town and its people well.

Richard and Annis Stockton left Princeton hurriedly on November 29. Annis packed the family silver and other valuable objects and had them buried in the garden—hopefully safe from British plunder. Richard and Annis, along with their twin girls Mary and Susan, now fifteen; eight-year-old Lucius Horatio; and three-year-old Abigail, drove off into Monmouth County to the home of John Covenhoven, "Federal Hall," some thirty miles away. They must have taken a wagon that carried whatever items they brought with them, as well as the children. Annis rode in the old family chair while Richard rode beside it on his sorrel mare.

Twelve-year-old Richard, who had just entered the college for his first year of study, is believed to have remained behind at Morven in the care of a trusted old slave. Whether young Richard was ill or the Stocktons thought that to completely abandon the property would provide an excuse for the enemy to mistreat it is not clear. It was not unusual for a fleeing man to leave behind members of his family, often including his wife, or even just a slave, for that reason. In any event, Annis and Richard were heartbroken to leave the house and gardens they had spent so much time and creativity developing during their life together. They knew that the American and the British armies would soon be crossing their land and perhaps fighting a battle on it. What would be left when, or even if, they returned?[85] Why Richard did not choose the shorter journey to Trenton and then cross the Delaware River to greater safety in Pennsylvania, like so many others decided to do, is not known. Everyone had to decide on an escape route quickly, lacking complete knowledge about the entire situation. Some chose well, and others did not.

While people desperately scrambled to get out of town and find protection for themselves and their belongings, Captain Ibbitson Hamar, no longer a prisoner of war, joyously married widow Sarah Howard on November 30, and became the owner of Castle Howard on December 12. Sarah had recently lost her husband, retired Captain William Howard of the British 17th Regiment of Foot. Howard had become an ensign in the 17th Regiment of Foot in 1735 when he was fifteen years old and lieutenant in 1741, purchased his captaincy in 1756, and came with his regiment to America, serving throughout the French and Indian War. Forty-seven-years old, when the regiment was preparing to return to England in 1767, Howard asked for permission to sell his commission due to poor health. He settled on a two-hundred-acre estate with a stone mansion that he purchased near Princeton on the road toward Kingston and married Sarah Hazard. His house became known as Castle Howard. Howard played a minimal role in the Revolutionary crisis, though his strong Patriot views were well-known to locals. According to tradition, he was a victim of gout and confined to his room by 1776. Sarah was an enthusiastic Loyalist and insisted on entertaining British sympathizers who passed through the community. The old veteran, forced to listen to their unwelcome political views, had painted over his mantel "No Tory Talk Here." He died sometime in 1776.[86]

A Proclamation of Amnesty

Amid the abject fear of some and matrimonial happiness of others, on November 30, the Howe brothers issued an amnesty proclamation. It looked like the Revolution would soon be over, with a British victory. Washington's army had consistently suffered defeat and retreat. The enlistments of several thousand New Jersey militiamen in the five-month levies that had fought alongside the Continentals in the New York campaign expired that day, contributing to the dissolution of Washington's army. The British were expanding the area they controlled across central New Jersey. Many people found the Howes' promise of "a full and free pardon of all treasons and penalties" and protection of person and property to be irresistible. Hundreds flocked to sign papers reading, "I, A.B. do promise and declare, that I will remain in a peaceable obedience to His Majesty, and will not take up arms, nor encourage others to take up arms, in opposition to His authority."[87]

By the end of the day on November 30, the amnesty proclamation first appeared posted in public places. That same day, the legislature Joint Meeting at Burlington elected Richard Stockton, Jonathan Dickinson Sergeant, and John Witherspoon to one-year terms as delegates to the Continental Congress along with Abraham Clark and Jonathan Elmer.[88] Stockton had already fled Princeton to hoped-for safety in Monmouth County, Sergeant had presumably left for Philadelphia, and Witherspoon prepared to depart rapidly. When would the American army, followed by the British, actually arrive in Princeton, and how long would they stay?

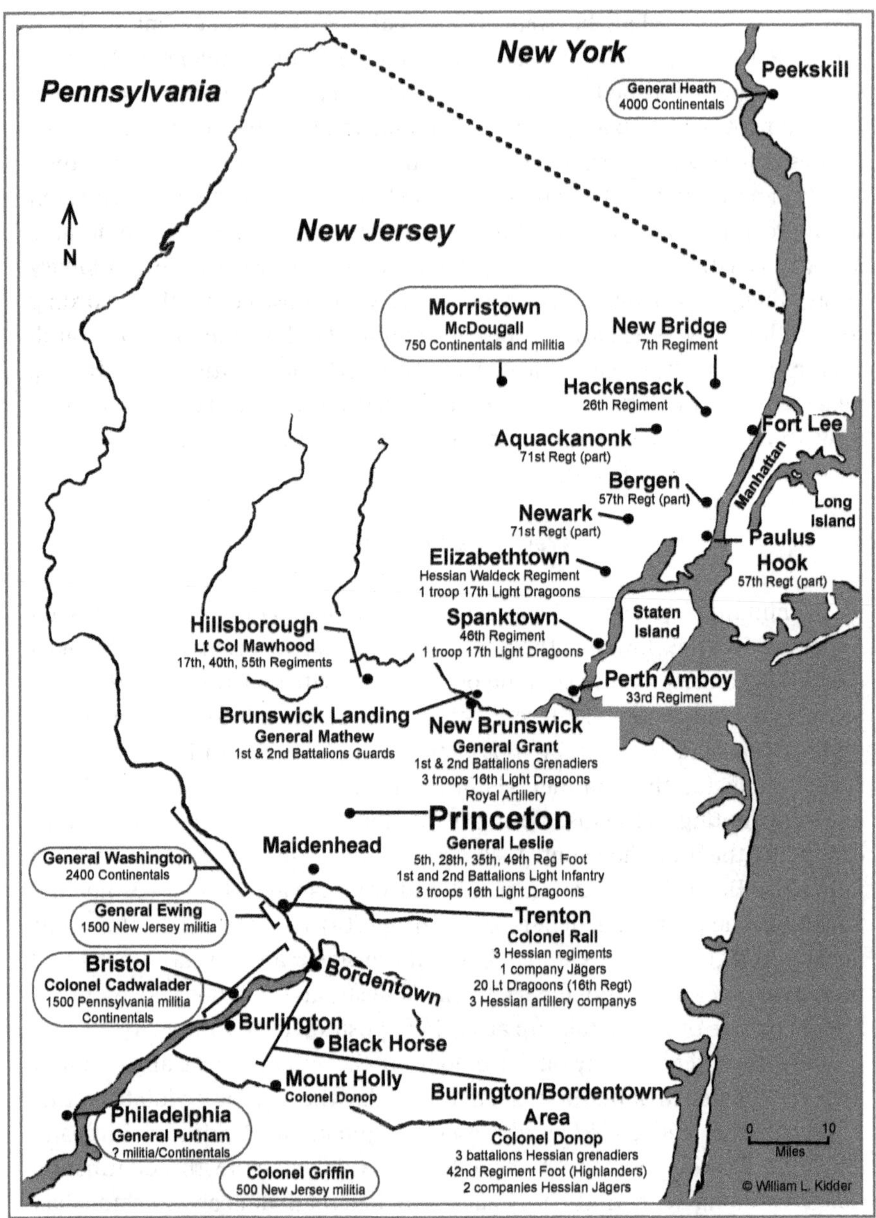

Map 6: British Occupation of New Jersey - December, 1776

Chapter 4

December 1776

The string of British battlefield victories in the five-month campaign for control of New York had resulted in the disastrous depletion of General Washington's army through battle casualties, prisoners of war, illness, and desertion. American and British leaders had expected to win the military conflict by the end of the year. Although it continued, both sides believed the struggle was nearly over. Both sides wondered just how long the Americans could maintain their fight for independence. For the people of Princeton, the question had immediate importance as they daily expected the arrival of the remaining American forces retreating ahead of British forces that would follow them through their town. They wondered whether the soldiers would just pass through town or whether there would be a battle that could devastate it. Based on what news they had heard about British actions in those parts of New Jersey the British had already passed through, Princeton residents feared the worst for their lives and property. They could not anticipate that first the Americans and then the British would station troops in Princeton throughout December, with no end in sight, and that their town would suffer as though hit by a natural disaster.

December 1

American troops marched out of New Brunswick after nightfall on December 1 following a stressful afternoon exchanging artillery fire with the advanced British forces arriving there. After trudging along the Post Road toward Princeton and reaching a safe distance from New Brunswick, the Americans took what shelter they could beside the road for the night. Some stopped as close to Princeton as Kingston. Word quickly reached Princeton that the army was retreating again and, unaware that General William Howe had ordered Cornwallis not to go beyond New Brunswick, the residents believed that both armies would soon pass through Princeton.

Trenton's Presbyterian minister, Rev. Elihu Spencer, received an urgent message the night of December 1. The British were headed toward Trenton, and he needed to escape quickly because, among other reasons, he had a one-hundred-guinea price on his head in retribution for work he performed in the southern colonies for the Continental Congress.[1] Before leaving, though, Spencer knew he had to protect his daughter, Margaret, living in Princeton and the wife of recently appointed Continental Congress delegate Jonathan Dickinson Sergeant. Jonathan was away, leaving seventeen-year-old Margaret and their infant son, William, at their new Princeton house directly in the path of the approaching armies. Fortunately, Margaret's neighbor living several blocks north on the Post Road, Dr. Absalom Bainbridge, a former classmate of Jonathan's at the college, came to her house about 2:00 a.m. He warned Margaret to make her escape and made sure she left immediately in the family carriage, heading west toward a Delaware River ferry. Dr. Bainbridge would be staying in his home.

The Witherspoons also made their escape down the Post Road toward Trenton, "bringing one wagon load of effects." College student Benjamin Hawkins from North Carolina drove John's wife Elizabeth in "the old chair," while John rode his sorrel mare, and student John Graham of New York drove his four young colts.[2]

Rev. Spencer quickly saddled one of his horses and rode hurriedly up the Post Road toward Princeton, hoping to find Margaret. He met the Witherspoon family headed toward Trenton and learned she had escaped Princeton. Witherspoon encouraged Spencer to turn around, hurry back to Trenton, and remove the rest of his family to safety. Arriving back in Trenton, Spencer locked up his house without removing any contents, left his cattle unattended, loaded his entire household into a large carriage, and drove several miles north up the river to Howell's Ferry, where he hoped to find Margaret.

When he did not find Margaret at Howell's, Spencer left his family there and continued north to Johnson's Ferry. Finding Margaret at Johnson's, he returned to Howell's and brought his family up to Johnson's. Soldiers had diverted most of the local boats to Trenton for use by the army. Despite severe difficulties and so many people wanting to escape, all the Spencers finally reached Pennsylvania. Margret recorded, "We were unspeakably delighted when we got over safely, and into a little hut, where we spent the night with a company of American soldiers, on their way to join General Washington."

Spencer's young daughter Lydia retained indelible images of that night. To her "youthful imagination they called up the day of judgment: so many frightened people were assembled, with sick and wounded soldiers, all flying for their lives, and with hardly any means of crossing the river."[3]

December 2

Just at dawn, back on the Post Road between Kingston and New Brunswick, after a cold night without enough tents or blankets, the American soldiers broke their makeshift camps and resumed their march toward Princeton. Anyone remaining in Princeton saw first the American advance scouts, some on foot and some mounted, between 8:00 and 9:00 a.m. Next appeared the advance party consisting of the remnants of Major Elisha Sheldon's Light Horse of the Connecticut militia, Maryland and Virginia riflemen in their variously colored long hunting shirts, and musket-armed remnants of several Continental regiments. Next came General Lord Stirling's brigade that included the 1st Virginia Regiment, along with the half dozen or so remnants of Colonel John Haslet's 1st Delaware Regiment, wearing what remained of their blue coats with red facings. Colonel George Weedon's 3rd Virginia Regiment was reduced to just 181 officers and men. Then the 6th Maryland Regiment marched without their colonel, who had been wounded and captured at Fort Washington.

General Hugh Mercer's brigade followed them: the 232 officers and men of the 27th Massachusetts Regiment; the 419 men of the 20th Connecticut; the 262 "shattered remnants" of William Smallwood's Maryland Battalion, also without its colonel; the 108 men of the Connecticut State Regiment; and, lastly, the 105 men of Moses Rawlings's Maryland and Virginia Rifle Regiment. Three Virginia regiments under General Adam Stephen followed Mercer. Shortly before they had left Virginia in October, observer Nicholas Cresswell described the 6th Virginia Regiment as "a set of dirty, ragged people, badly clothed, badly disciplined and badly armed."[4]

Washington and his staff, wrapped in dark cloaks or greatcoats, rode along on horseback accompanied by Washington's heavily armed and mounted Life Guard troopers. Civilian Thomas Paine, the author of the highly influential call for independence *Common Sense*, accompanied General Nathanael Greene as his secretary. Paine was already developing wording for a new pamphlet, *The Crisis*, reflecting the desperate situation now facing those who supported the war for independence. Next came the Pennsylvania Associators, groups of volunteer militiamen, of the Flying Camp under General James Ewing and Colonel Edward Hand.

Dispersed among the infantry units, horses drew artillery pieces through town, clattering and creaking on the uneven road. One artillery officer described as "a youth, a mere stripling, small, slender, almost delicate in frame" was about twenty-year-old Captain Alexander Hamilton, in command of an independent New York Artillery company. The artillery carriages carried some shot and powder. However, most of it was packed into the many horse-drawn wagons forming the baggage train that followed the army with extra ammunition, provisions for man and horse, any remaining tents, and other supplies for the soldiers, plus shovels, axes, saws, and other tools. Following behind everything else came whatever civilian merchants catering to the soldiers, known as sutlers, along with any soldiers' wives, children, and other camp followers, that remained with the army.[5] It was a ragged community on the march—not just soldiers.

Arriving in Princeton between 8:00 and 9:00 a.m., Washington wrote a letter to John Hancock and, according to tradition, had breakfast at the home of Robert Stockton, just beyond Morven toward Stony Brook.[6] Just down the road from Stockton's, college student Joseph Clark at John Johnson's farm now realized that it was impossible to remain in Princeton, so he prepared to send his possessions farther away from danger. While he discussed this with Johnson, American soldiers traveling ahead of the army to impress wagons and horses for army use came to Johnson's farm. Clark said, "with much difficulty we put them off for this time." But it was not long before they came back, and "we had but little hopes of keeping the wagon and horses."

Clark knew that, unless they removed all valuable items "while we had our wagons, they must necessarily fall into the enemy's hands." So, Clark acted and later recorded, "I took the opportunity while the press men were debating with Mr. Johnson, and took the wagons out of the stable and went off with them into the woods, and though they ran after me, they neither found me nor the horses." After the Americans left, Clark and Johnson packed up items they wanted to save, and Clark "carried them by hand to the woods where we had concealed the wagons." About daybreak the next morning, they set off to Amwell in Hunterdon County and arrived shortly before dark.[7]

Washington did not linger long in Princeton but continued marching on to Trenton. He left five Virginia regiments and Haslet's Delaware troops, altogether about twelve to fourteen hundred soldiers, under General Stirling at Princeton to watch for enemy movements and notify him if they came out from New Brunswick.[8] Lieutenant James McMichael of Colonel Samuel Miles's Pennsylvania Rifle Regiment found quarters in the village and was convinced that the remaining residents were primarily Loyalists.[9] As the ragged troops marched out of town on the Post Road, by tradition, Washington watched them from the porch of the Thomas Olden House.

At about this same time on December 2, the State government adjourned at Burlington, intending to meet next at Trenton the following February 18.[10] With British troops now occupying the middle portion of the State, government officials either went to their homes to protect their families, relocated to stay with family or friends outside the area occupied by British troops, or perhaps, like many residents, left the State entirely.

At his refuge in Monmouth County, Richard Stockton optimistically sent off an invoice to the New Jersey Assembly for his pay as a delegate to the Continental Congress.[11] Loyalists felt empowered by the presence of so many British soldiers in the State to seek revenge on Whigs, and some Loyalists had joined the New Jersey Volunteers, a formal military brigade of six battalions fighting with the British army. Local Monmouth County Loyalist Cyrenus Van Mater heard about Stockton and alerted some men of the Volunteers to his location. That night they took Stockton and Covenhoven prisoner. They turned Stockton over to the British, as an inflammatory account a month later reported, after "driving him, on foot, through rivers and creeks, with the greatest precipitation, particularly the Raritan, which at low water is fordable, to Amboy, where, we hear, he lies dangerously ill."[12] This account exaggerated the event to increase hatred for the British. From the common jail at Perth Amboy, the British sent Stockton to New York and incarcerated him in the notorious Provost Jail.[13]

December 3

On December 3, Joseph Clark and John Johnson met at John Drake's in Hopewell Township and rode to Princeton, where they found Stirling's American troops. Clark, coming down with an illness, returned to Drake's, hoping that the enemy "would not advance farther than Brunswick." The British did not advance, and Clark remained at Drake's until December 6, when he rode with Johnson back to Johnson's Stony Brook house and stayed for the night. The next day, December 7, the British renewed their advance toward Princeton, and about 3:00 p.m., about an hour and a half before the British arrived, Clark and Johnson set off once more to John Drake's house. The next day, they went to Amwell and stayed with Jacobus Johnson for a week, where Clark wrote he "was treated exceedingly kind."[14]

December 6–7

Continental Congress delegate Robert Treat Paine wrote to David Cobb on December 6 that Princeton's residents had "evacuated" the area on Sunday night, December 1, "with Pannic & Precipitation." Additional residents had left town by December 7, leaving behind their houses and most of their belongings due to lacking enough carriages to carry things away. Some sent away animals and other valuables to the degree that they could.[15] However, the British still had not proceeded beyond New Brunswick, and Paine believed they probably would not because "we heard yesterday that Genl [Charles] Lee with a large body of men was close in the rear of the enemy."[16] To some degree, the British did hesitate because of Lee's troops that Washington had left behind in northern New Jersey, anticipating the Americans might attack from two sides.

After crossing all essential military items to Pennsylvania at the Trenton ferries, Washington expected to be reinforced by New Jersey and Pennsylvania militiamen, along with General Lee's troops. With an expanded force, Washington hoped to make a stand at Princeton. However, he was concerned "by a strange dilatoriness and the confusion" resulting from the presence of the enemy in the State. The result was "the lukewarmness, not to give it a worse name," that allowed the enemy, with new orders from General Howe, to resume its march. The enemy would approach Princeton before Washington had enough men to engage them with any hope of success. Serving with Stirling's force, Lieutenant James McMichael paraded at Princeton at 2:00 p.m. on December 7 when the enemy came in sight, and he heard the orders to evacuate the town. Leaving town on the Post Road, the last American troops destroyed the Stony Brook bridge to slow down any British pursuit.[17] Washington had set out from Trenton for Princeton with some of his troops that morning, but on the road learned of the British advance. He reversed his troops and returned to Trenton, followed by Stirling's men, who arrived at Trenton about 10:00 p.m. and found temporary quarters for the night.[18]

While in Princeton, the American soldiers engaged to some degree in plundering, especially for firewood. Weaver James Finley lost twenty yards of linen, several pieces of furniture, and six cords of wood to the troops under Stirling. Thomas Robenson lost twenty bushels of potatoes and fifty new fence rails taken by Continentals.[19]

Two columns of soldiers commanded by Lord Cornwallis advanced into Princeton about one hour after Stirling's troops departed. Hessian Jäger Captain Johann Ewald recorded in his diary that "toward evening the two columns united at Princetown, in and around which place the army went into cantonment." Ensign Thomas Glyn of the 1st Battalion of Foot Guards noted that British and Hessian soldiers came through Princeton on their way to Trenton "in great expectation of making Philadelphia their winter quarters. The whole Jerseys seeming to submit to the British government & to give every possible assistance to the King's troops." British soldiers took up quarters in Nassau Hall, where they ransacked the college library, the Presbyterian Church, the Quaker Meetinghouse, and many of the vacated nearby houses. Ewald noted, "both Jäger companies were assigned posts in a wood a half an hour from the town on the road to Trenton, where we were repeatedly alarmed during the night by enemy parties and remained under arms the whole night."[20] The Americans retired in good order, and one British light horseman was shot from his horse by an American who fired from high ground across the Stony Brook before making his escape.[21]

Richard Cochran organized the repair of the Stony Brook bridge using his slaves and any local people he could convince to help. He then found General Howe and "presented him with an address in the names of the Loyalists in that part of the country offering him every service in their power." When he returned to his farm, he found that "a party of the king's troops & a number of women with them had plundered my house carried off my horses, my childrens and my own cloaths & such furniture as they could carry with them, among other things, they took with them a clock, which cost me £25 threatening to put any of my family to death that opposed them." He sent a message reporting this plundering, of an actively loyal citizen, to both Quartermaster General Sir William Erskine and General Howe but never got an answer or received any payment.[22]

December 8

On the morning of December 8, Cornwallis marched troops down the Post Road to Trenton, only to find the Americans had all crossed to Pennsylvania. They had stationed artillery that fired on the British party that came to the river's edge, and people in Princeton could hear it. They continued to hear cannon fire every day until the 13th, when the British decided to go into winter quarters.[23] Discovering that Washington had removed every boat to the Pennsylvania side of the river to prevent the British from following him, the British began to organize winter cantonments. General Alexander Leslie commanded the British troops at the Princeton cantonment consisting of the 5th, 28th, 35th, and 49th Regiments of Foot, the 1st and 2nd Battalions of Light Infantry, and three troops of the 16th Light Dragoons. Just to the north at Hillsborough, Lieutenant Colonel Charles Mawhood commanded the 17th, 40th, and 55th Regiments of Foot. Additional cantonment sites included the Hessians under Colonel Johann Rall at Trenton and British and Hessians under Colonel Carl von Donop in the Burlington and Bordentown area. The British established their New Jersey headquarters at New Brunswick with Major General James Grant in command. These cantonments formed the western portion of a line that stretched across the State and gave the British control of it. The presence of British troops and the absence of Continentals gave renewed hope to the New Jersey Loyalists while significantly discouraging the Whigs, who now felt abandoned.

Loyalist informers at Princeton, like Cochran, told the British which inhabitants had borne arms against them and especially any officers. British soldiers then plundered their property without any pretense of payment. The Loyalists even helped the soldiers find hidden objects. The British leaders considered anyone who had fled the area to have gone to the rebels, so the King's representatives could legally seize their belongings.[24] If Dr. Bainbridge had been conflicted back in July when named to collect surplus linens for the American military hospital, by December, he had resolved to support the Loyalist cause. Lieutenant Colonel West Hyde of the 1st Foot Guards recounted that, when he arrived at Princeton commanding a detachment of the Guards, he inquired as to which people were loyal to the government. One local person encouraged him to talk to Dr. Bainbridge. Hyde sought him out and "received every possible assistance from him & such intelligence as was of material consequence to His Majesty's Service in the situation the affairs of that country were, at that time." Hyde was so impressed with Bainbridge that he recommended him to the officer who came to replace him at Princeton.[25]

However, Bainbridge was not so extreme a Loyalist that he would endanger the lives of friends who did not agree with him—as shown by his recent kindness to Margaret Sergeant. Why Bainbridge chose the Loyalist side is a bit of a mystery. He may have been one who supported or was neutral about the protests against the acts of Parliament but then became conflicted with the declaring of independence. His relatives living in Maidenhead were active Patriots, while his wife's parents were fervent Loyalists. The Bainbridges were just one family in which members found it painful to matter which side each individual chose.

Richard Cochran did even more to help the British than Bainbridge did and not only provided Leslie with information and procured fresh provisions for the army, but also helped to administer the oaths and examine people seeking protections under Howe's amnesty proclamation. British Quartermaster General Sir William Erskine ordered Cochran to hire and impress wagons into the British service. A lieutenant colonel of the Guards arranged for him to seize cattle, hay, and other items for the use of the army. He was to take these items from inhabitants who had deserted their farms and taken up arms against the King, and Erskine appointed him Deputy Commissary. Some incensed local Whigs threatened Cochran with hanging and making him pay for all the items he took for the British. The insurgents attacked his house, took some property, and tried to burn his papers, except for some bonds that he had removed. His wife and children had to "flee to the King's army at Princeton in the middle of the night" from his farm just outside the village. While rebels carried his papers to the bonfire, some of them dropped along the way, and after he returned to Great Britain, Cochran reported they were "picked up by my Negroes & my wife sent them to me."[26]

British Occupation

From the time they arrived until the day they left Princeton, British troops either deliberately or accidentally destroyed several buildings, including the large new house from which Margaret Sergeant had escaped just days before. Resident Benjamin Plum saw that fire, which also consumed the new large kitchen, smokehouse, and the necessary house, and he firmly believed that British troops had set it. Also destroyed was a large garden and its almost new cedar post and five-rail fencing. The soldiers also took a large quantity of undressed flax in bundles. All these damages totaled over £620.[27] Jonathan Dickinson Sergeant's father, Jonathan, also suffered the loss of 190 panels of worm fence, 238 post and rails, 1 twelve-year-old mare, 1 almost-new riding chair, 12 good sheep, and a quarter of beef.[28]

The British collected bundles of flax, "whether rotted or not," to use in making defensive earthworks. Several people lost all the flax that they had, including 200 bundles from Robert Stockton, 20 from Thomas Olden, a hundredweight of undressed flax from Jonathan Dickinson Sergeant, a hundredweight of Thomas Stockton, and "a load" from William Scudder.[29]

General Howe had issued orders on December 10 that "as protections are given to the friends of government, only, for the security of their family's and property, the Commander in Chief is determined to punish with the utmost rigor any person who presumes to disturb or molest inhabitants or however under the sanction of a protection."[30] Tragically, these orders proved ineffective in protecting the local people, to which even Loyalist Cochran could attest, and their property. Giving the order was one thing; enforcing it was another.

The British soldiers required vast quantities of wood for warmth and cooking. Throughout their occupation of Princeton and the surrounding area, they burned up winter firewood supplies. They also stripped the siding from shops, houses, and even outhouses, and cut down many apple and other orchard trees for wood. Soldiers took wood from joiners and carpenters, and sent carriages out to collect the wood from farmer's fences. Plundering extended out at least four or five miles from the village.[31] Robert Stockton lost many items, including 689 panels of fence, harvested crops, animals, household furniture, and a well-painted pleasure sleigh with a good leather harness. James McCombs made soap and lost all his tubs and apparatus as well as household belongings. From his tanning business, he lost 146 hides in tan vats, part of the hides fit for use; 5 dozen calf skins; and 35 cords of tanning bark.

James Moore lost 275 hides nearly tanned and 145½ hides partly tanned, 10 dozen calf skins tanned, 5 dozen calf skins partially tanned, 4 dozen sheepskins, and 17 cords of tanning bark. Once hides were tanned, they were finished by currying to make them strong, flexible, and waterproof. The currier stretched the leather and burnished it to produce a uniform thickness and suppleness. It was then dyed, and other chemical finishes were applied to give the leather its desired color. Moore lost 10 sides of curried leather, a dozen curried calf skins, 20 gallons of train oil (whale oil used in currying leather), and a currying knife. Moore also lost many household and farm items, including 200 panels of post and rail fence and 150 sections of worm fence. He seems to have enjoyed driving and lost a pleasure sleigh with steel runners, a new sulky, and two harnesses. Isaac Updike and John Sanderson both witnessed British soldiers taking leather out of the vats and carrying it off, as well as taking harvested crops from Moore's barn and harvested winter wheat in the sheaf from Moore's field.[32]

Soldiers under Lieutenant Colonel Thomas Sterling of the 42nd Regiment of Foot stationed a "little out of the western end of the town" on one cold night "stripped both wheat fields and upland meadows setting fire not only to firewood and carriages but to all sorts of timber and especially fences." Because of this destruction, the farmers later had to expend valuable time and labor to cut and prepare wood before rebuilding their fences.[33] The soldiers did not limit themselves to destroying abandoned property but ignored any protection papers given to residents as part of the Howes' amnesty proclamation. Soldiers often went out at night to steal and kill sheep and cattle, normally skinning them and taking away the meat.[34]

Jonathan Deare lost a young orchard of 50 grafted apple trees about half a mile from the town and 6,000 cedar rails from the fence enclosing his lot. From his house in Princeton, he lost a large number of items, including furniture, clothing, kitchen utensils, silverware, many law and other books, and even his enslaved person's bed and bedding.[35] Quaker farmer Joseph Olden of Windsor Township lost 1 twelve-year-old mare, 5 six-month-old hogs, a ton of hay, several saws, a bushel of salt, 150 rails, a coopers adze, a pair of women's new cotton stockings, a new beaver hat, a quarter of beef, and 2 cords of sapwood, among other items.[36] Blacksmith Aaron Longstreet lost 300 bushels of coal, 200 bushels of iron and steel, and all the small tools belonging to a smith's shop, in addition to personal items.[37]

Stony Brook Quaker and leatherworker Matthew Clarke, living beside the heavily traveled Post Road near the bridge, lost quantities of harness leather, upper and sole leather, thick skins, calf skins, two sets of shoe maker's tools, a new saddle, and a set of chair harness. He also lost half a load of hay, some tallow, a feather bed, bedspread and blankets, pewter plates, dishes, spoons, a copper tea kettle, a frying pan, many household utensils, clothing, 15 pounds of hatchelled flax, his garden fence boards and panels, and many other items.[38] Thomas Stockton suffered the loss of a twenty-year-old barn, three hundred feet square, covered with cedar; 40 panels of board fence; 120 panels of five rail fence; 100 weight of pork; 100 weight of flax; 25 bushels of potatoes; 3 tons of the best hay; and damage to his dwelling house.[39] William Worth lost 200 bushels of wheat and 50 bushels of corn, 40 bushels of oats, 3 tons of clover hay, 5 hogs, 1 very large milch cow, bedding, kitchen furniture, a washtub, water buckets, and 2 smoothing irons.[40]

The British troops especially needed horses and wagons, and a group of Hessians took four horses from people living to the westward of town. Four "gentlemen farmers" lost two wagons, three horses, and an enslaved man for whom one of them had paid one hundred pounds some years before. From another farmer, they took one wagon, one horse, and a Negro man. From another, they took a wagon, a horse, and one Negro lad. Two soldiers mounted on broken-down horses came to David Olden's house and demanded his horses. Fortunately, he had sent them away "with all his household goods and provisions except what was absolutely necessary for present use." Others had acted similarly.[41]

Upon entering houses, soldiers sometimes ripped open beds and took away the "ticken," leaving the farmers with little to cover themselves. Officers and soldiers who boarded out in farmers' houses took their horses, Indian corn, oats, and the best fodder. A "Gentleman Farmer" living next to Thomas Olden's had to accommodate 170 men and officers. The officers took his best rooms and beds and ate "the best diet that the house afforded" while the men camped out, inhabited outbuildings, or created brush shelters. Soldiers also took "stalk tops and oats in the sheaf" to make temporary "sheds to keep them from the cold when they stood on guard, besides what their horses devoured." When they left, the owner unsuccessfully asked for reimbursement. He estimated his loss at fifty pounds, but they only gave him twenty shillings. At another house, an officer demanded to use all but one room, leaving the owner and his family only the kitchen. Sometimes officers bargained with farmers for things they needed based on prices the army had established for various goods, but then only gave receipts instead of money.[42] Thomas Olden lost a milch cow and 1 two-year-old heifer, 1½ tons of hay, flax in the sheaf, 120 rails in worm fence, and 120 stakes, 3 cords wood, and 2 loads corn stalks.[43]

Quaker William Clarke's widowed mother lived with him on his Stony Brook farm and occupied half the rooms in their house. A captain and company of regulars came to take up quarters there, and soon after, a second captain "of an overgrown size and terrifying countenance and with insolence equal if not superior to the huge bulk of his body demanded a room with a bed and fireplace" for his lodgings. William was not at home, but his pregnant wife, Ann, tried to deal with the captain. He abused her verbally, swearing and cursing at her so aggressively that "she fell into a violent disorder and soon after miscarried."[44]

It is not clear whether British soldiers took up quarters at John Witherspoon's Tusculum estate, a little over a mile out of town, but they plundered the property. Witherspoon had left a "Mr. Montgomery" in charge who proved very loyal to him, and even though Witherspoon, as a signer of the Declaration, was "the object of the enemy's distinguished hatred," the property survived with only limited losses. Many of his treasured books and most of his furniture remained intact. However, while fourteen "old and young" cattle somehow remained, the soldiers destroyed all of his sheep.[45]

British troops harassed people in many ways. At some point, four Hessians went to "a Gentleman's House (who is called a Quaker)...between 50 and 60 years old and small," and even though he had a signed "protection," one Hessian "laid hold of his hat on his head and pulled it off." The victim "laid hold of their champion and struck up his heels and threw him on the ground and clapped his foot on his sword and prevented his drawing it. And took his hat again from him. Upon that the three other poltroons drew their swords, and he was obliged to yield up a very good hat." They then stole his horse and hogs. According to residents, British generals Cornwallis, Grant, and Leslie observed this plundering and were amused to see their soldiers trying to catch the hogs in their pen. Most of the people the soldiers mistreated similarly were Quakers who had not taken up arms against them.[46]

A party of British soldiers arrested a neighbor of Robert Lawrence and held him in Trenton for some time before marching him with other prisoners through Princeton to New Brunswick and then on to a prison in New York. The guards crowded so many prisoners into one room that they could not lay down. The temperature was frigid, and when some prisoners tried to light a fire, some officers came in with clubs and knocked three or four of them down. One group of six prisoners was allowed only four and a half pounds of bread and a pound of pork for a week. Lawrence's neighbor did better because he had some hard money and kept himself going for three months and then escaped with two others to Staten Island. When he got home, he found his house plundered, and that a wagon, four horses, and several cattle, as well as some tools, were missing.[47]

Women were no safer than their men, and several cases of rape and molestation occurred in the vicinity of Princeton, especially in neighboring Hopewell Township and Pennsneck. Most women did not publicly accuse their tormentors due to the prevailing negative attitude toward women who suffered rape. The victim and her family wanted to keep her name secret, so most suffered in silence.[48]

On December 12, General Howe ordered that "small straggling parties, not dressed like soldiers & without officers, not being admissible in war, to presume to molest or fire upon soldiers, or peaceable inhabitants of the country [i.e., Loyalists], will be immediately hanged without trial as assassins."[49] Although Howe wanted to win the hearts and minds of the colonists, this new order could only alienate people because it reduced the militia to outlaws, even when on duty, given that militiamen rarely wore uniforms.

The next day, Richard Stockton's first cousin, Loyalist Captain Richard Witham Stockton, guided a party of British light dragoons commanded by Lieutenant Colonel William Harcourt to Basking Ridge where they captured General Charles Lee. He then led them safely back to Pennington the same day. For this service, General Skinner, Stockton's commander, promoted him to the rank of major in the 6th Battalion of the New Jersey Volunteers, and he became famous as the "land pilot" of the British.[50]

Some militiamen did wear uniforms. Abraham Golden of Hopewell Township joined a troop of light horse militia in Somerset County rather than serve in the Hunterdon militia, which did not yet have a troop. During the retreat across New Jersey and the British occupation of Princeton and Trenton, the Somerset light horse served almost continuously protecting local Whigs. One December night, Golden returned home exhausted, sank into bed still wearing his militia uniform, and fell into a deep sleep, only to be awakened by a squad of Hessians searching for rebel militiamen.

At sunrise, the Hessians set off for Princeton with their prisoners, including Golden's sixteen-year-old militiaman nephew, Jacob Lane Golden. Jacob was known as Little Jake because he was small for his age, looking more like he was twelve years old. However, he was quite boisterous and given to bravado. While the Hessians assembled their prisoners and plundered the neighbors, Jake made full use of a wide range of profanity in "expressing his contempt for the whole British nation and this squad of Hessian robbers in particular." While the Hessian sergeant pondered whether or not to take a mere boy into custody and confine him in Nassau Hall, Jake dramatically boasted that he could handle a musket better than a Hessian, so they took him prisoner. Marched to Princeton with the other prisoners, he gave the Hessians fits as they tried to deal with his colorful cursing without bursting out laughing.

At Princeton, the Hessians lined up their prisoners in front of Nassau Hall to be inspected by a colonel. The colonel was not amused by Jake and asked the sergeant why on earth he had brought along the "dirty nosed little brat." He slapped Jake across the back with the flat of his sword and told him to run along home to his mother. Awed and silenced by the many brilliant uniforms and polished equipment of his captors, Jake did as the colonel told him. Retelling the story after the war, Jake admitted that his size had always been a source of humiliation for him, but on that morning, he was thankful for it. All of the other militiamen prisoners were also allowed to return home, except Abraham Golden, considered a prisoner of war because he was in uniform. Abraham was imprisoned in the basement of Nassau Hall and later taken to New York and imprisoned there until exchanged on October 16, 1777. He must have been in poor shape when released, because his estate was probated about five months later in March 1778.[51]

On December 16, General Leslie received a letter from Hessian Colonel Donop at Bordentown in compliance with Howe's orders to communicate with him periodically. He brought Leslie up to date on his troop arrangements in the winter cantonments between Trenton, Bordentown, and Burlington.[52] At Princeton, Leslie was midway between the British troops at the extreme western end of the line of cantonments spreading across New Jersey and the British headquarters in New Jersey at New Brunswick. During December, he dealt continuously with communications between Hessian Colonels Rall and Donop near the Delaware River and General James Grant, commanding at New Brunswick.

The New Jersey militia was in total disarray during December, and men joined with others in random, makeshift units that had little relation to their officially established companies. Joseph Clark left Amwell on December 18 and crossed the Delaware River to join with elements of Captain Aaron

Longstreet, Jr.'s Princeton-area militia company, then apparently mixed with part of an Amwell company in a makeshift unit, which was with Washington's army in Bucks County. He found them, but since he had not brought a musket, he did not immediately join the company but did come back across the river with them the next day. They marched from the river after crossing, and at some point, Clark left them, and after getting a bit lost, "got home the next day about ten in the morning."

The following day he approached within a half-mile of the enemy at Princeton, where he obtained "a gun and accouterments." However, the treacherous traveling conditions in winter resulted in a sprained ankle. He came back to Amwell the next day, intending to cross again over the river, but the Amwell militiamen crossed back to the New Jersey side, and Clark rejoined them. During these mid-December weeks, members of makeshift New Jersey militia units crossed back and forth over the Delaware River to check on their homes and also to harass the British and Hessians occupying their state.[53]

Howe ordered Lieutenant Colonel Mawhood on December 17 to march "by Hillsborough towards Flemingtown" in Hunterdon County and General Leslie to make a circuit march to Springfield in Essex County, then south through Bound Brook in Somerset County to Princeton.[54] While these marches temporarily expanded the area controlled by the occupation forces and gave comfort to the Loyalists, they also reduced the strength of the various detachments, making them more vulnerable to American attack. While occupying New Jersey, the British army controlled about three hundred square miles, less than five percent of New Jersey, but even this much stretched British resources to their limit.[55] Leslie learned that Grant had arranged with Donop to have a light dragoon carry messages at express speed from Trenton to Princeton, where they would be forwarded to New Brunswick carried by a fresh dragoon. The answer would return the same way, also stopping at Princeton. Grant believed, "by that means the conveyance will be quicker and the dragoons less fatigued."[56]

By December 20, Continental Congressmen, such as Robert Morris, believed that Washington must drive the British out of New Jersey to save the Revolution. Princeton would play a significant role in that effort because delegates thought that the British had "their main body about Prince Town & strong detachments in all the other places" such as New Brunswick, Trenton, Penny Town (Pennington), Bordentown, Burlington, Morristown, Mount Holly, and Haddonfield. Washington received and welcomed the troops commanded by General John Sullivan that had been under General Charles Lee, until Lee's capture on December 13.

Additionally, Canadian campaign veterans under General Gates also arrived from the Fort Ticonderoga area. The British troops were so spread out in their line of cantonments that they were vulnerable to Washington taking them one at a time. Washington's major obstacle would be the danger from Loyalists providing intelligence about their preparations and movements to the British. The number of Loyalists had seemed to mushroom as one effect of the Howes' amnesty proclamation and occupation of the State. If the British continued to occupy New Jersey, Philadelphia would be in great danger.[57]

Both Grant and Leslie became frustrated with Colonel Rall's frequent requests to send additional troops to Trenton. Although couched in terms of his need for the additional forces in case of attack, Rall made these appeals more out of his desire to increase the prestige and importance of his command.[58] Responding to one such call, Leslie wrote to Rall on December 18 that he had ordered the 1st Light Infantry Battalion to be at Trenton by 10:00 a.m. on the 19th and that he was taking the 2nd Light Infantry Battalion and three hundred men from the 2nd Brigade to Maidenhead to act in support if needed. People in Princeton saw these troops leave. Leslie sent additional units on December 21, but they were ordered to return as soon as they reached Trenton.[59] Rall wanted a permanent post of soldiers from Princeton established at Maidenhead, but General Howe would not approve it. Instead, Grant told Leslie to send frequent patrols from Princeton to meet up with patrols from Trenton. Grant also sent out artillery ammunition and powder and balls for muskets so that Leslie's men could make up cartridges "at their leisure."[60]

By the third week of December, communication delays became frequent because of the demonstrated dangers in taking the road from Trenton to Princeton without an escort.[61] A Hessian captain with one hundred men and a piece of artillery marched into Princeton on December 20 with another message that Rall would like Leslie to station some troops at Maidenhead, "if only two hundred men." That morning, Rall had sent two dragoons to Princeton with letters, and a rebel ambush had killed one man and wounded the other man's horse. The survivor took the bag of messages, mounted the dead man's horse, and returned to Trenton.[62] Rall had responded by sending this strong escort force of one hundred men and the cannon, much to the critical amusement of the British officers at Princeton, who felt he had significantly overreacted. They advised him in the future to send messengers at random times over a variety of routes and suggested other measures to reduce the ambushes.

General Leslie sent the 1st Battalion of Light Infantry to Trenton on December 22, believing that a battalion of Rall's command had departed from

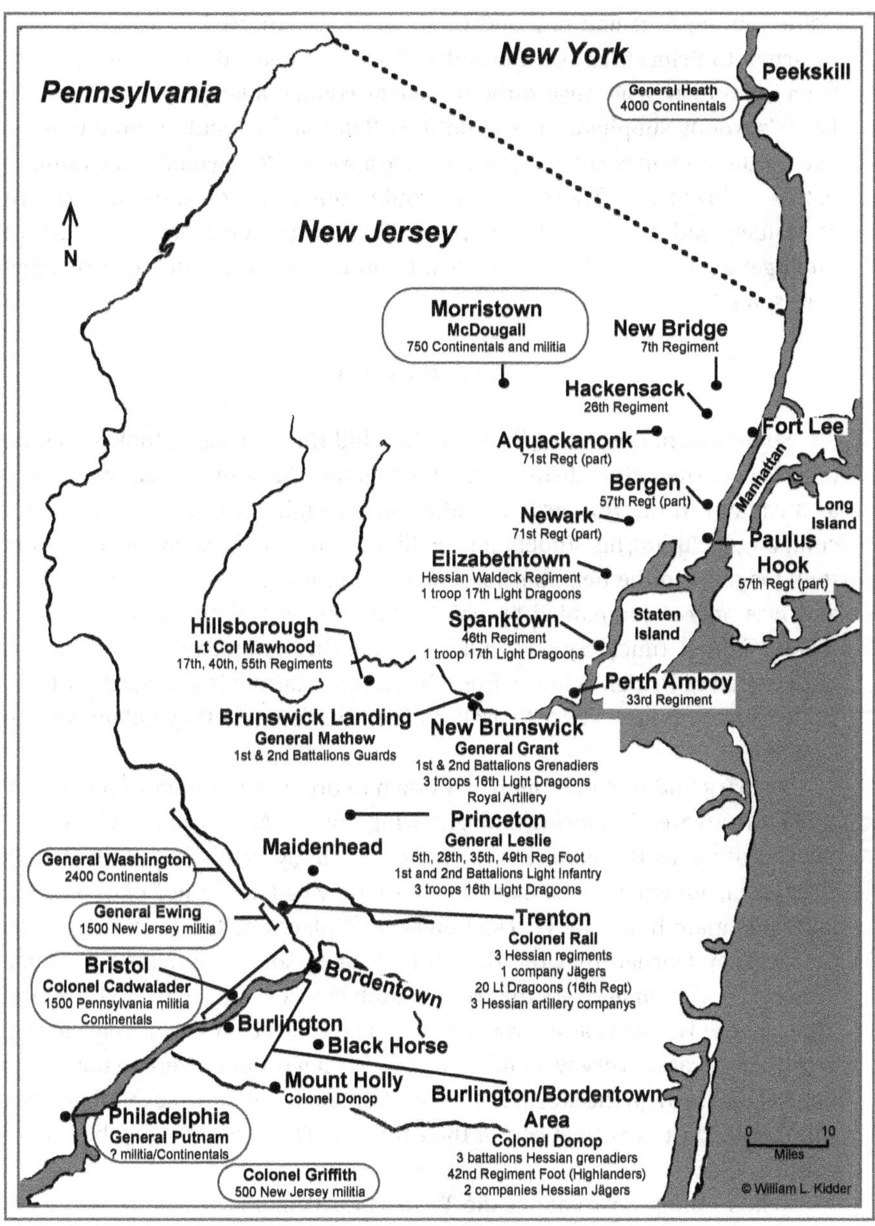

Map 7: British Occupation of New Jersey - December 25, 1776

there. But, since it had not, and there were no expected attacks, the force returned to Princeton.[63] On December 23, Grant needed to procure wagons from Donop's area because without them he could not keep both Donop's and Leslie's troops supplied.[64] Leslie notified Rall that he would send a twenty-five- or thirty-man patrol to Trenton twice a week if Rall would send a similar patrol to Princeton. These patrols would substitute for stationing troops at Maidenhead. Leslie sent a patrol to Trenton the next day, and it heard intelligence that Washington planned to attack either Trenton or Princeton very soon.[65]

December 24–26

Sometime in December, William Churchill Houston again took on militia duty. Due to the militia disorganization, this time he volunteered unofficially as a captain in the Hunterdon militia. On December 24, Captain Houston's company, including his student Joseph Clark, conducted a scouting patrol and took lodgings in the neighborhood. Clark's sprained ankle was very painful and was now accompanied by painful blisters on the bottoms of his feet, making him at times cry out while walking. On the morning of the 25th, a large squad of British soldiers from Princeton scouting in the neighborhood came near the house where Clark lay asleep. Fortunately, they did not stop to search it.

As Clark and the other men "sat down to breakfast, tidings of the enemy came, they were plundering a neighboring house." At that point, Clark says, "eleven of us, as there were no more of our body near, went immediately after them, but when we came to the house they had just gone." Clark's group joined its main body and checked on several places before returning to the house. They learned that the British had taken some militiamen prisoner. These were the same hours that Washington crossed the Delaware River and attacked the Hessians at nearby Trenton. The weather was severely stormy, and Clark became "very wet and lame, and having orders where to meet next day, I came through the storm to Jacobus Johnson's, where I stayed that night [the 26th]."[66] He was unaware of the events at Trenton unless he heard the gunfire.

When Donop heard about the Trenton disaster, his first concern was to protect the route to Princeton from being cut off. While trying to organize his dispersed command, he sent acting Quartermaster General Captain Thomas Gamble to Princeton to inform General Leslie of the Trenton news and how Donop proposed to respond to it.[67]

December 27

Clark felt better the morning of the 27th and set off to meet the militia company. He wrote that they "went to the old Meeting house, from whence most of the battalions had just departed in sleds. My ankle now grew very painful, still I followed on two miles, and from there rode in a sleigh, six miles to the battalion. In the afternoon we marched 10 miles around about road to the [Delaware] River. That night I lodged with part of the company at Mr. Oakham's; but my ankle was so swelled and painful I could not march with them in the morning [the 28th]," so he remained there until recovered enough to set out on January 1 to find his group.[68]

Some of the British light dragoons and Hessians who escaped capture at Trenton came to Princeton the night after the battle. They were terrified after their escape across the Assunpink Creek and trekking through muddy swamps and water.[69] Others had not gotten that far and were still looking for refuge. A farmer about five miles from Princeton took prisoner two armed Hessians using only his pitchfork and dog. His enslaved boy discovered them in his stable, seeking shelter among the horses. So before daylight the next morning, the farmer ran to the stable, got his pitchfork, and challenging them with it like a bayonet, commanded them to yield. One of them obeyed, but while the farmer was tying him up, the other ran away. The farmer sent his dog after him, who caught him by the coat and held him until the farmer secured the man. Both Hessians told him they had escaped from the battle at Trenton, and the farmer turned them over to American troops.[70]

Leslie now had about fifty fugitive Hessians and three officers from Rall's brigade at Princeton and wondered about the disposition of Donop's soldiers. They were then near Allentown, having left their cantonment area in the vicinity of Bordentown after hearing about Rall's defeat.[71] While marching his troops toward Princeton the next morning, Donop received orders from General Grant to join the garrison at Princeton. General Leslie received orders to send a patrol toward Trenton to provide cover for Donop's march and learn all he could about Washington's forces. Grant also ordered him to set up guard posts at Kingston and Six Mile Run and place the 2nd Brigade and the 42nd Regiment at Rocky Hill, from where they should put out pickets toward Pluckemin.[72] Grant and Leslie acted in ignorance that Sullivan's troops had joined with Washington and were no longer in New Jersey positioned to attack them from the flank and rear.

After arriving in Princeton, Donop reported his situation to General Grant. His first concern was that he no longer had Colonel Sterling with him, who had translated Donop's French into English for both other officers and the local people. Commenting on Rall's defeat, Donop believed that Washington had not taken more than five hundred Hessians prisoners, "which number cannot surely weaken our army." Even so, he said, "I acknowledge however that the shame is none the less for our nation to have lost six cannon, with fifteen banners and three regiments at one attack and this in a section of the country greatly demoralized." Grant had ordered him to establish a storehouse at Princeton, but Donop could not find Quartermaster Captain Gamble, whom he thought was with Grant. He requested orders as to whether the two six-pounder artillery pieces belonging to the 42nd Regiment should remain in Princeton. He also really wanted Leslie's men to depart the town to make room for his men and noted that "400 men slept last night in the open air. You can imagine what must happen to my men. All sick."[73]

December 28–29

Donop's troops arrived in Princeton about 2:00 p.m. on December 28 and took over the quarters of Leslie's departed brigade. The Minnigerode battalion took over houses in town, and the 42nd Regiment quartered near Stony Brook along the road to Maidenhead and Trenton. The Jäger companies found houses north of Princeton toward Kingston. The von Linsingen and Block battalions, and the men from the Rall brigade remained in Kingston. Ordered to bring the baggage wagons on to Princeton, Captain von Stein at Cranbury reported the night of December 29. General Leslie, who enjoyed being in Princeton, kept seeking ways to delay his departure while hoping for a change in orders allowing him to remain in command there.

Reports during the night of December 28 told of American troop movements in New Jersey, and the 42nd Regiment was sent toward Maidenhead to join the light infantry stationed there. The von Linsingen regiment replaced the 42nd at Stony Brook and extended toward Eight Mile Run, crossing the road to Trenton. Colonel Block's orders at Kingston were to march his men to the high ground at Nassau Hall on the slightest alarm. The Jäger companies became the rearguard, and Donop's baggage remained packed in its wagons in case of the need to head out quickly for New Brunswick. Donop ordered the construction of two small redoubts on the south side of Princeton village and made additional preparations for the anticipated attack from Washington's army.[74]

December 30–31

Donop heard another rumor on December 29 that Washington's army was approaching him at Princeton. The next day, Leslie at Maidenhead sent

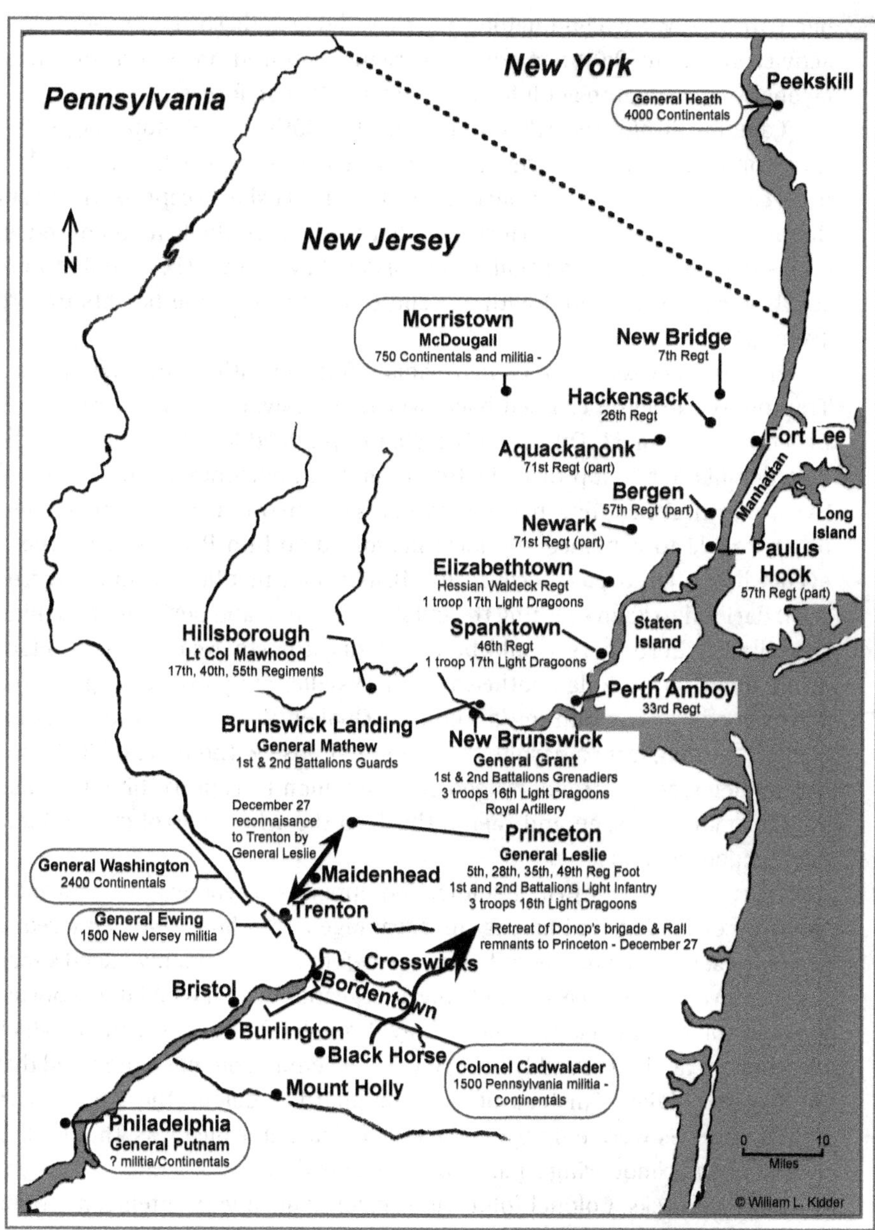

Map 8: Aftermath of Battle of Trenton - December 27-28

out patrols toward Pennington, but they did not discover any American activity. At about 9:00 a.m. some Hessians captured an American officer evidently on a scout to get information on the British forces.[75]

Captain Ewald recorded that "on the 30th the Donop Corps left Kingston and joined the army in Princetown, around which the army had been concentrated and cantoned under General Leslie, except for the Grant Brigade." In addition to quartering soldiers in houses, the British housed an entire regiment in Nassau Hall. Ewald also believed that "six redoubts were constructed and mounted with 12- and 6-pounders on the heights toward Trenton."[76]

Having recrossed to Pennsylvania after defeating the Hessians at Trenton, Washington crossed back over the Delaware River to Trenton on December 30 and 31. On December 30, Joseph Reed led six troopers of the Philadelphia 1st Troop of Light Horse on an intelligence-gathering patrol toward Princeton. They became somewhat frustrated during their ride, being unable to convince any local person to go into Princeton for them, even when offered pay, because the British had instilled so much terror. Reed decided to keep scouting the outskirts of town and perhaps get behind the village where there would be fewer guard posts. Near the John Flock farm, about half a mile southeast of Clarksville, his patrol emerged from some woods and, mounting a knoll on Quaker Road, observed a British soldier "passing from a barn to the dwelling-house without arms." Thinking the soldier was a marauder, Reed sent two men to capture him, but then another man was seen and then a third, so the whole patrol charged and surrounded the house.

As a result, "twelve British soldiers, equipped as dragoons, and well armed, their pieces loaded, and having the advantage of the house, surrendered to seven horsemen, six of whom had never before seen an enemy." Reed's men also captured a Commissary, and only a sergeant escaped who later reported at Princeton that he had to fight his way through fifty light horsemen, which his listeners no doubt readily believed. A Princeton resident commented that the British soldiers, "instead of being on guard to defend the Commissary and themselves were employed in a much pleasanter business, that was, in attacking and conquering a parcel of mince pies."[77]

At Crosswicks, Colonel John Cadwalader sent "a very intelligent young gentleman" to scout for information at Princeton. He arrived about noon and gathered vital data, but General Leslie and Lieutenant Colonel Robert Abercromby detained him when he tried to leave town that evening. The young spy escaped the village the next morning and returned to Crosswicks, where he reported that there were about five thousand enemy soldiers at

Princeton, about equally divided between Hessian and British troops. The British commanders in Princeton believed that the Americans had no more than five or six thousand men, many forced to serve, and many were deserting each day.

Based on the young man's information, Cadwalader drew a rough map of Princeton and the roads around it, indicating artillery emplacements and redoubts under construction or scheduled to begin building that morning. The young man saw no sentries on the back or east side of the village. He learned that some nights the men laid on their arms in expectation of an attack and paraded each morning about an hour before daybreak. Consequently, the soldiers were very fatigued and had suffered a food shortage until the previous night, when a large number of wagons arrived from New Brunswick with provisions. Troops, including Donop's Hessians, continued to arrive at Princeton. About fifty light horse troops were at Princeton, with half the men occupying quarters at Scudder's Mill to the east and the other half on the west side of town. The young spy was aware of the capture of the commissary and dragoons by Colonel Joseph Reed's scouting party.[78]

A vital element of the sketched map, soon called the "spy map," was that it showed a road leading to the back of Princeton on the east side that saw only light use and was not guarded by the British. This road was a makeshift country lane functionally linking the Stony Brook Friends Meetinghouse to a sawmill on Stony Brook, east of the village. Although declining in use after the late 1760s, it was still clear enough to be used by Washington as an approach to Princeton.[79]

Accurate information was hard to find, and many rumors spread on both sides. Ewald noted, "On the 30th reports came in almost hourly of the approach of Washington's army. Since Lord Cornwallis arrived at the army in Princetown, it was planned shortly afterward to give the enemy a beating and thereby repair the damage at Trenton."[80] Grant at New Brunswick and no doubt Donop at Princeton received an express late that night that Princeton should expect an attack. Two battalions of grenadiers, one battalion of the Guards, three regiments of the 4th Brigade, and a regiment of Hessian Grenadiers prepared to march and set off for Princeton about daybreak on January 1. They arrived in Princeton about 1:00 p.m. and joined the three Hessian Grenadier battalions, one Jäger company, two Light Infantry battalions, the 2nd Brigade, and the 42nd Regiment. All these troops prepared for combat because there had been a small skirmish at a piquet post in which the rebels lost four men. The 42nd Regiment of Foot and three Hessian Battalions of Grenadiers and the Jäger company advanced about a mile outside Princeton and bivouacked.[81]

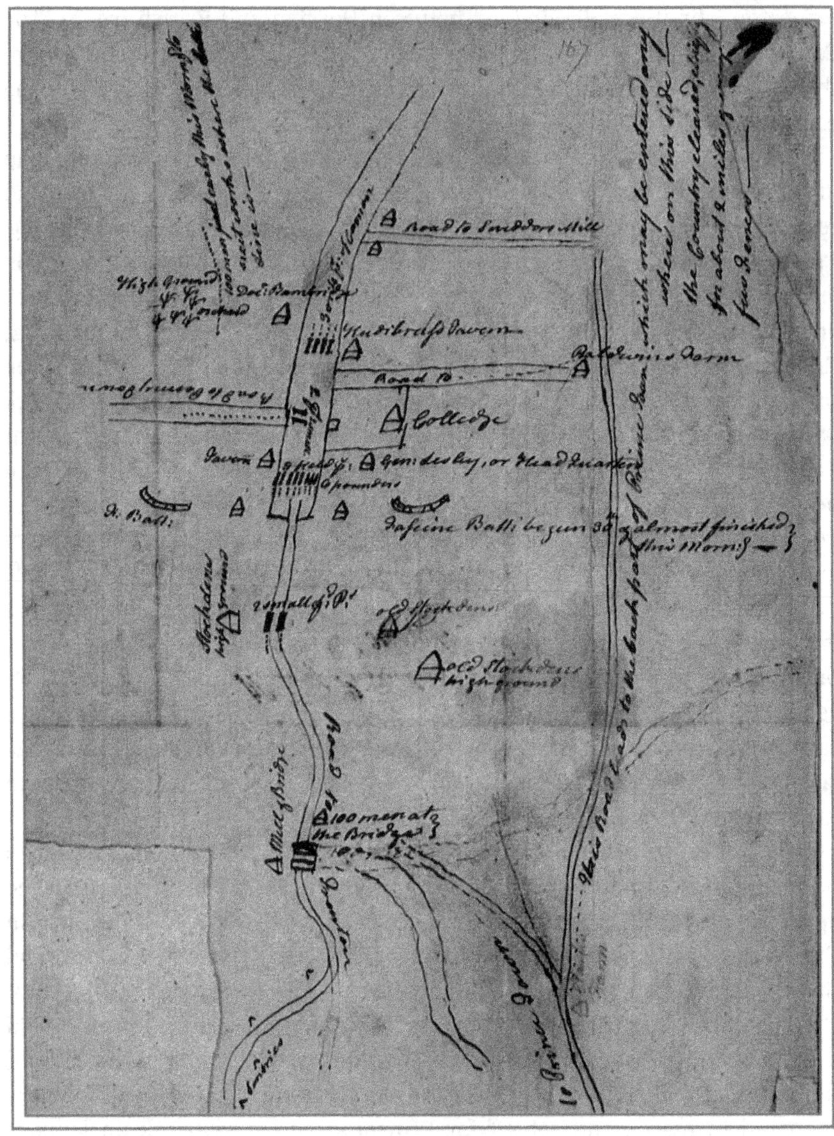

Map 9: The Spy Map

This map was prepared by or for Colonel John Cadwalader based on information acquired on December 30 from someone recently in Princeton.

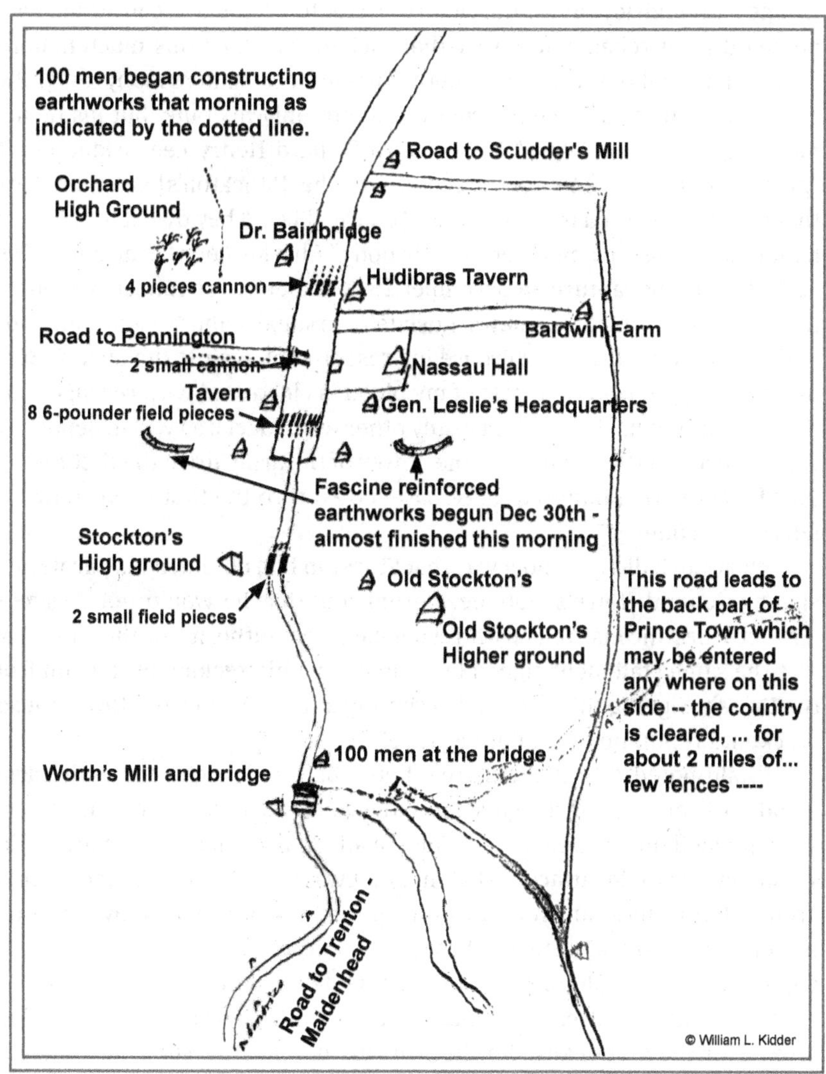

Map 10: The Spy Map

This modified map has been enhanced to reveal locations and modifications made by the British to defend the town. A key item is the back road on the right side of the map extending from the Quaker Road and passing the Baldwin farm to access the town from an unexpected direction.

On December 30, Dr. Benjamin Rush was at Crosswicks with Cadwalader's troops. Although joyous for the victory at Trenton, Rush was concerned when he heard from reliable authority that Richard Stockton, his much-honored "father in law who is now a prisoner with Gen Howe suffers many indignities & hardships from the enemy from which not only his rank, but his being a man ought to exempt him." He wrote to Richard Henry Lee, asking him to "propose to Congress to pass a resolution in his [Stockton's] favor similar to that they have passed in favor of Gen. [Charles] Lee. They owe it to their own honor as well as to a member of their body." Charles Lee was also in British custody after his capture on December 13, and there were concerns about his treatment. Reacting to the news, Rush felt personally abused and said, "I did not want this intelligence to rouse my resentment against the enemy. But it has increased it. Every particle of my blood is electrified with revenge—and if justice cannot be done to him in any other way, I declare I will in defiance of the authority of the congress, & the power of the army drive the first rascally tory I meet with a hundred miles bare footed thro the first deep snow that falls in our country."[82]

What Rush did not know was that Stockton had obtained his parole after signing General Howe's statement promising that he would not engage in any activities inconsistent with recognizing the authority of the King. This was the same statement signed by so many people seeking protection from the British. Signing this oath and accepting a full pardon from Howe caused Stockton's reputation to suffer negatively.[83]

Ewald noted, "On the 31st, two hours before daylight, the entire army stood to arms on the heights around Princetown, since the enemy had strengthened his position at Maidenhead and we had information that Washington would attack." That night, Ewald recorded, "In the evening around ten o'clock, an American officer was taken prisoner by a Scottish patrol. This man had sneaked through the outpost and posed as an English adjutant at a Scottish post, from which he demanded the password on the excuse he had forgotten it, having been sent off by Lord Cornwallis to look around for the Americans. But the Scots did not like this story, and held him securely until one of their patrols arrived, to whom they delivered him." When this man appeared before Lord Cornwallis, "he immediately identified himself and his mission. He was a major of riflemen, who intended to make a surprise attack on the Scottish regiment as soon as he had succeeded in learning the password."[84]

On December 31, British troops burned down William Scudder's grist mill, noted as "the best gristmill in these parts," along with the wheat and flour it contained. The soldiers also burned down his fulling mill, including a large amount of cloth. They burned the fabric even though the miller begged them not to because his customers would hold him accountable for it. They also burned down his six-room wooden house.[85] The British soldiers also took both wood and straw from neighboring farms and used some of the straw to sleep on and some to make shelters from the cold; they burned the rest.[86]

As the year 1776 drew to a close, Captain Ewald confided to his diary that "Thus had the times changed! The Americans had constantly run before us. Four weeks ago we expected to end the war with the capture of Philadelphia, and now we had to render Washington the honor of thinking about our defense. Due to this affair at Trenton, such a fright came over the army that if Washington had used this opportunity we would have flown to our ships and let him have all of America. Since we had thus far underestimated our enemy, from this unhappy day onward we saw everything through a magnifying glass."[87]

However, not all British officers had developed Ewald's respect for Washington and his troops. It would take just a very few more days to realize the effects of that lack of respect.

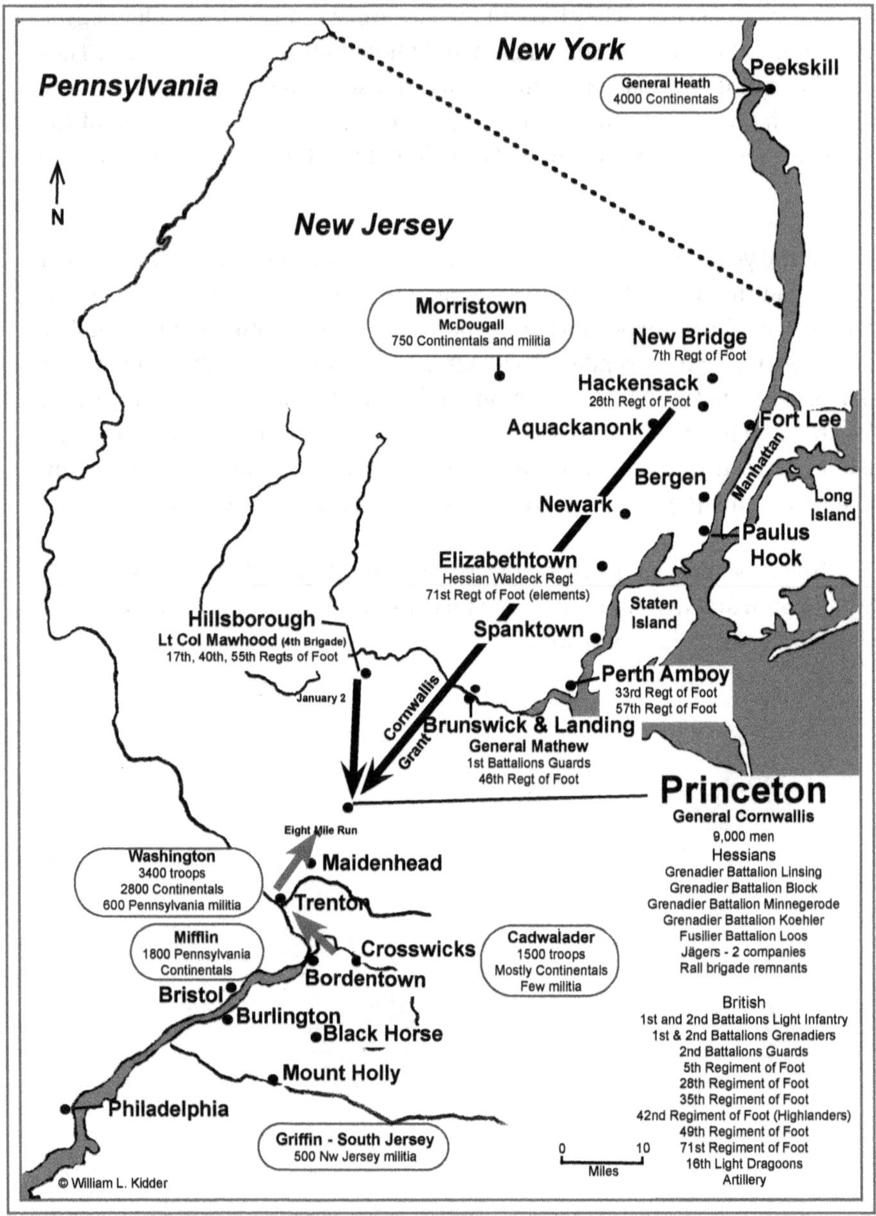

Map 11: Troop Concentrations at Princeton and Trenton, January 1, 1777

Chapter 5

January 1–3, 1777

January 1

Soldiers assigned to the advanced British guard posts outside Princeton received harassing enemy fire for several days and consequently had laid on their arms the past three consecutive nights.[1] At daybreak on January 1, a British force of light infantry under Lieutenant Colonel Abercromby, a mounted Jäger company under Captain Lorey, and Captain Wreden's Jäger company marched out of the village toward Maidenhead to dislodge enemy troops at Eight Mile Run. Jäger Captain Ewald took twenty of his men and two British light dragoons in the opposite direction to Rocky Hill, where they occupied the bridge across the Millstone River and covered the right flank of troops marching from New Brunswick to Princeton under General Grant. Ewald saw enemy parties several times, but they stayed out of rifle range. His men kept guard over the one family living on the Princeton side of the Millstone bridge and, to prevent the Americans from gathering any information about him, they did not allow anyone to cross the bridge. Ewald and his men experienced much discomfort in the deep snow and frigid afternoon temperatures. His men had no bread, and he had nothing to eat. General Grant's force successfully reached Princeton during the day about noon.[2]

British Ensign Thomas Glyn came to Princeton with General Grant marching through Kingston, where he says, "Lt. Col. Mawhood with the 17th 40th and 55th Regiments from Hillsborough followed in the rear of one column to Princetown." Mawhood's regiments were weakened because they left a strong detachment with their baggage at Hillsborough under Captain Scott of the 17th Regiment. Glyn's men took shelter in barns near the town.

Glyn also notes that Cornwallis had been on the verge of leaving on a ship for England but, having collected his forces at Princeton to "drive the enemy from Trenton across the Delaware and recover our former ground," he joined the army at Princeton that evening.[3]

During the day, Robert Lawrence at Thomas Olden's farmhouse observed a British light dragoon riding back and forth on the hillside across Stony Brook, then heard gunfire and saw smoke, indicating a small ambush. Soon after, a nearby farmwife was working in her kitchen, along with the British Adjutant's servant, whom she may have been boarding. While she worked, several soldiers returning from guard duty came in, and she overheard one of them say to the servant "that he could not do as Brown did today." He then told of a wounded man, unable to stand, who begged for his life while Brown placed his gun to the man's chest and fired.

Soon after, local farmers found the bodies of two militiamen with wounds similar to those described by the men in the kitchen—one shot in the groin and the breast and one shot in the hip and the head. The palm of that man's hand and the wrist band of his shirt on the other arm had gun powder burns, as though he threw up both hands for protection when he saw the British soldier aim at his head. The bullet hit him just above his eyebrow, shattering his skull, resulting in some of his brains lying on his face when he fell. These deaths may have been one result of Howe's December 12 orders concerning treatment of belligerents not in uniform and without an officer. A British light dragoon also suffered a wound in the brief encounter inflicted by a ramrod accidentally shot by one of the militiamen. According to Lawrence, the dragoon must have leaned back on his horse to avoid the flying ramrod, but it entered "under his chin and came out again at his nose near his eyes." The injured dragoon "languished a few days and died."[4]

Joseph Clark, having recovered from his sprained ankle, set out in the morning to look for his militia battalion. That evening he came to Benjamin Johnson's, where part of his company spent the night.[5] Princeton-born and -raised, Thomas Olden marched that night from Crosswicks to Trenton with the Pennsylvania militia squad he had joined. Olden then marched three miles on the road toward Princeton and joined an ambush party on the Post Road.[6]

General Cornwallis joined Grant at Princeton that evening with a large body of troops and established his headquarters at Morven. Overnight, British troops maintained a guard post at Eight Mile Run—about three and a half miles south of Princeton on the Post Road. Ewald, at the Millstone River bridge, did not receive orders to return to Princeton until 11:00 p.m. The cold weather began to break, bringing warmer temperatures and heavy rain that made their night march miserable.[7] Overnight, British troops built many fires while encamped alongside the main road for some distance, from the turning at Clark's corner down to near the bridge at Worth's Mill and up the road on Cochran's Hill on the other side of the creek toward the Province Line.[8]

January 2

On the morning of January 2, most of the soldiers quartered about Princeton mustered to begin a march to Trenton, no doubt to the great relief of their forced hosts. Captain Ewald arrived at Princeton from Rocky Hill about daybreak and "found the entire army under arms." He drew biscuit and brandy from the depot for his tired and hungry men and then joined the column of about eight thousand troops under Cornwallis marching toward Trenton. The temperature rose into the forties and turned the roads into deep mud.[9]

The 4th Brigade, commanded by Lieutenant Colonel Mawhood—consisting of the 17th, the 40th, the 55th Regiments of Foot, two troops of light dragoons, and several pieces of artillery—remained at Princeton as a rear-guard. During the day, individual soldiers who had been in New York on various duties, had recovered from illness, or were recent recruits came to Princeton following orders from General Howe to join their units in New Jersey. To keep track of them and maintain discipline, Mawhood formed these transient men into temporary, makeshift companies commanded by transient officers as they arrived at Princeton.[10] During the day, Mawhood's men carried out their usual garrison routines. Periodically, they heard the sounds of distant combat as British soldiers fought Washington's troops at various points on the Post Road in a series of actions planned out to delay their arrival at Trenton.

While the British troops marched toward Trenton, Joseph Clark and his militia company marched to Penny Town and drew rations. Continuing toward Trenton, they must have been very aware of the British advance on the town and did not go far, but halted and took lodgings for the night.[11] Local militiamen were more interested in protecting the local people from British patrols than in joining with the main army.

Late in the day, a British express rider sent by Cornwallis arrived in Princeton. He carried a message for Mawhood, ordering him to march early the next morning to bring numerous supplies and the bulk of his troops, all except the 40th Regiment of Foot, to Trenton. The muddy roads and delaying actions had slowed Cornwallis so much that he did not arrive at Trenton until too late in the day for a decisive attack. In the morning, he expected to renew

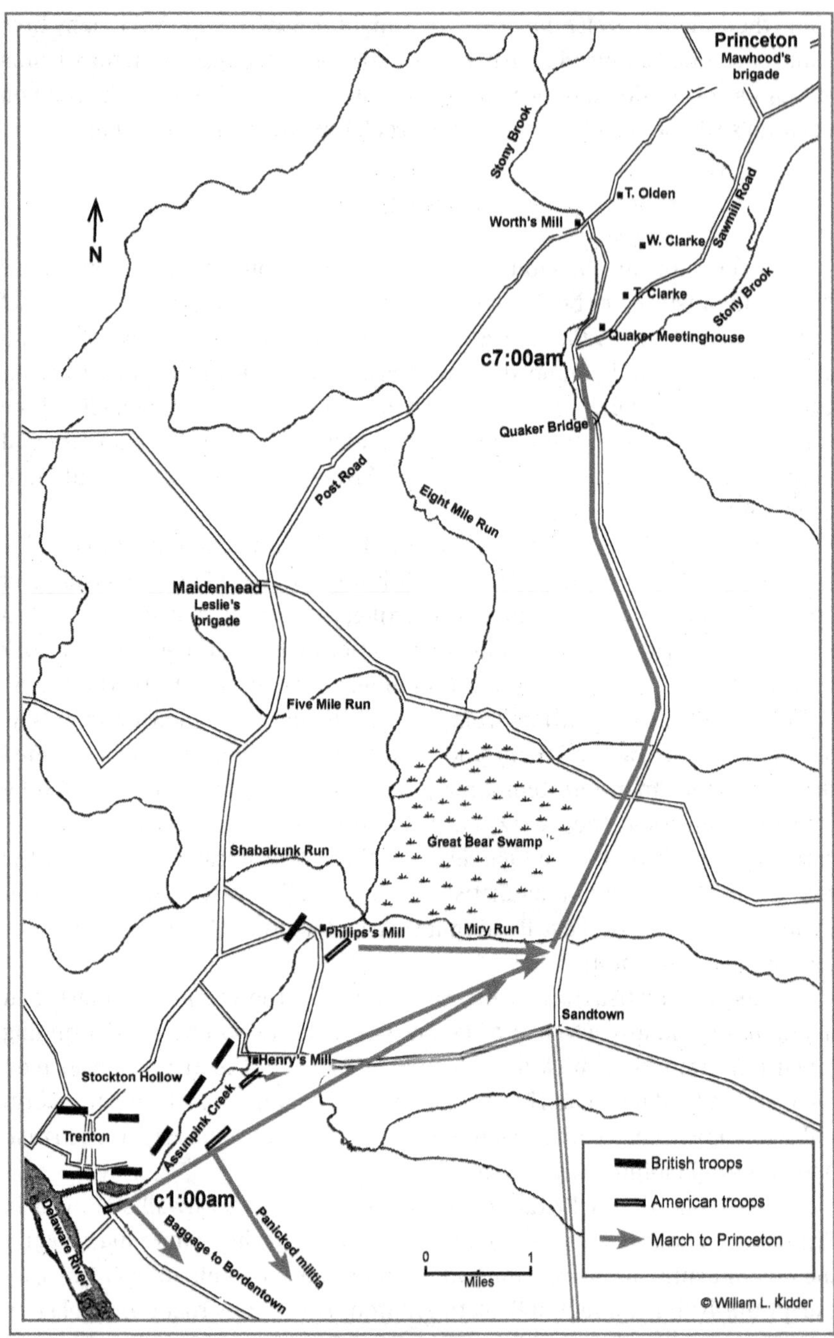

Map 12: Washington's Night March to Princeton, January 2-3, 1777

his attack on the American forces entrenched on Mill Hill, where he had left them at the end of that day's battle.

January 3

Mawhood's troops formed up in Princeton early on the morning of January 3, to begin their ordered march to Trenton. A captain, possibly grenadier Captain Thomas Williamson of the 52nd Regiment of Foot, temporarily commanding one of the makeshift companies of transients, forced a local man to go with him and his men in case they needed a guide to show them the way to Trenton. The man later told friends that when he expressed a reluctance to go with them, "the captain bid him step along nimbly, for if he did not he swore he would run him through with the drawn sword that he had in his hand, and the sergeant swore that if he did not lead them right he would shoot him."[12] Understandably, the man reluctantly agreed to accompany them.

Overnight, the temperature had plunged, solidly freezing the mud that men and horses had slogged through the day before. Just as day broke, Robert Lawrence once again saw British soldiers marching from the village toward Trenton, this time on the frozen road.[13] Captain Thomas Trewren with a troop of the 16th Light Dragoons led this force, followed by the 17th Regiment of Foot, several supply wagons, the 55th Regiment of Foot, some artillery pieces, a squad of dismounted dragoons, and the temporary companies of transients on their way to join their units. The 40th Regiment remained in Princeton to guard the town and British military supplies remaining there.[14]

Lawrence was unaware that a man he knew, a member of the extended Olden family, young Thomas, had been in the all-day battle on January 2, first during the delaying actions against Cornwallis and then at the cannonade across the Assunpink Creek that was only stopped by nightfall. Olden's militia unit, he recalled, had been ordered to fall back "into a copse of wood where we struck up a great number of fires & about one o'clock in the morning were ordered to march to Princeton." Olden was now with Washington's troops only about a mile from his hometown and preparing to attack it.[15]

Having marched all night on a frozen back road from Trenton, about 7:00 am, Washington halted his army at a wooded area along Stony Brook about two miles from Princeton, close to a recently discontinued British picket position.[16] Washington's men were on the edge of exhaustion after over thirty-six hours of nearly constant activity with little or no rest or food. Many had marched all night on January 1 to get to Trenton or had stayed alert at ambush sites on the Post Road. During the day on January 2, they had prepared for and

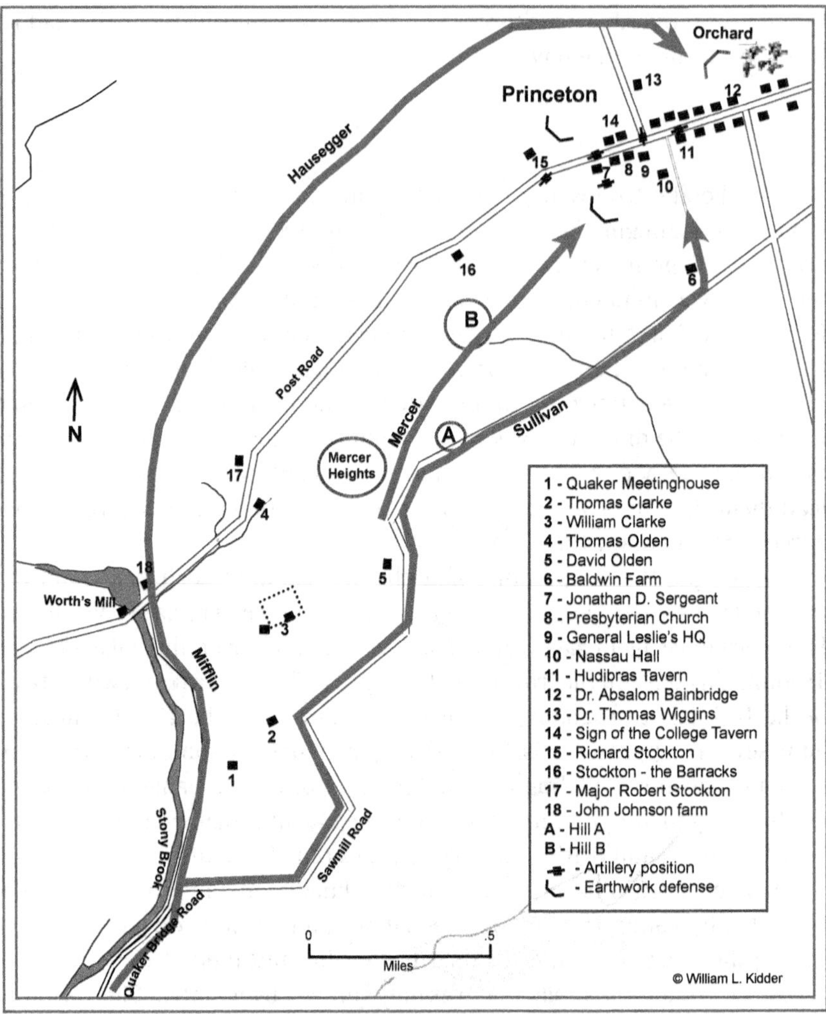

Map 13: Washington's Plan for attacking Princeton, January 3, 1777

then fought delaying actions, and finally exchanged fire with the British at the Assunpink Creek in Trenton until the battle ceased for the night. Then they had spent another night marching in the freezing weather to Princeton. This was not the same army that had fought at Trenton just a week before. Those troops who had successfully crossed the Delaware and were with Washington at Trenton were seasoned Continentals, for the most part. Washington's Continental troops now were those veterans who had agreed to extend their enlistments for six weeks. They could have gone home several days previously and avoided the dangers of further battles. Most of the other troops with him now were militiamen who had come out to join Washington after the success at Trenton and, while many had fought in small militia actions, most had not fought alongside Continentals in significant battles.

While the men briefly rested, Washington explained to his officers how they were going to surprise and envelop the British soldiers in the village from several directions, much like they had at Trenton the previous week. Washington's plan developed from the information placed on the Cadwalader spy map that had shown him the British defenses and the little-used back road, called the Sawmill Road, to Princeton that they had now reached by secretly marching around the British army at Trenton.

Washington divided his tired troops into three divisions. The first, under General Sullivan, would march to Princeton on the Sawmill Road and attack from the east across the Jonathan Baldwin farm toward Nassau Hall. Sullivan had about twenty-three hundred men consisting of St. Clair's brigade of New Englanders, the Virginia brigade, Hitchcock's New England brigade, and Colonel Hand's Pennsylvania riflemen, along with about thirteen pieces of artillery. These were some of his best troops and nearly half of his Continentals and artillery pieces.

A second division would march along Stony Brook and cross the Post Road, then head north to the back of Princeton to cut off any British troops retreating to New Brunswick, while engaging the British soldiers fighting to defend Princeton. This division numbered about two thousand men, including General Roche de Fermoy's Brigade, composed of the five hundred men of Colonel Nicholas Hausegger's German Regiment, reinforced by some Philadelphia Associators, and Mifflin's Brigade of about fifteen to eighteen hundred men from five depleted Pennsylvania regiments.[17] Fermoy himself was absent.

A third, and the smallest, division would "march straight on to Princeton without turning to the right or left." It consisted of about three to four hundred Continentals in Mercer's and Stirling's brigades and one thousand to fifteen hundred militia under Colonel Cadwalader. Mercer had two artillery pieces and Cadwalader six. Colonel Haslet, on foot, and General Mercer, on horseback, led Mercer's brigade. Captain Thomas Rodney's Delaware militia company marched on the right flank of the brigade, as Rodney noted, "in an Indian file so that my men were very much extended and distant from each other." Rodney marched in front, followed by Sergeant Jonathan McKnatt and Nehemiah Tilton.[18]

By about 7:30 a.m., Washington's army was formed up, the men had rested a bit, and many had downed their half a gill of gun powder–fortified rum.[19] Hausegger's brigade had set off early along Stony Brook, crossed the Post Road where the people living near Worth's Mill must have heard and wondered about them. They then headed north across farms toward the back of Princeton, out of sight of the main road. Mifflin's troops held back, to follow later and tear down the Stony Brook bridge.[20]

Soon after starting their march to Princeton on the Sawmill Road, the van of Sullivan's division passed the Thomas Clarke farmhouse, barn, and outbuildings. Thomas and his sister Sarah were already up and attending to morning farm chores although they had lost most, if not all, of their animals to British plundering. They must have been glad the bulk of the British army had gone south to Trenton the day before but no doubt believed the British would return at some point. But now they must have wondered about these several thousand unexpected troops trudging toward Princeton past their farmhouse on the Sawmill Road.

At the same time, most of Mawhood's troops marched down the Post Road toward Trenton, out of sight of Thomas and Sarah. As his troops reached the bridge at Worth's Mill, Mawhood must have wondered why the road showed disturbances caused by something that had crossed the road very recently. But Mawhood had explicit orders to get to Trenton as quickly as possible and did not stop to ask the local people about them or send out scouts; instead, he pushed ahead.

The Mutual Sighting

By around 7:50 a.m., Sullivan's large division, followed by Mercer and Cadwalader, had passed Thomas Clarke's house and was heading toward David Olden's. As the army trudged along the crest of a rise east-northeast of Clarke's home, several officers at the rear of Sullivan's division, possibly attracted to sunlight flashing off some metal, spotted two or three British light dragoons about a mile away on the high ground of Cochran's Hill.[21] Sergeant Nathaniel Root of the 20th Continental Regiment wrote that "we observed a light-horseman looking toward us, as we view an object when the sun shines directly in our faces."[22]

Simultaneously, Cornett Henry Evatt of the 16th Light Dragoons at the summit of Cochran's Hill looked around and spotted some unknown troops marching toward Princeton about a mile distant on the William Clarke farm. Cornett Evatt's commander, Lieutenant Simon Wilmot, immediately informed Mawhood, who "in the grey of the morning" believed they might be Hessians but sent Wilmot with a trooper down "to the edge of the wood to see what they were." Wilmot returned shortly and reported the troops were a

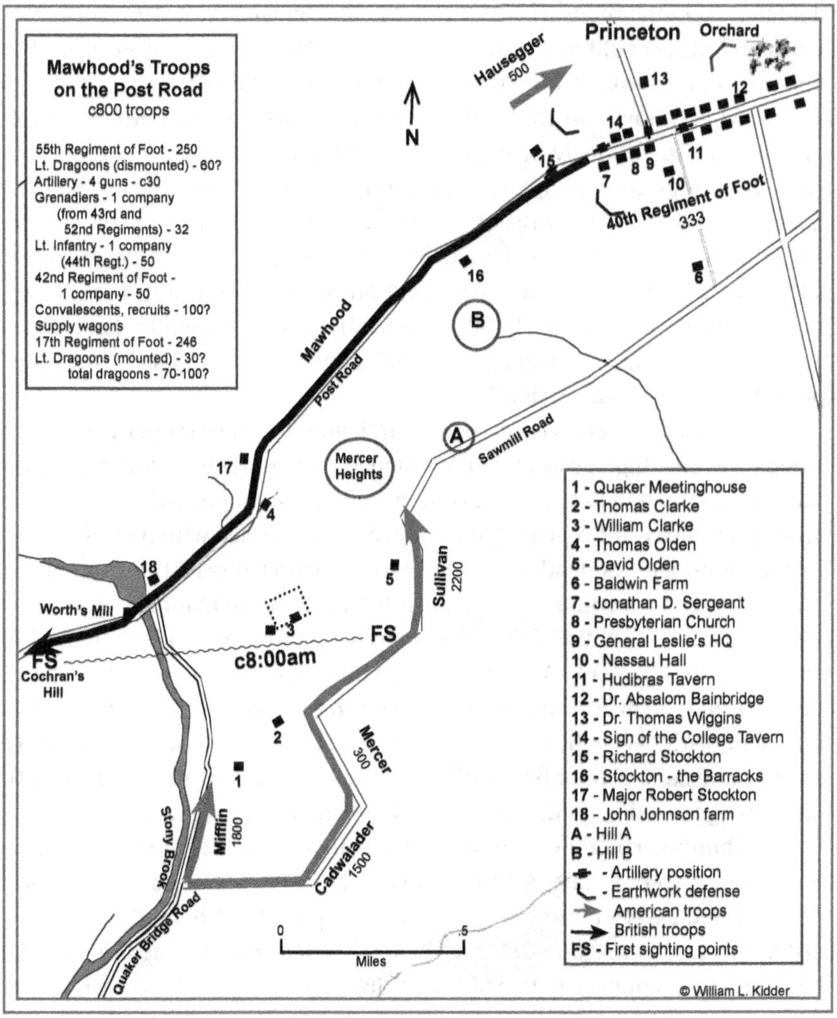

Mawhood's Troops on the Post Road
c800 troops

55th Regiment of Foot - 250
Lt. Dragoons (dismounted) - 60?
Artillery - 4 guns - c30
Grenadiers - 1 company (from 43rd and 52nd Regiments) - 32
Lt. Infantry - 1 company (44th Regt.) - 50
42nd Regiment of Foot - 1 company - 50
Convalescents, recruits - 100?
Supply wagons
17th Regiment of Foot - 246
Lt. Dragoons (mounted) - 30?
total dragoons - 70-100?

Princeton
Orchard
Hausegger 500
N
40th Regiment of Foot 333
Mawhood
Post Road
Mercer Heights
Sawmill Road
Sullivan 2200
Worth's Mill
FS
Cochran's Hill
c8:00am
Mercer 300
Cadwalader 1500
Mifflin 1800
Stony Brook
Quaker Bridge Road
0 .5 Miles

1 - Quaker Meetinghouse
2 - Thomas Clarke
3 - William Clarke
4 - Thomas Olden
5 - David Olden
6 - Baldwin Farm
7 - Jonathan D. Sergeant
8 - Presbyterian Church
9 - General Leslie's HQ
10 - Nassau Hall
11 - Hudibras Tavern
12 - Dr. Absalom Bainbridge
13 - Dr. Thomas Wiggins
14 - Sign of the College Tavern
15 - Richard Stockton
16 - Stockton - the Barracks
17 - Major Robert Stockton
18 - John Johnson farm
A - Hill A
B - Hill B
- Artillery position
- Earthwork defense
American troops
British troops
FS - First sighting points

Map 14: Battle of Princeton, January 3, 1777 - Initial Sightings c8:00am

Thomas Olden House

This house is at number 4 on the map above and is the site from which Robert Lawrence observed much of the battle and other events in early January 1777. Today it can be seen when driving Route 206 and is located on the grounds of Drumthwacket, the official residence of New Jersey's governor.

Historic American Buildings Survey (Library of Congress) HABS NJ-797 detachment of the rebel army marching in line toward Princeton and parallel to them. But he could not accurately estimate their numbers because of the distance and the intervening web of bare tree branches.[23]

Mawhood now had to decide whether to carry out his orders and get to Trenton expeditiously or engage this apparent enemy force of unknown size. His troops stretched back on the road toward Princeton, but he could have destroyed the Stony Brook bridge after all his troops crossed, to delay any pursuit. However, that would leave the 40th Regiment vulnerable to falling into enemy hands. He also could not justify to himself "the idea of a flight, before the people he had long since been accustomed to conquer and despise—[and] these considerations determined him to make a stand, and put it to the issue of an action."[24]

Mawhood decided to reverse his march and try to intercept the unknown troops on some high ground, today called Mercer Heights, before they got to the village. Mawhood's troops and horse-drawn equipment awkwardly turned around on the icy dirt road and marched in reverse order, with part of the 55th Regiment now in the lead, followed by the wagons, the 17th Regiment, and the 16th Light Dragoons. The makeshift transient companies under junior officers, such as Captain Williamson, marched in the space between the 17th and the 55th Regiments. While reversing direction, Mawhood sent orders to the 40th Regiment in the village to come to his aid. He then advanced his regiment with the light dragoons and the 55th Regiment toward Mercer Heights and sent Wilmot back out to learn more.[25] During this confusion, the local man pressed to guide Captain Williamson made his escape.[26]

Washington could not see the entire British force due to the terrain and intermittent web of barren tree branches blocking his view. He concluded the horsemen were merely a small morning patrol out from Princeton and ordered Mercer's brigade to leave the line of march and attack them, while he rode on to connect with Sullivan's division.[27] Surgeon's-mate Ebenezer Richmond, of the 11th Continental Regiment of Hitchcock's Brigade, later wrote that "Gen. Mercer with the Phila[delphia] Militia desired & were permitted the honor to begin the attack."[28] Mercer expected the British to remain on the Post Road, so he turned his brigade to the left and headed for the road across the icy, uneven Clarke farm fields strewn with crop stubble and residue, and some areas covered with winter wheat sprouts.[29]

As Mercer's men began to advance across the fields, Wilmot directed his horse toward the Americans until reaching a spot where "his retreat [would be] hazardous and difficult," and he came within rifle range of Mercer's men. From there, he could also see Cadwalader's column and realized there were significantly more men than he had seen initially. Mercer spotted Wilmot approaching on his scouting mission and ordered his riflemen "to pick him off." Visibility was now excellent, at about 8:00 a.m., but the temperature was only around twenty degrees with a light wind, and the riflemen standing in the middle of the farm field near Thomas Clarke's house were cold and tired from their all-night march. Following orders, though, several riflemen prepared to fire just as Wilmot "wheeled about and was out of their reach," galloping off to report to Mawhood that he had sighted two additional columns. Knowing that the escaping horseman would reveal his position, Mercer accelerated his advance toward the Post Road. He had about 120 men followed by another 200 but neglected to send out a screen of riflemen in advance. Cadwalader's brigade prepared to advance and support him.[30]

Lieutenant Wilmot found Mawhood on the Post Road and informed him there were at least three columns of rebels marching toward Princeton on the Sawmill Road, only about half a mile away. Mawhood realized he did not have time to intercept the most advanced column, Sullivan's, or to try and reach Princeton first, so he decided the 40th Regiment of Foot would have to defend Princeton alone as best it could. To intercept Mercer's column, Mawhood immediately formed up his troops with three companies of the 17th Regiment in the center, the dismounted 16th Light Dragoons on his right flank, and the mounted 16th Light Dragoons on his left. Joined by at least some of the makeshift companies of men from various regiments traveling with him, he ordered about 450 men and two artillery pieces up a slope to take position behind the orchard on William Clarke's farm.[31] The speed with which the British soldiers reacted and deployed for combat under those confused circumstances displayed Mawhood's outstanding leadership and the discipline of his soldiers. They would be well-prepared to receive Mercer's troops.[32]

Robert Lawrence now saw the British forces that he had observed marching out of town about half an hour earlier, returning at a more rapid pace. A portion of the 17th Regiment came into the field at his house and laid down their packs before forming up for battle "at the corner of our garden about 60 yards from the door." Lawrence saw them march "away immediately to the field of battle...in William Clarke's wheat field and orchard round about his house...plain within sight of our door at about 400 yards distance." Looking toward the developing battlefield, Lawrence saw a man fall before hearing any gunfire, and immediately afterward, "the report and smoke of a gun was seen and heard," followed by so much fire that he could not count the shots. Lawrence and those in the farmhouse with him "presently went down into the cellar to keep out of the way of the shot," and a neighbor woman visiting with them was "so affrighted that she imagined that the field was covered with blood."[33]

Hausegger's Force Reaches Princeton

John Hood of the 3rd Battalion of Philadelphia Associators with Colonel Hausegger reached the outskirts of Princeton at about daylight. His company came through some woods and a field at the back of the town, where they saw the defensive earthworks that British troops had begun constructing just days before. From the orchard-covered hill behind the house of Dr. Bainbridge, Hood could see Mawhood's column ascending Cochran's Hill, saw the column reverse its direction, and the beginning of the battle with Mercer's troops.[34]

Local Militiamen

Joseph Clark's militia company set out early in the morning on January 3 for Trenton, expecting the battle to resume there. Half an hour after sunrise, Clark says he "heard the engagement begin towards Princeton; we then immediately marched back to Penny Town, waiting some time for intelligence. Made two or three movements and lay in wait some time in the woods, for the enemy; but they, having got intelligence of us by some Tory, returned another road, and so escaped us. We then came to Levy Hart's, took lodgings, and cooked provisions."[35]

The Battle on the Clarke Farm

Major Apollos Morris, aide de camp to Washington, wrote of Mercer's troops crossing the farms that, "coming near the summit of the declivity," they encountered a fence between William Clarke's farmhouse and barn. They rushed through a gate, neglecting first to reconnoiter ahead, and entered into a thickly planted orchard only to discover they were facing a strong line of infantry supported by flanking units and two pieces of artillery. Morris recalled, "This line was in an open field, separated from the orchard only by a two bar fence." Mercer's men advanced through the orchard to gain possession of the fence and the slope just beyond it.[36]

Lieutenant John Armstrong, the college student who was now aide-de-camp to General Mercer, advanced rapidly with Mercer's men. He saw no enemy until reaching the area between William Clarke's farmhouse and barn, where they ran into the British line.[37]

Sergeant Nathaniel Root of the 20th Continental Regiment found that "as we were descending a hill through an orchard, a party of the enemy who were entrenched behind a bank and fence, rose and fired upon us. Their first shot passed over our heads cutting the limbs of the trees under which we were marching." His unit had just started to change direction when the corporal standing at Root's left shoulder "received a ball and fell dead on the spot."[38]

For Sergeant James McMichael of Miles's Pennsylvania Rifle Regiment, "Gen. Mercer with 100 Pennsylvania riflemen and 20 Virginians, were detached to the front to bring on the attack. The enemy then consisting of 500 paraded in an open field in battle array. We boldly marched to within 25 yards of them, and then commenced the attack, which was very hot."[39]

Jacob Hefflebower of Captain Smith's Company of the 3rd Pennsylvania Regiment encountered British fire upon reaching high ground, and his regiment kept the high ground advantage, with the smoke from their guns blowing toward the enemy so that the British shots fell short. At some point, Hefflebower received a severe wound in the forehead from a bullet. Fortunately, he was wearing a grenadier cap with a brass plate on the front, and the ball struck that plate, which helped save his life, although he fell to the ground.[40]

After the first British volley, Sergeant Root's company "formed, advanced, and fired upon the enemy," which retreated about forty-four yards to their packs laid in a line. Root recalled that he "advanced to the fence on the opposite side of the ditch which the enemy had just left, fell on one knee and loaded my musket with ball and buckshot."[41]

British Lieutenant William Hale estimated the American advance force to be eight hundred men, who held their fire until the British troops had advanced to within forty yards of them. The first, "very heavy discharge... brought down 7 of my platoon at once, [and] the rest, being recruits, gave way. I rallied these with some difficulty, and brought them on with bayonets." Although the rebels "poured in a second fire," the 17th Regiment "advanced in a most excellent order, and at length we drove them through the railings, barns and orchards."[42] The British had the advantage of bayonets fixed on their muskets, while Mercer's troops had very few of them because many of them were riflemen, and rifles did not mount bayonets.

Casualties began to mount. Among the flying bullets, grenadier Captain Thomas Williamson of the 52nd Regiment of Foot, who had pressed the now-escaped local farmer as a guide for his temporary command of returning transients, fell dead. Ensign Martin Hunter of the 52nd Regiment of Foot respected Williamson as "a most accomplished man" and noted he was the third captain of the 52nd Regiment Grenadiers killed in the war.[43]

Twenty-five-year-old Captain William Leslie of the 17th Regiment of Foot took musket balls in his left breast and side, falling on his back with his right arm extended as he dropped his sword. His servant, Peter McDonald, rushed

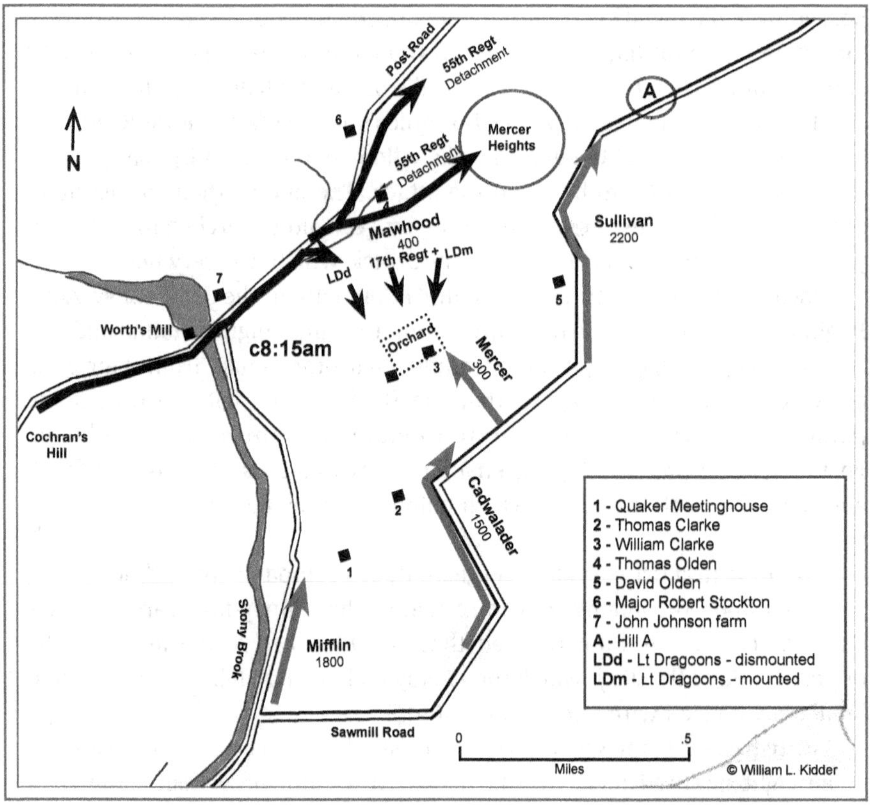

N
Post Road
55th Regt Detachment
Mercer Heights
55th Regt Detachment
Mawhood 400
17th Regt + LDm
LDd
A
Sullivan 2200
Worth's Mill
c8:15am
Orchard
Mercer 300
Cochran's Hill
Cadwalader 1500
Stony Brook
Mifflin 1800
Sawmill Road
0 .5 Miles
© William L. Kidder

1 - Quaker Meetinghouse
2 - Thomas Clarke
3 - William Clarke
4 - Thomas Olden
5 - David Olden
6 - Major Robert Stockton
7 - John Johnson farm
A - Hill A
LDd - Lt Dragoons - dismounted
LDm - Lt Dragoons - mounted

Map 15: Battle of Princeton, January 3, 1777 - c8:15am - 8:20am

The Thomas Clarke House

This mid-19th century drawing from Benson J. Lossing's *Pictorial Field Book of the Revolution* (1859) shows the post-1777 addition to the right end of the house. The drawing gives an impression of the farmland battlefield and its relation to the house. William Clarke's farm house is located on the hill seen in the distance just to the left of the Thomas Clarke house. Today, the Thomas Clarke house still stands as an integral part of the Princeton Battlefield State Park.

up to him and found him still alive, but unable to speak. Leslie gestured to McDonald to take his pocket watch and then succumbed in McDonald's arms a few seconds later. As the fighting continued, McDonald placed Leslie's body in a baggage wagon and stayed close by to protect it, until having to leave to avoid capture. Lieutenant William Armstrong of the 17th Foot believed of Captain Leslie, the nephew of General Alexander Leslie, that "a more amiable man never existed."[44]

Sergeant Root thought he "heard Gen. Mercer command in a tone of distress, 'Retreat!'" But Delaware militia Captain Thomas Rodney found the British "onset was so fierce that Gen. Mercer fell mortally wounded and many of his officers were killed, and the brigade being effectually broken, began a disorderly flight."[45] John Chilton of the 3rd Virginia Regiment saw that Mercer "staid too much behind to conduct our retreat and was inhumanly murdered with bayonets."[46]

Cary McClelland of Captain John Marshall's company of Pennsylvania rifles took a wound to the groin about the same time and fell. In the wild storm of the fighting, he saw his comrades push against British bayonets on the right and left wings, and General Mercer receive seven bayonet stabs.[47]

As the British advanced rapidly with bayonets leveled, the wounded Mercer shouted to Captain Daniel Neil of the New Jersey Artillery to fly and save himself. A blow to the side of his head from a British musket butt used as a club brought Mercer to his knees, half stunned, and before he could regain his feet, he was surrounded. Noting Mercer's uniform, British soldiers running up to him began shouting, "The rebel General is captured!" and, "with a dozen bayonets" pointing at Mercer from all directions, one soldier shouted, "Surrender, you damned rebel!" To which Mercer, gasping in pain, yelled back, "I am no rebel," and instead of calling for quarter, determined to die fighting. Mercer lunged from the ground toward the man, confronted him, and immediately received bayonet stabs. He fell as though dead, and after administering a few additional bayonet thrusts into him to assure he was gone, the British infantrymen moved on.[48]

Artillery Captain Neil, deserted by his men, became surrounded and was bayoneted while endeavoring to reload his cannon. General Nathaniel Greene said the enemy refused to grant Neil quarter after wounding him. To Greene, this action painted the "horrors of war beyond description." The British captured Neil's two guns, and British Lieutenant Hale believed they kept possession of the orchard for about twenty minutes and turned one of the captured field pieces on the Americans.[49]

Colonel John Haslet of Delaware, Mercer's second in command, had marched into the battle on foot beside Mercer on horseback. The march was extremely painful for Haslet because he had fallen into the Delaware River at about 3:00 a.m. on the return to Pennsylvania after the victory at Trenton on December 26. This had caused Haslet's legs to swell, and he developed other bodily discomforts that still flared. When Mercer went down, Haslet took his place in command, but a short time after, a British musket ball struck him in the head and killed him.

Amidst the fearsome melee of the battle, each individual experienced, observed, and remembered different things that stayed with them. Mercer's aide-de-camp, college student John Armstrong, found himself briefly pinned under his wounded horse before being rescued.[50]

Captain John Chilton of the 3rd Virginia Regiment saw 1st Virginia Regiment Captain John Fleming fall dead. Then, he saw Lieutenant Bartholomew Yates of the 1st Virginia fall into enemy hands after receiving a "slight wound in the thigh," and the enemy "immediately butchered him with the greatest barbarity."[51] Lieutenant Yates was only mortally wounded and would live in pain until his death on January 9.[52]

Virginia rifleman Jonathan Grant in Captain Graham's company witnessed Colonel Haslet, Captain Fleming, and many other officers killed. When Lieutenant Abraham Kirkpatrick fell wounded, Grant carried him from the battlefield.[53]

Sergeant William Young noted that, after an officer became injured in one leg, "a soldier came and knocked his brains out with the butt end of his gun. A young lad that was wounded they stabbed 3 times in his side with his bayonet, which so exasperated our men that seeing two Hessians behind a tree ran at them, shot one and run the other through and that the militia behaved to [a] miracle."[54] There were no Hessians units in the action, but these two men may have been transients, or were simply mistaken for Hessians.

For the occasional fortunate man, the strenuous battle exertions somehow relieved or repaired earlier wounds. Captain John McKinstry of the 15th Continental Regiment had "received a ball through his thigh in Canada" in December 1775, and "his nerves, irritated with the wound, became contracted," causing him to be lame. He recovered enough to rejoin his unit. He found that "at the affair of Prince-Town, after traveling eighteen miles on foot, he happening to leap over a fence, [and] by this effort the contracted nerves broke or rather lengthened themselves," ending his lameness.[55]

After the battle, Sergeant Root's experiences caused him to exclaim, "O, the barbarity of man!" He was particularly struck by the brutal treatment of the American wounded during the battle. He says, "On our retreat, we had left a comrade of ours whose name was Loomis from Lebanon, Ct., whose leg was broken by a musket ball, under a cart in a yard; but on our return he was dead, having received several wounds from a British bayonet. My old associates were scattered about groaning, dying and dead. One officer who was shot from his horse lay in a hollow place in the ground rolling and writhing in his blood, unconscious of anything around him. The ground was frozen, and all the blood which was shed remained on the surface, which added to the horror of this scene of carnage." In the confusion of battle, Sergeant Root says he "looked about for the main body of the army which I could not discover—discharged my musket at part of the enemy, and ran for a piece of wood, at a little distance where I thought I might shelter."[56]

Mercer's Brigade Retreat and Cadwalader's Reinforcement

Mercer's men retreated in some disorder on the William Clarke farm and ran into Cadwalader's troops coming out of a woods onto the field near Thomas Clarke's house. The 17th Regiment advanced on Cadwalader's militia now mixed with Mercer's retreating men and also put them in some disorder.[57] As Cadwalader lined up his forces, he saw about fifty British light infantry posted behind a fence about one hundred yards away.[58] To counter that threat, he sent off Captain Henry with about one hundred light infantry.[59] Henry's men, assisted by an artillery barrage from Captain Joseph Moulder's two cannon placed on high ground to the right of the Thomas Clarke farmhouse, stopped the advance of the 17th Regiment, when "the first discharge from our field pieces on the left, drove them up to the main body."

Cadwalader recorded that at that moment, "I just then saw a considerable party of horse [mounted dragoons under Cornet Staples] moving off to our right, to take advantage of the confusion, but a discharge or two from the [Moulder's] cannon immediately dispersed them. I asked the General if it would not be proper to form about an hundred yards in the rear."[60]

Lieutenant Charles Willson Peale, serving with Cadwalader's militia, wrote: "We marched on quickly and met some of the troops retreating in confusion. We continued our march towards the hill where the firing was, though now rather irregularly. I carried my platoon to the top of the hill, and fired, though unwillingly, for I thought the enemy too far off, and then retreated, loading. We returned to the charge, and fired a second time, and retreated as before. Coming up the third time, the enemy retreated."[61]

Zebulon Applegate of Moulder's artillery company says, "after we got into the field we formed a line with the artillery in the center and the other troops on each side." They had gone about three or four hundred yards when they saw two British artillery pieces emerge from behind "a large barn and orchard and fired at us." Moulder's artillery "returned the compliments and

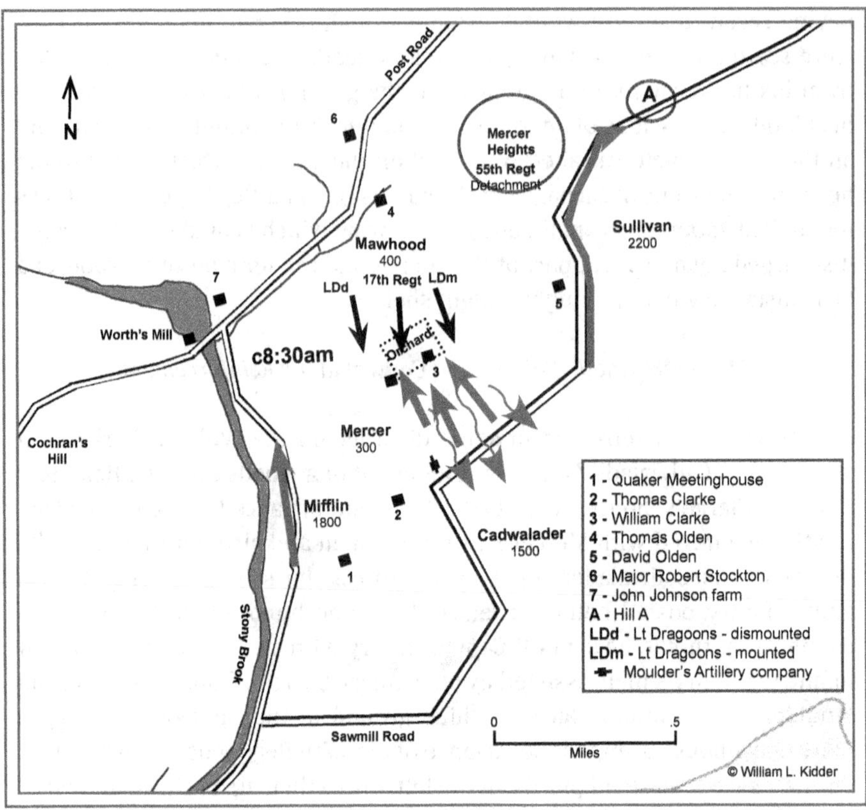

Map 16: Battle of Princeton, January 3, 1777 - c8:30am - 8:40am

kept a heavy fire until they retreated[, then] we advanced. When the battle first begun we had a bad piece of ground going down the side of a hill and after one or two rounds we received orders to retreat." Then, "as soon as we began to retreat the British huzzaed all along the line—we retreated about twenty or thirty yards" until told "not to go any further but to dispute the ground."[62]

The British fired high over the heads of Moulder's men, while Moulder "mowed them down in rows as if they had lain down to rest."[63] Thomas Rodney noted that even British prisoners captured at the battle believed the Americans served their artillery more effectively than the British and that "almost every shot from ours was placed in the thick of them while theirs flew harmless o'er our heads."[64]

At the time Mercer's Brigade retreated in panic into Cadwalader's militia, an attack from the 55th Regiment of Foot supporting the 17th Regiment could have defeated them. However, the 55th Regiment failed to answer repeated calls from Colonel Mawhood, apparently because they saw "such a slaughter among the first rank of the 17th that their commander felt it was over."[65]

So far, most of the action had taken place between the houses of Thomas and William Clarke, and Cadwalader's men never reached the orchard. The reforming of his forces about one hundred yards in the rear took place under cover of the hillside on the south side of Sawmill Road toward the wood. As Cadwalader reformed his troops, he "collected some of the brigade and some New Englandmen, and advanced obliquely to the right, passed a fence, and marched up to the left of the enemy. Two small parties were formed on the left, and advanced at the same time, and bravely pushed up in the face of a heavy fire. The enemy then left their station and inclined to the left, and gave us several heavy fires, in which two were killed and several wounded."[66]

During the battle, a woman who had experienced a recent miscarriage was bedridden in her home, and after a shot came through a window of her room, her husband and nurse carried her to the cellar for safety.[67]

Washington Saves the Day

The van of Sullivan's column had advanced past Mercer Heights to a small hill nearer town when Washington realized the magnitude and disarray of Mercer's engagement near the Clarke farms. He ordered Colonel Daniel Hitchcock's and Colonel Edward Hand's brigades to advance on the British flank to assist Mercer and Cadwalader. The remaining forces under Sullivan's command, still sixteen to eighteen hundred men strong, halted to await further orders. While the number of men is one indicator of an army's strength, another is the structure of its units and the experience of its officers. Hitchcock's substantially depleted brigade only had about five or six hundred men. Colonel Christopher Lippitt's regiment had 16 platoons but only 8 men in each, so it had about 128 men. On the right, Lieutenant Colonel Nixon commanded his brother's regiment. Next came Colonel James Varnum's Rhode Island regiment command by Lieutenant Colonel Archibald Crary because Varnum had resigned. In the middle came Colonel Lippitt's Rhode Island regiment. To its left came Colonel Hitchcock's Rhode Island regiment, commanded by Major Israel Angel because Colonel Hitchcock was ill. On the left flank came Colonel Little's Massachusetts regiment commanded by Lieutenant Colonel William Henshaw.[68] Major Angell, as the senior officer present, gave Hitchcock's men an inspiring short speech, "encouraging them to act the part that became brave soldiers, worthy of the cause for which we were contending."[69]

Personally leading Hitchcock's and Hand's brigades, Washington galloped across what is today known as Maxwell's Field toward the fighting. By the account of Surgeon's mate Ebenezer Richmond of the 11th Continental Regiment of Hitchcock's brigade, they advanced while firing five volleys and within six minutes had eliminated the British artillery threat and pushed on to rout the enemy. Two officers in Colonel Lippitt's Rhode Island regiment recalled they formed up about two hundred yards from the enemy and began firing within one hundred yards, fired two or three times in covering the one hundred yards. The enemy retreated to their artillery of two pieces, which the Rhode Islanders rushed and took. The enemy broke and retreated but recovered several times, formed ranks, and fired before fleeing again.[70]

Lieutenant Stephen Olney of the 1st Rhode Island Regiment noticed the enemy near them just before thirty or forty of the British fired a volley on the front of the column, which broke it, and the men came running through the Rhode Islander's ranks. Captain Jeremiah Olney ordered these men to join him, and about a dozen did, while the remainder headed for the woods. Lieutenant Olney said, "when clear of the woods and other obstructions, our column displayed and marched in line; at this instant the enemy made a full discharge of musketry and field-pieces, loaded with grapeshot, which made the most horrible music about our ears I had ever heard, but as they overshot, there were but few but what continued the march, looking well at the colors, which were carried steadily by Ensign Oliver Jencks, of Cumberland, (no fool of a job to carry colors steady at such a time)." The enemy was surprised that "we were not all dead and that we continued to advance in order with a reserved charge for them, [and] turned their backs and fled in disorder."[71]

Seeking shelter in the mayhem, Sergeant Root saw Washington at the head of the troops coming on to help Mercer and Cadwalader's retreating forces. He heard Washington yell, "Parade with us, my brave fellows, there is but a handful of the enemy, and we will have them directly." Root, along with others near him, "immediately joined the main body, and marched over the ground again."[72] At one point, a cannonball hit and splintered a fence rail while Washington was receiving some information about the enemy, slightly wounding John Keen of Captain Richard Humphreys's company of Cadwalader's brigade.[73]

Major Apollos Morris saw order restored by this advance led by Washington that combined with "some rounds of grape fired from two [of Moulder's] field pieces opportunely advanced on their left flank," while Cadwalader and the remnants of Mercer's brigade still engaging the British front. Some troops from Mifflin's brigade also now appeared and attacked the British right flank.[74] Mifflin's men had been advancing along in the Stony

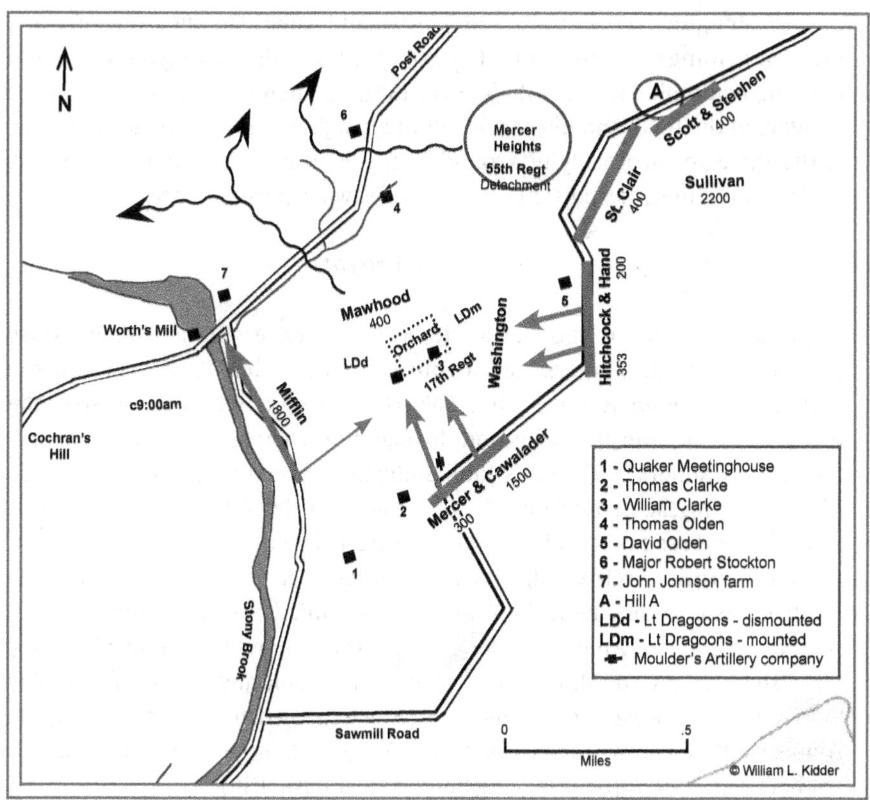

Map 17: Battle of Princeton, January 3, 1777 - c8:40 - c9:00am

Brook ravine and could not see the battlefield above them to their right, although they certainly heard what was going on. Mifflin ordered several units to climb out of the ravine and head for the battle, while the majority pushed on to destroy the Stony Brook bridge. Washington's troops now threatened to encircle Mawhood, and as British troops began to retreat, the defeat threatened to turn into a rout. The "fox chase" was on.

Referring to this portion of the battle, James Read with the Philadelphia Associators later commented to his wife, "O my Susan! It was a glorious day and I would not have been absent from it for all the money I ever expect to be worth. I happened to be amongst those who were in the first and hottest of the fire and I flatter myself that our superiors have approved of our conduct." He felt compelled to add "a few words respecting the actions of that truly great man Gen. Washington, but it is not in the power of language to convey any just idea of him. His greatness is far beyond my description." Referring to how Washington rode between the British and American lines, encouraging his men, leading many to fear that one of the hundreds of flying bullets would kill him, Read told Susan, "I shall never forget...when I saw him brave all the dangers of the field, and his important life hanging as it were by a single hair with a thousand deaths flying around him. Believe me I thought not of myself. He is surely America's better Genius and Heaven's peculiar care."[75]

The British Retreat

Near the end of the battle, Robert Lawrence at the Olden house saw seven British soldiers "fall at once."[76] As Mawhood's troops fled the battlefield, Captain Rodney said, "We then pushed forward towards the town spreading over the fields and through the woods to enclose the enemy and take prisoners."[77] Generals John Sullivan, Adam Stephen, and Arthur St. Clair, watching the battle from afar, saw that the tide of the battle had turned favorably and resumed their advance toward Princeton.

As his troops retreated, Mawhood ordered his mounted dragoons to the front, where they kept the Americans occupied and slowed down their pursuit. While the Americans focused on those horsemen, believing they were the rear guard, Mawhood's infantrymen took advantage of a thickly wooded area to prevent the Americans from quickly discovering their escape routes.[78] While individually displaying very gallant behavior, the British soldiers retreated rapidly, leaving behind their casualties.

Washington came upon wounded Captain-Lieutenant John McPherson, shot through the lungs, and assured him that the American troops would treat all the wounded men of the 17th Regiment with the same respect as their officers, "on account of their gallant behavior."[79] Several weeks later, a newspaper reported that "General Washington perceiving a wounded soldier belonging to the enemy laying on the field, came up to him, and after inquiring into the nature of his wound, commended him for his gallant behavior, and assured him that he should want for nothing that his camp could furnish him." As Washington began to move on, an American soldier, thinking this wounded man was dead, "came up in order to strip him; the General see[ing] it, bid the soldier be gone, and ordered a sentry to stand over the wounded prisoner till he was carried to a convenient house to be dressed."[80] Three British soldiers lay dead "in and near the main road that Washington ordered put in wagons and taken to town." He then asked "the country people to bury the dead" of both sides, and several that lay near the battlefield were buried in other places over the next few days. Lawrence also commented that Washington saw the British "packs lying in ye field where they had left them, and set a guard over them with orders that nobody should meddle with them until further orders." Lawrence saw a guard stand by them until the Americans departed.[81]

Colonel Mawhood escaped south to Maidenhead with a remnant of the 17th Regiment and joined with General Leslie, father of the deceased Captain Leslie. Later that day, Loyalist Joseph Stockton guided Mawhood to New Brunswick.[82] George Inman of the 17th Regiment escaped with Mawhood. He later commented, "We suffered much," and "sustained a loss of 101 rank and file, killed and wounded and much the greater part by the first fire received." He felt fortunate, commenting that "I being the only officer in the right wing of the battalion that was not very much injured receiving only a buckshot through my cross belt which just entered the pit of my stomach and made me sick for the moment."[83]

During Hausegger's march north toward the back of town, he sent out reconnaissance scouts who remained undetected but discovered Mawhood's troops marching out of Princeton. This surprise proximity to British soldiers led to a heated discussion between Colonel Hausegger and Major Ludowick Weltner. Unable to inform Washington of his discovery, Hausegger wanted to attack. However, Weltner urged caution because their gunfire might disrupt Washington's battle plan, and they did not yet know the strength and location of the enemy forces. Colonel Hausegger was not convinced and ordered his regiment to leave the back road and head for the enemy forces on the Post Road, with Hausegger riding ahead. By then, Mercer's and Cadwalader's troops were fully engaged with the 17th Regiment.

Aware of the battle raging around William Clarke's orchard, General Sullivan vainly tried to get word to Hausegger to rejoin the army. Suddenly, Hausegger, with a ten-man squad, rode into a woods heading toward the firing. He was surprised and captured by a party of enemy troops. The story of Hausegger's capture was controversial at the time and continues so today. It is unclear whether the British captured him or, as was generally believed at the time, he deserted. He always maintained his innocence, even demanding a court-martial, which Washington denied him. At some point that morning, there was fighting at a Princeton orchard between Hausegger's men and men from either the 40th Regiment of Foot or troops retreating from the primary battle. During this action, twenty-four-year-old Jacob Saylor, who often played his fiddle for the diversion of Hausegger's battalion and was a favorite among the men, received a cut on the face from a British bayonet, a wound that eventually cost him the sight of one eye.[84]

The British Attempt to Defend Princeton

While the action on the Clarke farms developed, elements of the 55th Regiment of Foot hurried toward Princeton, as Mawhood ordered a detachment under Captain James Taylor Trevor to secure a hill ("Hill B") in the path of the Americans and the rest of the regiment hurried toward Mercer Heights.[85] Sullivan and Trevor kept a frustrated eye on one another, yet they found themselves unable to move. Trevor's detachment was not strong enough to attack Sullivan, but neither could he go to Mawhood's aid. Sullivan dared not march on Princeton without better knowledge of British strength there.

When it became clear that the momentum of the battle favored the Americans, Colonel Charles Scott's Virginians headed for the fray. Scott called out to his men, "boys there are 250 red coats on yonder hill & about 250 of us, we can beat them." Ensign Robert Beale's men, with a great "Huzzah," rushed from their position on "Hill A" to "Hill B" but found Trevor's detachment had already abandoned it. Seeing Mawhood retreating, Trevor proceeded to Princeton to support Captain Robert Mostyn, commanding the 40th Regiment. Just outside the village, Beale's men came upon a small defensive earthwork that had been thrown up along the Post Road to protect the road into town, but found it empty. They continued toward the college and, looking back down the hill, saw the British running.[86]

Sullivan's and St. Clair's brigades continued marching along Sawmill Road to the northern edge of Frog Hollow ravine, about half a mile southwest of Nassau Hall. At Frog Hollow, Captain Mostyn, with men from the 40th and 55th Regiments that he had collected, briefly delayed Sullivan's advancing troops.[87] Major Apollos Morris reported that "some of the 40th appeared pouring out of the back gate of the college and taking possession of a dike [Frog Hollow] which extended from thence down the hill." The Americans attacked across the depression. While they ascended "the opposite side within sixty or 80 yards of the enemy, who were still concealed from our view by the acclivity," the British turned around and headed for the college.[88] Mostyn's hopelessly outnumbered force was soon dislodged by the Americans, aided "by the fire of two field pieces," which also killed Mostyn.[89]

Hauling their cannon from near Thomas Clarke's house toward the college, Moulder's artillerymen encountered wounded British soldiers begging for quarter. They reassured the wounded men they were safe, because "we are after live men," and then handed the grateful men their canteens of warm whiskey.[90]

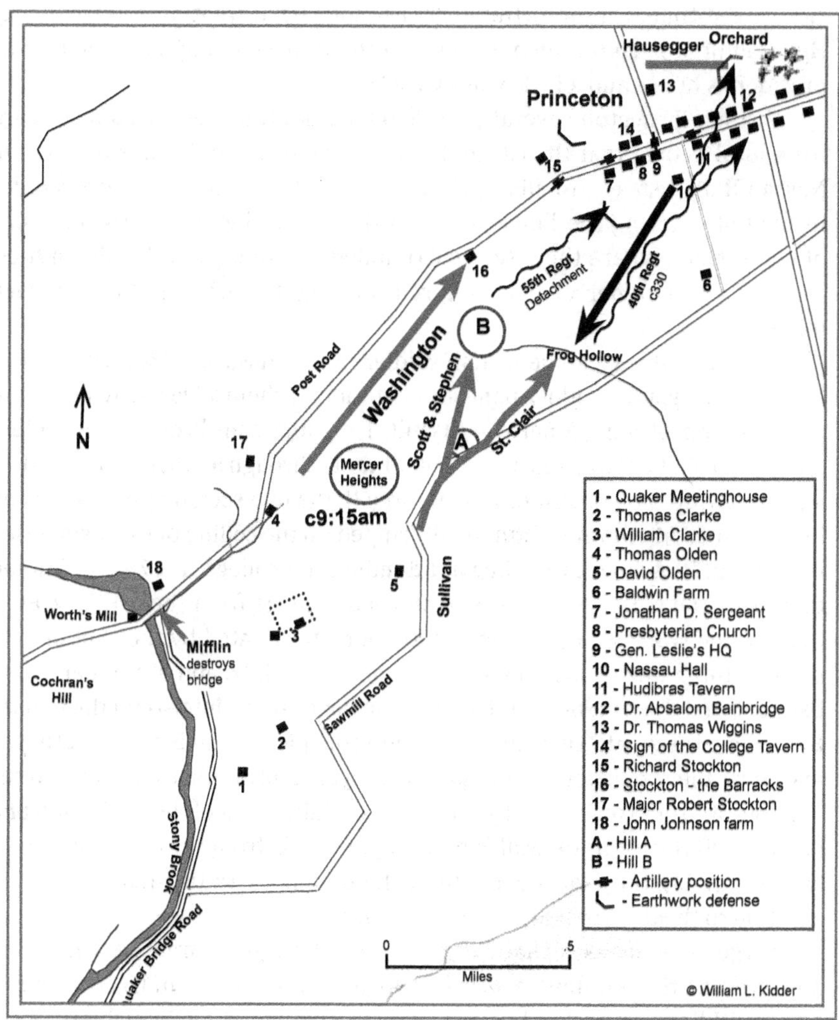

Map 18: Battle of Princeton, January 3, 1777 - c9:00am - c9:15am

Final Action at Nassau Hall

While the disorganized mob of British soldiers streamed back into Princeton as fugitives, some fled out today's Witherspoon Street, passed through Rocky Hill, and headed toward New Brunswick. Sporadic fighting in the village consisted of mop-up actions in which many British became prisoners. Local accounts and memories of British surrenders varied widely in detail. Princeton militiaman Lieutenant James Hamilton, though he was sick at the time, captured three British soldiers retreating toward Rocky Hill. Hamilton lived on the north side of the Post Road opposite the college president's house and a little ways west.[91]

Visiting Princeton several years later, the Marquis de Chastellux heard from local people that British soldiers did not seek a defensive position in Nassau Hall. Instead, "to all appearance their officers were bewildered, for instead of entering the house, or even the court, they remained in a sort of wide street, where they were surrounded and obliged to lay down their arms, to the number of one hundred and eighty, not including fourteen officers."[92]

However, at least some British soldiers entered Nassau Hall, where they knocked out glass window panes and stationed themselves at windows to repel the approaching American assault. The Americans brought up artillery and fired a shot or two, and a cannonball came through a Prayer Hall window and destroyed the portrait of King George II, the one seen by John Adams on his tour in 1774. Another cannonball "ripped up the ceiling of the dismantled prayer-hall."[93] Ashbel Green began attending the college in 1782 and noted then that "the whole building" still showed damage from the artillery. Even though "the stone walls, indeed, could not be perforated by the shot of field pieces,...the impressions they made were long visible, and a number of the balls entered the windows, and made great havoc in the interior of the house." By one local account, "One ball had made a conspicuous hole in the south wall in or near the projection containing the prayer-hall; another had entered the window of a room on the south side of the building west of the projection and had pierced the partition wall separating the room from the long corridor or 'entry' running through the length of the building." All this damage was in addition to the destruction of the painting.[94]

Sergeant Root says that "after two or three discharges, a white flag appeared at the window, and the British surrendered," and according to Charles Willson Peale, "we huzza'd victory." Root found the British prisoners to be "a haughty, crabbed set of men, as they fully exhibited while prisoners, on their march to the country."[95] By one local tradition, Captain James Moore and his local militia company burst open the door to Nassau Hall and demanded the British surrender, and the British complied.[96] However, Moore was not yet captain; Aaron Longstreet was, and at least part of the company was at Penny Town during the battle and did not appear in Princeton until after the British surrendered or fled.[97] The time was a little after 9:00 a.m. In the space of about two hours, Washington's army had struck another chip from the myth of British invincibility. But their stay in Princeton would be short.[98]

With the British garrison remnants in Princeton all fleeing sure capture, the several Loyalists who had been working with them also fled town for their lives. Dr. Bainbridge went with them. He left behind at least one slave, the young man named Prime, who remained in Princeton for a time and then went to the house of John Taylor, the father of Mrs. Bainbridge, in Monmouth County.[99] Richard Cochran later reported, "When the Kings troops were attacked at Princeton I had not a minutes warning & was in such danger of my life; that I would have surrendered myself a prisoner, had I not been informed that the rebels threatened to treat me with the utmost severity. When I got to Brunswick I had not so much as a second shirt."[100] Likewise, Captain Ibbitson Hamar and his wife Sarah left Castle Howard and joined the retreat of the British army to New Brunswick before continuing on to New York.[101]

Americans in Princeton

When the American army entered Princeton village, Mercer's and Cadwalader's brigades remained about a quarter mile outside it, under Nathanael Greene, while Sullivan's division occupied the town. Upon entering and searching Nassau Hall for any British holdouts, Sullivan's men liberated from confinement several Continental prisoners and about thirty civilians accused of being or assisting rebels. British prisoners took their places.[102]

Sergeant Joseph White searched through the rooms of Nassau Hall and discovered in one of the rooms an excellent uneaten breakfast left by a fleeing British soldier. White carefully went in, locked the door behind him to preserve the bounty for himself, sat down, and ate it. He also liberated a pair of shoes, a Bible, and a British officers' coat from the same room. However, later discovering that he would not be permitted to wear it, he sold the jacket to an American officer.

After leaving the room, White observed American soldiers grabbing fresh British blankets and throwing away their old dirty ones, so he grabbed himself a new one also. White saw men plundering outside Nassau Hall. Some filling wagons with as many barrels of flour from the British stores as they could hold and smashing the remaining barrels. Artillery Captain-Lieutenant Joseph Crane found a British military box containing hard money. He put it into a small ammunition cart "on the spur of the occasion" to keep it for himself rather than divide it among his company.[103] Washington had ordered that if a group of men takes booty from the enemy they must divide it equally among them, but this order went largely unenforced.[104] Not all men stayed around to plunder. Both individuals and groups deserted. In one case, a whole company departed except for "a lieutenant and a lame man."[105]

Jonathan Lowber and Mark Coudratt of Thomas Rodney's Delaware militia volunteers deserted.[106]

Aftermath of Battle

When the fighting ceased, the local people who had taken shelter reemerged. As the people at Thomas Olden's house came out of the cellar, Robert Lawrence said the hysterical woman visiting them "called earnestly to us to look out and see how all the field was quite red with blood. When none was to be seen at that distance." He was struck to see "what strange mistakes sudden frights with the fear of death may put us into." He also recalled that "almost as soon as the firing was over our house was filled and surrounded with General Washington's men, and himself on horseback at the door." Lawrence exclaimed, "It really animated my old blood with love to those men that but a few minutes before had been courageously looking death in the face in relieving a part of their country from the barbarous insults and ravages of a bold and daring enemy." Lawrence recalled that some of Washington's soldiers who entered the house were "laughing outright, others smiling, and not a man among them but showed joy in his countenance." It did not seem to matter that they were both starving and thirsty.[107]

Lawrence was greatly distressed by the way he heard the British soldiers had treated wounded Americans, showing a complete lack of mercy. He felt it was a result of "that vast pile of bribery and corruption under which the inhabitants of Great Britain now groans." The accounts raised his concern that humanity had lost virtue. However, the actions of the Continental soldiers relieved those concerns. Two American soldiers carried two enemy soldiers into his house "on their shoulders and their cloaths much besmeared with their blood." Other American soldiers brought large numbers of wounded enemy combatants into other homes that were near. These men suffered "the spoiling of their cloaths which they had rather bear than to leave their wounded enemies that could not stand by wallowing in their blood in the field." Lawrence saw more than twenty wounded men carried into William Clarke's house, and another sixty men taken to Princeton but did not know how many individuals in each group were regulars. Two of the men brought to William Clarke's died soon after.[108]

One of the two men Lawrence saw carried into Thomas Olden's house "was shot in at his hip and the bullet lodged in his groin, and the other was shot through his body just below his short ribs[.] he was in very great pain and bled much out of both sides, and often desired to be removed from one place to another, which was done accordingly and he died about three o'clock in the afternoon." Lawrence noted, "the other [man] also bled much and they put a cloth dipped in vinegar to the wound to stop it and three of them stayed with the wounded men near an hour after the others were gone." He commented that "they was both used very tenderly by the rebels (as they call them)"[109] and was struck by how different that was "from that barbarous cruel usage of the Regular Army when in the same battle."[110]

Pennsylvania militiaman Ensign John Hendy helped carry General Mercer and several other wounded men into Thomas Clarke's house. He heard Mercer exclaim "as he was carried along 'Cheer up my boys the day is ours.'" They put Mercer in a bed, and by tradition, even a hundred years later, the bloodstains on the floor by the bed were discernable.[111]

In addition to the wounded, a neighbor told Lawrence that 31 regulars and 19 provincials were found dead on the battlefield, and 175 British were prisoners.[112] Some wounds were relatively minor. Sergeant Root lost the end joint of a forefinger to a musket ball but was completely unaware of it until after the battle, when an officer saw blood on his clothes and found his finger "bleeding profusely." Checking himself out for other damage, he also found bullet holes in the skirt of his coat and noted, "my pack, which was made fast by leather strings, was shot from my back, and with it went what little clothing I had. It was, however, soon replaced by one which had belonged to a British officer, and was well furnished." He did not have it for long, though, because it was stolen from him soon afterward.[113]

Some civilians received wounds during the action. A woman living on the Post Road on the Princeton side of Stony Brook lost her leg when a cannonball, thought to be from an American cannon, smashed her ankle early in the fighting.[114]

Cornwallis Returns from Trenton

Knowing that Cornwallis would be marching his army back from Trenton as quickly as possible, about an hour after the battle ceased, Washington gave orders to be ready to march in half an hour. This order caused plundering to accelerate, with the items taken divided among nearby soldiers, and the men destroyed anything that they could not carry off—even rum from the local stores.[115] Before leaving town, the American forces had to be reorganized and gathered together, whether from looting or pursuing individual British soldiers still hiding out in the area.[116]

Colonel James Potter, of Mifflin's brigade, ordered a party of Major John Kelly's Northumberland County militia to dismantle the Stony Brook bridge to delay Cornwallis.[117] Kelly worked alongside his men, not willing to order other men to take on something people might accuse him of being too cowardly to do himself. As they worked, the British were approaching, and British Sergeant Sullivan recalled that they engaged the rebels with two six-pounders. In response, William McCracken of Captain Thomas Strawbridge's Company of the Chester County militia heard the firing of the two guns of Captain Forrest's company protecting Kelly's squad. Stephen Olney described hearing that "our cannon, which we had left at the [Stony Brook] bridge, west of Princeton, began to play at the enemy we had left at Trenton, who having lost sight of us last night, were in pursuit of us this morning."

While under fire, as Kelly cut "the sleeper of the bridge," it fell and, according to militiaman George Espy, took Kelly "with it into the creek." Believing Kelly to be dead, his men quickly departed. British Sergeant Sullivan saw that the British cannon fire "in a few minutes drove them from the bridge, which they had cut down, and retreated into the woods."[118] However, Kelly was alive and, through great exertions, managed to reach the river bank through the high water and floating timbers. Although weighed down by his wet, frozen clothes, Kelly followed after his retreating men and even took an armed British scout prisoner and brought him to camp.[119]

From his viewpoint at Thomas Olden's house, Robert Lawrence then saw that "the regulars were obliged to cross the brook at the ford with their artillery almost middle deep in water (the back water of the mill being then up)."[120]

Washington Leaves Princeton

Washington's original plan had been to advance on to New Brunswick, further hurt the British by destroying supplies, and perhaps help his cause by capturing the British £70,000 war chest. Stephen Olney noted they could have done this with four or five hundred fresh troops. But the previous nights' marches, "the first through mud, snow and water, the last over frozen ground, with the hardships of the day, seemed to have nearly exhausted both men and officers—some of whom were almost as bad as barefoot." They were also short of food, but "no one complained" because they "had been too busily engaged to think of hunger." In general, "we rejoiced to find ourselves so much better situated than we were the preceding night at Trenton," seemingly on the verge of a desperate climactic battle.[121] Instead of New Brunswick, Washington decided to go directly to Morristown, where he would be able to watch the British during the winter and prepare for the upcoming campaign. The Americans would then have a substantial presence in New Jersey after the ten-day campaign. Importantly, Washington was no longer retreating from battlefield defeat. He was achieving victories while choosing to avoid decisive actions—even when he seemed to be inviting them, as at Trenton the previous day. He was defeating enemy forces he outnumbered, as he had just done at Princeton.

When reports sounded that the British were nearing, Captain Rodney was ordered to march out with "a number of carpenters...and break up the bridge [over the Millstone], which was done."[122] Sullivan's division marched out for Kingston to take position on the high, defensible ground between Kingston and Rocky Hill. As they left, the British supplies remaining in Princeton were burned to prevent the returning enemy from using them.[123]

Cadwalader's and Mercer's brigades followed and did not stop in town. Cadwalader's brigade had captured several artillery pieces, but not all of them could be carried off due to lack of horses. However, to upgrade his weapons, one particularly nice brass six-pounder was taken by Thomas Proctor in exchange for a less-desirable iron three-pounder. The departing Americans threw one British cannon into a well. Another gun and an ammunition wagon were later recovered by the British from the area where Mercer and the 17th Regiment had engaged.[124]

The Americans could not take many of the abandoned British wagons "by reason of the enemy's [40th Regiment] cutting the traces, and taking the horses out before our people got up."[125] Thomas Olden, the Princeton man in the Pennsylvania militia, departed with the army for Morristown.[126]

To slow down the approaching enemy, and cover the army's evacuation of Princeton, Washington assigned Moulder's artillery company as the rearguard. Moulder was to keep the enemy "in check as long as safe to his men, then spike and leave his guns, and save his men by following with all speed after the main body of the army." However, when their retreat became necessary, Moulder's men refused to abandon their guns and earn the derogatory name among their fellow artillerymen of "grass-combers." Forty men attached ropes to each gun carriage and successfully dragged the cannon up the road while protected from a company of British horsemen pursuing them by the 1st Troop of City Cavalry under Captain Samuel Morris.[127]

Several days later, Washington reported that, after capturing Princeton, "We took two brass field pieces but for want of horses could not bring them away. We also took some blankets—shoes—and a few other trifling articles." They even burned the hay collected at Nassau Hall that the British had used as a stable and "destroyed such other things as the shortness of the time would admit of."[128] When Washington departed for Somerset Courthouse, he left some British prisoners and some his own men to care for the sick and wounded from both armies.[129]

Captain John Polhemus of the New Jersey Continentals was a local man serving with Washington in-between commissions in the 1776 and 1777 versions of the Continental Army. He said, "I was left behind with a rearguard to secure stores and bury the dead, which we did by hauling them in sleds to great holes and heaping them in. I was then relieved by Colonel Chamberlain" and his 3rd Hunterdon County militia regiment.[130] A local woman, Amy Cheston, was at Princeton that afternoon, where she saw her husband, John, for the first time since he had left for Canada a year before with Polhemus.[131]

The British Return to Princeton from Trenton

General Leslie got to Stony Brook from Maidenhead at about 10:30 a.m. but decided not to advance into town without support. He finally entered the village at about 12:00 noon; Washington had left at about 11:00 am.[132] Upon leaving Trenton, Cornwallis had "marched back at quick step," but once again, the road was sloppy due to warmer temperatures.[133] Ensign Thomas Glyn recorded that Cornwallis's column had "marched with all possible dispatch through Maidenhead[,] forded the rivulett [Stony Brook]," and "came to the ground where the action had commenced."[134]

In the afternoon, when the British army arrived at William Clarke's house, they "sent for the man out of his house to ask him some impertinent questions." Other soldiers began insulting "his sick and feeble wife and robbed her of the cloak that she wore over her shoulders in bed." Not intimidated, "she asked them if they robbed women of their cloaths." In response, "one of them swore that if the dam'd rebel bitch said a word more he would run his bayonet threw her heart." While this exchange took place, "they plundered the house of most of the valuable goods, and then drew their bayonets and run them threw the feather bed that the sick woman lay on." They ignored questions about why they did that and "swore that there was rebels that was hid under it, but damn them they would fetch them out." They destroyed the bed.

While they did this, more than twenty wounded men, mostly fellow British, lay on straw in the next room where Washington's soldiers had delivered them immediately after the battle. The British soldiers paid no attention to their wounded, some of whom were near death, and moved on. Robert Lawrence later wrote, "Thus those hardened wretches went on without having the least compassion either on their wounded fellow soldiers or the helpless woman that they made the object of their brutal sport, whereby they have shown themselves to be a pack of insolent poltroons rather than valiant English soldiers."[135]

Marching back through Stony Brook, four or five regulars paused at the shop of a fifty-nine-year-old blacksmith. Noticing that he wore a good pair of shoes, they took him prisoner and made him walk about a mile to find the rest of their company. One soldier needed shoes, so they confiscated the blacksmith's shoes for him. British Captain Thomas Dowdeswell of the 1st Battalion of Foot Guards wrote that "The first thing our English soldiers look for is shoes, we are much in want of them, many of our men not being able to march with us, on that account."[136] Then they forced the blacksmith to march in his stocking feet from Princeton to New Brunswick, where they kept him a day and a night. When released, a friend helped him to get another pair of shoes and limp home. The British had taken three civilians prisoner, two men, and a woman. The younger man escaped, and because the woman was unable to march, they left her at Princeton. The old blacksmith was the only prisoner taken to New Brunswick. Both harassed men had protections, as did the husband of the woman. All three were Quakers.[137]

When the British arrived near Thomas Olden's house, Lawrence saw them begin "to plunder their fellow soldiers packs taking out what they pleased and leaving the rest in the dirt." The plundering soldiers robbed one another. Lawrence saw that some of the men had tried to better secure their packs by throwing them into the garden over the board fence. He now saw a Hessian go into the garden and throw them back over the fence into the field. He "opened one of them and took out some things." However, a British regular standing guard also wanted those articles. The Hessian refused to give them up, "and then the regular laid hold on him and took them from him by force and kicked his breech when he had done, one or two more scuffles of the like nature we saw but at a far greater distance."[138]

Hessian Captain Ewald recorded, "we found the entire field of action from Maidenhead on to Princeton and vicinity covered with corpses...In the afternoon the entire army reached Princeton, marching in and around the town like an army that is thoroughly beaten. Everyone was so frightened that it was completely forgotten even to obtain information about where the Americans had gone. But the enemy now had wings, and it was believed that he had flown toward Brunswick to destroy the main depot, which was protected by only one English regiment."[139]

Cornwallis visited both the British and American wounded, left Mercer as a prisoner on parole, and assigned "five privates and one surgeon" to stay behind to tend the wounded.[140] But not all of the wounded received prompt care. Lawrence later reported that "the man that lived was left at our house above two days and one night with his wound not drest, before the regulars that was left to take care of the sick and wounded would take him away, though they had notice that day after the battle."[141]

As they approached the town, the British saw that "the [military supply] magazines at Prince Town were burning." They found no enemy soldiers in town. Searching for stragglers, they sent several companies into a wooded area where they found several 17th Regiment wounded men, an artillery piece, and an ammunition wagon, which they secured.[142]

While in Princeton, British troops searched for belongings they left behind when they had marched to Trenton the previous day. Some plundered the already-picked-over town, especially the homes of anyone they considered to be a rebel supporter. Princeton symbolized much of New Jersey, which Thomas Rodney described as "almost totally ruined & nothing can equal the brutal cruelty of the savage slaves of Brittain—what they cannot carry away they burn & destroy—nothing is sacred to their unhallowed hands. The infirmities of old age, the innocent weakness of babes, and the delicate form of the female, it is their sport to insult and distress—in no form has distress been seen to meet from them one humane act."[143]

The British Depart for New Brunswick

To save the military stores at New Brunswick, Captain Ewald wrote, "Hurriedly the army was issued three days' rations of biscuit and brandy, left behind the stores, all the sick, the wounded, and the greater part of the baggage, and moved with such haste toward Brunswick that, although it was only a five-hour march, over one thousand wagoners first reached Brunswick toward evening on the 4th. If the enemy had pursued them with only a hundred horsemen, one after another would have been captured." The Hessians often received biscuit instead of bread. So much so, that they got accustomed to it and began to prefer biscuit.[144]

Troops that had been sent out to Princeton from New Brunswick did not arrive in time to engage Washington's forces before they left town. However, they secured the cannon lost in the battle, and Cornwallis's troops soon joined them.[145] Portions of the 17th Regiment from Maidenhead passed back over the field of battle about 4:00 p.m.[146] After Donop's rearguard from Trenton and Mawhood's troops who had escaped to Maidenhead arrived back in Princeton, Cornwallis was ready to advance. As reported by Ensign Glyn, Cornwallis, "having left a Flag of Truce with the sick and wounded in Prince Town was determined to make a forced march to relieve Brunswick had Genl. Washington marched to possess it or to recover General Lee. We marched at five in the evening a very hard frost and snow on the ground."[147] Before his main force left Princeton, Cornwallis sent some infantry and carpenters toward Kingston to monitor Washington's movements and repair any damage to the Millstone bridge. He also sent "a strong party of horse [up]...the road to the left of the Millstone" toward Rocky Hill.[148]

Ensign Martin Hunter of the 52nd Regiment noted, "We only halted two hours at Princetown, and continued our march all night in hopes of coming up with Washington, but he was too far before us, and got into the Blue Mountains. I never experienced such a disagreeable night's march in my life. It was as dark as possible, and a very cold hard frost, and the horses being tired, the guns got on so slowly that we did not arrive at Brunswick before ten the next morning. We had been eighteen hours in marching sixteen miles."[149]

The Evening of January 3

After student-turned-militiaman Joseph Clark had "laid about 3 hours with my blankets on cords" they set out about 3:00 p.m. from Penny Town toward Princeton. After a round-about march, they came to the battlefield where they "had a most dismal prospect of a number of pale mangled corpses, lying in the mud and blood. I felt gloomy at the awful scene." They returned by a rough, tedious march to Hopewell, and the unpleasant marching caused his ankle to swell again and grow painful.[150]

As daylight faded, most people in and near Stony Brook and Princeton village had to deal with the after-effects of the battle rather than look forward to a night's sleep. Caring for the wounded of both sides was the immediate concern. The bodies of the dead would freeze overnight, so burial could wait a bit. Casualty estimates for the Americans range from 25 to 44 killed and about 40 wounded and for the British from 18 to 100 killed and 58 to 70 wounded. The lower figures for British casualties come from General Howe's official report.[151] Several months after the battle, Stephen Kemble wrote in his journal that British losses were a captain, a sergeant, and 16 rank and file killed; a captain, 4 subalterns, 5 sergeants, and 48 rank and file wounded; and, a captain, 3 subalterns, 5 sergeants, 4 drummers, and 187 rank and file missing, for a total of 276.[152] The actual casualty figures are difficult to assess, and one should not overlook the prisoners.

At Thomas Clarke's house, Thomas, Sarah, Susannah, and young Huguenot David de la Force no doubt stayed up all night helping to care for General Mercer and the other wounded men brought to them. Not far from the Clarke's lived the Opdyke family, where the mother and her young daughter had gone to the cellar in terror of the battle. Probably like most houses, theirs was ransacked for clothing and other cloth that could be torn up and used to care for the wounded. The Opdykes lost all their clothing except for a few pieces remaining in a washtub. The local people also noted bloody handprints on trees. The Opdyke daughter was scarred for life by this battle, and her granddaughter "never forgot the expression of deep distress upon her grandmother's face" when talking of it.[153]

Anthony Morris, Jr., an officer[154] of the Pennsylvania Associators, died at the Thomas Clarke house three hours after being wounded. Anthony was the brother of Captain Samuel Morris of the 1st Troop of Philadelphia City Cavalry, who also fought in the battle. Morris had been a brewer from a well-to-do Philadelphia Quaker family. As soon as possible, his remains were taken to Philadelphia and buried at the Friends' burial ground at 4th and Arch Streets, without military honors at the request of the family because of their Quaker beliefs.

Thomas Clarke collected all of Morris's clothes and belongings to send to Philadelphia. Doctor Enoch Edwards of Philadelphia listed these items on a receipt that he signed and dated January 11, stating that Thomas Clarke had given them to him. This list is the only surviving document stating the actual possessions of a soldier killed in battle during the American Revolution. It includes one regimental coat, one blanket surtout (a loose-fitting overcoat), one waistcoat, a pair of leather britches, one pair of shoes, a wig, cartridge box, a bayonet belt & gun case, two silk handkerchiefs, a fur cap, a pair of mittens, a black stock, a tobacco box, two knives and forks, a pair of knee and shoe buckles, a stock buckle, gold sleeve buttons, a silver watch, three flints, five keys, seventy-seven and two-thirds dollars, and one pound seven shillings.[155]

Several days later, Dr. Jonathan Potts came to Clarke's house and noted that Morris had received three wounds: one on his chin, one on his knee, and the third, the mortal wound, on his right temple, inflicted by grapeshot. He also found that some British soldiers had robbed the wounded General Mercer, "as he lay unable to resist on the bed, even to taking his cravat from his neck, insulting him all the time." However, Potts could positively declare that the British had "never been so shamefully drubbed and outgeneraled in every respect. I hourly expect to hear of their whole army being cut to pieces or made prisoners."[156]

Because Quakers had suffered so much during the British occupation, Robert Lawrence commented that "By the joy that I felt myself I cannot help but be of the opinion that the most strict of them all against bearing arms in our own defense (if they have any love for their bleeding country) but must in some degree or other rejoice with the rest of their neighbors and others for that days happy relief that it pleased God to bless us with."[157]

Commenting on the multiple military changes during January 3, Lawrence said, "So unconstant is the State of War and so certain and sure the mischiefs and miseries attending it that it is a wonder that wise men should ever depend on it."[158]

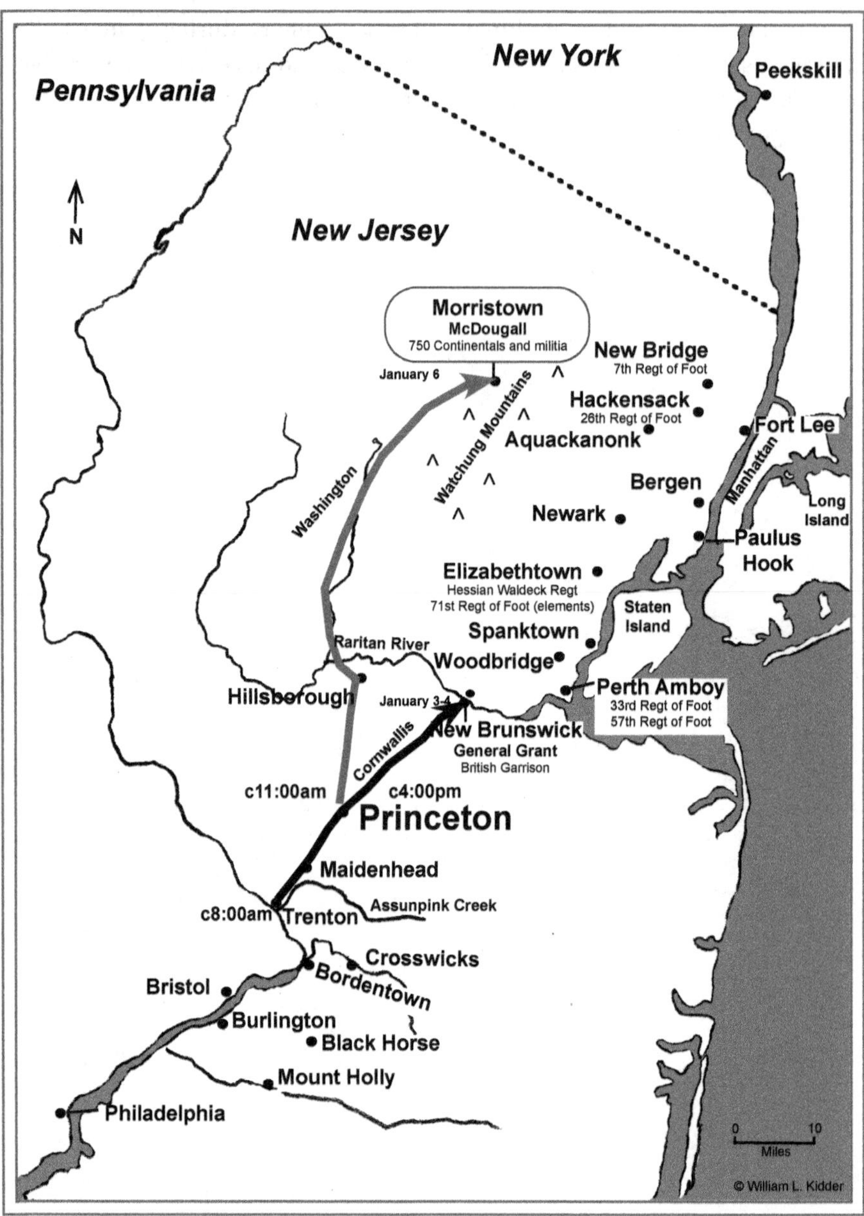

Map 19: Aftermath of Battle of Princeton - January 3 - 6, 1777

After the Battle of Princeton, Cornwallis took his forces to New Brunswick and Washington took his army to Morristown for winter quarters. The ten days between December 25, 1776 and January 3, 1777 went a long way towards removing the British troops from most of New Jersey.

Chapter 6

January 4–December 31, 1777

The January 3 battle climaxed the Ten Crucial Days, reversing the psychological state of people on both sides of the conflict. The British now doubted their ability to put down the rebellion quickly, and the Americans gained new confidence in the correctness of their cause and their ability to achieve their goals. However, the significance of that one event cannot allow us to forget the challenges that played out in Princeton as the town began the process of recovering from a month of military occupation, culminating with the battle. Nor can we overlook how the village became the scene for many military and political functions supporting the struggle that continued for another six and a half years. The war did not leave Princeton alone to clean up from the occupation and battle damage; instead it continued to confront Princeton in military and political ways that daily affected its inhabitants.

The Quaker Meetinghouse, Nassau Hall, and the Presbyterian Church had all sustained significant damage during the occupation and battle.[1] John Witherspoon's personal library was destroyed, and a friend noted, "It grieves him much that he has lost his controversial tracts. He would lay aside the cloth to take revenge of them. I believe he would send them to the Devil if he could, I am sure I would."[2]

From a recollection of Ashbel Green, who came as a student in 1782, "The British had rifled the [college] library," and some of the books later turned up in North Carolina, left there by troops of Lord Cornwallis. Green said, "What was left did not deserve the name of a library." Other teaching materials also disappeared, and "nothing remained but the orrery, a small telescope, and an electrical machine, with a case of coated jars." The British had placed a guard on the impressive orrery, "intending to transport it to Britain." However, after the battle, American soldiers "deranged" the "delicate machinery" and removed many of its wheels to keep as curiosities or souvenirs when they took possession of Nassau Hall. Samuel Stanhope Smith years later commented that this "was no more than to be expected from a number of ignorant men, so imperfectly disciplined as, at that time, they were."[3]

The college prayer hall had lost its bench-like pews, the rostrum, the pillars supporting the gallery, and the high pulpit, all removed for firewood. The organ pipes were gone, and only the case for the organ and "the coat of arms of Governor Belcher" remained. Virtually all the windows of the building were broken. The brick wall surrounding the college courtyard was badly damaged, and virtually no fences remained in Princton.[4]

Soldiers had stripped the Presbyterian Church of its pews for firewood. British troops had built a fireplace where the pulpit had been, and a brick chimney extended through the roof, on one sides of it. All windows had been broken.[5]

Benjamin Rush discovered that the town had been turned into "a deserted village; you would think it had been desolated with a plague and an earthquake, as well as with the calamities of war; the college and church are heaps of ruin; all the inhabitants have been plundered." He was most concerned about his wife's family home and found "the whole of Mr. Stockton's furniture, apparel, and even valuable writings, have been burnt; all his cattle, horses and hogs, sheep, grain, and forage, have been carried away."[6] However, the battle had given the British pause. Rush noted that "the enemy in their advance upon our troops through the Jersies, called them the rebel army," and now he said they had more respect for the Americans. On "their retreat through the same Jersies, they called them the provincials, and sometimes the continental army."[7]

Fears of enemy reprisals plagued the people of Princeton during the remainder of the year. The British occupied New Brunswick, leading to constant concern about what they might be up to, especially as the spring campaign season approached. The British did send out many foraging parties that Washington's troops and local militiamen harassed. These encounters throughout the winter and early spring became known as the Forage War. After the Battle of the Short Hills* on June 26, General Howe evacuated New Jersey, loaded troops aboard ships in July, and sailed for the Chesapeake Bay to attack Philadelphia from the head of the bay. These actions taken by the British to capture Philadelphia affected Princeton in several ways. The village militiamen became involved in the Battle of Germantown on October 4, and the increasing need for the military hospital kept it functioning at Nassau Hall

*The battlefield is located in today's Edison Township and should not be confused with today's community of Short Hills in Millburn Township.

and other local buildings. While combat in the town itself and the immediate surrounding area had ended on January 3, the wartime atmosphere continued throughout the year. Washington established a military post at Princeton, and the town became a link in the supply chain for the militia and Continental Army. Throughout the year, the people of Princeton adapted to these things going on around them and tried to live their lives as normally as possible. A primary concern was to get the college back to normal as soon as possible. The rift between Patriots and Loyalists became even stronger, while those wishing to remain neutral, including the Quakers, found themselves suspect.

After Battle Clean-up and Care for the Wounded

On January 4, a farmer named Drake living between two and three miles from Princeton saw four British regulars standing together in a field. Putting a stick under his greatcoat and holding it there as though it were a gun, he approached the men boldly and ordered them to surrender. To his relief, they did, even though two of them had real muskets. The other two men had been captured the day before and then escaped without their weapons. After getting help from his neighbors to secure the four men, Drake caught a fifth man, again with his fake gun. By tradition, several other farmers in Somerset and Middlesex Counties captured wandering British soldiers searching for their army.[8]

Robert Lawrence recounted how local people walked over the littered battlefield to get to the wounded and assess damage to their property after the battle. One item they found was a British orderly book containing the orders of December 12, about hanging non-uniformed men, and of December 14, for going into winter quarters. It must have been ironically amusing also to see Howe's orders against plundering and to honor protection papers. Lawrence also reported that local people buried fifteen dead Americans and twenty-one British regulars in an unspecified stone quarry.[9]

The freezing weather made burying the frozen corpses in the rock-hard ground problematic. Within a day or two, local Quakers temporarily buried Anthony Morris and Pennsylvania Marine Captain William Shippin in the Stony Brook Friends' burial ground.[10] Captain Shippin, twenty-seven years old, had joined the Pennsylvania Marine Service and, returning from a cruise shortly before the battle, had gone to camp and joined Washington's forces. He left four young children.[11]

On January 5, Dr. Jonathan Potts reported to Owen Biddle that "General Mercer is dangerously ill indeed. I have scarcely any hopes of him; the villains had stabbed him in five different places." He also confessed to Biddle that "It pains me to inform you that on the morning of the action I was obliged to fly before the rascals, or fall into their hands, and leave behind me my wounded brethren."[12]

In his January 5 report to Congress, Washington repeated the erroneous report given to him that General Mercer was dead.[13] Expecting that the British would seek revenge for their recent losses, Washington also wrote to General Israel Putnam, then at Trenton with about one thousand men, ordering him to march his men to Crosswicks and keep a close watch on the enemy. He advised Putnam to send out as many spies as possible and in his verbal and written communications to always describe his force as being at least twice its actual size. He should forward on to Washington all troops and baggage belonging to the main army and keep him informed of any threatening enemy movements. But Putnam would not march from Trenton until January 8.[14] Putnam erroneously heard at Bristol that the British had left about two hundred men at Princeton to care for the wounded. Although Putnam thought about attacking them, he did not pursue that idea.[15]

People took some of the injured soldiers to private homes in the area near Princeton, where local doctors treated them. On January 6, Hopewell Township doctor Benjamin VanKirk dressed the wound of a soldier at the home of John Drake and then visited the homes of John Polhemus and the Andersons to dress soldiers' wounds. VanKirk made follow-up visits over the next few days.[16]

Four days after the battle, Doctors Rush and Cochran transported their patients in horse-drawn wagons from Bordentown to Princeton.[17] Approaching the village, Rush commented, they "passed over the field of battle still red in many places with human blood. We found a number of wounded officers and soldiers belonging to both armies. Among the former was General Mercer, and a Capt. McPherson, a British officer [of the 17th Regiment]." The British surgeon's mate caring for them committed them over to Dr. Rush. When Rush examined General Mercer at the Thomas Clarke farm, he found that the Virginia doctor had received bayonet wounds "in his belly in several places" and also an injury on the side of his head made by the butt of a musket used as a club. Rush wrote to Richard Henry Lee, begging him to "immediately dispatch an express to Mrs. Mercer to inform her that the General is considerably better and there are reasonable hopes of his recovery. I have attended him since yesterday and shall not leave him till he is out of danger." Rush described the wounds as seven bayonet wounds but said, "He is in good spirits drinks plentifully, sleeps tolerably well, and talks cheerfully on all subjects, as usual." It seems that because he needed a surgeon when he fell, "he was obliged to give his parole in order to procure a surgeon from the enemy, and he is now their prisoner."[18]

Moving on to where Captain McPherson lay with a wound to his lungs that had resulted in a substantial loss of blood, Rush was introduced by name to the Captain, who asked, "Are you Dr. Rush, Capt. Leslie's friend?" When Rush told him that he was, McPherson exclaimed, "Oh! Sir...he loved you like a brother." Rush had stayed with the Leslie family in Scotland during his medical training and got to know the family well, so Rush and McPherson joined together "in tributes of affection and praise" to Leslie's memory. Rush was so overcome by Leslie's death the he "wept, for the first time, for a victory gained over British troops."[19]

Washington wrote again to Congress with the good news that "I am happy to inform you, that the account of General Mercer's death, transmitted in my last, was premature, though it was mentioned as certain by many who saw him after he was wounded." Washington now knew from competent sources that Mercer was alive and expected to do well, although Washington believed "unhappily he is a prisoner."[20] Washington seems to have assumed that the British retook control of Princeton and the wounded he left behind were all prisoners, although perhaps on parole.

Princeton's Military Hospital

Doctors Rush and Cochran established a makeshift hospital in damaged Nassau Hall to care for the wounded from both sides. Their staff consisted of other American medical officers and a British surgeon and five privates left behind to care for the British wounded. The British injured included four men who had their legs amputated on Rush's order, and all recovered.[21] Rush and Cochran also cared for patients taken to private homes, such as General Mercer at Thomas Clarke's home.[22] Rush also visited with his father-in-law, Richard Stockton, recently released by the British, and as soon as he believed his "wounded patients were out of danger" set off to attend Congress on Saturday, January 11.[23]

Jacob Hefflebower of the 3rd Pennsylvania had been severely injured in the forehead by a bullet. After the battle, John Gundrum carried him from the battlefield to the hurriedly established hospital where he recovered until spring, when the medical men sent him to Philadelphia. His wound remained visible for the rest of his life.[24] Less fortunately, Lieutenant Thomas Parsons of the 1st battalion of Philadelphia County militia was wounded in the knee but died soon after, probably from infection, leaving a widow and two children.[25]

Surgeon's Mate James English from nearby Cranbury came to Princeton to help with the wounded. He had been a regimental surgeon's mate for one of the Five-Month Levy regiments in the New York campaign. The Surgeon

General at Princeton, twenty-seven-year-old Dr. Charles McKnight, accepted his help gladly. McKnight, also from Cranbury, knew James English and his family, especially James's mother, who had suckled McKnight as an infant when his mother was unable to.[26]

General Mercer died on January 12, by tradition in the arms of twenty-year-old Captain George Lewis, a fellow Virginian who had graduated from the College of New Jersey in 1775. Lewis's father married George Washington's only sister, making Captain Lewis Washington's nephew. Again by tradition, Lewis was with Washington on the way to Morristown when they received word that Mercer had not been killed and was recovering at Princeton as a prisoner. Washington arranged for Lewis to travel under a flag to General Cornwallis, requesting adequate care for Mercer and that he allow Lewis to remain with Mercer and help care for him. Cornwallis agreed to both, ordering his staff-surgeon to check on Mercer.[27]

That surgeon examined Mercer and believed that, although he had many severe wounds, they would not be fatal. However, Mercer was a trained doctor and told Lewis to "raise up my right arm, George, and this gentleman will there discover the smallest of my wounds, but which will prove the most fatal. Yes sir, that is a fellow that will very soon do my business." While Lewis was with Mercer, he described the "extreme indignation which prevailed in the American army, together with threats of retaliation at the inhuman treatment it was supposed the general had received from the enemy, viz., that he had been bayoneted after having surrendered and asked for quarter." However, Mercer told him that story was false and that "My death is owing to myself. I was on foot, endeavoring to rally my men, who had given way before the superior discipline of the enemy, when I was brought to the ground by a blow from a musket. At the same moment the enemy discovered my rank, exulted in their having taken the rebel general, as they termed me, and bid me ask for quarters. I felt that I deserved not so opprobrious an epithet, and determined to die, as I had lived, an honored soldier in a just and righteous cause; and without begging my life or making reply, I lunged with my sword at the nearest man. They then bayoneted and left me."[28]

By May, controversy arose over whether or not to maintain a hospital at Princeton for sick soldiers. Dr. William Shippen wanted General Sullivan to remove all the sick troops under his command to Trenton. He believed the "inconvenience or danger of moving any sick from your division to Trenton, will be vastly less than will arise from establishing a separate Hospital at Princeton." Congress had forbidden "Regimental Hospitals" and ordered that any soldier needing hospitalization must receive treatment at a Continental Hospital. Shippen did not seem to realize that the Princeton hospital had been established as a general hospital and not one limited to a specific regiment or division.[29] In spite of Shippen's orders of May 29, the Princeton military hospital continued in operation, and the persisting need for it soon became apparent.

The army brought the seriously wounded from the Battle of Brandywine on September 11 to hospitals, such as Princeton, in open wagons accompanied by medical personnel. Dr. James Tilton came with one group that proceeded very slowly to Princeton, stopping at Philadelphia, Bristol, and Trenton. Tilton complained that the quarters given his men at the Trenton hospital were not clean and his patients contracted a putrid fever. At least one soldier died of a fever, rather than his wound, after they got to Princeton. The Trenton staff rejected his complaint, insisting that they had cleaned the rooms and that no patients had suffered from putrid fever during the previous three weeks. However, soon after arriving at Princeton, Tilton and some of his wounded did experience "languor and listlessness of the whole body, and a peculiar sensation of the head, as if it were tightened or compressed." Several days later, their "pulse began to sink, a dry tongue, delirium" developed.[30]

After the Battle of Red Bank along the Delaware River on October 22, the army sent additional wounded soldiers to the Princeton hospital. One man was an apparent twenty-three-year-old Hessian deserter named Johann Buettner, "struck by a rifle bullet that entered under one of my shoulder blades, passed over my spinal column and out through the other shoulder blade." While first under the care of Hessian surgeons sent to care for the wounded, he says, "a few days later all the wounded Hessians were taken in closed carriages to the main hospital in Princeton, where they were cared for." Commissary General of Prisoners Elias Boudinot visited the Princeton hospital in early November to check on the condition of the Hessian prisoners there. He "found them in want of cloaths &c to a very great degree" and had a surgeon make up a list of their needs. Boudinot felt frustrated in his attempts to secure proper winter clothing for the prisoner patients.[31]

Buettner came to America from Saxony as a redemptioner and had joined the American army with the permission of his owner. He fought at the Battle of Short Hills, where he deserted to join General Knyphausen's Hessian regiment, with which he fought at Red Bank. In Princeton, he encountered a man from his former American regiment who recognized him. Buettner made up a story that he had been forced to join the Hessians and made his escape at Red Bank. Dr. Tilton overhead this discussion and also learned from it that Buettner had training as a barber-surgeon and had practiced that trade briefly. Tilton decided to take Buettner on as his servant, to feed and saddle his horse, to perform domestic duties, and, when sufficiently recovered, to assist him in his hospital duties. He and Tilton talked about many things, including the disagreements behind the Revolution, which Buettner often found amusing as reasons why anyone would go to war. Just how long Buettner served with Tilton is not known. However, he was still serving on February 17, 1778, when Tilton wrote a letter that indicated his presence and also that Tilton for the most part believed his story. At some point, Buettner told Tilton that he wanted to return to Europe and asked for a pass to Philadelphia where he could take ship. Tilton very reluctantly complied, and Buettner went through more adventures, again serving in the Knyphausen Regiment, before returning to his home country at the end of the war.[32]

After the battles of Brandywine, Germantown, and Red Bank, Tilton described the Princeton hospital, along with others, as being so "crowded as to produce infection, and mortality ensues too affecting to be described." He served as prescribing surgeon in the Princeton hospital and noted, "the sick and wounded flowing promiscuously without restraint into the hospital, it soon became infectious and was attended with great mortality." However, he knew other hospitals were even worse.[33] On November 24, the Princeton hospital had 139 sick, 130 wounded, and 10 convalescent for a total of 279 patients.[34] Ebenezer Stockton, son of Robert, was commissioned as surgeon's mate of the army's general hospital on September 20 and served until August 1, 1780.[35]

Toward the end of November, Washington was concerned about the safety of men in the Continental hospitals threatened by the British occupation of Philadelphia. On November 25, he wrote to General Greene that the hospital at Burlington should be well guarded or removed to a safer place. He was also concerned that "the hospital at Princeton also will be left naked if the enemy should move farther up, you will therefore leave them some cover, if you think there will be some occasion." Then, in a P.S. he noted, "as leaving a guard at Princetown will still divide our force[,] if the patients could be removed further from thence, I think it would be for the better. I told Dr. Shippen when he fixed it there it would be dangerous."[36]

At the end of November, orders came to remove the sick from the hospitals at Burlington, Bordentown, and Trenton and take them to Princeton. The army moved them, but without making any provision to accommodate them. The Princeton hospital was without hospital furniture or means of cleanliness. No tubs, pots, or kettles, and "in short, every article of accommodation was wanting." The sick, in general, had putrid diseases and were very dirty, filthy, and lousy. At Princeton, they numbered about five hundred, making their quarters very crowded, and the lack of cleanliness produced many infections, often leading to death. Even the caregivers got sick, and six of eleven surgeons could not do their duty. Tilton himself became ill and had to leave Princeton, leaving Dr. Samuel Finley as the presiding surgeon. Washington feared that Princeton might become an enemy target and urged the Princeton hospital to move its patients into the interior of Pennsylvania. However, they remained at Princeton.[37]

One of Tilton's complaints at Princeton was that "the wine was of an inferior quality and in sparing quantity, and the sick did suffer for want of it." However, "all the stores have been in greater plenty, since the purveyorship was taken out of Dr. Shippen's hands, than before. When I was sick I was obliged to procure Madeira wine elsewhere." Thomas Stockton, Hospital Commissary at Princeton, recalled having once received twelve or sixteen gallons of spirits or wine for the sick, which he thought had been adulterated.[38]

Benjamin Rush, who visited his wife in Princeton, reported in early December that he had about five hundred sick and wounded soldiers, "many of whom have complaints so trifling that they do not prevent their committing daily a hundred irregularities of all kinds." Because the physicians and surgeons had no "power to prevent or punish them," he asked General Greene to "send immediately two or three officers, or even one if more cannot be spared, to take the command in this place." He believed the sick and wounded needed to be under the same military discipline they experienced in their regular units. As it was now, the men were losing all sense of military discipline while hospitalized. He noted that, in the British army, "the hospitals constantly feel the influence of military authority. An officer of note is always stationed near a hospital who is called a Military Inspector." He set up guards, had the roll called, visited the wards, and reported all deficiencies to the post commander. Rush begged for more attention to be paid to the health of the soldiers. As it was, "the character of our officers, nay even our cause, suffers by the many monuments of sickness and distress which are left by our army in every village in New Jersey and Pennsylvania."[39]

Rush wrote in a similar vein to Dr. William Shippen the same day and emphasized, "We go on rapidly in preparing good accommodations for the sick and wounded in this place. The college and church are palaces when compared with the buildings [the barracks] at Trenton and Burlington." He also intended to seize the Quaker Meetinghouse and to repair Castle Howard on the road to Kingston east of Princeton, the residence abandoned by Loyalist Captain Ibbitson Hamar and his wife, Sarah. These additions would allow the hospital to treat one thousand men. To complete the accommodations, though, "we want hospital furniture, especially implements of cookery. Frequent changes of straw must supply the place of bed cases. In comfortable quarters the sick are happy without them. Mr. Stockton (our commissary) cannot be too much commended. We shall derive credit from his management. I have lent him 400 dollars on account of the hospital." Looking to the immediate future, he asked, "Is not this the time to lay in stores for next year? Every day increases their scarcity and high price. Suppose you send Dr. [Thomas] Bond to New England for that purpose." He needed one hundred pipes of wine, fifty hogsheads of sugar, and one hundred hogsheads of molasses. He also hoped "Dr. Forster may spare him some of his linen, sheets, &c., with which he abounds. What do you think of a magazine of Indian corn—a most wholesome and agreeable diet for the sick? It is rising [in cost] and perhaps will not be to be had in the spring?"[40]

In a December 8 letter to William Duer, a New York delegate to Congress and friend, Rush made a detailed argument for refining the medical department, again comparing things to how the British army did them. After describing the powers of the many officers working in the British system, he said, "The director general possesses all the powers of the above officers. He is chief physician, inspector general, purveyor or commissary general, physician and surgeon general. All reports come through his hands, by which means the number of sick, wounded, and dead may always be proportioned to his expenditures and to his fears of alarming Congress with accounts of the mortality of diseases. He can be present only in one place at a time but is supposed to be acquainted with all the wants of his hospitals. This is impossible."

The result of this system is that the sick "must suffer, for the surgeons of hospitals have no right to demand supplies for them, the director general being the only judge of their wants. Lastly, his accounts are not certified by the physicians and surgeons general, so that the sick have no security for the stores and medicines intended for them. A director general may sell them to the amount of a million a year without a possibility of being detected by your present establishment. All that the Congress requires of him are receipts for the purchase of the articles intended for the sick." The current system provided the temptation to the director-general to accumulate personal wealth at the expense of the sick and wounded. To prevent this, the person in charge of directing the hospital program should never be the same person who acts as a commissary. His statements should not be taken to imply the current surgeon general was corrupt—just in a vulnerable position. He believed that the army suffered from more than the expected amount of sickness and that "trifling diseases are prolonged and new ones often contracted by the negligence, ignorance, and wants that are entailed upon us by the establishment." Rush went out of his way to state that he did not make his concerns known out of any personal desire to rise in rank or displace anyone. He only wanted to help the soldiers who require the care of the medical service.[41]

Rush wrote again to Duer on December 13, indicating that instead of the estimated three thousand patients in the military hospitals, it now appeared there were actually five thousand, and there were only enough hospital supplies for fifteen hundred. In Princeton alone, "What do you think of 600 men in a village without a single officer to mount a guard over them or to punish irregularities? This is the case at this time in Princetown, and the consequences are: old disorders are prolonged, new ones are contracted, the discipline of the soldiers (contracted at camp) is destroyed, the inhabitants are plundered, and the blankets, clothes, shoes, &c., of the soldiers are stolen or exchanged in every tavern and hut for spirituous liquors." Rush had witnessed all this for the past six months and complained of it to the director-general, the Congress, and the generals of the army without achieving improvement.[42]

By the middle of December, Rush was very concerned and noted one building was only capable of handling 150 men but had to deal with 400, and over three days, 12 patients had succumbed to putrid fever. Since the spring, 6 of the surgeons had died of various fevers. And, he still did not have guards to enforce discipline.[43]

Rush wrote to Washington on the first anniversary of the Battle of Trenton, expressing his concerns about the medical department. He believed that "I am safe when I assert that a great majority of those who die under our hands perish with diseases caught in our hospitals." He added, "When I consider the present army under your excellency's command as the last hope of America, I am more alarmed and distressed at these facts than I have words to express. I can see nothing to prevent the same mortality this winter among our troops that prevailed last year. Every day deprives us of four or five patients out of 500 in the hospital under my care in this place." One problem was crowding, and Rush commented, "I have seen 20 sick men in one room, all ill with fevers and fluxes, large enough to contain only 6 or 8 well men without danger to their health."[44]

Governor Livingston wrote to Henry Laurens on December 25, apologetically reporting on the situation of the army hospitals, especially the one at Princeton. While the New Jersey Assembly sat at Princeton between November 3 and December 12, he had resided in the village. In many conversations with local people, he heard that the soldiers in the hospital "were destitute of many articles absolutely necessary for persons in their condition." This led him to investigate, and he reported the following disturbing facts. In addition to overcrowding, patients were not provided with hospital sheets, shirts, and blankets, but had to lie in their campaign clothing. They were only provided with half the amount of wine and other necessary stores, and "suffer greatly from a meat diet." There were no military guards to prevent mobile patients from wandering about and indulging in spirituous liquors, often purchased with money gained from the sale of their arms and clothes. Wandering patients also often plundered the residents, producing "less humane" feelings about the hospital. There were currently five thousand men in hospitals in Pennsylvania and New Jersey, and the Princeton hospital had been losing about four to five men out of five hundred per day. All the hospitals combined were losing fifty each day, and if that rate continued, forty-five hundred would die by the first of April. Most men who died in a military hospital did so from diseases contracted there, not from what brought them to the hospital. The hospital directors had to spend too much time acting as commissaries and quartermasters rather than as doctors. Both Rush and Livingston critically compared the Continental system with that of the British army, which they considered superior, but had trouble finding Continental medical officers who agreed with them.[45]

American Occupation of Princeton—General Israel Putnam

General Israel Putnam's troops were reinforced at Bordentown on January 6 by about five hundred militia and some Continental troops who had been "left by accident by Gen. Washington at Trenton on the night of his march to Princetown" on January 2. Putnam expected to proceed to Trenton that afternoon with about one thousand men but was concerned that a whole company of Pennsylvania militia had deserted the previous night. He heard questionable intelligence that the British baggage had gone to South Amboy, and the troops were prepared to retreat to New York if the American forces continued to pressure them.[46]

General Putnam expected to march from Trenton to Crosswicks the next morning, where he hoped the militia would continue to join him.[47]

Several days before the attack on Trenton, Rall's regimental quartermasters had sent wagons to New York for badly needed supplies, and the Hessian prisoners taken to Pennsylvania still needed them. On January 8, Washington arranged for Cornwallis to send the wagons, escorted by a Hessian sergeant and twelve unarmed men through Princeton and Trenton to Philadelphia. Additionally, in recognition that Cornwallis no longer controlled Princeton, Washington arranged for him to send a British surgeon and a supply of medicine there without molestation from the army. Washington did warn him, though, that he could not control the militiamen "who are resorting to arms in most parts of this State, and exceedingly exasperated at the treatment they have met with from both British and Hessian Troops."[48]

General Putnam finally marched to Crosswicks, where he received a letter from Washington ordering him to advance his men to Princeton. However, Putnam hesitated, still concerned about British attacks, and awaiting the arrival of reinforcements for which he had sent.[49]

Washington ordered the American baggage train that had been sent to Bordentown when the army marched to Princeton on the night of January 2 to come up to Morristown. The wagons passed through Trenton and Princeton on January 9, reaching Morristown on January 12.[50] Putnam reported that there had been several encounters with British and Hessian troops at Spanktown (Rahway) the past Sunday, and the heavy firing was heard as far away as Princeton.[51] Washington must have understood that his only military presence in Princeton was medical, making it vulnerable to British troops who might try to occupy it again. To prevent this, Washington wanted General Putnam to establish a garrison at Princeton. He was very frustrated that Putnam had not yet marched his troops there, even after receiving several messages, and wrote to Joseph Reed with instructions for Putnam.

Putnam should prepare Princeton for any possible enemy attack from New Brunswick. He should only keep two or three days of provisions, and only as many supplies as his men could clear out with an hour's warning. He should continuously maintain scouting parties and should retreat to Morristown if compelled to leave Princeton. Putnam should also take control of all flour from the mills on the Millstone River to prevent the British foraging parties from taking it. His men should be out searching as often as possible for forage in the area of New Brunswick and compel the farmers there to bring in forage to him. This would significantly distress the enemy.

Although Washington had given consent for Cornwallis to send a surgeon to oversee the care of the British wounded at Princeton, he was concerned that this provided an avenue for intelligence gathering. He suggested sending the less-severely wounded to New Brunswick, perhaps in exchange for American prisoners. Washington told Reed that he had sent General Howe a copy of the statement of Bartholomew Yates about his mistreatment after being wounded and had "remonstrated sharply on the treatment of our prisoners."[52]

Rush reported to Richard Henry Lee that Yates had received a wound in his side that caused him to fall. He begged for quarters when British soldiers approached him, and a soldier stopped and, after loading his musket in front of Yates, shot him in the chest. Then, Rush said, "finding that he was still alive, he stabbed him in thirteen places with his bayonet, the poor youth all the while crying for mercy." When the British were forced to retreat, he was struck on the side of the head with a musket stock used as a club. He lived for a week in great pain. Rush diagnosed that it was the wounds he received after he had surrendered himself and begged for mercy that killed him. Rush wrote another letter to Lee on January 14 from Philadelphia, noting that he had left Mercer the past Saturday when he was out of danger but still too weak from blood loss to be moved. Although he was still considered a prisoner by the British, the commanding officer at New Brunswick had given him permission to ride or go where he pleased while still under parole.[53]

Washington again wrote to Joseph Reed on January 15 about his distress that Putnam was not yet at Princeton. He was concerned about militiamen removing stores from there without orders and his inability to secure a quartermaster to serve there and take charge of the stores. Washington also wanted the militia organized and ordered out to engage in foraging and annoying the British troops at New Brunswick. Word of Mercer's death had not yet reached him, so Washington asked Reed to extend his best wishes to him and let him know that he did not come to see Mercer after the battle only because he received word that he had died on the battlefield.[54]

Putnam was actually making efforts to establish a garrison at Princeton by calling for militiamen, but was running into opposition. For example, the owner of the Pennsylvania salt works wrote to the Pennsylvania Council on January 18 that Putnam was calling out all the militia and this was preventing the operation of the salt works.[55]

Delaware General and Declaration of Independence signer Caesar Rodney arrived in Trenton on January 19 to command a garrison stationed there. About the same time, General Putnam finally took command of a small garrison at Princeton. Putnam was concerned that he was losing men to enlistment expiration, and they would not remain until recruits could replace them. He was very concerned the British would take advantage of his small force and attack Princeton.

The next day, Trenton merchant and former leader in the State government Samuel Tucker traveled up the Post Road to Princeton. Tucker had been a State Treasurer and had made a mistake similar to Richard Stockton's. Tucker had chosen to stay in New Jersey and hide his valuable property, including a vast amount of New Jersey currency lacking only his signature (one of three required) to become legal tender. He entrusted the money, his papers, and some valuables to a friend living on a farm near Trenton, but away from the main thoroughfare. A Loyalist betrayed Tucker, and the British found his goods and the State money. They forced Tucker to sign a loyalty statement to receive protection for his family and property. Still, the British took his belongings to the Morven quarters of Lieutenant Colonel

Robert Abercromby of the 37th Regiment of Foot. He had been appointed by General Howe on October 23, 1776, to command the 1st Battalion in Brigadier General Alexander Leslie's light infantry brigade.[56] Having heard that someone had seen his papers at Morven, Tucker was now on his way to retrieve anything he could.

When Tucker got to Morven, he found many of his bonds and mortgage papers in a desk drawer. Stockton's "old negro man" gave him a box of papers he had swept up after British soldiers had spat upon and dirtied them on the floor. Some of the deeds had their wax seals cut off. Someone had thrown other papers about, and local people had picked up some of them. Tucker found one woman who gave him six crucial deeds. A British officer had purchased Tucker's confiscated phaeton and horse and driven off to New York, taking Tucker's silver plate, his wife's jewelry, and other items.[57]

Now at Princeton, Putnam reported that two companies of Pennsylvania militia had deserted, leaving only a lieutenant, a sergeant, and drummer. He was concerned that desertions would increase unless these men were apprehended and brought back to duty, possibly for an extended term of service. He believed that severity was necessary, or "we shall in a few days have not a man of the militia left."

An enemy foraging party of about one thousand men with one hundred wagons and four field pieces came as far as Somerset Courthouse on January 20. They collected a great deal of plunder before a small party of New Jersey militiamen attacked them and forced them to give way. The militia could not oppose the artillery, but when reinforced by about four hundred men they renewed their attack and put the enemy to flight, retaking the items plundered along with about fifty British wagons, one hundred horses, and eight prisoners. The militiamen had three men killed and several wounded, but the enemy left no dead. This encounter, known as the Battle of Millstone, was an early action in what became known as the Forage War that winter, in which the British did not do well.[58]

One wounded man Putnam encountered while commanding at Princeton was Scottish Captain McPherson, whom Washington had told would receive proper care. However, he had not received needed medical attention, at least partly because his chest wound was considered fatal. Putnam came to McPherson's aid and ordered that his treatment be improved and everyone treat him kindly. A grateful McPherson is said to have asked Putnam for his nationality. Putnam, a Connecticut resident descended from Puritans going back to 17th-century Massachusetts Bay, replied that he was an American. McPherson said he found that hard to believe and replied, "I did not think there could be so much goodness and generosity in an American, or, indeed, in anybody but a Scotchman!"

At some point, McPherson asked Putnam if he could arrange for a British officer friend currently at New Brunswick to visit him before he died. Putnam worried that such a visit could provide the British with information about the minimal size of his force. However, he wanted to accommodate McPherson and agreed. Under a flag of truce, he sent a messenger to New Brunswick and arranged for the officer friend to come to Princeton after dark. When the officer arrived, Putnam had created an illusion for him. Every window in town had been fitted with a candle, illuminating the village. While the two British officers met and talked, Putnam's men walked multiple times by the window of the building, giving the impression of a much larger force. When the guest officer returned to New Brunswick, he reported Putnam's garrison to be many times larger than it was in reality.[59]

Washington issued a proclamation on January 25 requiring every person who had submitted in any way to Howe's offer of amnesty to, within thirty days, either swear an oath of allegiance to the United States or remove themselves and their families behind British lines. This command alarmed New Jersey Congressional delegate Abraham Clark, who believed it violated a March 9, 1776, resolution of Congress forbidding military officers to demand test oaths from civilians. Clark introduced a motion on February 6, opposing the proclamation because it "may in some particular States, interrupt the due course of the laws made therein for the trial and punishment of traitors and other offenders against the peace and liberties of the same." To prevent this, he asked Congress to resolve that the "Proclamation shall not in any wise take effect in such manner as to prevent the free exercise of the laws or regulations, enacted or provided in any of the United States...or in any instance to interfere with or oppose the free exercise of the Legislative or Executive powers of any State." Jonathan Dickinson Sergeant seconded the motion, and Congress sent it to a committee of five, including Sergeant. That committee determined that the proclamation did "not interfere with the laws or civil government of any State; but considering the situation of the army was prudent and necessary." However, after receiving the report on February 27, Congress tabled it to avoid a divisive debate. Therefore, the proclamation stood and had a similar effect to that of the Howe brothers the previous November 30. People sought out officers, such as Putnam at Princeton, to take the appropriate oaths and receive protection.[60]

General Putnam undertook actions in January against the Loyalists in Monmouth County, whom he believed were worse than the Hessians "in their savagery." He also kept a strong guard at Kingston and sent out scouting parties to within a mile or so of New Brunswick. He energetically sent forward troops in the newly formed southern regiments, such as the

9th Virginia Regiment that arrived on January 18, about 4:00 p.m., on their way to join the army at Morristown.

Putnam was critical of the way Washington dispersed the army by placing part of it at Morristown while other parts were detached, such as at his Princeton post. If all regiments joined together, he believed they could take New Brunswick. In the meantime, small skirmishes with British pickets and foraging parties had caused the British leaders to keep their whole army under arms.[61] By January 25, delegates in Congress optimistically believed Putnam had "not less than 6000" men at Princeton.[62]

Late in January, John Witherspoon chaired a congressional committee looking into British and Hessian atrocities. He established its headquarters in Princeton, where he obtained leave in February to give his personal business some attention.[63] He frequently tried to find a reason to go back to Princeton to see to both his affairs and those of the college.

On January 31, Putnam sent fifteen prisoners taken "by different scouting parties" to Philadelphia along with several British deserters, including two tradesmen who "would be glad of employ. You will please to notice them." He warned the Council of Safety that the Pennsylvania militiamen were all going home because "no arguments can prevail on them to stay a day beyond their 6 weeks." Things were better now in Monmouth County, and he hoped people would return to the cause, especially with militia Colonel David Forman sent to command there. Prices of everything were exorbitant, but he appreciated the work of the New England governments and the committee of the various states that recently met at Providence, Rhode Island, and "fixed the prices of every article and employment, even to the barbers."[64]

Putnam and the Council of Safety dealt with complaints lodged by Whigs about seemingly Loyalist actions they had observed in their neighbors during the British occupation. On February 5, Francis Shivers and Peter Head reported that they "heard one Robert Barns in Amwell Township drink a health to King George and success to General Howe and Damnation to General Washington and the Congress and all their proceedings."[65] Putnam sent Barns to Haddonfield, where he appeared before the Council of Safety on March 19. The Council examined and then discharged him after he took the required Oaths of Abjuration and Allegiance.[66] The Barns case was just one of many examples of men whose actions taken to avoid British harassment during the occupation got them into trouble after the Battle of Princeton.

Putnam reluctantly had to dismiss Pennsylvania militia units when their enlistments expired. On February 5, he wrote to Major John Davis of the 3rd Battalion of Cumberland County Militia, "I am much obliged to you for your activity, vigor and diligence, since you have been under my command. You will now march your men to Philadelphia, and there discharge them, returning into the store all the ammunition, arms and accouterments you received at that place." These men had engaged in several skirmishes of the forage war, and their genuinely significant achievements had encouraged other militiamen to turn out confident of success.[67]

However, not all militia groups had behaved well, and too many militiamen plundered residents on the excuse of suspected Loyalist tendencies. This infuriated Livingston, who believed that this practice "is not only repugnant to the laws of the land, whereby every man's property is secured and protected until it is declared forfeited by judicial process, but hath a manifest tendency to inflame the minds of the sufferers; to excite jealousies and contentions between the inhabitants, at a time when we ought to be peculiarly studious of cultivating unanimity and concord." He provided detailed instructions to militia officers to prevent this from happening.[68]

Putnam sent the British prisoners who had remained at Princeton to care for the sick and wounded to Philadelphia: Corporal Gibson, William Hamilton, William Taylor, and Robert Henderson.[69] Daniel Putnam, aide-de-camp to General Putnam, notified the officer commanding the Philadelphia prison that these men "have behaved themselves very orderly & sober, I do therefore recommend that they may have their liberty & not be put in close confinement."[70]

On February 10, Putnam wrote to Livingston about his concern that many militiamen were refusing to turn out when called. He had authorized a colonel from Salem County to apprehend such delinquents and make them either serve or pay the required fine. He also hoped that the Legislature would pass a new militia act which, among other things, would "adopt some new mode of treatment of the Quakers which shall render it no man's interest to be conscientious against bearing arms." He asked for a copy of any revisions to the law regarding Quakers, "for these gentlemen are at present extremely troublesome."[71]

Livingston responded quickly to Putnam, praising his energetic efforts to get the militia out. However, he disagreed with him that men should be allowed to pay a fine instead of serve, even though permitted by law. He had two primary concerns. First, they needed militiamen, not money. Second, paying fines raised the issue of the unequal ability of men to pay the fines. It made the poor more susceptible to having to serve. He went into lengthy detail about his frustrations with the Legislature for not passing an adequate militia bill. Livingston also cautioned Putnam about criticizing the Quakers, reminding him, "as for the people called Quakers, they cannot be compelled to fight without violating those conscientious scruples which they have always professed as a people. But I hope they are, in other respects valuable subjects, & will give government no trouble."[72]

Putnam replied that he really did not like the idea of men paying fines because no sum "can be really equivalent" to service in a time like this. He recognized that the fines had been introduced for the Quakers, but "I detest the practice of admitting it and (as members of Society) the Sect for which it was introduced." He reacted to Livingston's comment that Quakers could not be compelled to fight, by expressing his doubt whether "these drones of society [can be] permitted to remain unmolested." The Burlington militia "finally brought their Quakers before me. If I had detained them their month it must have been by keeping them constantly under guard, but this would have been gratifying spleen to very little purpose. I did not ask them to fight, and they did not choose to fatigue but, were willing to submit to the fine imposed by State, they did so and were dismissed."[73] Quakers refused to even perform non-combat labor duties, fatigue, because those duties supported combat. On February 22, Washington wrote to Livingston that he had written Putnam and ordered him, "immediately to put a stop to the practice of extorting fines from reluctant militia."[74]

As part of the harassing attacks on the British troops around New Brunswick, Middlesex County militia Colonel John Neilson used information learned from a deserter to lead a February 17 attack on a Loyalist outpost about sixteen miles from Princeton at Bennett's Island on the Raritan River. The outpost commander was Loyalist Major Richard W. Stockton, now known as "the enemy's RENOWNED land pilot" after guiding Lieutenant Colonel Mawhood to New Brunswick after the January 3 battle. Neilson informed General Putnam of the planned attack, and Putnam sent him fifty Bedford County, Pennsylvania, riflemen to reinforce his attacking force.

Neilson told his men that their mission was to disarm the Loyalists at Bennett's Island, capture Major Stockton, and deliver him to headquarters at Princeton. Colonel Neilson reported to Major General Philemon Dickinson that his roughly 150 men engaged 60 New Jersey Volunteers for only about one minute and the enemy lost 4 killed and 1 wounded, while the Americans suffered 1 killed. They also captured 63 muskets, which Putnam felt should go to the Middlesex Militia. Neilson commended his second-in-command, Major William Scudder of the 3rd Middlesex militia regiment, for behaving "in a very soldierlike manner, and executed his orders with the utmost punctuality and firmness." The Pennsylvania militiamen, especially those Bedford riflemen, also performed excellently. Colonel Neilson arrived in Princeton the next day with his prisoners.[75]

On March 8, Stockton and two other captured officers were manacled together in irons and marched out of Princeton for Philadelphia. Although

Putnam was well known for being lenient to his prisoners, he ordered the officer taking them to Philadelphia that "You will observe that uncommon vigilance is necessary to secure persons whose acquaintance with the country and whose desperate situation, gives them every advantage, and every incitement to escape from an injured and exasperated community into whose hands they have fallen. Those in irons are to remain so while under your care. Let no indulgence be allowed them which affords a possibility of escape, they are to have no communication with any stranger whatever; double your centinels within and without doors and take every other precaution which your discretion would point out to secure villains resolved on flight. You will not take too much room for their quarters, but stow them as thick as possible. Remembering you stand accountable for every misconduct." The Philadelphia officials imprisoned Stockton at Carlisle, Pennsylvania, where the officers were treated very harshly until exchanged in September 1779. He later moved to Canada and died in New Brunswick in 1801 at the age of 68.[76]

When Washington learned of these actions, he wrote to General Gates at Philadelphia on March 10, "I am informed that General Putnam sent to Philadelphia in irons, Major Stockton, taken upon the Raritan, and that he continues in strict confinement. I think we ought to avoid putting in practice, what we have so loudly complained of, the cruel treatment of prisoners." Washington wanted the men treated well, stating that Stockton, "I believe, has been very active and mischievous, but we took him in arms, as an officer of the enemy, and by the rules of war, we are obliged to treat him as such, and not as a felon."[77] It may be that General Putnam and the officers who held Stockton were so disgusted by the actions of Loyalists in New Jersey that they desired to make Stockton's life as miserable as possible.

On February 27, Putnam sent several prisoners, including a Hessian deserter, to General Gates at Philadelphia and believed some of the prisoners would be willing to enlist in the Continental Army. He then quoted from a letter dated February 24 that, the previous day, General Maxwell's brigade engaged with about two thousand enemy troops, took seven prisoners, and kept the ground with one man killed and three or four wounded. The enemy "were seen to carry off several wagon loads of dead & wounded." Putnam also asked him to send newspapers because at Princeton, "we scarce see one in an age, and then by accident."[78]

The British strengthened their forces at New Brunswick toward the end of February, leading Washington to believe they planned another move toward Philadelphia by way of the Delaware River, as they had hoped to do in December before going into winter quarters. Such a move would bring them through Princeton, so he advised Putnam to be on the alert and prepared to meet any advance the British might make. Should they appear to be heading for Philadelphia, Putnam was to cross the Delaware immediately with his forces, take command of the militia there, secure all boats on the Pennsylvania side of the river, and make all arrangements to facilitate crossing the rest of the army if forced again to leave New Jersey. Fearing a reprise of November and December, Washington was determined to defend New Jersey inch by inch.[79]

Artillery Colonel Thomas Proctor arrived at Princeton on the evening of February 28 after checking on artillery in various locations. He found things in good shape, and the "men are in exceeding high spirits." He mentioned a skirmish near Quibletown or Samptown the previous Sunday and also how the enemy soldiers were not doing well.[80]

Aaron Burr quartered with Putnam in Princeton as his aide-de-camp. Although quite ambitious, Burr wrote to a friend from Princeton on March 7 that he did not seek a promotion at present because he was very content, and "I am at present quite happy in the esteem and entire confidence of my good old General."[81] Burr was also quite familiar with Princeton. His father was president of the college when Aaron was born and he had attended the college as part of the class of 1772, where he got to know James Madison (class of 1771) and Henry (Light Horse Harry) Lee (class of 1773).[82]

British Assistant Quartermaster General Captain Thomas Gamble was a prisoner at Princeton in March in the process of being exchanged. He had asked to go to New Brunswick on the 7th but was told by General Putnam that "he would meet General Howe at New York on the 9th."[83] Gamble was still a prisoner at Princeton in May when Livingston wrote to Witherspoon that he had asked Princeton merchant Major Enos Kelsey to inquire into complaints of misconduct by Gamble and also by Doctor Stapleton, the British doctor permitted to attend Captain McPherson there. The Continental Congress had ordered this to be done on May 10 and expected Washington to be informed of the results. The two men were removed from Princeton.[84]

A notice from General Putnam dated Princeton, March 10, 1777, and signed by aide-de-camp Aaron Burr, thanked Colonel Cox of Lancaster County for the "diligence and activity with which he commanded at an advanced post." He also praised the conduct of his militiamen, and now that their time of service for which they engaged was over, they were discharged with honor and permitted to return to their homes.[85] Putnam also wrote to Livingston on March 10 that one Moses Ivins had been brought to him as an enemy of the State. He understood that Ivins had previously given his bond to the Provincial Congress for his good behavior but had then strayed. Therefore,

Putnam was sending him on to Livingston for disposition. He had at present twelve or fourteen men under guard similarly accused of being Loyalists that he would also forward. He ordered that no more Loyalists be sent to him from Monmouth. In a follow-up note, Putnam indicated he had heard from Washington about a plan requiring his assistance. However, his very weak manpower put him in no position to assist in the effort until reinforced.[86]

Major Hall and Lieutenant Keen of the 1st Salem County Regiment, with two sergeants and twenty-four privates, were ordered by General Putnam on March 14 to convey several Tory prisoners from Princeton to Haddonfield. This service necessarily detained them three days longer than the time for which they had drawn pay or rations, and Keen received twenty pounds to settle things.[87]

On March 17, Putnam informed John Hancock that two wagon loads of supplies for the British and Hessian prisoners in American hands conducted by a flag and carrying a letter had come through Princeton. He found the contents of the document "so obnoxious and unjust and ungenteel" that he took it and sent a copy to Hancock and the original to Washington.[88]

Between April 5 and 8, Putnam informed Congress of all enemy movements known to him. From Colonel Neilson, he learned that fifteen transports had lately sailed from Perth Amboy.[89] Then, "By a light horseman just arrived from Cranbury, who has been at South Amboy, I have the following intelligence." There were a large number of ships in Amboy harbor, and six or seven hundred Hessians had been seen paraded in Amboy. Ships carrying troops had been seen going from New Brunswick to Amboy, where soldiers were loading their baggage on ships. Also, "They have burnt several houses and taken all the boards of the barns at the round abouts, they have continually a party cutting and hewing ranging timber which (it's probable) is to make platforms on board their ships for the conveniency of transporting their troops."

Everything seen at New Brunswick and Amboy, Putnam said, "has the appearance of moving soon somewhere or other, they plunder the inhabitants that are in their reach of every thing they can carry off, without giving them any reward." Putnam promised to keep his spies out and report any further signs of movement, which was expected. He offered his "wish that the troops in Philadelphia were armed and accouter'd, and the militia ready to turn out at the shortest notice—for by their movements and our intelligence we have the greatest reason to think that Philadelphia is their greatest object at present in view."[90]

In early April, Captain John Noble Cumming's company of Colonel Israel Shreve's 2nd New Jersey Regiment was at Princeton and, while there, suffered a dozen desertions.[91] There were also desertions from the 4th Virginia Regiment and from Captain Andrew Hynes Company of the 7th Maryland Regiment around the same time.[92] Putnam continued to deal with Loyalists and the work of the Council of Safety. On April 11, Governor Livingston, acting for the Council of Safety, informed him that Captain Thomas Webb, who held an office under the King, had appeared before the Council and was to be allowed fourteen days to settle his affairs and remove to the enemy with a flag.[93]

As the time for the spring campaign neared, rumors that the British were about to leave New Brunswick became rampant, and the expectation was that they would aim for Philadelphia by crossing through New Jersey.[94] Nathanael Greene proposed an attack on New Brunswick and other British outposts, no doubt in response to a request from Washington, which would include the troops at Princeton under General Putnam. However, in the council of war called to discuss the plan, the officers unanimously decided that they did not have sufficient force and that the troops lacked the discipline needed for success. Even Greene voted against his proposal.[95] On April 29, Putnam forwarded a New York paper and expected, "the enemy will make a move. It would give me great satisfaction to see our troops come faster to camp."[96] Between May 3 and 10, General Putnam had Hazen's Regiment, the 9th Pennsylvania Regiment, the Delaware Regiment, the 4th Maryland Regiment, and some artillery at Princeton.[97]

In late April, militiamen under Major William Scudder apprehended two men about three miles from the British lines at New Brunswick who were seeking to join the British troops. Scudder obtained a confession from at least one of the two and sent them to General Putnam at Princeton, who then sent them on to the Council of Safety at Bordentown.[98] Putnam was dealing with several other men arrested because they were going in and out of New Brunswick without passes.

Also, an Elisabeth Brewer was in custody, having been taken coming out of New Brunswick, and gave information on several other people. She was probably the wife of Peter Brewer and listed as widow Brewer in the February 1780 Middlesex County tax rateables. She told Putnam that she had previously worked at the Princeton military hospital and would like to be a nurse there. The surgeon attested to her good character, so Putnam detained her at Princeton for that purpose. If her actions raised any objections to that, he would send her to Livingston immediately.[99]

Putnam left Princeton in mid-May to take command in the New York Highlands. During his four winter months at Princeton, troops sent out by Putnam took nearly 1,000 enemy prisoners and captured more than 120 baggage wagons, along with a substantial amount of valuable supplies and provisions.[100] When General Putnam arrived at Peekskill on May 22 to take command, he jokingly confessed to Jeremiah Wadsworth that "I was three months in Princeton and what with comers and goers I drank there 2 casks of wine which was 12/ more than my wages so that I grow rich fast."[101] Putnam's replacement, General John Sullivan, arrived at Princeton in May with 1,500 men, soon augmented by troops coming up from the south.[102]

American Occupation of Princeton—General John Sullivan

Colonel John Hawkins Stone, stationed at Kingston, received an order from General John Sullivan on May 18 to furnish a captain for a court of inquiry. However, Stone notified him that "there is but one Captain at this place who is not on duty and he was only relieved this morning, so that its impossible for us to furnish any—the duty at this place is hard on the officers, our guards are extensive considering our numbers—if the troops at Prince Town could take the Mill Guard which they have done till within these few days and which would not be more than their proportion of duty it would make us much more compact and our duty lighter." He also believed that "we are scattered in such a manner that we can be of no other use than that of alarming the other posts, if the enemy approach."

Stone also did not know what he was actually expected to do. He told Sullivan, "I have been stationed at this place for near a week without the least order for regulating my conduct, and as I think, and dare say you will think it necessary, that the line of conduct I am to pursue should be pointed out, I shall esteem it a particular favor if you will be pleased to give me such instructions in writing as you may think proper." One specific concern was that "we have four different passes to guard and there is still one left unguarded, which I think of consequent, it's the road that the most part of our deserters take and where, I am informed, many of the inhabitants who are disaffected pass to go to Prince Town."[103] Stone wanted orders as to how he could best use his troops to help the cause.

Not knowing Putnam had left Princeton, General Schuyler wrote to Generals Washington and Putnam on May 22, asking them to detain James Fisher of Philadelphia, "a notorious Tory and one capable of giving much information to the enemy." Fisher was accompanying Mrs. Alexander Graydon on her journey to New York to seek the release of her son, a prisoner of war held by the British.[104] Schuyler requested that, if Fisher came to Princeton, the generals would "give directions to have him apprehended and sent under guard to Philadelphia and to prevent him from passing our lines at some other place. I wish you to give notice to the respective officers commanding the out posts and order them to secure him."[105]

Mrs. Graydon, of Reading, Pennsylvania, had been planning to go to New York for some time and found that her Whig friends were against it and her Loyalist friends for it. The Loyalists felt it would give a good impression of General Howe, while the Whigs thought it would not work, and if it did, it would help the Loyalists by showing the human side of the British. She finally resolved to go, purchased a horse and riding chair, and set out for Philadelphia, where she met Fisher, a Scotchman and relation of her grandmother's, who offered to drive her to New York. Graydon suspected, though, that "as he was a retailer of dry goods, his object, no doubt, was traffic; and to bring home with him some scarce light articles in the chair box." Mrs. Graydon was unaware of Fisher's political mind and accepted his offer. Just before they reached Princeton, a detachment of light cavalry caught up with them. General Mifflin did not want Fisher to get to New York and had sent the horsemen to apprehend him. After taking Fisher into custody, the horsemen took Mrs. Graydon to General Sullivan's quarters in Princeton. She remained there until arrangements were made to get her back to Philadelphia "under an escort of horse." Back in Philadelphia, she went to army headquarters to obtain the proper passes to go to New York and did visit her son.[106]

On May 29, General Sullivan informed Congress about British ships sailing from Sandy Hook. Several were warships, and all appeared heavily laden.[107] On May 31, the Delaware detachment was the only unit listed as serving under Putnam at Princeton, but he had departed by then, and Sullivan had taken over.[108] On June 1, Sullivan had Hazen's Regiment; the 1st, 2nd, 3rd, 4th, 5th, and 6th Maryland Regiments; Captain Dandridge's troop of horse; and some artillery at Princeton.[109]

By June 1, General Benedict Arnold, who had taken over at Trenton from Caesar Rodney, expected the enemy would soon open the spring campaign and send ships to the Delaware River to make a feint at Philadelphia, if not an actual attack. He told General Sullivan that troops were coming from Philadelphia with all possible expedition, and "boats & men will be ready at or near Trentown, on the shortest notice."[110]

Among those troops was Delaware Captain Enoch Anderson, who had missed the battles of Trenton and Princeton, having been sent to do some recruiting back home. He said the recruiting had gone slowly until the two victories at Trenton and that Princeton gave it a new life. His company was ready to march in the early spring, along with Captain Kirkwood's of the same regiment. They marched to Philadelphia, where they obtained supplies, and after a few days, "our two companies all in new regimentals, new arms and fully supplied with ammunition" arrived in Princeton by June 7 for duty under General Putnam, who had recently departed. Anderson said, "We found we were the only regular troops here, the others were militia;—perhaps in all not more than three hundred men." He continues, "From Princetown to Brunswick was eighteen miles. We were all in a dangerous situation. Perhaps our whole force was not more than four thousand, and the British at Brunswick amounted to fifteen thousand. But such was the art of our old General that he made the enemy believe he had thousands, when he had not hundreds."[111]

On June 14, the people of Princeton heard rumors that the British were advancing in two columns from New Brunswick and that one would pass through Princeton on the way to Trenton and the other by Griggs's Mill and Sourland Meeting on the way to Coryell's Ferry. The British had indeed marched out of New Brunswick, hoping to lure Washington out of his defensible position in the Watchung Mountains in Morris County. At Coryell's Ferry, General Arnold received intelligence from Washington at 4:00 p.m. that seven thousand men under Howe and Cornwallis had encamped at the Somerset Courthouse. In response, they understood General Sullivan had marched to intercept the column heading for Coryell's, and people had heard heavy firing toward Trenton.[112] At this time, Captain Enoch Anderson's partial regiment received orders to join the main army, and the rest of his men soon joined it, along with regiments from other states.[113]

According to Stephen Kemble, "At Hillsborough, a Battalion of Light Infantry fell in with a body of rebels, took a few prisoners, and killed five or six, with the loss of one man killed and three wounded," including Captain Lysaght of the 63rd Regiment of Foot. The soldiers left their tents and baggage behind, "supposed in hopes of bringing Mr. Washington to an engagement; but, not succeeding in that," they returned to New Brunswick on the 20th, after spending five days.[114]

Arnold knew that the New Jersey militia was turning out in high numbers, and Sullivan had gone to Flemington. Arnold sent on to Sullivan any troops that arrived at Coryell's but feared the British would return to New Brunswick before he had sufficient troops to make a battle reasonable. He expected to have more than twenty thousand men within four days. He knew that Washington had ordered Putnam to send him four thousand men from the Highlands immediately. His main problem was that the militia had very little ammunition.[115]

On June 19, General Sullivan's aide-de-camp Major John Eustace informed General Mifflin that the British had recrossed the Millstone and were returning to New Brunswick. Eustace had seen large fires in the area of Middlebush and asked, "You must excuse this shocking scrawl, as I am obliged to write on my knee." He then noted that "We have dispatched our Light Horse to Princetown to reconnoiter that road. Should they proceed that way we shall acquaint you of it."[116]

Then, on June 22, Kemble noted, "General Howe evacuated Brunswick this day; the rear of the army attacked; had five or six men killed, and about forty wounded; the rebels had by accounts upwards of 30 men killed."[117]

Commenting on the recent British actions, General Putnam at Peekskill wrote to Jeremiah Wadsworth on June 24 that he believed that when the Americans converted one person to the Whig cause, General Howe created ten "by his cruelty & cheating the inhabitants in the Jersies while he was there." In contrast, Putnam judged that when he commanded at Princeton he "endeavored to win [people] over to our side.... By every salutary measure I was capable of & have reason to flatter myself it had a good effect." The response against the British that month he saw as proof of his efforts.[118]

After refusing Howe's offer of battle, Washington brought his troops down from Middlebrook to Quibletown and sent Brigadier General Lord Stirling to the Scotch Plains area north of New Brunswick, to guard Washington's left flank and harass the British. Howe came out again in June, and this led to the Battle of the Short Hills on June 26. After this, the Maryland Line and the Delaware regiment were at Morristown under General Sullivan, instead of at Princeton.[119]

Militia—The Forage War—Philadelphia Campaign

After the Battle of Princeton, local militiaman Thomas Olden had marched with the army to Morristown, where he stayed until ordered to Middlebrook. There he became an express rider for General Sullivan and served part of the time at Princeton. He fell from his horse about August 20 and received an injury on his right side that forced him to leave that position, and he returned home.[120]

After spending the night at Thomas Drake's, on January 4, Joseph Clark and company went to Penny Town "to take some hides, &c. from Cochran's." They came back to Hopewell that night. On the 5th, the company went to Hart's, and in the evening, a party set off for Penny Town. Clark served as their guide to "lead them the nighest way through the woods," and they got there about bedtime. The rest of the battalion came in the next day, and they went to Penny Town, where they were "employed to take care of the Stores taken from the enemy." Clark was "appointed to take care of a Lieutenant wounded in the late action, tended him till Friday night (10th), when he died."[121]

On the night of January 10, Clark's militia company received orders to march to join General Washington at Morristown, and most of the men left early the next morning. However, Clark stayed behind, temporarily appointed a lieutenant, and was given "orders to press 2 wagons and horse to ride" to take ten British regulars, one Hessian, and two Tories with a guard of four men and deliver them to Trenton. After delivering them the next day, he returned that night toward Amwell with his guards and horse. For the next week or so, they kept moving around in the area of Flemington and toward Bound Brook. They fought with the British foraging party on January 20, which severely hurt the British army's ability to gather food from the countryside.[122]

Captain Longstreet had dismissed his company for three days shortly after the battle on January 3 and instructed them to join him at Cranbury. There they became employed scouting about on the lines for some time and then marched to Monmouth Courthouse. They remained for a few days and then went to Middletown, and the refugee Loyalists left when they came. They then went to Shrewsbury and back to Monmouth Court House, where they remained until the goods taken from the British could be sent on to Burlington. Then they returned to Princeton by way of Cranbury and were stationed there to take charge of the military magazine, stores, and prisoners.[123]

During the nearly six months the British occupied New Brunswick, there was constant anxiety about movements that Howe might make. When General Sullivan commanded at Princeton, Longstreet's company was frequently called out for duty, along the Millstone River toward Somerset Courthouse and in the region north and east of Princeton, to keep an eye on any British movements. When serving in the town, they received prisoners taken in the Forage War around New Brunswick and along the sea coast of Monmouth and Burlington Counties. Sometime during the summer of 1777, the Rev. James Caldwell of Elizabethtown, Commissioner of Prisoners, appointed Captain James Moore deputy commissary of prisoners at Princeton. Moore was to take charge of all prisoners who should be sent there, convey them to headquarters at Morristown or wherever ordered, and parole the officers.[124]

Many changes in leadership took place in New Jersey militia regiments during the first months of 1777. On March 28, Abraham Quick resigned as colonel of the 2nd Battalion of Somerset Militia. Lieutenant Colonel Henry VanDike became commander, Benjamin Baird lieutenant colonel, Peter D. Vroom first major, and William Vanbryck second major.[125] Enos Kelsey officially resigned his commission as second major on March 30 because he had been appointed Deputy Quartermaster and Commissary.[126]

Captain Longstreet resigned to become a commissary of stores procurement. On April 24, the Council of Safety sent three blank officer commissions to Lieutenant Colonel VanDike, to be filled in with the names of the officers elected by the Princeton militia company. He was to also submit the names to the Council. On April 28, James Moore was named captain, James Stockton first lieutenant, and James Hamilton ensign. Princeton residents Benjamin Plum and John Updike witnessed the certificate of their election.[127]

At this time, Major William Scudder had apprehended three men, whom he sent to Princeton and placed in the guard-room until the Council of Safety could hear the charges against them.[128]

A general alarm called out the militia when the British came out in force from New Brunswick toward Somerset Courthouse in mid-June. Private Abraham Skillman's company assembled in Princeton and marched to Buxtown to join the Middlesex regiment commanded by Colonel Jacob Hyer and Major William Scudder. Skillman was from South Brunswick Township, living about half a mile from Kingston in Somerset County. The next day they marched down to one of the branches of the Raritan and joined with the Somerset County militia. They went to Sourland Mountain, then to Steels Gap, and then joined Washington's army. Skillman, along with John Gulick, William Vantilburgh, and others, were selected as part of a squad to make a scout under the command of Captains Longstreet (not the Princeton Longstreet), Williamson, and Chambers. Skillman stayed out on duty for several months, alternately serving for himself and as a substitute for his father.[129]

Between August 26 and September 3, Captain James Moore's company was on duty at Princeton for four days.[130]

In September, many Princeton-area militiamen lost the colonel of their regiment when his actions indicated he had switched sides in the conflict. A Joint Meeting of the Legislature elected Lieutenant Colonel Jacob Hyer on September 6 to replace John Duychink, who had "taken protection from the enemy," as colonel of the 3rd Regiment of Middlesex County militia, and promoted Major William Scudder to lieutenant colonel.[131] Then, on October 13, upon the recommendation of Colonel Hyer and Lieutenant Colonel Scudder, they appointed Robert Dix as first major and Thomas Egberts as second major of the battalion.[132]

In the spring, Captain Moore's company served along the Millstone River about Somerset Courthouse to help prevent enemy incursions from New Brunswick. When a large British force departed Perth Amboy on July 23 and headed for the Chesapeake Bay to attack Philadelphia, militia duty in New Jersey had to adapt. Although seldom sent out of the State, Captain Moore received orders to join General Washington's army in Pennsylvania on September 15.

He marched there under General David Forman of Monmouth County, joining the army several days before the Battle of Germantown on October 4.[133]

At the Battle of Germantown, a friend of Ensign James Hamilton was killed. Before he died, he requested Hamilton to take charge of his watch and buckles and deliver them to his mother, which Hamilton did. John Hulfish, Hamilton's next-door neighbor, was also at the battle in Moore's company. He recalled that Hamilton became separated from the company near the end of the action and was not able to rejoin until the next morning. Hulfish stated that Hamilton "was esteemed in his company as an active and faithful officer and true friend to his country." The company was discharged on October 9, a few days after the battle. About this time, Stephen Morford served as one of the guards under the command of Captain Samuel Stout of Middlesex, marching some prisoners from the Princeton college to headquarters at Valley Forge. After the battle, Moore returned to Princeton to continue with local duties, such as taking charge of prisoners, stores, magazines, and the alarm gun. At times he took his company out on scouting parties in various directions.[134]

John Witherspoon's son, James, brigade major with General Maxwell's Brigade at Fort Ticonderoga in New York, came south in May to upper New Jersey and then in August to Germantown. He may have fought at Brandywine and was killed at Germantown. He was buried in a common grave with other men and then moved to the burial ground at St. Michael's Church in Germantown. He had never married, but left his parents and siblings in mourning, no doubt supported by their many friends in Princeton.[135]

After the Battle of Germantown, Captain Moore's company divided into eight classes, as was typical for the militia. Grouping the men in this manner helped assure that men from the same family or immediate neighborhood would not all be absent at the same time when the militia was called out. One or more classes from one company combined with some classes from other companies to form temporary companies for the duration of the call out, usually about a month.[136] The number of classes called out depended on the expected need for that month. One month two classes might be called out, while the next month four might go out.

Thomas Olden continued at home after the fall from his horse in August, and sometime in December he volunteered in the Brunswick Artillery Company, part of the Middlesex militia. The company kept one gun stationed at Princeton under the command of Lieutenant Hamilton, and Olden was one of the crew. Militiamen could volunteer to serve in the artillery company rather than their normal infantry company. Elias Woodruff, Quarter Master of the Military Stores at Princeton, employed Olden "in the laboratory making cartridges, &c."[137]

The Legislature adjourned for the year on December 12. The next day, Governor Livingston ordered every captain or commanding officer in the militia to make a return of the number of men in his company, their accouterments, and ammunition and to give it to the colonel or commanding officer of his regiment. That information would then pass up through the ranks to the governor.[138] Members of Captain Moore's company served for a week, from December 18 to December 24, commanded by Governor Livingston and probably serving as his bodyguard. The Legislature had been meeting at Princeton but had adjourned until February.[139]

Military Supplies

Establishing an American garrison in Princeton in January 1777 placed enormous demands on the local people for firewood and other items, including forty wagons to move some sick and wounded to the Bethlehem, Pennsylvania hospital, and five two-horse sleds to haul corn (Indian meal). Putnam also set up a system of alarm guns and beacons.[140] It also meant that local citizens would become involved as officials in the poorly regarded army supply system that was still developing. They would encounter a series of uncomfortable challenges for the duration of the war.

Princeton merchant Enos Kelsey was appointed Deputy Quartermaster and Commissary at Princeton in about April and was receiving barrels of flour for the Continental Army by April 9. During April and May, he received quantities of flour, sometimes in barrels and sometimes in bags, and also 495 pounds of beef on May 6. In June, Kelsey supplied 74 rations and 376 gills of rum to Captain Dean's company of the 7th Maryland Regiment. In mid-June, he paid at least half a dozen men as bakers and continued to receive flour and meat. He also took care of live animals and paid for the pasturing of 14 head of cattle and 40 sheep by David Davis. The flour and meat continued arriving in August, in addition to 199½ gallons of rum and whiskey.[141]

The 1st Virginia Regiment marched from Virginia to camp as part of a detachment of troops in July. Lieutenant David Thomson found that a quartermaster at Trenton pressed a wagon into service to carry their baggage. It accompanied them as far as Princeton, "at which place the waggoner went off, carrying his horses and leaving his wagon," which eventually caught up with the regiment at Camp.[142]

On August 29, the military magazine at Princeton received 8 barrels of flour, 3 barrels of biscuit, 100 pounds of soap, 10 pounds of candles, and 11 barrels of herring. The shipment receipt indicated that some items were damaged. Things they probably expected, but that were not part of the shipment, included beef, rum, whiskey, Codfish, slat, peas or beans, lard, rice, pork, or bacon.[143]

The Council of Safety meeting in Princeton on October 13 agreed to procure and send to Major Kelsey about "150 weight of powder," so that Kelsey could make up cartridges with the lead he already had. The powder would be sent in the wagon that took prisoners to Princeton "in the care of Captain [Samuel] Stout." The Council also ordered paying Jacob Bergen's bill for £115.4.1. He had supplied some prisoners captured fleeing toward Staten Island and their guards while they were at Princeton. They also paid Colonel Jacob Hyer for providing "250 weight of Continental bread & flour & two barrels of fish" for the prisoners and their guards.[144] On October 22, the same day as the Battle of Red Bank, the Council of Safety ordered 1,256 pounds of lead and some cartridge boxes sent to Princeton and delivered to Major Kelsey at the magazine, very likely his house.[145]

The Legislature appointed David Olden on November 25 to be a commissioner of clothing for Middlesex County. Although selected for Middlesex, he occasionally also purchased items in western Somerset County, no doubt because of the county line situation at Princeton. Just four days after his appointment, he bought one blanket and one pair of shoes from Robert Lawrence. In late November and through December, he purchased blankets, shoes, stockings, cloth, thread, and "sundries." On December 5, he spent several days obtaining and delivering money to the Assembly and put in for travel and carting expenses.[146] Purchasers like Olden did not make orders to large manufacturers or suppliers of things the army needed. Instead, they went from house to house and talked people into selling them items they could spare for the military or perhaps agree to make up in a small quantity of needed supplies. Almost everyone became involved in supplying the army, but not in an organized way that maintained the needed amounts in the supply chain.

The College

John Witherspoon was anxious to reopen the college. On March 24, he placed an announcement in the *Pennsylvania Evening Post* that classes would begin on May 10. He advised all prospective students not to delay arriving, "for it is proposed by assiduous application to recover what has been lost by the public confusions, and therefore it will be impossible, by extra-attendance, to bring up those who fall behind their classes." Because of the damage to the building and its current use as a hospital, he was not sure just where students would live and attend classes, but he would give public notice as soon as a location was arranged.[147] Because British movements were expected in late May and then in June, Witherspoon felt he should find a safer location than Princeton. Instead, he delayed the reopening.

The college trustees met at Cooper's Ferry on May 24 to consider whether it was possible to gather the students together and "endeavor to proceed with their usual instruction." They agreed that, should the British depart the state, "Dr. Witherspoon is desired to call the students together at Princeton, & to proceed with their education in the best manner he can, considering the state of public affairs." Witherspoon would be the only instructor unless enough students gathered to justify hiring additional teachers, in which case he could hire one or more instructors.

John Witherspoon, Richard Stockton, and Rev. Elihu Spencer "were appointed a committee to determine what repairs are necessary for the convenience of the students, & to order them to be made." However, repairs should be limited to only those necessary "to save the building & to accommodate those students who may be collected." They asked Witherspoon to work with Congress "to resolve that troops shall not hereafter be quartered in the college." Due to the death of college treasurer Jonathan Sergeant, the trustees formed a committee to settle accounts and take care of financial matters.

On a more scholastic subject, the previous graduating class had not officially been granted their degrees and received their diplomas. The trustees voted that those students should obtain them as "soon as the confusions of the war will admit of it."[148]

Although reopening in May or June did not materialize, Witherspoon optimistically submitted a notice to the newspapers that the college would begin on Tuesday, July 8. Potential students were advised "to take all possible pains to provide themselves with books, according to their standing and future studies, which are already known to them." Books were not available at the college, and because it had been so long since students had attended classes, he hoped they had been studying on their own. Upon returning, students were to expect to work diligently to recover the ground lost due to the war. Seniors, in particular, were to prepare to attend classes until the end of September when the examination for bachelor's degrees, usually held in the middle of August, would occur immediately before commencement.[149]

Instruction finally did resume in July, but with only a handful of students. This led Witherspoon to repeat in the July 10th newspaper the announcement that classes had resumed on the 8th. Nassau Hall was in such bad condition that recitations took place in the president's house, where Houston and a tutor did most of the instruction.[150]

The college had no money for repairs, so the President's residence continued in use during the winter of 1777–78. Joseph Scudder had entered the college in 1775 and left it just before the British arrived in the fall of 1776. Returning now, he found that a hospital occupied Nassau Hall, so that students no longer lived there, but instead boarded out in private homes and recited at the college president's house. Professors Witherspoon and Houston both spent part of their time attending Congress. To keep things going, "either one or the other of them would come home and hear the students recite about once a week, and sometimes once in two weeks."[151]

On July 17, a memorial dated July 15 from the trustees of the College of New Jersey was read in Congress and referred to the board of war. It stated that, in its effort to reopen the college, the trustees were unable to make the necessary repairs. This was true because "every party of the Continental Troops, marching thro' this place, take possession of it as barracks; and partly thro' wantonness, and also under pretense of not being supplied with firewood, are daily committing the greatest ravages upon the building, in breaking up the floors, and burning every piece of wood they can cut out of it." They asked Congress to order the army to cease using the college as a barracks. Instead, it should appoint a quartermaster to reside in Princeton and arrange for quartering soldiers in vacant houses, barns, and other unoccupied structures. The State Legislature should pay rent to the owners. The trustees suggested John Malcomb and Jacob Hyer as good candidates for this position.[152]

Partly because of requests such as this one from the college, Washington included in his July 25 general orders specific requirements aimed at ending plundering, including the widespread use of fence rails for firewood. He admonished, "How disgraceful to the army is it, that the peaceable inhabitants, our countrymen and fellow citizens, dread our halting among them, even for a night and are happy when they get rid of us?" He placed the solution squarely on the shoulders of all his officers of every rank.[153] Congress followed up and on August 6 appointed John Malcomb, of Princeton, to act as quartermaster, "for such detachments of the army as may be passing that way, till the quarter master general shall give further directions on this subject; and that he take care that no damage be done to the college at that place." Malcomb would work with the local magistrates and only use the college when "one or more magistrates find it absolutely necessary and in that case said quartermaster shall take effectual care that no damage be done."[154]

The Community

Just when Richard Stockton returned home from British imprisonment is not known, but it appears to have been before the period of January 7–11 when Benjamin Rush spoke with him. The fact that Stockton was set free after a relatively short imprisonment and apparently signed a loyalty oath to the King has led to much discussion about whether, even though he signed the Declaration of Independence, he should be honored as an American patriot of the Revolution.[155]

Stockton had been granted a full pardon by Lord and General Howe by December 29, 1776, and was entitled to all his property. A letter to Loyalist Colonel Elisha Lawrence stated that Stockton, "having informed that his horse, bridle and saddle were taken from the ferry [at Perth Amboy] by some of the people under your command, you will upon receipt of this restore the same horse and such other of his effects as shall come within your department to the said Mr. Stockton at the house of John Covenhoven in Monmouth."[156]

While the details of Stockton's captivity cannot be verified, it is evident that he signed some form of agreement to discontinue acting in support of the Revolution. Just why he would agree to this raises questions about his character. In considering his actions, though, it is crucial to understand the situation in which he found himself. During the first three weeks of Stockton's incarceration, the British forced Washington to cross to Pennsylvania with his army, leaving the British in authority in New Jersey. The State government ceased to meet and was altogether disrupted. Governor Livingston's location was not known, although he probably had gone to Pennsylvania like many others. People in New Jersey feared greatly that the British would continue to occupy the State and then attack Philadelphia, which also feared that attack.

Stockton was captured just two days after General Howe and Admiral Howe announced their proclamation of complete amnesty to anyone who, within sixty days, reaffirmed their loyalty to the King and stopped taking actions against the British government. New Jersey people by the thousands took advantage of this offer, feeling abandoned by their government and the Continental Congress with the removal of Washington and his troops from the State. Throughout the new states, people felt the Revolution was doomed to imminent failure. Loyalists, like those who captured Stockton, felt confident that the British were going to prevail and reestablish Royal authority. Since the Declaration of Independence and the formation of the new State government, Loyalists had felt a loss of their liberties and suffered at the hands of the new Patriot government. Now, they could exact revenge. Whether or not Stockton was threatened with physical violence or death if he did not sign a loyalty oath, other patriot men, including at least a few government officials, also signed oaths under duress, often at the hands of Loyalists.

Stockton had long been in favor of a separate local government in the colonies that was not under the control of Parliament, but remained loyal to the King and hoped this would be accomplished without a war. He could have been convinced by Howe that his amnesty program was one step toward a possible accommodation to those ideas. The Howes wanted peace as much as Stockton did.

We tend to evaluate the actions of prisoners of war as reflections of their loyalty to their ideals and government. In December 1776, it was difficult to envision a new government in the colonies and there was a real possibility that they would lose and have to deal with the British government. The colonists had already shown the British that they were willing to die for their cause. Now, they might be in a position to negotiate a settlement. It is unclear just what motivated Stockton's actions. But, in pondering them, it is essential to remember his very complicated situation. He had no explicit knowledge of just where things were going and how those things he held dear, both ideals and people, would fare over the following decades. He was a thoughtful man, obviously well respected before being taken prisoner, and did what he thought was best at the time. Alternatively, he may just have been weak as some judged him then and do now.

Upon returning home, Stockton learned that Morven had been occupied by British light dragoons under Lieutenant Colonel William Harcourt. Stockton's brother-in-law, Elias Boudinot, reported the dragoons had removed bonds, notes, and other personal property totaling about £4,000 to £5,000 in value. His son-in-law, Benjamin Rush, noted that "The whole of Mr. Stockton's furniture, apparel, and even valuable writings have been burnt. All his cattle, horses, hogs, sheep, grain, and forage have been carried away by them. His losses cannot amount to less than £5,000."[157] Abraham Clark notified New Jersey Assembly Speaker John Hart on February 8 that "Mr. Stockton by his late procedure cannot act," and the Assembly must select a replacement for him in Congress.[158] The next day, John Hancock told Robert Treat Paine that "Stockton it is said, & truly, has received General Howe's protection."[159]

On February 2, John Witherspoon wrote to his son David, reporting to him that, "I have been at Princeton, and find that by Mr. Montgomery's care, not many of my books are gone, and but little of the standing furniture is destroyed. John Goodman has been exceedingly careful and faithful about the farm; so that upon the whole, though I was the object of the enemy's distinguished hatred, I have escaped, through divine goodness, much better than I expected. Our sheep are all destroyed. There are, I think, old and young, fourteen of the cattle saved."[160]

Washington's February 3 General Orders at Morristown announced that "any officers, or soldiers of the American Army, who are possessed of bonds, or other papers, belonging to Mr. Stockden, are strictly ordered to deliver them to the Adjutant General at Head-Quarters." It may be that some of the soldiers heard about Stockton taking an oath of loyalty to the King and felt he had turned on the cause. They may have added to the plunder of Morven, or perhaps found some of Stockton's papers scattered around the area thanks to the British. This order was presumably issued to get the papers back to Stockton and is just one indication that there was no suspicion he had betrayed the cause and provided information to the British.[161]

Due to the destruction of his Princeton house, Jonathan Dickinson Sergeant moved his family to Philadelphia. Over time they became citizens of Pennsylvania, and Jonathan became Attorney General on July 28, 1777,[162] prompting his resignation from the Continental Congress. He stated that while "public affairs have taken a much happier turn & my own private circumstances have assumed rather a melancholy complexion, I hope your honorable body will excuse my wishing to retire to the management of my private concerns." His life had become very complicated due to the war. He reasoned that "the loss of my house is the least part of my misfortune, as my attention to politics during these unhappy times has at once superseded my business & prevented the collecting my accounts 'till the greater part of my debtors, it is to be feared, are either ruined or not to be found." His work in Congress made supporting his family problematic. However, he pledged to stay until a replacement could be appointed and served until September.[163]

John Witherspoon wrote to his son David on March 17 that he had been to Princeton and conveyed the news that old Jonathan Sergeant had died of smallpox. Witherspoon also noted that Richard Stockton was ill and "much spoken against for his conduct" in giving Howe "his word of honor that he would not meddle in the least in American affairs during the War." He also told the story that Loyalist Richard Cochran's wife had been sent under a flag to New York. When her husband came to meet her, he said to the officers with her "that Judge Stockton had brought evidence to General Howe to prove that he was on his way to seek a protection when he was taken." Stockton denied that, "yet many credit it." However, "Mr. Cochran's known quarrel with him makes it very doubtful to candid persons."

As for his Tusculum estate, he reported that "John Graham has been a very faithful servant. He has threshed and sold above a hundred bushels of wheat since the enemy fled & could he get hands would soon sell all that remains." Witherspoon ordered his books to be put in boxes and sent away to safety in case the enemy should return. At present, Witherspoon said, "There are also about 300 bushels of my potatoes left which I have directed to be sold. Probably I will go again to Princeton the end of this week to see further about my affairs."

Witherspoon noted that Mr. McDonald, one of the three men from the West Indies who ran into difficulties because of the Continental Association in 1774, had returned and "taken the oaths to the State of New Jersey & behaves well." In news of the war, he reported, "Hitherto everybody has expected the enemy to push this way but now it begins to be judged that their intention is to go up the North [Hudson] River to effect a junction with Carlton if possible which was the last years scheme. If so it will be a happy circumstance for us & I hope no loss to the public."[164]

On April 4, Mary Bainbridge sold their enslaved man Prime to her father, John Taylor, for seventy pounds, along with a horse and a riding chair at fifteen pounds each for a total of one hundred pounds. This transaction took place only with the consent of General Putnam, since Loyalist property was involved.[165] Ezekiel Clarke freed his ten-year-old mulatto boy Felix on August 16, to take effect on January 1, 1788, when he turned twenty-one. Thomas and Benjamin Clarke witnessed the manumission paper.[166]

Variations in racial mixture stood out to all. Traveler Ebenezer Hazard, originally from New York, came through Princeton in early August and noted that he "lodged at Hyer's [Hudibras] where I saw a child, the son of a Negro woman but of a white father, who could not be distinguished either by his color, skin or hair from the children of white parents; in short, he appeared to house nothing of the Negro in his composition." His only other comments about his visit concerned the devasted condition of the town.[167]

Ephraim Manning of Princeton placed a notice dated May 14 in the *Pennsylvania Journal* that his wife, Sarah, had left him and "taken considerable of his effects with her, without any just cause or reason." He announced that he would no longer be responsible for any debts she incurred after that date.[168]

The June Stony Brook preparatory meeting informed the quarterly meeting that Joseph Olden had administered the oath in the course of his office as coroner under the former government. He also had been concerned in promoting military measures in the present time of commotions. Several members were appointed to meet with him.[169]

The New Jersey Legislature at Princeton

The New Jersey Assembly began meeting at Princeton on September 29, but did not have a quorum until Thursday, October 2. They named Ethan Smith Doorkeeper to the Assembly.[170] Two joint committees of the Assembly and Council were ordered to meet on October 8. One was to settle the accounts of the Treasurer of the State, to meet at Jacob Bergen's tavern at 6:00 p.m. that evening, and the other was to settle the accounts of expenditures of the last $100,000 drawn from Congress for payment of the militia, to meet at Mrs. Lott's tavern at 7:00 a.m. the next morning.[171] The legislature adjourned at Princeton on October 11 to meet next at Trenton on October 28.[172] The Assembly began meeting again at Princeton on Monday, November 3 and named Andrew Jobs Doorkeeper to the house.[173] The Joint Meeting of the Assembly and Council began meeting on November 6 at Jacob Bergen's tavern. Also, in November, the Joint Meeting elected John Witherspoon and Elias Boudinot to Congress. On November 7, the Council of Safety met at Princeton with Governor Livingston present.[174]

On November 27, the legislature established two post rider routes from Isaac Collins's printing shop in Bordentown to the nearest continental post office. One courier would take the road from Bordentown and ride through Trenton and Pennington to Joshua Corshon's near Ringo's Tavern in Hunterdon County, and return by way of Princeton, Cranberry, Allentown, and Crosswicks to Collins's shop. They also asked the Postmaster General to establish a Continental post office at or near Corshon's.[175]

The Legislative Council recommended on December 10 that the legislature no longer meet in Princeton. The village not only accommodated "the General Hospital of the sick and wounded of the Army" but was just too small. Even when not overrun with troops, it could not properly accommodate the members of the legislature. All of this retarded the work of the legislature. However, moving the site of legislative meetings, unless absolutely necessary, would give the appearance of instability as well as subjecting the members to great inconvenience. Therefore, a location needed to be chosen that could be used until a permanent seat of government was established. That could not take place until the war was over, and threats from either New York or Philadelphia were removed. The legislature adjourned on December 12 with the intent of meeting next at Trenton on February 11, 1778.[176]

Actions of the Council of Safety

The Council of Safety was active, demanding people take Oaths of Abjuration and Allegiance. Joseph Horner of Princeton did so on March 19 at Burlington.[177] The Council summoned several local people to appear before it on November 17, to take their oaths of Abjuration and Allegiance to the New Jersey government. These included: William Bryant, Benjamin Clarke, Isaac Clarke, James Clarke, John Clarke, Matthew Clarke, Samuel Clark, Thomas Clarke, William Clarke, John Heath, John Hedges, Joseph Horner, William McDermott, Alexander McDonald, Andrew Morgan, Joseph Skelton, Ezekiel Smith, John Stockton (son of Joseph), Robert White, Thomas Wilson, and Samuel Worth. The same day, Colonel William Scudder took his seat on the Council.[178]

Mathew Clarke took the prescribed oaths on December 19 and was dismissed. However, a group of Quakers received Warrants of Commitment for failure to take the oaths and submit bonds. The warrants ordered them to appear before the next Quarterly Court of General Sessions of the Peace for Middlesex County. These men were Joseph Horner, Isaac Clarke, Benjamin Clarke, William Clarke, John Clarke, Thomas Clarke, and Robert White.[179] The next day, Jacob Hyer gave a surety of £300 each for two men ordered to appear in court for refusing the oaths. The Council also dismissed for the present Quakers Isaac Clarke, Benjamin Clarke, William Clarke, John Clarke, Thomas Clarke, and Robert White, after they gave their word to be present the following Wednesday.[180] Several influential Princetonians pledged their own money in bond for the proper conduct of their Quaker friends and neighbors.[181] Richard Stockton appeared before the Council of Safety on December 22 and took the required Oaths of Abjuration and Allegiance.

The Council authorized money to pay Captain Moore and twenty-four men of his company for guarding the Council of Safety between August 26 and September 3. It also paid Moore for removing the wife of Thomas Russell to Staten Island and for taking some prisoners to Morristown and Philadelphia. It paid Lieutenant Bergen and twelve of his men for guarding the Council of Safety and securing prisoners. Bergen was also reimbursed for providing the guards with wood, candles, and other items. The Council agreed to pay Andrew McMakin for making up cartridges and Jonathan Baldwin for taking charge of the musket balls and cartridges from McMakin. McMakin lived on the north side of the Post Road in the village and earned local praise for his service in the militia at Germantown.[182]

The Council authorized Colonel Joseph Ellis to remove cattle (except for milch cows), sheep, and hogs from any places where they might fall into enemy hands. Any owners refusing to let him remove animals were to take full responsibility for them. The Council then agreed that the prisoners taken with Richard W. Stockton in February should be treated as prisoners of war. Finally, John Holton, William Drake, Jeremiah Turner, and James Pyatt were dismissed, having taken the required Oaths of Abjuration and Allegiance.[183]

The Council of Safety agreed on December 3 to allow Edward Taylor his parole, backed by a one hundred pound bond, to stay within a mile of the college unless obtaining permission from the Council. He would be freed once the British released prisoner Thomas Canfield and allowed to return home.[184]

Loyalists

Princeton Loyalist Joseph Stockton died in March at New Brunswick while employed as a guide to the British army in the forage war. His wife was deprived of their property in 1777 and lost his 300-acre farm and 150-acre wood lot, both near Princeton. In addition to his confiscated wheat, cattle, and horses, he lost two male slaves and one female slave, leaving his wife, Sarah, and eleven children to the mercy of "an unfeeling world."[185]

In August, 104 people with Loyalist sympathies, "wearied out with the oppression and persecutions of the rebels," assembled and tried to get to New York. Fifty of them captured in Hunterdon County the first night were "made to march loaded with irons, and tied together." They were taken first to Trenton, then Burlington, next to Princeton, and finally to Morristown, where they were jailed. Two were executed, while others enlisted in the Continental Army to save themselves, although several then deserted, and others remained in jail.[186]

In August, the Legislature sitting in Princeton passed a law for confiscating and selling the estates of Loyalists who had acted openly in support of the enemy. They would each have the opportunity to show repentance by a certain date, but when that time expired, their property would be sold.[187]

Princeton Loyalist Richard Cochran left America in November and went to England. His health suffered from the hardships he had endured with the army, and he could be of no further service. Cochran went to London in January 1778, although without means of support. Losing his land forced his wife, daughter, and two sons to go to New York. His wife and daughter were never allowed to return to New Jersey. His two sons initially remained in New York, because he had no means to support them, but they were eventually able to join their father at Glasgow.[188]

At the end of 1777, the people of Princeton could take some comfort that the British had, for the most part, exited their state. However, they now had armies in both New York and Philadelphia, and the battles of Brandywine, Germantown, and Red Bank were still fresh memories. The events of late 1776 and 1777 had also allowed people on both sides of the struggle to inflict damage on their opponents. Both sides employed plundering to attack their opponents, and families became split in their loyalties. Robert Lawrence told the story of a loyalist farmer living near Princeton whose brother was a schoolmaster and left his school to join the New Jersey Volunteers. He convinced his farmer brother to join with the British also, but his wife was a committed Whig and remained at home, where some overzealous Whigs abused her and plundered the house because of her husband's choice. Her father was also a Whig, so he was plundered by the British and left with too few bedclothes to keep him warm at night. He got cold, became sick, and died. The loyalist farmer was at Princeton during the occupation, and the rebels took him prisoner near New Brunswick after the battle on January 3.[189]

The destruction of property by both sides was universal. Robert Lawrence believed that "if it provokes and grieves us to be plundered by the British and Hessian soldiers, our professed enemies, then how much more must it be so to the sufferers that are plundered by their pretended friends." To Lawrence, those "blind zealots (a zeal without knowledge) that plundered the woman did not consider that they were committing that very crime of oppression that the other Whigs have drawn their swords against, and by that have transformed themselves into Torys and did not know it." This was true for Lawrence because "the word Tory as it now is understood among us signifies oppression or at least an accessory to oppression: and when any person is oppressed the accessory in aiding or assisting is as guilty as he that does it, and therefore these plunderers may properly be called Torys." The situation had become so disheartening to Lawrence that he could only despairingly conclude, "What a melancholy sight it is to see our own people guilty of the crime that we are opposing with the hazard of some of our lives."[190] The war for independence was indeed also a civil war.

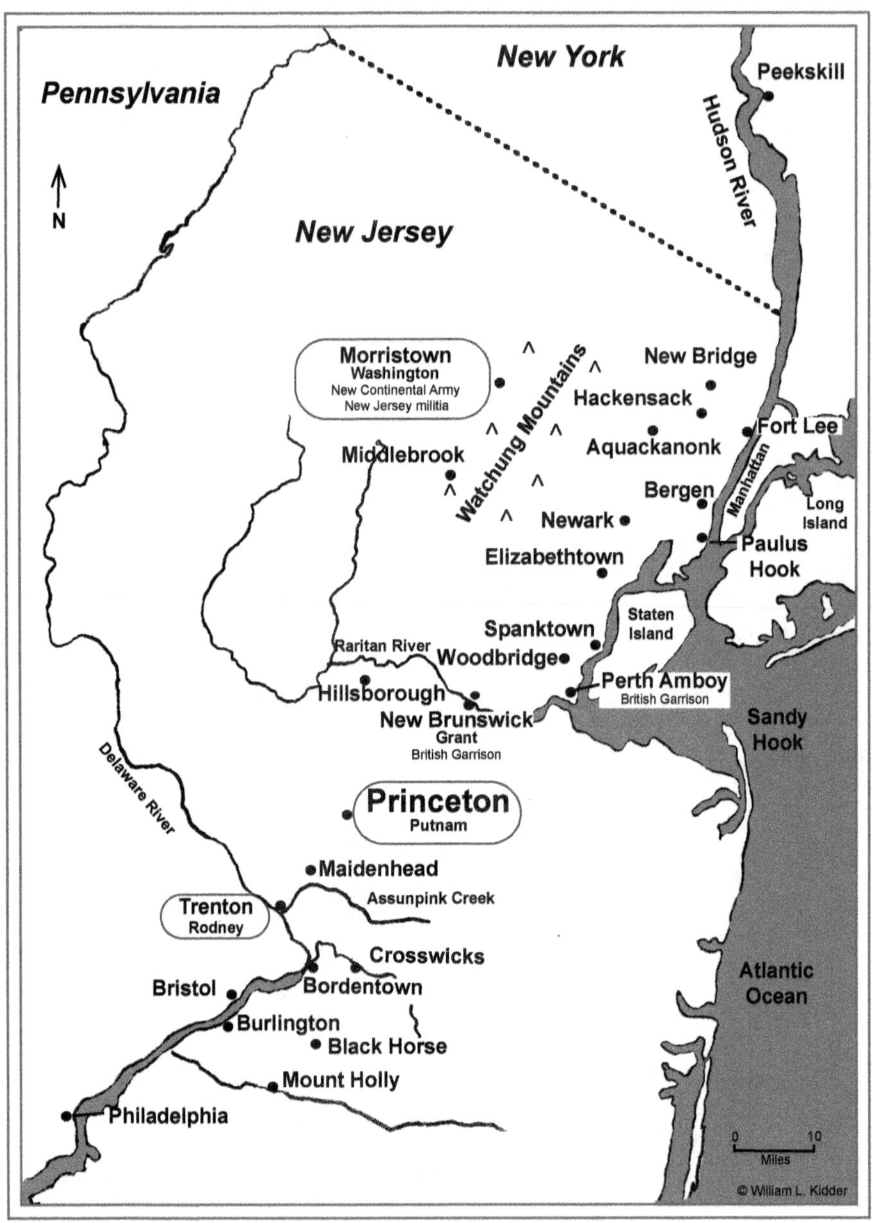

Map 20: New Jersey - 1777

Chapter 7

1778

The victory at Saratoga in October 1777—after the crucial victories at Trenton and Princeton, and the establishment of an alliance with France in February 1778—had raised hope that the war could be won and independence achieved. However, the war continued with no clear end in sight, and the year began with most of Washington's troops in winter quarters at Valley Forge and British forces occupying both New York City and Philadelphia. This put the people of New Jersey in constant fear of British foraging raids and other incursions. Another worry was that the British troops in Philadelphia would return to New York by marching through New Jersey. The first fear led to the frequent call out of Princeton militiamen to protect other parts of the state against British raids. The second fear was realized in June and resulted in the Battle of Monmouth on June 28 that affected Princeton and its residents in several ways.

The lingering war complicated farmers' decisions on just how much of each crop to plant. Should they plant just enough for their family, or should they go beyond that in hopes the surplus could be sold? There was a ready market for food and forage in the Continental Army, but actually receiving payment for it was not always realized. People had learned that in wartime, with at least one army almost always in the neighborhood, maintaining ownership of farm produce and other possessions could be problematic. Even soldiers from friendly armies and militias might simply take items they needed that had not been adequately supplied to them by the State Legislature or the Continental Congress. The military supply system needed to be significantly improved, and Princeton people became part of it, if even in a small way.

The Revolution and the Battle of Monmouth

The Assembly began a session at Princeton on April 6, and at about that time, people heard speculative rumors of a change in British government policy.[1] Loyalists who had relocated to England reported that the government was prepared to offer the colonies peace terms that should be acceptable. Mostly they would restore things to the way they had been in 1763. People considering themselves to be "good whigs" began to fear that Congress would accept this offer. Benjamin Rush heard the rumor in Princeton and declared, "I hope ancient habits of subordination will not make us forget that we are an independent power. Suppose you treat the bill as King George treated our petition to restore us to 1763. Throw it under the table."[2] The perceived offer was too little too late for solid Whigs.

Meanwhile, there was growing concern about the British forces occupying Philadelphia. Elias Boudinot took advantage of a military courier sent to Elizabethtown and wrote to his wife, Hannah, who was visiting her Stockton relatives in Princeton on June 13 from Valley Forge. He confessed, "We are still in expectation of the enemy leaving the City every moment," but reassured her that "I am still persuaded you will not be troubled with them in the Jerseys altho' there are different opinions."[3]

At about the same time, William Livingston at Princeton received two New York Loyalists, Major Moncrief and Theophilus Bache, along with four slaves. They had been taken in a raid on Long Island led by a volunteer William Marriner and Lieutenant John Schenck of the Monmouth County militia with about a dozen militiamen. In the American newspaper account of this incident, the Americans behaved "with the greatest bravery and prudence." In a New York Loyalist account, "At Mr. Bache's they behaved in their usual savage stile, they gave Mrs. Bache several blows on her intreating them not to use her husband ill, wounded one of the female servants with their bayonets, plundered the house of what plate they could find, and dragged away Mr. Bache without giving him time to put on his cloaths." Nathaniel Scudder reported on this incident to Elias Boudinot and derisively noted that Major Moncrief and Mr. Bache were at Livingston's and "really look silly enough."[4]

The issues of depreciated currency and price controls made life difficult for everyone. Jonathan Baldwin found himself in trouble in June for selling sugar without a certificate and for a higher price than the regulated one. On June 19, the Council of Safety fined him £6 and ordered him to forfeit the £88.13.6 he made selling the sugar. He had to pay the Council treasurer, his friend William Churchill Houston. William Sloan also paid a fine of £6 for purchasing the sugar at higher than the regulated price.[5] On June 20, the Legislature passed an act to prohibit the exportation of provisions including wheat, flour, rye, Indian corn, rice, bread, beef, pork, bacon, livestock, and other provisions until November 15. Any of these provisions found being exported on ships were subject to confiscation, with the profits divided between the state, the custom-house, and any informers.[6] William Scudder was elected to a committee of the Princeton Association to prevent trade and intercourse with the enemy.[7]

Elias Boudinot was still at Valley Forge on June 20, and "in the coffee house amidst the confused noise of multitudes of joyous fellows," when an opportunity to send another letter presented itself. He quickly wrote to Hannah, "I have time only to acquaint you that the enemy are gone quite off—I suppose they quarter this night in Mount Holly—From the best intelligence, their left column or flying Army will pass through Princeton—I wish you to go home [to Baskinridge] without delay." He tried to reassure her, saying, "Genl Robinson has promised me to direct his aid to quarter at Mr. Stocktons & Mrs. Noels to protect &c."[8] Two days later Boudinot wrote again that "the enemy are bound thro' Princeton & Brunswick I believe—I take it for granted that our Army will pass thro' Baskinridge—if so pray get some gentleman of our acquaintance to lodge in the house—I wish Elisha [his brother] could be with you."[9] People in Princeton once again expected British soldiers to be coming through and disrupting their town.

About a week before the end of June, Joseph Plumb Martin, of Colonel John Chandler's 8th Connecticut Regiment, passed through Princeton. He was part of a detachment of one thousand light infantry troops sent out to intercept the enemy's route and maintain close enough contact to pick up any deserters or stragglers. Martin recalled, "Our detachment marched in the afternoon and toward night we passed through Princeton; some of the patriotic inhabitants of the town had brought out to the end of the street we passed through some casks of ready-made toddy[.] It was dealt out to the men as they passed by, which caused the detachment to move slowly at this place." As he passed very slowly through the village, Martin noticed that "the young ladies of the town, and perhaps of the vicinity, had collected and were sitting in the stoops and at the windows to see the noble exhibition of a thousand half-starved and three-quarters naked soldiers pass in review before them." Martin, "chanced to be on the wing of a platoon next to the houses, as they were chiefly on one side of the street, and had a good chance to notice the ladies, and I declare that I never before nor since saw more beauty, considering the numbers, than I saw at that time; they were all beautiful." After passing through Princeton, Martin's detachment "encamped on the open fields for the night, the canopy of heaven for our tent. Early next morning we marched again and came up with the rear of the British army."[10]

On the morning of June 27, General Washington marched his army, both Continentals and militia, to Monmouth Courthouse. Captain James Moore had orders to remain with his militia company at Princeton as a guard for the supply magazines and to receive and take charge of all prisoners that might be sent there.[11] Other militiamen from the Princeton area no doubt participated in the Battle of Monmouth on June 28 as part of the Somerset or Middlesex County militias. Less than a month after the battle, Jacob Hyer placed a notice in the paper that a "pistol, brass mounted, the barrel about six inches long, marked on the lock GABBITAS," had been lost on the morning of the battle. He offered a reward for its return to him.[12]

The Militia

Militia units continued to experience changes in leadership. In January or February, Colonel Jacob Hyer and Lieutenant Colonel William Scudder informed Governor Livingston and the Council of Safety sitting in Princeton that their regiment, the 3rd Middlesex, presently had neither a first nor second major. They asked for someone to be appointed to those positions and recommended Captain Robert Nixon for first major and Adjutant Thomas Egberts for second major. These appointments were made.[13] Later in the year, at a meeting at Jacob Bergen's tavern on October 2, the Joint Meeting of the Legislature received Jacob Hyer's request for his resignation as colonel of the 2nd Middlesex County militia regiment and accepted it.[14] He was another man simply trying to do too much.

Militia units out on guard duty or to prevent trading with the enemy while the British occupied both New York and Philadelphia took many prisoners that needed to be guarded. The Council of Safety agreed on April 4 that prisoners currently under guard at Trenton should be brought to Princeton by Captain Quigly.[15] On April 11, Lieutenant Joseph Schenck, of Colonel Jacob Hyer's Middlesex regiment, with six privates, took prisoners from Princeton to Morristown and spent four days out on that duty.[16] Between May 24 and June 4, men from Captain James Moore's Company turned out to guard Princeton and the prisoners held at headquarters there.[17]

In June, the Council of Safety agreed to reimburse Abraham Hyer for money he spent supporting a five-man guard at Princeton.[18] At about the same time, Colonel Jacob Hyer decided that he could not give proper attention to his duty in the militia because the frequent call-outs interfered with his business and his obligations in the Quartermaster Department. He spoke with friends and decided he must resign his commission as a colonel in the militia. But, with things heating up due to the anticipated departure of the British from Philadelphia, he did not resign just yet.[19]

Between June 19 and July 3, members of Captain Moore's Company served as guards at Princeton and also accompanied prisoners to Morristown and Philadelphia. The Council of Safety ordered Captain Moore on June 20 to send three prisoners to Morristown if he thought there was any danger of them being rescued by the British forces expected to march through the State.[20] After the Battle of Monmouth on June 28, Captain Moore conducted the prisoners he received to jail in Philadelphia and then was on militia duty almost all of the rest of the year, frequently called out to perform duty guarding the lines between New York and New Jersey.[21] The Council of Safety met at Princeton on July 1 and ordered Captain Moore to make a list of the names and regiments of his British prisoners and furnish twenty men with an officer to take those prisoners to Philadelphia.[22] Captain Moore's militia company served again from September 25 to October 7.[23]

During the latter part of the year, Princeton militiamen continued to act as guards for various prisoners brought to Princeton. Sometimes those prisoners were put on parole and mixed with the regular population. A British galley had wrecked near Shrewsbury in a recent gale, and its thirty crewmen became prisoners on parole in Princeton in August.[24] On December 14, Princeton lodged about sixty prisoners, seamen from an English ship that became stranded on the New Jersey coast on a voyage from Halifax to New York. Since they had surrendered themselves to New Jersey inhabitants not then on militia duty or in any away in the pay of the United States, Governor Livingston considered them to be prisoners of New Jersey and asked Washington for his thoughts on that.[25]

Some militiamen served individual tours in addition to company tours. On July 3, the Council agreed to pay William Seaman for service as a light horseman messenger for the Governor and Council of Safety between May 11 and June 21, and John Vandike from June 5 to July 3, and Jacob Vandyke for June 23 to July 3.[26]

When a man changed his residence, even temporarily, to another county, he might get caught up in that county's militia. John Hulfish temporarily relocated to Maidenhead to do some work as a journeyman weaver. He was a member of Captain Moore's company and had been an apprentice weaver to James Finley of Princeton. While at Maidenhead, he was called out in Captain Phil Phillips's company of the Hunterdon County militia. That company served more than a month guarding prisoners at Morristown.[27]

The Military Hospital

The military hospital continued to see heavy use this year, and especially after the Battle of Monmouth in June. By early January, the Hessian prisoners at the Princeton hospital had been sent to Easton, Pennsylvania.[28] Benjamin Rush wrote to George Washington from Princeton on February 25, reporting on the state of the hospitals and his resignation from the hospital service. He said the departure was not due to his well-known conflict with Dr. William Shippen, although he remained a significant critic of Shippen. Part of his report included that, over the past four months, between eighty and ninety men had died at Princeton, and sixty had died in December and January. He noted that the overall death rate in the military hospitals was chiefly from "putrid fevers caught in the hospitals."[29] About a week later, on March 9, Rush noted to Congressional delegate Daniel Roberdeau that Princeton's hospital mortality rate between November 1 and March 1 was above one hundred. He also explained to Roberdeau why he was resigning. Rush had suggested changes to the Hospital Department, and Congress had resolved on February 6 to make changes that even went beyond the suggestions he offered. However, before that action, Witherspoon had told Rush that Congress was only going to make "very trifling alterations," one of the top officials must be relieved, and it would be him. However, after resigning, Rush learned that things were better than he had been told.[30]

The Princeton military hospital continued to receive items donated by civic groups. A March 18 newspaper notice publicized two such gifts. One from the congregation of Rev. Jacob Hardenbergh at Raritan consisted of 180 pairs of stockings, 60 good shirts, 43 shirts partly worn, 20 pairs of linen trousers, 5 linen breeches, 2 linen jackets, 111 shirts, 50 woolen jackets, 25 woolen pairs of breeches, 17 coats, 4 blankets, and 5 pairs of shoes, besides a quantity of old linen and woolen cloth. Another donation from Rev. Jeremiah Chapman's congregation in Newark Mountains (today's Orange) brought in 10 blankets, 19 sheets, 45 shirts, 9 coats, 40 vests, 27 pairs breeches, 105 pairs of stockings, 2 pairs of shoes, 3 surtouts, 3 watch coats, 15 pairs of trousers, 94 yards of new linen, 5 yards of linsey, 1/4 yard cloth, 4 pillowcases, 1 coverlet, 1 table cloth, and a quantity of old linen. Potential donors learned that "a proper assortment of all kinds of clothing will be kept in the hospital for the entertainment and refreshment of the sick and wounded soldiers in general of the Continental Army, who shall be sent to this hospital, and the residue will be distributed to them who are fit for service, paying a particular attention to the regiments of this state, whether in hospital or camp."[31]

The Princeton hospital remained open during the winter and early spring of 1778, even though many others were being consolidated or closed. It was one of only two located east of Philadelphia that stayed open. As of April 8, the Princeton hospital had just 53 patients. From January 14 to April 8, 52 patients had died at or deserted from the hospital and 135 returned to duty.[32]

After the Battle of Monmouth in late June, the army carried along with it many of its wounded in jarring wagons until the end of July, before sending wounded men to hospitals at Trenton and Princeton.[33] Joseph Scudder, a Princeton student who had departed the college in November 1776 and was now back hoping to return to his studies, found Nassau Hall in use as a hospital. Scudder frequently visited the hospital and boarded with Aaron Mattison, the coffin maker for the hospital. Scudder recalled "seeing numbers of them piled up in the college entry."

Scudder left Princeton in the summer of 1778, a short time before the Battle of Monmouth and returned again in September 1778, a few days before commencement. He learned that many of the wounded brought to Princeton after Monmouth "did not get their wounds dressed in something like two weeks, owing to the difficulty in getting them to the hospital, and it was thought by many that some of them died in consequence of their wounds being neglected." He described the hospital at this time as "large and convenient," and that "a great many soldiers were brought there from Pennsylvania and other places." On one occasion, he saw Dr. McKnight and also Dr. Bloomfield performing amputations on two wounded men.[34]

The Princeton army hospital appears only sporadically in the records between mid-1778 and the end of 1781. It seems to have been open in the summer of 1778, when a typhus epidemic was raging.[35] Although the hospital occupied Nassau Hall, commencement services occurred in the college prayer hall. Scudder recalled that a large portion of the audience was convalescent soldiers, to whom Scudder and his fellow graduates delivered their commencement speeches.[36]

James English turned out with the militia for a month in 1778 when the British marched across the State.[37] His stepfather's house was only a couple of miles from the Monmouth battlefield, and various officers dined there before the battle. Dr. McKnight, who served with the army at Monmouth, came to the house immediately after the battle and stayed with his servant for two weeks or so. McKnight often visited the English home and called Mrs. English "mother." Pennsylvania Colonel Ramsey, who had been slightly wounded, stayed with them for a week.

At the time of the battle, English served in Colonel John Neilson's militia regiment. Shortly after the battle, McKnight was staying at the Englishes' house and sent James off to Princeton to continue serving under him as a surgeon's mate at the hospital, believing this service would help prepare James for a medical career. While working at the Princeton hospital, James occasionally visited his family near Englishtown, which was named for his family, who were early settlers. His mother frequently washed his clothes and sent them to Princeton. Sometime in the fall, James became sick, and his sister Margaret came to Princeton for about two weeks to nurse and attend him.

When partially recovered, his stepfather sent to Princeton for him, and he was brought home in a bed. Captain Thomas Arnold of the 1st Rhode Island Regiment had been wounded at Monmouth and his leg amputated. He had been staying at the English house before being removed to the Princeton hospital. James came home in the same wagon that brought Arnold to Princeton. Arnold had been at their home for two or three months, attended by an Englishtown physician. After his release from duty at the hospital, James began his medical practice in the Englishtown neighborhood, residing at his family home. His sister Ann later said, "She was young at the time and the transactions of that period made a deep impression upon her mind."[38]

To keep a local eye on the use of Nassau Hall as a hospital, the Council of Safety met at Princeton on October 2 and ordered that Dr. Moses Bloomfield attend the following morning at 8:00 a.m. He was to bring a list of the physicians, surgeons, and surgeon's mates attending at Princeton and the number of sick in the hospital.[39]

The Supply Departments

Not only was the hospital department seeing changes, but also the supply departments. On February 2, William Churchill Houston listed his complaints about abuses in the various supply departments at Princeton. He commented that, if court judges or the Council of Safety had only had the power to stop these abuses, "they would have saved at this place within three months past three thousand dollars within my knowledge and probably double or thrice that sum." He called for immediate action to be taken.[40] Basically, the departments were seen as overly expensive while also extremely ineffective in supplying the soldiers with what they needed to be effective. One problem was supplying both the Continental Army and the State militia through two different systems.

The Continental supply departments had not been able to maintain the soldiers and supply them with clothing, weapons, and ammunition. A significant change took place in March, when Washington convinced General

Nathanael Greene to take over the Quartermaster Department. The reluctant Greene proved capable of making many improvements. But the system was never provided with enough money to function correctly. One result was that men who worked in the department became disillusioned when they were unable to pay for items they purchased for the army with sound currency. Because the system did not work smoothly, many officials came under fire for incompetence or seeking merely to enrich themselves. This led to a frequent turnover in personnel. People in Princeton became involved in this unsatisfactory system and suffered some of the consequences.

One problem was simply the large number of supply officials at both the Continental and State level. As Washington's aide, Tench Tilghman, wrote to him, "there is not a cross road or village of three houses but a deputy Commissary and Quartermaster is fixed there—to do nothing." People objected to the pay and rations provided all these people while also suspecting that the large numbers of personnel slowed down the work and prevented the soldiers from getting their severely needed food and equipment.[41]

Responding to this concern, Congress resolved on February 9 that State Executives could suspend any staff officer not appointed by Congress for misbehavior or neglect of duty and replace him with a temporary appointment. They could also remove any civil officers who "appear to be supernumerary"—that is, no longer needed. Livingston spent three days in late February at Princeton examining the quartermaster and commissary departments. He then wrote Washington that he believed "that by removing the supernumeraries, & regulating a few abuses the £64.10.3 which that department now costs the continent per diem to supply about 200 sick with wood & provisions, may be reduced to £21.15.2." He promised to "give Congress the clearest proofs, of the most unparalleled mismanagement."[42]

Then, on March 5, Livingston reported to Congress that he had removed several men who appeared to be supernumerary. These were Deputy Quarter Master's Clerk Abraham Hyer, Waggon Master William Hyer, Forage Master David Hamilton, Issuing Commissary for the marching troops Stephen Lawrie, and his clerk Benjamin Rankson. Livingston explained the reasons he felt each man was no longer needed and the savings that would be achieved. He also directed the Deputy Quarter Master to discharge all but six of his wagon men and likewise his woodcutters.

Regarding the hospital, he noted "Mr. Stockton, the commissary of the Hospital who lives here being able & willing to do all the business that is now done by Mr. Lowrie's clerk." In general, he noted the overall weak system and "the indolence" of employees, such as the wagoners. This was "why the hospital has been so badly supplied that some of the sick have actually perished with cold." Overall, Livingston felt "The Quartermaster has a sufficient allowance for doing all the business & he may easily do it upon setting diligently about it. At present his office is a nice sinecure." Livingston closed with estimates for the expense of procuring wood and issuing suitable provisions to two hundred soldiers each day.[43] Livingston also wrote to Henry Laurens on March 5 that, if his report to Congress were carried out, it "may save the public some millions. In that insignificant department, as affairs are now managed, there is above £19,600, per annum clearly thrown away."[44]

Aside from the supernumeraries, Livingston identified the current department employees, including Deputy Quartermaster Colonel Jacob Hyer, stable attendant Thomas Maxwell, baker John Clemond, Steward of the Hospital Hugh Montgomerie, Commissary of the Hospital Thomas Stockton, and his clerk James Hamilton, as well as a coffin maker, butcher, and tallow chandler.

On March 17, Livingston let Congress know that he was pleased it had approved the suspension of the identified supernumerary officers. However, he told Congress that removing Stephen Lowrie as Issuing Commissary for marching troops at Princeton, along with "his clerk & attendant at the scales," had been a mistake. This was because "our prisoners begin to pass & our recruits soon will." Therefore, he appointed Thomas Stockton, the Issuing Commissary to the Hospital, to fulfill that need and adjusted his and his clerk's salary accordingly. He had confidence in Stockton due to his reputation for "punctuality & integrity." The Continental Congress approved Stockton on March 26.[45] Although much of the public denunciations of supply department personnel were unfounded, those men who served often bore the brunt of public dissatisfaction, and that did not help morale already diminished by the constraints that made them feel less than successful.[46]

There was still the ever-present need for ammunition, and the Council of Safety agreed on March 17 to pay Jonathan Deare for hiring Andrew McMackin to cast musket balls and cover his expenses.[47] The Council of Safety on April 2 ordered all gun powder remaining with Colonel Sullivan to be removed to Princeton.[48] On the 20th, Livingston wrote to Nathaniel Scudder about Congress approving his removal of the supernumeraries. He declared, "From my observation on the conduct of these cormorants here, I believe Princeton will appear a mere paradise to this Augean stable of corruption, and everything that defraudeth the continent. I have not yet been able, upon account of other business, to grasp the besom of destruction and sweep them into official nonentity."[49] However, he also commented on officials resigning over inadequate compensation and other issues.

The State also continued efforts to supply the troops with clothing. The Assembly ordered that David Olden, as one of the commissioners for purchasing clothing for the New Jersey regiments, should be paid £350 to use for securing clothing.[50] On May 22, the Council of Safety, per an act of the Assembly, gave directions to Major Enos Kelsey, a commissioner for purchasing clothing for the New Jersey regiments. Because various accounts indicated that the men needed shirts more than any other item at present, Kelsey should especially obtain linen to be made into shirts. If he could not get enough, then he was to purchase flax to be made into linen. Wool of the courser sort was also to be purchased. Homespun thread was to be furnished in sufficient quantity to make up shirts for those that could not be obtained readymade.

Curiously, commissioners for purchasing clothing often also purchased lead for ammunition, and the Council directed Kelsey also to buy a ton of lead. The Assembly followed up on June 10, raising the amount to be purchased to a ton and a half and to store half of it at Morristown and the other half at Princeton under the care of Jonathan Baldwin. Governor Livingston had put Baldwin in charge of distributing ammunition throughout the State. As a member of the Princeton Council of Safety, Baldwin had been responsible for the town's "balls and cartridges." Frustrated by his failure to get the State magazines adequately supplied, Livingston asked Washington to send any spare cartridges to Baldwin for distribution. However, if the Continental stores were empty of cartridges, Washington could just send lead, if possible, because Baldwin had enough powder to make up cartridges. Livingston had persuaded the Assembly to pass a resolution to seize powder for the public use. Anticipating action against the British, he noted that "our militia appear in high spirits; & I trust they will fight if they can be equipped for the battle."[51] At this time, Jacob Bergen hired various people to make cartridges for the use of the State.

Membership on the Council of Safety varied, and on May 31, William Churchill Houston served as a member and soon became treasurer. Several days later, the Council agreed to pay Houston to cover the expenses incurred by Colonel Henry VanDike to erect warning beacons at or near his farm.[52]

The money advanced to Kelsey on April 18 for purchasing clothing had proved inadequate, and a large purchase of clothing was needed immediately. So, on June 21, the Assembly authorized Kelsey to draw a sum of not more than £6,000 for clothing. The next day, the Assembly also authorized Kelsey and David Olden, another commissioner for purchasing clothing, to contract with James Finley, a weaver of Princeton, to furnish whatever quantity of linen on which they could agree. That contract was to have the agreement of

Jonathan Deare, John Hart, Benjamin Van Cleve, William Churchill Houston, and Jacob VanDyke, or any three of them, before submitting the contract to the Legislature. Then, because of the impending British march across the State, the Legislature adjourned to meet next on September 9.[53]

So many transactions had taken place while purchasing supplies and transporting them that, on June 22, the General Assembly passed an act for collecting, adjusting, and settling the Accounts of the State. The committee appointed to carry out this act announced on August 10 that anyone entrusted with public monies by the State or anyone with unsettled vouchers from the state needed to settle their accounts. The committee was to receive all accounts before the next sitting of the legislature on September 9. The announcement was signed at Princeton by William C. Houston and James Mott, Jr. It would affect Princeton people such as Kelsey, David Olden, Jonathan Baldwin, and others who had taken public money to purchase clothing, munitions, and the like.[54]

After the Battle of Monmouth, Livingston wrote to the New Jersey Delegates to Congress from Princeton on July 3 that "the distressed condition of our brigade from want of clothing induces us to desire you will use your utmost endeavors on this occasion." He had heard that General Arnold at Philadelphia had a large quantity of cloth and linen. While expecting New Jersey to get its share, he asked that New Jersey's portion be sent to Kelsey, who had "persons now in the employ of the State, who will be forthwith set to work in making up the cloths." Livingston felt Kelsey could have the cloth made into clothing more rapidly than the Clothier General could.[55]

Having no doubt paid the fine for his illegal sugar transaction and suffering no lingering disfavor, Jonathan Baldwin, along with William Churchill Houston, received orders from the Legislature to proceed to Philadelphia to receive $30,000 from Congress to use for purchasing clothing. Baldwin also continued to be in charge of the ammunition stored in Princeton.[56] On August 19, the Council of Safety met at Morristown and ordered Kelsey at Princeton to send the 15,000 flints he had to Colonel Hathaway at Morristown.[57]

The Assembly resolved on October 8, to provide Kelsey with £6,000 to purchase clothing for the New Jersey regiments. Also, since his current wages were not adequate to cover the expenses he incurred in his duties, "The Legislature will provide for and defray such proportion of his expenses as shall appear reasonable, in consideration of the present advanced prices of the necessities of life." It also authorized Kelsey to appoint one or more people to distribute clothing to the New Jersey troops, and the Legislature would provide payment for them at their next sitting.[58] On the same date, the Council and General Assembly passed an act to supplement the law passed in 1774 for regulating roads and bridges. Primarily, it raised the fines for those who did not turn out for their tours of annual road maintenance. The depreciated currency was behind this move. The act was good for only one year.[59] The Assembly then adjourned with no date for reassembling. In late October, Kelsey placed a notice in the *New Jersey Gazette* requesting the County Commissioners to purchase clothing for the New Jersey Continental troops and bring whatever they had collected to Princeton. The Council and Assembly had empowered him to receive them.[60]

Captain Moore's company provided a small contingent of militiamen to guard the clothes gathered by Kelsey and David Olden going from Princeton to Elizabethtown between November 26 and 30.[61] However, the soldiers always needed additional clothing, and in early December the Assembly ordered, and Council concurred, that a box of linens at the Quarter Master's store in Trenton be immediately forwarded to Kelsey to make up items for the use of the New Jersey Continentals.[62] A few days later, the Council sent a message to the Assembly indicating that the clothing supply was being handled by Kelsey and the other Commissioners as well as possible without the need for a new law; they only needed more money. The Assembly authorized Kelsey to draw up to £7,000. The need for ammunition for the militia was also a never-ending concern, and the Assembly approved a purchase in Morris County for one ton of powder. Half of it was to be sent to Jonathan Baldwin at Princeton for distribution to the New Jersey regiments as directed by the Governor or Commander in Chief. The Morris County source was also ordered to forward a third of the lead now in his possession to Baldwin for distribution in a like manner.[63]

Throughout the year, David Olden, as a commissioner for purchasing clothing, made purchases from many people of Princeton, even from fellow supply purchasers and Quakers who did not want to support the war but still had sympathy for the welfare of the soldiers. In January, he purchased two blankets and a pair of hose from Jonathan Baldwin, a pair of hose from Colonel William Scudder, and some buttons from Thomas Olden. In February, David Olden purchased more buttons from Thomas Olden, paid Joseph Olden for carting, and bought three pairs of hose from Matthew Clarke. He also purchased forty-four pounds and six ounces of pewter from Elias Woodruff, no doubt for casting buttons. In March, he paid Aaron Longstreet for casting buttons, Mary Olden for breaking the flax for thirty-five yards of linen, and Robert Lawrence, Jr., for one blanket. In April, James Hewes sold him a pound of thread, Thomas Clarke eight yards of cloth, and Jonathan Baldwin a button mold. In May, he purchased two yards of fabric from Elizabeth Longstreet and paid Aaron Longstreet for casting buttons, selling him twenty-nine button molds, and for casting forty-one dozen pewter buttons. Jacob Bergen carted goods from Philadelphia to Princeton for him in July. In August, John Updike sold him thread, and Abraham Updike did some carting. Isaac Updike did some additional carting for him, and Hannah White sold him a pair of hose in November.[64]

Despite all these efforts to acquire sufficient clothing for the troops, by December 26, the New Jersey Continental Line officers seemed ready to resign en masse. In their view, the Legislature seemed to be doing nothing in response to their requests for action regarding clothing. A bill to appoint a Clothier General had not passed. There was a concern that the authority given the Clothier General was too extensive and the salary too liberal. Instead of passing the bill, it appeared that additional powers had been granted to Kelsey, but Livingston was not sure just what those were. The officers seemed willing to give it only a few days for things to be settled, or they would resign. Livingston needed the Assembly to let him know quickly.[65]

The College

Getting the college back to its regular operations had proven impossible due to the many military demands being made on Nassau Hall. The college trustees met at Princeton on April 16 and unanimously resolved to apply to the State Legislature "to confirm the charter of the corporation" and to make several alterations in its wording, including those "as the late revolution & our present circumstances may require." A significant need was to reduce the number of trustees required to constitute a quorum, because the war made travel so difficult. The revised charter would be put before the board at its next meeting. Another concern was the worry of students and teachers over conflicts with military service. The trustees agreed "to present a petition to the Council & another to the Assembly, requesting them to enact a law, to exempt the masters & students of the college, from military duty." They firmly resolved, "that an attempt shall be made to revive the college studies, so long interrupted by the war; & Dr. Witherspoon was desired to publish in the New Jersey, Lancaster, & Fish-Kill papers, that due attendance will be given to the instruction of youth in the college after the 10th of May next."[66]

The grammar school opened on April 13, but students were slow to arrive. A newspaper notice dated April 20 advised that anyone sending their children should do so without delay so the children could start together. It also informed the undergraduates that vacation ended on May 10.[67]

The annual commencement took place on September 30, beginning with a highly impressive procession covering the short distance from the President's house to Nassau Hall. Candidates for bachelor's degrees, marching two by two, led the parade, followed by candidates for master's degrees, two by two; Governor Livingston, President of Board of Trustees; Dr. Witherspoon; other members of the board and faculty; members of the Legislative Council; members of the General Assembly; clergymen; graduates; and other gentlemen present. After the prayer came five orations and then the granting of five bachelor's and seven master's degrees, including one to David Witherspoon. The ceremonies concluded with a speech by Dr. Witherspoon. The next session of the college was announced to begin on November 10, while the grammar school simply continued without a vacation.[68] Things were hardly back to normal, but Witherspoon would not miss an opportunity to promote his college.

The Community

Life in Princeton continued along mostly standard patterns, exclusive of the war. In early June, Andrew Hunter put a house and lot next door to the Sign of the College tavern up for sale. Prospective purchasers could see either him or Richard Stockton for details.[69] William M. Dermott also advertised the sale of many items at his house in Princeton. The list provides a snapshot of commonly owned possessions and the standard of living. They included household and kitchen furniture, such as chairs, tables, candlesticks, teapots, a teakettle, a coffee mill, one iron pot, a griddle, pails and tubs, a new churn, four candle molds, bedsteads, one set of curtain rods screwed together, smoothing irons, one good (little) spinning wheel, a Dutch cupboard, a cradle, a good milk cow, empty casks, and a broadax. He also had goods from his shop, including needles per hundred, trowels, one scythe, a crosscut saw, plane irons, centerbits, slates, and a pair of large, good steelyards.[70]

In late December, merchant John Denton advertised that he had for sale, in the lane opposite the college in Princeton (today's Witherspoon Street): snuff in bladders or smaller quantity, needles by the thousand, imported salt at seven pounds a bushel, writing paper, sewing silks of various colors, and sundry other articles. He also had almanacs for the year 1779, by the gross or dozen, as low in price as could be purchased at the printers, and the high Dutch almanacs by the dozen or singly.[71]

The newspapers containing these advertisements came to Princeton by post rider from Trenton, Philadelphia, or New York, where the papers were published. People could arrange with local merchants to either send out letters or receive a personal copy of a newspaper. The cost at Princeton for one year of a paper was about one dollar.[72]

Men required to serve in the militia still had their regular jobs. Daniel Manning, who served periodically in Captain Moore's militia company, placed a newspaper notice in September that he "continues to carry on the distillery at William Savage's, within four miles of Princeton, where he intends to use the utmost of his endeavors to give final satisfaction to all who please to favor him with their custom, which he flatters himself he is capable so to do, as he has already provided a number of hogsheads, in order to relieve those that are sent with the commodities that are to be distilled, and as casks at present become a scarce article. N.B. Said Manning proposes to distill at the moderate rate of one gallon of the spirit each barrel will produce when distilled."[73]

Both horses and men strayed. On November 11, Princeton merchant Thomas Moody took up two stray old bay horses and placed an ad to notify their owners to come to get them or he would sell them in two weeks.[74] Colonel Ephraim Martin of the 4th New Jersey Regiment placed a notice about the November 20 desertion of a recruit. Colonel Martin asked that he be returned to him at Princeton if apprehended.[75]

People were still feeling the effects of the British occupation that had ended with the battle on January 3, 1777. In August, Dr. Thomas Wiggins posted an offer for a reward of fifty dollars for a lost item damaged by the British during the occupation. A new copper still had been considerably bruised when the enemy was at Princeton and pulled down his still house. The still was marked sixty-one gallons, and the maker's name, B. Town, was stamped on it. Wiggins noted it might have been "carried to the back parts of Pennsylvania, as there was a number of the militia from those parts stationed at Princeton about that time" when it disappeared.[76]

Quakers continued to suffer, whether they supported the Revolution or not. The Quaker community continued to question Joseph Olden's actions in administering oaths and serving on committees during the "late commotions." They notified him of the charges against him and of his right to appeal.[77] The civil government continued to harass Quakers about loyalty oaths. On August 5, the Council of Safety agreed to dismiss William Clarke after he provided security for his appearance in court at Monmouth.[78] Reacting to Quaker religious concerns, on October 1, the Legislature passed an act allowing anyone with a religious objection to swearing an oath on a Bible to do so by raising their hand.[79]

In a letter to his wife Julia in August, Benjamin Rush discussed family concerns, especially the health of their son Jack: "I wish you would try to get me a dozen pounds of purging salts of Mr. Kelsey or Mr. Robt. Stockton."[80] Meanwhile, Rush's father-in-law, Richard Stockton, developed a cancer on his lip that spread into his throat and neck.[81] By December, he was in Philadelphia consulting doctors and wound up having the malignancy cut out there rather than at home, where it would have upset his wife Annis and the children. He reported to her on December 9 that "I did not utter a sigh, or move a muscle. I have also abundant reason to bless God for the ease and comfort I feel now—I have not the least pain, and a comfortable night, the last." He expected to return home the following week.[82] Unfortunately, the cancer was not cured and he would suffer great pain for the next few years.

People considered Loyalists faced prosecution and loss of their estates. A notice of inquisitions against Somerset residents considered disaffected persons—Joseph Stockton, Richard Cochran, Charles Roberts, John Harris, Benjamin Worth, William Drake, and John Drake—appeared in the *New Jersey Gazette* in August. These inquisitions were conducted in accordance with a law passed on April 18, 1778, at Princeton. Jacob Bergen was one of the Commissioners for Somerset County for dealing with Loyalist property.[83] At the end of the year, Bergen posted a notice that, because a judgment had been entered at the last Court of Common Pleas for Somerset County against Richard Cochran, Joseph Stockton, and Charles Roberts, anyone having a claim against their estates was to appear at Henry Harrison's inn at Rocky Hill on February 15. Likewise, anyone indebted to them were to pay as soon as possible. Anyone holding any form of property of these men were to deliver it immediately to Bergen or another commissioner, "or they must expect to be proceeded against as the law directs."[84]

Dr. Absalom Bainbridge's enslaved man Prime found himself behind enemy lines on Long Island in 1778, where Bainbridge had sought shelter with the British and signed on as surgeon with the Loyalist 3rd New Jersey Volunteers regiment. Prime escaped from him about August 20, and in the reward notice submitted by Dr. Bainbridge, he was described as twenty-three years old and five and a half feet tall, with hair "of a remarkable light colored woolly kind."[85] Prime returned to Princeton, where, as confiscated Loyalist property, he was taken into custody and became a "Slave of the State of New Jersey." Although Bainbridge's property was in Hunterdon County (he had only rented in Princeton), Somerset Commissioner Bergen took an interest in Prime. Bergen believed that selling Prime "like a beast of the stall" would contribute to the moral inconsistency of "contending for Liberty under an appeal to Heaven and at the same time selling for account of the public, the bodies and service of human beings into perpetual bondage." Although there was no legislation backing him up, Bergen advised Prime to enter military service as a way to gain his freedom. Taking this advice, Prime faithfully served the American army as a wagoner during the rest of the war, as was later attested to by William Churchill Houston, who saw him several times in that service.[86]

Princeton celebrated the anniversary of the Declaration of Independence on July 4 "with the greatest demonstrations of joy for our happy deliverance from tyranny and arbitrary power, and the glorious prospect of transmitting freedom and happiness to our lasts posterity." The American army had been revitalized as a fighting force at Valley Forge under Baron von Steuben and had fought the British at Monmouth very respectfully, even if they did not achieve complete victory. Coming on top of the crucial victories at Trenton and Princeton in 1776–77 and the Saratoga victory, things seemed to be moving in a positive direction. At 6:00 p.m., "the solemnity commenced by the discharge of thirteen rounds of cannon, being some of the brass field pieces taken from General Burgoyne." Afterward, three cheers rang from the large crowd. Then Governor Livingston and any members of the legislature in town, officers of the army and militia, and the gentlemen of the place "repaired to the Governor's quarters, where they passed the remainder of the day with great festivity and decorum, and drank" thirteen patriotic toasts. "In the evening the inhabitants testified their joy by a general illumination of the village."[87]

The year had seen the continuation of the effects of the war on Princeton and its people. As the new year approached, the people must have wondered whether success could finally be achieved. However, although the future was difficult to read and realty must have tempered their hopes, the spirit of the July 4 celebration reflected their enthusiasm to proceed with their efforts.

Chapter 8

1779

After the British army returned to New York from Philadelphia, Princeton's residents hoped they would not be revisited by British troops, although the possibility remained as a cloud over their heads. Militia duty continued to challenge men to fulfill their full-time civilian jobs while frequently absent on militia call outs. Many men found it necessary to supply a substitute, pay a fine, or simply refuse to turn out for a one-month tour. The supply department and the military hospital kept Princeton actively involved in supporting the war for independence. The college maintained its often frustrating efforts to return to normalcy, and the community continued to undergo changes in population as well as make efforts to support the war and deal with its disruptions. This year, in a very peaceful manner, Princeton would become more aware of events that had been taking place in the west, out in the Fort Pitt and Ohio regions. People involved in those events would come to town, some for meetings and some to stay and become residents.

Militia Duties

Throughout 1779, Princeton-area militiamen frequently served on the lines in eastern New Jersey. A primary job was to prevent plundering excursions of the enemy and trade with the enemy in New York. Captain James Moore and men from his company served at Elizabethtown, Newark, Pompton, Bergen, and other points along the lines. Typically, militiamen were away from home for about a month each time they were called out. That month did not include the two or three days' travel time often needed for a particular duty station, so the tour of duty could extend into an unpaid period of days of as much as a week. The Princeton men also performed more police-like activities closer to home, such as guarding military prisoners and Loyalists. In April and May, Princeton accommodated several prisoners hoping to be exchanged, and Livingston himself got involved.[1]

On February 26, Captain Moore ordered Sergeant Isaac Cool to conduct eight prisoners of war from Princeton to Elizabethtown and deliver them to Elias Boudinot, the Commissary of Prisoners for New Jersey. Then, on February 29, Boudinot ordered Captain Moore to take some captured British sailors with him back to Princeton. He expected to exchange these men for an equal number of American prisoners held on prison ships in New York.[2] Prisoners of war became a common sight in Princeton. In March, the prize master and three hands from a recaptured sloop (driven ashore in a snowstorm and carrying rum, molasses, coffee, and cocoa) came to Princeton for a while.[3]

Trying to live a normal life and also meet the militia requirement could be complicated. Princeton resident John Hulfish went to Burlington County for a while to do some journeyman work. In May, he was called out on militia duty with a local company to pursue some Loyalists and was absent from his job for about a month. Sometime afterward, he moved back to Middlesex County and in the fall served in Captain Samuel Stout's company on active duty tours in the region of Rahway and Elizabethtown.[4]

Thomas Olden continued to serve in the Brunswick Artillery Company until May or June, when he said he volunteered to serve in Major "Lighthorse Harry" Lee's cavalry. He supplied his own horse and equipment and participated in the capture of Paulus Hook. Olden served with Major Lee for four months but was never paid. His old injury became so bad that he became unfit to perform duty as a horseman, and he left the service in the fall.[5]

The first week of June, Governor Livingston notified Middlesex County Colonel John Neilson that all the ammunition available to the militia was in the hands of Colonel Hathaway at Morristown and Elias Woodruff at Princeton. He also ordered that militia classes should be relieved monthly until further orders. At this time, militiamen were not turning out in sufficient numbers, making it difficult to protect that area from British incursions and prevent people from trading with the enemy. Neilson had been in command at Elizabethtown for some time, so Livingston ordered Colonel William Scudder to relieve him for one month. He told Scudder to arrive at the post a day or two early to get information from Neilson to ensure the transition went smoothly.[6] For personal reasons, Scudder asked not to be assigned that month, but the Council felt that his "appointment to that Post cannot be dispensed with consistent with the public weal." However, they assured him that he would be relieved the following month by Colonel Frelinghuysen, with a one thousand-man regiment called the "New Levies."[7] The constant militia duty was taking a toll on everyone involved.

Continental troops continued to pass through Princeton. On May 6, a sergeant and a private from the 10th and 2nd Pennsylvania Regiments deserted at Princeton.[8] Avoiding having these troops occupy Nassau Hall was always an issue as the college continued efforts to return to full business.

The College

A notice in the *Pennsylvania Packet* reminded the college trustees to attend the board meeting at Nassau Hall beginning on April 21 at 9:00 a.m. It noted, "The business is of such importance to the institution, that it is hoped no member will be absent."[9] Although not well, Richard Stockton attended. One lingering issue was that the Princeton Presbyterian Church still had not fully paid for the land on which their church stood, so the trustees made arrangements to negotiate a settlement. They also agreed to continue paying the salaries of Witherspoon and Houston, "notwithstanding the interruption of the college exercises by the war." Rather unnecessarily, they based this on the understanding that "they are, however, to give as much attention to the instruction of such youth as may be sent to the college as their circumstances, & those of the place will admit, till the building shall be repaired, & the state of public affairs will afford opportunity to conduct the education in the college, in a more complete manner." This is precisely what Witherspoon and Houston had been doing.

Regarding Nassau Hall's restoration, the trustees "agreed, to repair the roof of the College, as soon as possible, & next to glaze the windows in the front of it; & then to repair the chambers in the second story." The trustees requested Elias Woodruff to take charge of making of those repairs. But he was only to repair the roof, unless Congress provided money to repair the damage done by its troops. Witherspoon, Richard Stockton, and Rev. Elihu Spencer continued to oversee repairs and to receive any funds provided by Congress. Witherspoon's records show payments of £300 for glass and labor on window repairs and, in the spring, £400 for nails, £675 for carpenter work, and £350 for lime for plastering. In September, Witherspoon paid £600 for boards to repair damaged flooring and in September and November, £1400 for glass, putty, and brushes, and £255 for glazing labor. Then, in December, he paid £600 for "nails and oil." All payments, of course, had to be made with depreciated currency.[10]

Securing a new treasurer to replace the deceased Jonathan Sergeant had proven difficult, partly because the trustees felt it should be someone living close to the college. So they chose William Churchill Houston for that position, but it would be in addition to his teaching. They then agreed on new wording for the college charter to be presented to the Legislature and initiated additional money-raising efforts to get Nassau Hall back in repair. This would involve travel by several people to other states to seek contributions.[11]

An April 23 newspaper notice signed by Witherspoon and Houston gave an update and answered some of the many questions they had been receiving. They noted that "last summer the college was entirely given up to us, but in so ruinous a state as to be very unfit for accommodating the scholars." Several students lived in Nassau Hall during the winter session, and recitations were also held there. They could report that "tradesmen have been at work for some time repairing the fabric; that a good part of the windows are put in; that we expect the roof will be made entirely sound in a few days; and that chambers will be fitted up sufficient, it is supposed, to receive those who may come for the summer session, which begins on the tenth of May." Students living at the college would need to obtain their meals from local families and pay for them. The grammar school had reopened in April the year before and now had nearly thirty boys. It would begin its next session on April 26.[112]

At commencement time in late September, the college trustees met again, with Governor Livingston present and with the number of students increasing. They chose Samuel Stanhope Smith of Hampden-Sydney in Virginia to be a Professor of Moral Philosophy, and he began his duties on December 12, when he arrived from Virginia. Witherspoon gave up half of his salary to Smith, vacated the president's house for Smith's use, and moved to his home at Tusculum. Due to being away from the college so much because of his work in Congress, Witherspoon also gave Smith many of his college administrative duties.[13]

At the September 28 commencement, young James Rock was one of just six graduates of the grammar school admitted as freshmen to the college. That evening "the College Hall was lighted up, and in presence of the Governor of the State, the Trustees of the College, and a numerous assembly of Gentlemen and Ladies who had come up to Commencement, the six young undergraduates gave orations."[14] James was the son of local carpenter and craftsman James Rock, who had frequently made routine repairs to Nassau Hall and its furnishings even before the British occupation. He supplied or repaired bedsteads, mended tables and, once, a large picture frame in the prayer hall, repaired damage to doors, and installed locks as needed. His house was on the main street across from the northeast corner of the college grounds.[15]

Only six young men graduated in the commencement exercises on September 29. Three local students gave orations. George Merchant gave the

Salutatory oration, Aaron Woodruff the Valedictory address on the subject of affability, and Richard Stockton, son of Richard and Annis, gave a discourse on the principles of true heroism. Even the small number of graduates signaled that the college was "beginning again to rise from its ruins, and to recover from the desolation it has suffered in the present unnatural war."[16]

The next session for the grammar school began on October 27 and for the college on November 8. Recognizing the complications caused by the war, and that education had not progressed evenly for many students, the faculty had to evaluate each student and put him into the appropriate class. To encourage students to return to campus on time, the college allowed students choose their rooms based on length of time in residence at the college rather than on class standing. Students who did not show up on time lost their opportunity to choose and took whatever remained. Despite some complaints about the reduced educational opportunities caused by the war, the grammar school had many students. The *New Jersey Gazette* reported that the significant difficulties preventing full operation of the college had been largely removed, and "the repairs of the building are in great forwardness and will go on without interruption, so that there will be comfortable accommodations for as many as probably may attend this fall." While the number of students the previous session had been only ten, no matter how many students now attended, both the President and Professor Houston were working, along with Professor Smith and a newly added tutor. Boarding remained the same price, "making allowance for the state of the currency," and French was currently being taught.[17]

Use of Nassau Hall for military purposes could not yet be totally eliminated, but Quartermaster Robert Stockton of Princeton reported that, between November 1778 and September 1780, American troops passing through town seldom used it. However, two rooms had been assigned by Dr. Witherspoon to the tailors of the New Jersey Brigade and occupied by them from October 1779 to April 1780.[18]

Supply Department Issues

Since the military activities and the assembling of the Continental Army took place before a support system had been put in place, and because it was unclear where the responsibilities of the State and Continent began and ended, the supply system fell far short of exemplary achievement. This meant that supply problems were endemic and never-ending. Men who signed on to work in a supply department with the best intentions found their work hampered continually and their reputations suffering. Men who signed on with less laudable aims could take advantage of the fragile system to benefit themselves. With the way the system developed early in the war, it became easy for everyone to find fault with those it employed. A fundamental flaw, however, was the inadequate and untimely funding that resulted in the purchase of items with a promise of future payment, complicated by the unstable currency situation.

Purchasing supplies with a government receipt and only the promise of payment led to many complaints against the supply departments and their agents. The departments had been reorganized in 1778, but many of the debts incurred by the old departments were still outstanding. Rev. James Caldwell came to Princeton on January 5 and 6 to "discharge the debts of the Quarter Master department" contracted between October 5, 1776, and March 3, 1778, when the new system began.[19] Anyone needing to settle accounts with the "late" Quartermaster General's department while it was under General Mifflin should see him. Paperwork could be left for Caldwell with Colonel Jacob Hyer at Princeton. Caldwell was making the rounds rather than just taking paperwork at his office in Springfield.[20]

As the Legislature attempted to settle the State debts, on June 12, James McCombs of Princeton was added to the Committee of Publick Accounts and authorized "to proceed as fast as may be" to examine and prepare all accounts for settlement. To settle any account, McCombs needed at least one other member of the committee to agree. Committee members received fifty-five shillings per day in addition to their pay as Assembly members.[21]

Clothing

The Legislature on April 30 authorized Enos Kelsey to draw up to £7,000 to purchase clothing for the troops of the State, and he must provide receipts for expenditures to settle accounts. Kelsey was also responsible for the proper use of money, authorized to provide officers who had been on service for at least one year with clothing to the amount of £200. Naturally, this was complicated by some officers having already received some clothing.[22]

Because New Jersey Continental troops were deployed in May on the Sullivan Campaign against the Iroquois in New York State, Kelsey's actions to provide clothing to officers and men could not be completed, so he received instructions to give individuals money instead of clothing when needed.[23] He had been authorized on May 26 to pay $40 to each non-commissioned officer and private of the three New Jersey regiments involved, and Kelsey wanted to include the ten men drafted from these regiments to serve in Washington's guard. The Legislature approved this, essentially allowing men to purchase their own clothing if they could.[24] Then, on June 11, an act repealed two previous ones on the requisition of clothing for the New Jersey Brigade and established the position of State Clothier to purchase clothing with public funds. The Joint Meeting appointed Kelsey to that post on June 12, and his duties were spelled out in a March 23 congressional resolve.[25] On June 15, Kelsey, Robert Stockton, and Joseph Olden signed for a bond of £20,000, and Kelsey promised to "faithfully and uprightly perform and discharge the duty of Purchaser of certain articles for the better subsistence of the troops of the State of New Jersey in the service of the United States of America in accordance with the act of the Legislature passed June 11."[26]

In addition to Kelsey, David Olden also purchased clothing and related items for the troops. He bought more pewter from Elias Woodruff in March, nineteen and a half pounds of pewter from Jacob Hyer in April, and two pairs of stockings from Sarah Clarke, sister of Thomas, in June.[27]

In mid-June, Kelsey once again informed the Assembly that the money authorized for purchasing clothing was insufficient. The Assembly authorized an additional £5,000 and also approved to provide Kelsey £30,000 for his use in purchasing and forwarding supplies to the troops.[28] As Kelsey got deeply involved in his work supplying the New Jersey soldiers on the Sullivan Campaign, he placed an ad in the *New Jersey Gazette* in July for "a sober regular person to go to Wyoming [Pennsylvania] to issue certain necessaries to the Jersey brigade. His business will be easy, and wages generous. None need apply without producing the best recommendation."[29]

No-doubt frustrated or exasperated, Kelsey informed the Legislature in October that he continued to have great difficulty purchasing the necessary clothing for the army and that clothing items would be much cheaper if he could buy them in Boston; however, the dangers and expenses of traveling there were beyond his present allowance as Clothier General. The Legislature agreed to pay all necessary costs incurred by him and a servant if he found it necessary to go to Boston. He was also authorized an additional £45,000 for clothing.[30] In November, he received authorization for an additional £50,000 for clothing, shortly after another £50,000,[31] and in December another £50,000.[32]

Ammunition

The Legislature noted on May 1 that the state ammunition magazines did not have sufficient supplies to furnish the militia. It authorized Princeton merchant John Denton to purchase two tons of powder along with lead, flints, and cartridge paper in proportion. He should provide half a ton of powder and lead, flints, and cartridge paper in proportion to Elias Woodruff at Princeton for the use of the Hunterdon, Somerset, Middlesex, and Monmouth county militias and other amounts to other locations for other counties. The Legislature told Woodruff to employ people to make up several sizes of cartridges and to keep them in proper boxes, labeled to identify the size of the cartridges they contained, under safe conditions. Different styles of firearms required different sizes of ammunition, so there was no one standard size. He must make returns on the ammunition every six months. It authorized Denton to draw from the Treasury any amount up to £15,000 to pay for these articles. Denton was to be paid for his time and expenses in purchasing and conveying the ammunition, and the Legislature would also pay any men who worked for him. It also directed Jonathan Baldwin to deliver the ammunition in his care to Woodruff. On May 10, it authorized Denton to purchase an additional half a ton of musket powder with lead, cartridge paper, and flints in proportion and deliver a third of it Woodruff.[33] Seven days later, it authorized Denton to take wagons to New England to procure lead because the Board of War did not have a supply in Philadelphia.[34]

In September, Denton informed the Legislature that various "small articles are necessary for the use of the artillery belonging to this State, to fit them for service, which he is not authorized to purchase by the resolutions of the Legislature, empowering him to purchase ammunition." The Legislature then directed him to purchase these items, which included primed tubes, canisters, portfires, and match rope. He was to deliver them in appropriate quantities to the State Magazines at Princeton and Morristown.[35]

As the year was coming to a close, on December 25, the Assembly ordered Woodruff to go to Mount Holly and bring all of the cartridges, lead, and other ammunition items kept there to the magazine at Princeton. The Legislature would pay his expenses to do this.[36]

Complaints

Complaints against those working in the supply departments seemed endless and significantly stressed men like Kelsey who were trying to do their jobs well despite inadequate resources provided by the Legislature. Governor Livingston even called on citizens to inspect the conduct of the Quartermaster or the employees of the Commissary General's department. A notice appeared in the *New Jersey Gazette* in September that "there has been a general complaint against some of those at Princeton." Therefore, a meeting of magistrates from the Princeton area would take place at Jacob Bergen's tavern on September 11, from 1:00 p.m. until the evening. The magistrates would "receive and record any complaints or information against any person in either department."[37] The magistrates meeting that day were Joseph Olden, Elias Woodruff, John Johnson, and Jacob Bergen. They issued subpoenas to several people they were told had complaints against the "person then acting in the Quartermaster General's department in Princeton," Robert Stockton. After examining those people under oath, the magistrates found "no cause of complaint against the person now acting as quarter-master in this place, and that the said information is false and groundless."[38]

Although redeemed, Quartermaster Robert Stockton reported a horse stolen from the continental stable at Princeton the night of October 24. The horse was branded "CA" on the near shoulder and buttock.[39] Stockton issued certificates of payment for goods and services he purchased in November and December. These included one to James McCombs on March 1 for his pay as clerk.[40]

It was not always clear when a man was discharged whether it was for misconduct or elimination of the position. Livingston wrote to Jeremiah Wadsworth on October 15 that, in line with the Continental Congress resolution of July 9, he had discharged Thomas Stockton from his post as a purchasing commissary for the hospital because he was no longer needed.[41] This could cause confusion because, as Livingston wrote to Samuel Huntington (the recently elected president of Congress), from Princeton on October 29 he had received private complaints regarding Stockton's mismanagement of his office. However, after examining the charges, he did not find "any part of his conduct inconsistent with the character of an honest man; tho' till his explanation, several facts proved against him naturally tended to furnish his accusers with sufficient grounds for suspicion." However, "as to his being a supernumerary, I had no doubt."[42]

On October 15, Livingston also mentioned that he should have discharged one of the two deputies of Robert Stockton in the Quartermaster General's department. However, Stockton assured Livingston that he needed both men until the end of the month due to the quantity of forage that still needed to be collected at Princeton. Although Livingston consented, Aaron Mollison, one of the deputies, resigned and removed the need to discharge him. Livingston was concerned by the persistent complaints about the supply departments. He believed the allegations were due to the minds of many men becoming "wholly occupied in amassing riches, & our patriotism I fear, as much depreciated as our currency." If he was re-elected to office, Livingston expected to "adopt a more effectual mode for investigating both the mismanagement & the unnecessary number employed in those departments if any such abuses do really exist."[43]

Community Changes and Events

The Stony Brook Meeting informed the Monthly Meeting that James Olden had "transgressed the rules of our discipline by being concerned in military services and neglects the attendance of our religious meeting." The Meeting appointed William and Isaac Clarke to inform him of these charges and report at the next meeting.[44] The August Monthly Meeting found that some members took care to bring up their children in plainness while others neglected it. No slaves had been imported or purchased, and those few members holding slaves were under care. However, the religious education of freed slaves had been much neglected.[45]

Probably due to the continuing concern over slaveholding, on February 10 the Clarke siblings freed their thirty-year-old enslaved woman Susannah, who had helped care for the wounded after the Battle of Princeton in January 1777. Samuel Worth and Benjamin Clarke witnessed the manumission paper. For some reason, she had been kept enslaved longer than other men and women held by Quakers in the Princeton area. Ezekiel Clarke had freed his ten-year-old mulatto boy Felix in 1777, and other slaves manumitted that year included fifty-year-old Francis by Samuel Worth in August, forty-eight-year-old Richard by Samuel Olden in April, and fifty-year-old Elizabeth by Joseph Horner in April.[46]

Enos Kelsey maintained his store in Princeton while working in the supply department and advertised in March that he had available for purchase a collection of patriotic poems on the struggle for American liberty, including Burgoyne's defeat.[47] Kelsey announced a sale to be held next to his house in April. Items included "a cow and heifer; a neat book case; large and small tables; looking glasses; knives and forks; chairs; a variety of mens wearing apparel; bedding; queen's and delft war; kitchen furniture, and sundry other articles."[48]

Jacob Bergen announced on April 17 that he had moved from the Sign of the College to the stone house almost opposite, where Mrs. Livingston formerly lived. He intended to call his new tavern The Sign of Thirteen Stars.[49]

Princeton merchant Isaac Anderson began "carrying on the chair-making business, at his shop in Princeton, where he has chairs and sulkeys; likewise desks, drawers, tables, &c. also an eight day clock, either of which he will dispose of for country produce, or continental currency, as may best suit the purchaser." He was also looking for a "good blacksmith, and likewise a body-maker."[50] He also made carriages in addition to furniture.

Princeton goldsmith Samuel Stout reported a robbery in July in which he lost "one chamber or spring clock, maker's name Edward Clark, Cornhill,

London, with a silver washed face; one pair of half worn silver shoe buckles, two pair of sleeve buttons, several broaches, &c." Colonel George Morgan patronized Stout and had him repair a clock in 1780.[51]

In August, John Johnson, Jr., reported two four-year-old cows strayed or stolen from his land near Princeton sometime in May or June: one red with some white and a white face, and the other brown with white spots. Both marked by the owner with a crop in the near ear.[52]

Colonel George Morgan Moves to Princeton

By early April, Jonathan Baldwin sold his farm behind Nassau Hall to Colonel George Morgan.[53] Morgan had been working on behalf of the Continental Congress as its agent for Indian affairs in the western district, working out of Fort Pitt. Morgan had been an advocate for dealing fairly with the Native American nations, but this put him at odds with many people, including fellow government officials, who speculated in western land sales. Morgan was not without interest in western lands and was deeply involved with the Indiana Company, but he did not want to swindle Indians. He came under increasing attacks from other officials working with the Indians who did not share his beliefs.[54]

The Delaware nation adopted Morgan and bestowed the name Tamenend on him as a testament of their appreciation for his honest and supportive efforts on their behalf, as well as their affection for him. Tamenend had been a historically significant chief, known for his peaceful and affable manner in dealing with people. The name evolved into Tammany, in which form it has found several uses. Delaware Chief Killbuck had described Morgan as "the wisest, faithfullest, and the best man I ever had anything to do with."[55]

Morgan became extremely frustrated and had tried to resign in the spring of 1778. Still hoping to leave, Morgan departed Fort Pitt and headed east, where he settled on his farm purchased from Jonathan Baldwin. Morgan arrived in Princeton at age thirty-seven and began many years as a gentleman farmer surrounded by a happy family and pursuing his curiosity about nature and raising plants and animals, demonstrating the very best that American farmers of his time could achieve. He was not a typical eighteenth-century American farmer that Europeans regarded as being behind the times.

His farmhouse, on the property that he named Prospect, faced eastward toward his farmland; it was built of stone and stood two and a half stories high, with three dormer windows. Near the house, he would establish a three-acre garden plot bordered by the barns, milk house, stables, and kitchen.[56] His "accomplished and lovely" wife, Mary Baynton, was glad to finally have him with her in the same home after a series of long separations in previous years. The Morgans had three children: John, about nine years old; Ann, seven; and Mary, five. Morgan also owned several enslaved persons and servants who were part of his household. Mary had given birth to four other children who did not survive.

Morgan also was caring for eight-year-old Tommy Hutchins, son of Thomas Hutchins, Geographer of the United States, and a lifelong friend of Morgan's.[57] Tommy had been born in September 1771 at Fort Pitt. An illegitimate child, he knew about but had not seen his father. Hutchins arranged with Morgan about 1777 to care for his son and Morgan became a surrogate father for Tommy.[58] Shortly after moving to Princeton, Morgan purchased clothing for Tommy including three pairs of stockings, two pairs of shoes, three shirts, and three pairs of trousers. Morgan began establishing relationships with local craftsmen, such as Stephen Morford, who lived on the northeast corner of today's Witherspoon Street, made or repaired several pairs of shoes, and was paid in December.[59]

At the time Morgan was settling in at Prospect, a delegation of ten Delaware chiefs was heading east to meet with Congress and Washington. Morgan offered to have them stay at his newly purchased farm, and the chiefs, accompanied by three Indian boys, arrived in May and set up their camp on the farm. Several days after their arrival, Dr. James Thacher described them as they must have appeared to the people of Princeton, but not in a way that Morgan would have approved. Thacher wrote in his journal that the chiefs were "a singular group of savages, whose appearance was beyond description ludicrous. Their horses were of the meanest kind, some of them destitute of saddles, and old lines were used for bridles. Their personal decorations were equally farcical, having their faces painted of various colors, jewels suspended from their ears and nose, their heads without covering except tufts of hair on the crown, and some of them wore dirty blankets over their shoulders waving in the wind. In short, they exhibited a novel and truly disgusting spectacle."[60] Thacher exhibited the feelings of whites toward the Indians as less than human that Morgan was attempting to overcome—without a great deal of success. The people of Princeton must have felt similarly to Dr. Thacher regarding the visiting Delawares.

One of Morgan's best Delaware friends, Chief White Eyes, who had named his son after Morgan, had died, most likely murdered, and Morgan offered to receive the deceased chief's son and several other young men at his home. He would see that they received an education in the ways of the white men, hoping to achieve greater understanding between whites and Indians, and ultimately better relations. The government agreed to pay their expenses. The three boys were eight-year-old George Morgan White Eyes, son of the deceased Chief White Eyes; sixteen-year-old John Killbuck, son of Chief Killbuck; and eighteen-year-old Thomas Killbuck, half-brother of Chief Killbuck. Morgan treated them like his own sons while they were with him.[61]

Morgan secured quarters for the three Indian boys with Princeton merchant Thomas Moody, whose home and store stood directly across the road from the college president's house. In June, Morgan had tailor Josiah Harned make, at government expense, trousers—two pairs for John, two for Thomas, and one for George—from ten and a half yards of sheeting he provided, and also a vest and breeches for the boy's tutor, local college student George Merchant, from three and a half yards of jean.[62] Merchant would graduate in a few months in the class of 1779 and become a teacher at the Nassau Hall grammar school. Morgan continued to engage him to tutor the Indian boys privately and probably Tommy Hutchins also. Young Hutchins did not enter the college as a freshman until 1785.

While the Delaware delegation camped at Prospect, Morgan talked with them and wrote down those things they wanted to communicate to Washington, so he could help interpret.[63] Washington agreed to meet with the delegation of chiefs and wrote to Morgan on May 11 that he would be able to talk with the Delaware chiefs and those with them the next day at 5:00 p.m. at his headquarters at Middlebrook. They could all come or just send a delegation, but Morgan should accompany them. Washington delivered the chiefs a message the following day.[64] Although the tone was cordial, the Indians received little encouragement from him because Congress planned to sell Indian lands to help pay off the nation's debts. But he did not want them to know that just yet, while trying to keep them from siding with the British. The Congressmen did not share Morgan's values and saw him as a hindrance to their plans.[65]

When the time came for the chiefs to depart Princeton, they offered Morgan the gift of a tract of land in their country. Morgan was grateful but told them he could not accept because he was paid a salary by the United States, for whom he had done his work with their nation, and could not accept the gift. Morgan also realized that taking the gift would only inspire other men whose motives were their own enrichment to seek similar favors. Washington became aware of death plots against the Indian delegation and provided them military protection on their journey to Philadelphia to meet with Congress and then on their return home. After the chiefs left, Morgan offered his resignation to Congress on May 28 as agent for Indian affairs in the western district, and it was accepted.[66]

Colonel George Morgan Farm - Prospect

India ink drawing, artist unknown, probably early 19th century. Colonel Morgan built the house sometime after he purchased the farm from Jonathan Baldwin. The house was replaced in 1850 by the current one designed by John Notman.

Courtesy of Princeton University Library. American Drawings and Paintings Collection (GC059); Graphic Arts Collection, Department of Special Collections.

When Morgan took up residence at Prospect, the house and farm were in bad condition. Jonathan Baldwin reported that the damage to the farm from British occupation troops included the loss of 2,000 panels of fencing, a woodshed, a plow, and harrow. He also lost 100 bushels of potatoes, 150 bushels of oats, 100 bushels of corn, 400 bushels of wheat, 22 tons of hay, and 300 pounds of flax in sheaf, along with 2 cows hamstrung and an eight-year-old mare stolen. He also lost many personal possessions, including clothing, furniture, china, iron pots, and other items. Baldwin appears to have really enjoyed cider in several forms and lost a lot of it.[67]

Morgan noted that during the British occupation, soldiers "burned & destroyed all the fences of the farm and most of the apple trees for firewood." They did leave nine large cherry trees in the oval near the house, four trees southeast of the house, a single tree in front (measuring eight feet and one inch around, one foot up from the ground), and three cherry trees in a row, with one Mulberry tree south of the house. All the cherry trees bore an abundance of fruit. Two white mulberry trees standing southeast of the house near the well—brought to the farm in saddle bags from Bethlehem, Pennsylvania, in 1762, according to the locals—measured about four feet in circumference, one foot above the ground. There were also several scattered young walnut, willow, mulberry, cherry, and ordinary apple trees.

Baldwin had become so busy with his work for the Revolution that he may have neglected the farm, which is perhaps the reason he sold it. Morgan began its restoration soon after his arrival, first making repairs to the house and rebuilding fences. He paid several men, including a mason, to dig drainage ditches in swampy land and sink a new pump. Morgan purchased from local man Thomas Fleming a four-year-old bay mare, thirteen or fourteen hands tall. For fieldwork, he bought a wheat drill and a manure machine, a pair of harrows, and a roller that all came by boat up the Delaware from Philadelphia to Trenton and then by wagon to Prospect. For tools, Morgan purchased three garden rakes, twenty-three harrow teeth, a set of gate irons, three spare gate hinges, and one small pitchfork, all from Thomas Shelton. These were just a few of the many items he purchased to improve the farm.

Morgan got busy growing wheat, oats, hay, and Indian corn that would be sent to Trenton and then down the river to Philadelphia, and also raised pigs, sheep, and cows. In addition to any slave labor, Morgan hired several local men periodically, whom he paid in wheat, buckwheat, or corn. Or in money, when available.[68]

June was a haying month, and Morgan paid local man Michael Hoy and several others to work for him mowing and making hay. The mowers sliced off the long grass stems at ground level with a scythe and then made hay by raking the grass, turning it, and letting it dry thoroughly before gathering up, loading onto wagons, and taking the hay to its storage place.[69] Also in June, Morgan paid weaver James Finley for weaving quantities of linen and jean.[70] He also put up a lot of fencing during the summer, paying for hundreds of posts and rails and the labor of digging post holes. Ditching fields also continued. In July, he paid Dr. Thomas Wiggins for medicine and attending his enslaved girl Katy, as well as his family.[71]

On November 8, Benjamin Rush wrote to Colonel Morgan that Richard Stockton was recuperating from an operation to remove a small growth on his lip and that all his doctors believed his recovery to be complete. In a postscript, he passed on the premature news that Congress had resolved to leave Philadelphia on May 1, and members were talking about "purchasing a few square miles of territory near Princetown and erecting public offices and buildings of all kinds for the accommodation upon it. A more central, healthy, and plentiful spot I believe cannot be found on the continent."[72]

Hessian Prisoners of War Working in Princeton

By mid-November, many people in Princeton were concerned about Hessian prisoners being brought to Princeton to work in various capacities. A group of inhabitants, including Jacob Bergen, signed a petition directed to Governor Livingston complaining about such men working for Witherspoon on repairs to Nassau Hall. Witherspoon also received a copy of the petition and asked Livingston if he was supposed to take any action. He assured Livingston that the men were "behaving in a very orderly manner & very useful both in the repairs of the college & to himself." Witherspoon spoke to several people about the issue and said he found only a small number who were not satisfied with the prisoners' behavior. There had been one case of a man behaving "indiscreetly" at Dr. Wiggins's house, and he had been sent away in consequence. The local people had been told the same would happen to any others who misbehaved. Witherspoon knew that several of the prisoners had no desire to return to the British and did not want to upset anyone. Should any problems arise or the inhabitants desire more action, Livingston told Bergen he would seek the advice of the Council. Even Livingston had asked his daughter Catharine, visiting Philadelphia on November 16, to obtain a Hessian prisoner in Philadelphia to be a servant for him.[73]

Livingston subsequently learned from Bergen that the inhabitants definitely wanted the prisoners removed from among them. The Privy Council, in consultation with Livingston, directed that all but ten prisoners be removed and that Witherspoon should decide which men to send away based on the behavior that the inhabitants found "obnoxious."[74]

By December 31, Witherspoon had not yet seen to the dismissal of the prisoners. Livingston wrote him that day, a little exasperated, saying, "It is some time since that I acquainted you by letter that the Privy Council directed me to request you to dismiss all the prisoners under your direction at & about Princeton." Then he softened his stance, saying, "as that letter may probably have miscarried I thought it my duty to leave this in my way [homewards]."[75]

The issue persisted into the New Year, with Witherspoon delaying the loss of the benefits provided by the prisoners. This caused Livingston to write him on January 29, 1780, that the Governor and Council had made it clear they wanted the prisoners removed, except for ten. Those ten should be selected "without any distinction between those employed in your service, or in any other manner whatever in the repair of the college." He closed by saying, "if there was any ambiguity in my letter on that head, I hope it is hereby removed."[76]

Loyalist Property Confiscations

The lack of money available to keep the army supplied with necessities created the specter of either confiscation of food for man and horse, as well as other items, or increased taxation. Seizure was problematic because so much had already been "purchased" with questionable money or certificates. Also, many farmers had given up growing surpluses to sell and planted only enough to feed their families and livestock. This was widespread in New Jersey. Rather than raise taxes, one expedient every state resorted to was the seizure and sale of Loyalist property to raise the needed funds. States had previously refused to do this but now succumbed.[77]

Newspaper advertisements noted the sale on March 15 of Richard Cochran's land one and a half miles from Princeton.[78] Another notice mentioned the sale of Joseph Stockton's property "lying on the Princeton road, about three miles distant from Princeton," sixty acres, adjoining Stony Brook and the lands of John Johnson and Robert Stockton. The thirty to forty acres of property of George Stainforth near Princeton, adjoining lands of Aaron Longstreet and others, along with three small houses and lots in Princeton belonging to Cochran, were also sold. The sales affected properties in both Somerset and Middlesex Counties, requiring different Commissioners. Jacob Bergen served as one of the Commissioners for these actions in Somerset County, and William Scudder did the same in Middlesex County.

Richard Cochran later enumerated his losses as a Loyalist. These included his farm and four houses and lots in Princeton, along with his household furniture and clothing. He lost 8 enslaved persons—4 men, 2 women, and 2 children—taken by the rebels and sold. One man, Mingo, had cost £110 and "was esteemed the most valuable Negro in New Jersey." He also lost 6 horses, including a pair of black carriage horses and a breed mare, 20 head of cattle, and some sheep and hogs, along with farming utensils and wagons. Crop losses included about 600 bushels of wheat, 200 bushels of Indian corn, about 30 tons of hay; he had a crop of winter wheat growing when he left in January 1777. Other items included about 250 cowhides and a large amount of tallow along with wine, rum, cider, beef, and pork. He also lost his library of 30 volumes. His total losses were over £10,000.[79]

In 1779, Princeton's people knew any family members or friends in the New Jersey Continental Line regiments had spent much of the campaign season in upstate New York in General John Sullivan's army, seeking to destroy Iroquois villages and their ability to carry on war on behalf of the British. By the end of the year, they were back in New Jersey in winter encampment at Morristown for one of the worst winters of the century. The weather also caused suffering in Princeton, yet there were no significant concerns over movement by the British army into New Jersey. The war went on with no end in sight, but with the action now further removed from Princeton.

Chapter 9

1780

At the end of 1779, John Witherspoon voluntarily retired from Congress as the war continued to disrupt everyone's life. He commented to a friend in Scotland early in 1780 that "I have now left Congress, not being able to support the expense of attending it, with the frequent journeys to Princeton, and being determined to give particular attention to the revival of the college." He also noted that "the members of Congress in general, not only receive no profit from their office, but I believe five out of six of them, if not more, are great losers in their private affairs." Professor Houston would serve as a Congressional delegate for 1780, although he expected to leave it himself in November. Rev. Samuel Stanhope Smith had arrived in December and took residence at the college president's house while Witherspoon "retired" to Tusculum, his "house in the country, at the distance of one mile, and in sight of Princeton."

He told his friend he had wanted to move to Tusculum for some years and now "intend to spend the remainder of my life, if possible, in otio cum dignitate. You know I was always fond of being a scientific farmer. That disposition has not lost, but gathered strength, since my being in America." However, the continuing effects of the British occupation hindered his ability to jump into farming. He noted that British soldiers had "seized and mostly destroyed my whole stock, and committed such ravages that we are not yet fully recovered from it." Speaking of the war, he wrote, "It seems to be yet uncertain whether we shall have peace soon. Greatly do I, and many others in America, desire it, and yet, were our condition ten times worse than it is, nothing short of the clear independence of this country would be accepted."[1] The war continued to involve Princeton and its people. There would be several battles in New Jersey with British forces from New York before the year ended.

Militia Call-Outs

During the spring, Thomas Olden turned out in his old company, the Brunswick Artillery, and continued performing periodic service till the close of the war in 1783. He was probably part of the crew for the alarm gun stationed at Princeton that someone disabled on May 27, by driving an iron spike into the touch hole used to fire it. The cannon barrel had to be heated to remove it. The Philadelphia papers commented that "It is hoped this villain will be discovered and meet a proper reward."[2]

The British made forays into New Jersey beginning in early June. Jonathan Baldwin received an express stating that General Greene, "with about 3,000 regular troops was to attack them today [June 7]. We have heard a great firing & long to hear the result." He could not help but add, "What a pity it is we are not always ready." Baldwin wrote to Livingston on June 8 that "this morning about one o'clock I was called upon by a waggoner who came for ammunition from the Scotch Plains who informed me that the enemy were at Springfield about 4 or 5,000 strong, but no orders came for the militia till two o'clock P.M. I was much surprised at it; Captain Moore upon his being informed thought best to fire the alarm gun which you have heard."[3]

Captain Moore's company turned out, having missed the June 7 Battle of Connecticut Farms, and was relieved on June 15, a few days before the June 23 Battle of Springfield. During the time they were out, they saw no significant action, but Stephen Morford recalled that Baron Steuben ordered the men to lie on their arms in the open fields during the night.[4]

On June 27, shortly after the Battle of Springfield, Colonel Henry VanDike ordered Captain Moore and his officers to meet at Mr. Allen's on the 29th to class the men at 10:00 a.m.[5] From that point to the close of the war, various classes from Moore's company turned out many times to guard prisoners, stores, and magazines, parole officers, and march to eastern New Jersey to prevent plundering by parties of the enemy from New York and Staten Island and trading with the enemy.[6]

Five months later, on November 28, Livingston ordered Major Thomas Egberts of the 3rd Middlesex County Regiment to "provide some suitable person at Princeton to put the alarm gun there in readiness. And to direct the person having the care of the same to fire said gun three times upon the first authentic intelligence that the enemy are actually landing in force on any part of this State." Livingston had received information that the British intended to send troops out to the Woodbridge area. The Council authorized Livingston to call out four classes from each of five militia regiments along with two companies of light horse. Residents of the Woodbridge area received orders to remove all livestock and personal possessions from the area and prepare an alarm gun to warn of the enemy landing.[7]

About the same time, on November 27, Colonel William Scudder wrote to Livingston, reminding him of a conversation they recently had in Princeton. He repeated his belief of the "unreasonableness of hiring a person on every emergence to alarm & collect our regiments at our expense which you conceived ought to be at the expense of the public." In light of that, Scudder enclosed an account of the expenses that he hoped Livingston would present to the Legislature. Scudder repeated that "I am not in a capacity to serve the public at my own expense."[8]

College Restoration

Witherspoon still wanted to get the college back to functioning in its pre-1776 manner. To promote his school, he submitted a long article to newspapers advising teachers and parents of prospective students now that things were getting somewhat back to normal. His message ranged from the physical restoration of the still-damaged Nassau Hall to his theories about how to get the most out of an education. It was partly advertising to attract new and returning students and partly just general advice on education.[9]

At commencement time, on September 26, the grammar school students gave public evidence of their proficiency in Latin and Greek, grammar, the orthography of English, and pronouncing English orations. Among the standouts was John Morgan of Princeton, the ten-year-old son of Colonel George Morgan.

The trustees met on September 27, but Richard Stockton could not attend "on account of his indisposition"—that is, his worsening cancer. The good news reported was that the Legislature had confirmed the college charter, but the bad news was that it had not agreed to reduce the quorum needed to conduct trustee business, one of the main charter revisions they had sought. It was not easy in regular times for the trustees to travel to the college, but in wartime, it was even worse. In desperate need of funds for the restoration of Nassau Hall, the trustees directed Witherspoon to prepare an account of reasonable sums to charge the State for renting the college to use as a barracks and hospital, and to "endeavor to recover the money as soon as possible."

The trustees also authorized Witherspoon to "offer to the trustees of the [Presbyterian] congregation of Princeton, a deed for the church & lot, upon their paying the money with interest due to the corporation, or their executing bonds with sufficient security for the same."[10] The college badly needed money for restoration.

Commencement exercises that afternoon included "A dialogue on the present state of the college, the prospect of its restoration, and of the revival of letters throughout America, along with the return of peace and the establishment of our independence." The afternoon opened with an oration on "the power of the people to constitute their own governments, and to alter and reform them for their own advantage." Six students received bachelor's degrees, including Ebenezer Stockton, son of Robert. Several alumni received master's degrees, while several college presidents and politicians accepted honorary doctoral degrees.[11]

By October, the student body consisted of seventeen or eighteen undergraduates, in addition to sixty to seventy grammar school students. Dr. Witherspoon and Rev. Smith were doing the teaching, while Houston took Witherspoon's place in Congress.[12]

Supply Department Problems

Several Princeton men continued to be heavily involved in procuring supplies of ammunition, clothing, and food for the militia and Continental Army. In January and February, Quartermaster Robert Stockton issued certificates for goods and services previously purchased. These certificates were for providing wood, carting provisions, carting hospital stores, carpentry work, smith work, and occasionally rent of a room. In terms of Princeton people, there were several certificates to members of the Updike family for providing wood and carting service, James Moore for carting, Thomas Stockton for house rent and carting, Aaron Longstreet for carting, Jacob Hyer for carting, Thomas Wiggins for rent of a room, David Hamilton for carting, Robert White for blacksmith work, and perhaps others.[13]

Ammunition

On March 7, Livingston advised the Assembly that Colonel Hathaway in Morristown did not want to continue to act as an ammunition custodian. Not surprisingly, Livingston noted that replacing him would be difficult because "few persons are willing to receive gun powder in large quantities into their dwelling houses." He suggested that "it may perhaps be requisite to build a particular depository for the purpose." Those men at Princeton who took charge of munitions must also have been using their private property for its storage. Furthermore, Livingston noted, the supplies of ammunition both at Princeton and Morristown "must by this time be considerably diminished; & as we shall probably be obliged to depend the ensuing campaign on our own militia for the defense of the State, it is the dictate of prudence to make seasonable provision for a suitable quantity of ammunition."[14]

To work toward that goal, on March 18, the Assembly authorized Jonathan Baldwin to immediately purchase enough supplies to have three tons of musket powder and enough cartridge paper to make it up into cartridges. He was to also purchase enough cannon powder that, when added to what was already in the magazine, there would be three-quarters of a ton with a proportional quantity of shot and flannel. He was to procure enough flints to have twenty thousand, and he was to keep two-thirds of the musket powder and half the cannon powder under his charge at Princeton and send the remainder to Morris County.

The Assembly ordered him to employ proper people to make up appropriate cartridges and to keep them in labeled containers for delivery when needed. Baldwin was to also take possession of all cartridges, lead, and other ammunition at Mount Holly and anything kept by Elias Woodruff at Princeton. The Legislature said it would pay his expenses and also authorized him to draw from the Treasury up to £40,000 for ammunition and submit accounts on his expenditures. The Assembly ordered the new person at Morristown, Abraham Kitchel, to send returns to Baldwin every three months, of the ammunition in his care and the quantity issued and to whom, and what remained in the magazine, so that Baldwin could report to the Governor and Legislature. The Assembly also directed the Auditor of Accounts to immediately call on John Denton to settle his accounts of money drawn from the treasury and his ammunition purchases.[15]

Men in the supply departments continued to risk drawing complaints as they attempted to carry out their duties with inadequate funds and other obstacles. On May 13, the Assembly heard that Jonathan Baldwin had not acted in his office to purchase ammunition for the militia. In response, the Assembly appointed Elias Woodruff of Princeton to take charge of procuring powder to be made into cartridges and take over from Baldwin. It authorized Woodruff to draw up to £40,000 and directed him to collect and take charge of all ammunition belonging to the state and make a return of it. The Assembly made void all official acts concerning Baldwin and Kitchel, authorizing them to draw money.[16]

Baldwin felt he was a victim and responded on May 25 with a petition "setting forth his losses by reason of the depreciation of the Continental Currency, and the injustice that has been done him under cover of the Tender

Laws, and praying if a law should be enacted to amend the Tender Laws, it may retrospect as far as September 1778."[17] Whether or not Baldwin was at fault, he was blamed.

On October 7, the Assembly received a report of people owed money by the State for various reasons. These included the expense of Colonel Asher Holmes in sending a two-horse team to Princeton to obtain ammunition for the use of his regiment at Freehold Courthouse in April; Joel Fithian for the use of Daniel Maskell for taking artillery ammunition from Princeton to Cumberland County for the militia in May; and Jacob Doremus for taking ammunition from Princeton for the use of Colonel Theunis Dey's Bergen County regiment in April.[18]

On November 1, the Assembly authorized Woodruff, now Keeper of the Magazine at Princeton, to deliver to Nathaniel Scudder eight thousand cartridges and one thousand flints for use by the Monmouth County militia and a detachment of the State Regiment stationed there.[19]

Clothing

Adequate clothing supplies continued to be an issue. On March 20, the Assembly authorized Enos Kelsey to draw money from the Treasurer during the recess of the Legislature up to £300,000 for clothing and other articles of subsistence for the Continental troops of the State.[20] The next day, it authorized Kelsey a sum of £2,800 per year, in addition to his salary, for acting as State Clothier and purchaser of supplies for the better subsistence of the Continental troops of the State since October 13, 1779.[21]

By May 15, officers from various New Jersey regiments were again complaining to the state legislature about Kelsey's performance. In a petition to the legislature, some of them wrote, "It is necessary to inform the House that a number of vests and breeches were produced to the Committee, which were evidently too small for the most minute person...and which the officers declared were left after providing the smallest men, and even boys with those articles; some shirts were also shewn to the Committee, which had been delivered to the men, much too small for them, by reason whereof they were greatly worn out, tho' but seldom used." The legislature wanted to investigate these claims and ordered a joint committee of the Assembly and Council to meet on Wednesday, May 24, at 10:00 a.m. at Jacob Bergen's tavern, where both the officers and Kelsey could produce evidence to support or negate the charges.[22] Several days later, on May 29, Kelsey gave the Assembly a return of the clothing and State stores issued by him as Clothier of the State since January 1.[23]

By June 19, Kelsey was replaced by Israel Morris as Clothier and Purchaser of Stores for the New Jersey troops. On June 19, Morris was authorized and required to call on Kelsey to acquire any articles of clothing and stores that he might still have had.[24] After his removal, as late as October, men appointed by Kelsey to distribute clothing to the troops and make purchases found Kelsey unable to help them settle their accounts and applied to the Assembly for relief.[25]

On October 7, the Assembly received a statement for David Olden, commissioner for purchasing clothing in Middlesex, indicating they owed him £4374.13.6.[26]

Food

The supply departments also collected food for man and horse at Princeton. On April 17, Livingston informed Azariah Dunham that supplies needed to be deposited at various locations, including 200 tons of hay and 2,000 bushels of corn at Princeton. Beef deliveries were less defined and "the proportion from time to time must of necessity be governed by the occasional requisitions of the Commissary General, which he adds must also be the case with respect to the salt & its ultimate place of deposit."[27] On July 20, Quartermaster General Nathanael Greene informed Livingston that 6,857 bushels of grain forage were to be delivered monthly at several places, including Princeton. This was in response to a requirement established by a Committee of Congress.[228]

Help From the New Jersey Ladies

In July, the women of Princeton joined a group initiated by several ladies living in Trenton as part of a statewide effort in New Jersey, "emulating the noble example of their Patriotic Sisters of Pennsylvania, and being desirous of manifesting their zeal in the glorious cause of American Liberty." They organized to promote "a subscription for the relief and encouragement of those brave men in the Continental Army, who, stimulated by example, and regardless of danger, have so repeatedly suffered, fought and bled in the cause of virtue and their oppressed country." Several women from each county were to immediately open subscriptions and correspond with each other to raise the money. This effort was led by several women in Trenton who expanded it to include the entire state. Three Princeton women became part of the group. Frances Deare and Mary Morgan represented Middlesex County and Annis Stockton Somerset County. A newspaper notice commented that their "well known patriotism leaves no room to doubt of their best exertions in the promotion of an undertaking so humane and praiseworthy, and that they will be happy in forwarding the amount of their several collections, either with or without the names of the donors, which will be immediately transmitted by Mrs. Moore Furman, treasurer, to be disposed of by the Commander in Chief, agreeable to the General Plan." Mary Dagworthy in Trenton was the group secretary, who could answer any questions and provide proper subscription papers.

As might be expected, when word of this effort circulated, all departments wanted to get hold of some of the funds raised.[29] However, Mary Dagworthy wrote to General Washington on July 17 that on behalf of the ladies she was transmitting by Colonel Thompson $15,488 to be used as Washington thought proper to benefit his soldiers. She would send additional sums as they were received. After graciously thanking the ladies, Washington asked them to hold any additional sums until things could be coordinated with the Philadelphia ladies.[30] Washington told the ladies that he preferred they would send articles of clothing, especially shirts and socks, or cloth, rather than money, which would inevitably be used frivolously and cause behavior problems. While they continued to raise money, at the end of the year, the New Jersey ladies also sent 380 pairs of stockings to New Jersey's Deputy Quartermaster General John Neilson, whose wife was also on the committee, that he should forward to Washington.[31]

The Princeton ladies, like those in Philadelphia, had no doubt been influenced by Esther Reed's broadside *The Sentiments of an American Woman,* published on June 10. Esther was Pennsylvania's First Lady, wife of Joseph Reed, and had lived most of her life in England. However, she was a firm believer in liberty, and the sentiments expressed in her broadside revealed the depth of her thinking. After lengthy comments on the Revolution and the sacrifices of the soldiers, Esther introduced the idea of women doing all they could to alleviate soldier suffering. She challenged American women: "Shall we hesitate to wear a clothing more simple; hair dressed less elegant, while at the price of this small privation, we shall deserve your benedictions. Who, amongst us, will not renounce with the highest pleasure, those vain ornaments, when she shall consider that the valiant defenders of America will be able to draw some advantage from the money which she may have laid out in these; that they will be better defended from the rigors of the seasons, that after their painful toils, they will receive some extraordinary and unexpected relief; that these presents will perhaps be valued by them at a greater price." Esther believed, everyone needed to sacrifice for the cause, much as they had done concerning tea and other boycotted items in the protests leading up to the war. Tragically, Esther died of dysentery only a few months later on September 18 at age 34.[32]

Community Developments

During the year, Colonel George and Mary Morgan became the parents of a new baby they named George. He followed two previous babies they had named George in 1776 and 1777, neither of whom lived for very long. This third George lived for 49 years. In January, Colonel Morgan continued his farm reconstruction efforts and paid Richard Scott for 15 1/2 days of masonry work, and then in February paid Stony Brook Quaker Robert White the large sum of £148.17.6 for blacksmith work. In March, he paid his state tax of £201.5.0 for his 210 acres of land, 3 horses, 7 cattle, 9 hogs, 1 slave, 1 riding chair, and 1 covered wagon on springs. He continued to pay for posts and rails, including payment to Daniel Manning for 400 broad oak and chestnut rails, 100 white oak posts, and carting them to Princeton. After the wheat harvest, neighbor John Mollison paid him for the one day's use of 5 horses for threshing wheat and later in the month for a day's use of 3 horses. Also, in August, he paid his £135 tax for raising substitutes for the 6-month service, another State militia service like the 5-month levies of 1776.[33]

Morgan combined his scientific interest in farming with the restoration work and, in April, planted 2 rows of cherry trees flanking the lane leading from Princeton to his house. On the west side, he planted 20 trees, all with their branches a little shortened. Their trunks ranged from 8 to 12 inches around or 2 1/2 to 4 inches in diameter, 1 foot from the ground. The 20 cherry trees on the east side of the lane were taller and trimmed of all their branches up to the very top so that they looked like poles. Morgan noted in his journal that they were "an experiment." He also planted a row of cherry trees ranging east to west from the east side of his house. These were planted with all their branches, but shortened, and were from 6 to 8 inches around and 1 1/2 to 3 inches in diameter.[34]

Opportunities to buy or rent properties indicated changes taking place in the community. Some people had reasons to relocate for business or personal reasons while others sought to take up residence in the town. One advertisement placed by William Scudder announced the availability for rent of Castle Howard, identified as "late the property of Lieutenant Hayman [Captain Hamar], (and some time before of Capt. Howard, deceased) near Princeton." This property was available due to the disruptions of the war and the seizure of Loyalist property. The rent for the property would be determined at a vendue, public auction, to be held on March 31 at 3:00 p.m.[35]

In mid-May, Jacob Bergen advertised that he had removed from his tavern in Princeton at the Sign of the Confederation and taken over the inn of Samuel Henry in Trenton.[36] Samuel Stout announced that he carried on the silversmith business in Princeton and employed an experienced hand in the watchmaking business—both mending and repairing.[37]

It appears that merchant Enos Kelsey was forced to resign as Clothier for the State, although not formally reprimanded, in June. Shortly afterward, on July 10, Kelsey advertised for sale the house where he lived "situated in the healthy and agreeable village of Princeton. The house is a large, neat, convenient, well finished brick building, with every conveniency of stores, stables, garden, &c. &c. to render it perfectly agreeable either for a merchant or private gentleman."[38] He was still living in Princeton in 1783 and advertising his store in 1782.

Princeton's Quakers were still conflicted about participation in the war and other disapproved actions by their members. In August, the Monthly Meeting could report that members were mostly clear of military services but not wholly, even though they made great efforts to convince members to avoid it. In November, James Olden acknowledged having participated in military actions and turning out as a soldier in the militia. After hearing him, the Meeting, after receiving a good account of him from some of his neighbors, agreed to welcome him back into membership. However, in December, he requested a certificate of removal to Philadelphia. Although many Quakers had freed their slaves, some members still owned a few. On the positive side, no members distilled spirits out of grain, made use of spirits, or kept taverns.[39]

Toward the end of January, John Witherspoon learned that Alexander McDonald, the West India man who ran afoul of the Association boycotts in 1776, was returning to the islands. Governor Livingston had assured him that he could receive a pass for leaving the State with his family and property as soon as he had put his affairs in order. However, Livingston did not believe he needed a pass to go to New York to obtain passage to the West Indies, so he denied that part of his request.[40] McDonald was apparently still in Princeton on June 29, when he advertised his "plantation" located on the road to Trenton about a quarter-mile from Princeton village for sale. He described it as having "more than 300 acres of excellent good land, 100 acres thereof is good woodland, 20 acres of meadow, and as much more may be made with very little trouble, a never failing stream of water runs through the center of the place. On the plantation is a well finished large stone dwelling house, fit for any family, likewise a large barn, and an exceeding good stable, that will hold 20 horses, with other out houses; also a large garden."[41]

McDonald was still in Princeton on February 7 when someone stole a horse from his stable in the night.[42] Theft of horses and horses straying continued to occur often. On the night of January 19, Samuel Worth had a horse stolen from its stable at Stony Brook, and on February 1, Aaron Longstreet had a grey horse come to his farm.[43] In April, an advertisement for a stolen horse gave the hospital at Princeton as one of several military hospitals it could be turned into for the reward.[44] On July 1, a gray mare belonging to James Hamilton became lost, strayed, or was stolen from a pasture between Princeton and Rocky Hill.[45] In September, James Riddle had a sorrel mare stray from Princeton and offered a $200 reward. The mare could be delivered to Captain James Moore in Princeton to collect the reward.[46]

Slavery

Runaway slaves continued to cause concerns augmented by their possible connections to the war. Colonel Morgan reported that his mulatto slave, Michael Hoy, ran away on May 20, supposedly encouraged to "carry letters or intelligence into New York." Morgan described him in detail, as near six feet tall, "strong and well made" and included that he "had on, and took with him, a variety of clothes, but, those he will most probably wear are, a suit of superfine mixt broad cloth, a new red great coat, white stockings, half boots, a black velvet stock and a beaver hat, but little worn. He appears to be 40 odd years of age, speaks good English, reads and writes a tolerable hand, and is a decent and well behaved ingenious fellow, capable of a variety of works." Hoy also took with him one of Morgan's horses, and it was thought that he accompanied a white man, so he might try to pass himself off as his servant. The same night, Rev. Samuel Stanhope Smith had a horse stolen, possibly by Hoy's white accomplice.[47] Most of the runaway enslaved people advertised from the area of Princeton were single and under thirty years old, and about 20 percent were women. Since not every runaway appeared in a newspaper advertisement, it is impossible to know just how many made an attempt and what their success rate was. At some point during the year, twenty-three-year-old Peter Stockton ran away from his owner, Robert Stockton, living on the Somerset County side of the Post Road in the Stony Brook area.[48]

In November, Princeton resident John Denton offered an eye-popping reward of $1,000 to apprehend his runaway slave Caesar. "There is good reason to believe that he has been advised to go away," wrote Denton, and "any substantial evidence who will discover the fact (if the plot be by a white person) on full conviction, shall have a reward of Six Thousand Dollars; if a black person, Five Hundred." Denton suspected that Caesar had taken British protection on Staten Island. Caesar was about twenty-five years old, and was "marked with the small-pox; had on a blue camblet coat worn out at the elbows, a pair of new buckskin breeches, straps without knee buckles, old pumps with a hole in one of the toes or a new patch, a small felt hat." As a good businessman, Denton also noted in the ad that "The subscriber has for sale, bar-iron, rock & shore salt, spelling books and almanacs by the gross or dozen as low as at Philadelphia, and sundry other kinds of merchandise."[49]

Slaves for sale also appeared infrequently in the newspapers. Again, many of these transactions remained private affairs, so it is hard to tell how often they occurred and to what degree they upset the lives of the men and women involved. For example, in November, when Rev. Samuel Stanhope Smith offered for sale a "likely negro boy, between eleven and twelve years old," one wonders if he was breaking up a family.[50]

A Visit from the Marquis de Chastellux

Major General François Jean de Beauvoir, Marquis de Chastellux, arrived in Princeton about November 27. He described the town as "situated on a sort of platform not much elevated, but which commands on all sides: it has only one street formed by the high road; there are about sixty or eighty houses, all tolerably well built, but little attention is paid them, for that is immediately attracted by an immense building, which is visible at a considerable distance." This was Nassau Hall, the entrance to which "is by a large square court surrounded with lofty palisades." When he got to the gate, he said, "I dismounted for a moment to visit this vast edifice, and was soon joined by Dr. Witherspoon, President of the university. He is a man of at least sixty, is a member of Congress, and much respected in this country."

Witherspoon addressed him in French, but Chastellux "perceived that he had acquired his knowledge of that language, from reading, rather than conversation." However, Chastellux did not embarrass him, and their conversation continued in French. Chastellux felt "this is an attention which costs little, and is too much neglected in a foreign country." Commenting on Nassau Hall, he noted, "This useful establishment has fallen into decay since the war; there were only forty students when I saw it. A handsome collection of books had been made; the greatest part of which has been embezzled."

As a military man, Chastellux admired Washington and wrote, "I confess also that I was rather anxious to examine the traces of General Washington, in a country where every object reminded me of his successes. I passed rapidly therefore from Parnassus to the field of Mars, and from the hands of President Witherspoon into those of Colonel Moyland. They were both equally upon their own ground; so that while one was pulling me by the right arm, telling me, here is the philosophy class; the other was plucking me by the left, to shew me where one hundred and eighty English laid down their arms."[51]

Fourth of July Celebration

Celebrating the anniversary of the Declaration of Independence had become a highly anticipated event each year. This year, the president and faculty of the college, with the students, the officers and soldiers of the army and militia, and other inhabitants, assembled at 6:00 p.m., when thirteen guns fired salutes. Before each gun firing, a statement was read by militia Major Egberts and the whole assembly gave three cheers. The remarks were like toasts, such as "The United States of America—May they prosper and flourish to the latest ages." Afterward, everyone adjourned to Nassau Hall, where Witherspoon delivered a discourse that covered three main points: the importance and necessity of Independence at the time it was declared, the events of Providence in the course of the contest, and the duty of all ranks in the present crisis. After sunset, the town and Nassau Hall were illuminated, "and the whole was concluded with the greatest good order."[52]

By year's end, things did not look so encouraging. The Continental Army continued to have problems and, quite unexpectedly, a large number of angry American soldiers would very soon occupy Princeton.

Chapter 10

1781

Morale in America had reached another low point as 1781 began to unfold. The continual dragging on of the inconclusive war had created or exacerbated many problems, including the depreciation of currency and Loyalists' efforts to disrupt the revolution. The thirteen new states had not even come together to ratify the Articles of Confederation. Maryland still held out. This constitution could not take effect until March 1, when Maryland finally ratified it. There was still a great division between those favoring a strong central government and those advocating for strong state governments. No one was happy about the condition of the army and the suffering of the soldiers. Events seemed so inconclusive that, for many Americans who had persisted and suffered in the fight, it appeared that an inevitable outcome would be some form of reconciliation without independence. Many people began to accept, or revert, to this idea of accommodation, while others feared that those favoring reconciliation would regain control of Congress as they had before mid-1776. This year of 1781 looked to be decisive.[1] It would begin with a Continental Army mutiny that once again brought the fear of military occupation to Princeton, but would then end celebrating a great victory at Yorktown after American and French troops had marched south through the town.

January 1 (Monday)—Pennsylvania Line Mutiny

As the residents of Princeton awoke on the morning of January 1, they no doubt were very aware that soldiers in the Continental Army had many grievances. However, they were not aware that ugly events had taken place overnight near Morristown that would soon bring over one thousand angry Continentals to their town, along with a great deal of stress and fear. It had been four years since the British occupation of their village and its surroundings in December 1776 and the first days of 1777, and the town had not yet fully recovered. New Year's Day was the date designated to implement a new arrangement of the Continental Army regiments based on their changing size and employment. Throughout the army, these structural and personnel changes came on top of continuing deficiencies in clothing, food, and pay, along with confusion over the lengths of individual enlistments. When soldiers of the Pennsylvania Line at Morristown were told their enlistments must continue because they had signed on for the duration of the war—a very questionable assumption in many cases—about fifteen hundred of them mutinied on January 1 and began marching off in groups commanded by sergeants in the direction of Philadelphia, by way of Princeton.[2]

They were not a violent mob, but rather soldiers loyal to the cause of independence, marching in a disciplined manner, led only by sergeants because they no longer trusted most of their commissioned officers. At Philadelphia, they planned to confront the Continental Congress and the Pennsylvania legislature to redress the grievances of the soldiers with their officers and fulfill the contracts made with their recruits regarding the term of service, pay, food, and clothing. As they marched toward Princeton, the mutineers presented a well-disciplined military force complete with camp followers, just like any eighteenth-century army, and driving nearly one hundred cattle. The only elements missing were commissioned officers.[3]

The exact nature of the revolt was not clear to everyone, and some top American officers feared that British agents had instigated the mutiny and the men would desert and join a British force attacking New Jersey from Staten Island. Upon hearing of the revolt, Massachusetts Congressman James Lovell wrote to John Adams, then serving as an envoy in Europe, despondently noting that the Confederation was now not only bankrupt but it had a mutinous army.[4] Could the Revolution survive?

While their officers remained behind at Morristown, the mutineers allowed only three respected officers—Major General Anthony Wayne, Colonel Richard Butler of the 9th Pennsylvania, and Colonel Walter Stewart of the 2nd Pennsylvania—to accompany them but did not allow them to command.[5] These three officers, regardless of personal risk, remained with the mutineers for about two weeks, helping to mediate the various efforts made to settle their grievances with their officers and the Pennsylvania State and Congressional authorities.[6]

January 3 (Wednesday)

Small groups of soldiers continued to collect and march off through January 3 to join those already on the march. At about 8:00 p.m., the eighty or so commissioned officers left behind received orders from General Wayne to obtain horses, arm themselves, and set out for Rocky Hill just outside Princeton. At about 9:00 p.m., the officers moved out, heading for Bound Brook, led by Colonel Robert Craig of the 3rd Pennsylvania Regiment. Major James Hamilton of the 2nd Pennsylvania and Major Thomas Moore of the 9th Pennsylvania detached and headed toward Princeton to inform Wayne of the approach of these officers and "the position they meant to take."[7]

Congress received word of the revolt and, at 6:00 p.m., appointed a committee of three delegates—John Sullivan, John Mathews, and John Witherspoon—to meet with the "supreme executive" of Pennsylvania, President of the Executive Council Joseph Reed.[8] The mutineers left Middlebrook and headed toward Princeton. The New Jersey Privy Council anticipated a British incursion to take advantage of the mutiny and ordered General Philemon Dickinson to call out and command the militia companies of Hunterdon and part of Burlington counties. The Burlington companies would take up station at Crosswicks and the Hunterdon companies headquartered at the Baptist Meetinghouse in northeast Hopewell Township until they received further orders.[9]

General Nathaniel Heard ordered New Jersey militia companies to deploy between the mutineers and any British forces that might come from Staten Island. Several 1st Hunterdon composite companies, consisting of classes from several companies, turned out under Colonel Joseph Phillips and served in the vicinity of Princeton, to help quell any disturbances the mutineers might cause and to prevent individuals or groups from heading east to join with the British.[10] Captain Phil Phillips's Company of Maidenhead was stationed for a month in the neighborhood of Princeton, where Hopewell privates Oliver and Israel Hunt "were both billeted together at the house of James Moore in Princeton." Members of Captain Ralph Guild's Company marched from Hopewell to Somerset Courthouse and then to Princeton. During their one-month tour, they spent time at Princeton to "prevent stragglers from going to New York."[11]

At Princeton, Rev. Samuel Stanhope Smith confessed in a letter to Governor Livingston that same day that, although the soldiers were said to be behaving very well, he was worried for the people of Trenton. In a replay of December 1776, an army marching across the State was preparing to cross the Delaware at Trenton and descend on Philadelphia. Smith had heard that, just like in 1776, some Continental officers had been ordered to Trenton "to secure the boats upon the Delaware, in order to prevent these troops from passing." Smith feared that, if true, this action would enrage the mutineers and put the people living along the river near Trenton in danger of reprisals. Smith advised that authorities should instead help the mutineers to get across the river to Pennsylvania. Placing the Delaware River between the mutineers and the British would better secure the negotiations from enemy interference and alleviate fears that the mutineers would join with the British if they did not get their way.

Smith emphasized that Princeton residents feared being once again plundered of their provisions and firewood and asked permission to supply the mutineers with public stores in Princeton. Smith also argued that the mutineers were Pennsylvania soldiers, although many were foreign-born, so it was proper that "their own state ought to be exposed to the inconveniences which they may occasion rather than the Jerseys." Smith also feared that, although the people living in and near Princeton wanted to accommodate the material needs of the mutineers, the mutineers would still plunder them for firewood and provisions. Smith requested that, if the mutineers impressed private property, the State would replace it or reimburse the owners. Princeton had suffered mightily when occupied by the British army in December 1776, and no matter how well-behaved the American mutineers might be, the people still feared them.[12]

The mutineer army arrived in Princeton by the evening of January 3 and began setting up camp, having agreed to General Wayne's request to meet with him the next day to discuss their grievances. Princeton's Robert Stockton wrote to Livingston, noting that the mutineers had "behaved orderly since they came here." However, Stockton must have been greatly concerned when the sergeants leading the mutineers told Stockton that they planned to stay in Princeton until their grievances were redressed and that they had detained wagons and teams to draw wood for their stay.[13]

During the week of occupation, at least three residents—Thomas Olden, Joseph Olden, and John Johnson—supplied multiple cords of firewood for the use of the Pennsylvania troops. Also, James Moore provided three horses for use by the soldiers for four days. Robert Stockton purchased the wood and rented the horses for the Quartermaster Department, so these citizens received pay for their services, although not until about a year and a half later.[14]

January 4 (Thursday)

The mutiny leaders decided to halt the army at Princeton while a committee of sergeants continued on to Philadelphia to present their grievances to Congress. While in Princeton, the soldiers encamped on Colonel Morgan's "Prospect near Princeton" farm, while the sergeants took up quarters in Nassau Hall, leaving General Wayne and Colonels Butler and Stewart to find lodging in one or more of the taverns.[15]

The mutineers set up their guard posts and conducted themselves in proper military fashion as they settled in at Princeton. The guard posts prevented all but the very few officers they trusted from coming in to negotiate with them. For example, arriving at the edge of Princeton from Bound Brook, the eighty distrusted officers confronted a mutineer guard post, where they met "with a great deal of insolence," leading them to divert to Allentown by way of Cranbury. At about 7:00 p.m., they arrived at Allentown, about twelve miles southeast of Princeton.[16]

General St. Clair heard that the mutineer posts established at Princeton were "well chosen, and the guards very regularly mounted, and a committee of sergeants manages their business." It was also encouraging that "they have as yet done very little injury to the inhabitants, and profess, that they do not mean any."[17]

In agreement with Wayne's orders of the previous day, a sergeant from each regiment met with him, Butler, and Stewart to convey their grievances concerning enlistment expiration dates; lack of pay, exacerbated by its declining value due to depreciation; and lack of clothing.[18] During the conference, Wayne told the mutineers that he would ask for representatives of Pennsylvania to meet with the soldiers at Trenton or another location. The sergeants were not happy with that plan and told him they would meet with "any gentleman of rank" right where they were, in Princeton. If the government wanted to settle their grievances fairly, its representatives would come to them and not require the victims of government actions to travel to it.[19]

At some point during the day, forty-three-year-old Colonel Stephen Moylan of the 4th Continental Dragoons arrived, without his regiment, "to give any assistance that may be in my power, as the enemy will, in all probability, come out," and was allowed to join General Wayne's staff. Moylan was Irish, and there were many Irishmen in the Pennsylvania Line.[20]

Fears that the British would take advantage of the mutiny remained palpable, and Wayne received intelligence that the British were making plans "to come out to make a descent on Jersey," and they expected that the mutineers would join them.[21]

January 5 (Friday)

The Pennsylvania officers at Allentown left at 11:00 a.m. and halted at Trenton, and then set out for Pennington, where at 3:00 p.m. Major Moore wrote to Wayne that he and Hamilton were now at Pennington with the eighty officers arranged in two companies commanded by Lieutenant Colonel Josiah Harmar of the 7th Pennsylvania Regiment.[22]

General St. Clair and the Marquis de Lafayette, hoping to help things, set out from Philadelphia and arrived at Trenton at about 3:00 p.m. The mutineers allowed them to come into Princeton, and although "there was an appearance of satisfaction in the countenances of the troops," St. Clair and Lafayette "were not allowed to have any communication with them." The only communication allowed had to be with the committee of sergeants. St. Clair suspected there were enemy agents among them.

Learning that the soldiers were not happy with their presence in town, St. Clair and Lafayette only stayed for about an hour and a half before leaving, fearing that staying longer would result in being detained by the soldiers. St. Clair erroneously heard that Wayne, Butler, and Stewart were prisoners of the mutineers and judged that the most "alarming circumstance is, their having organized themselves, and appointed all the necessary officers" from their sergeants. St. Clair returned south to Maidenhead in order "to be able to get them early tomorrow, before they have opportunity to intoxicate themselves." He said he would communicate to Reed if anything critical happened overnight.[23]

January 6 (Saturday)

General Nathaniel Heard informed Governor Livingston that the militia companies ordered out were at their posts, although at least one Hunterdon County company, Captain William Tucker's, was still organizing at Trenton.[24] Captain James Moore's company turned out to guard the Princeton magazine and provide guards for ammunition sent to New Brunswick for the militia assigned there between January 6 and 14.[25]

The eighty Pennsylvania officers at Pennington maintained a patrol between Pennington and Princeton. During the night, there was a hard rain.[26]

President Reed conveyed the issues involved in the negotiations with the mutineers to the Committee of Congress. He told them, "I mean to go within four miles of Princeton this afternoon, where I have written Gen. Wayne to meet me, and to inform the troops that I am ready to hear any reasonable complaints decently offered." The situation seemed very fluid, with some things looking good and others looking ominous. Reed saw no signs of British involvement, except for a few of the sergeants "who have been imprudently raised from the ranks to that office." He suspiciously wondered if they were British deserters who had joined the army. It was also unclear whether Wayne and the two officers with him were prisoners.[27]

Hearing that Reed had doubts about his safety if he met with the sergeants in Princeton, Sergeant William Bouzar, secretary for the sergeants, wrote to Reed that "yr Excellency need not be in the least afraid or apprehensive of any irregularities or ill treatment—that the whole Line would be gratified in settling this unhappy affair."[28] On behalf of the sergeants, Bouzar also wrote to General Wayne reminding him that the articles of clothing he had mentioned to the sergeants the day before "would tend to a great pacification if you would procure them as early as possible, as the men in general is in great want and profound necessity for the same." They wanted to know how soon they would get the clothing. Wayne replied that "he will take the proper measures to procure an immediate and full supply of shirts, shoes, socks, and overalls."[29]

The Committee of Congress remained at Bristol, incorrectly believing the mutineers were going to march to Trenton that night.[30] President Joseph Reed of Pennsylvania, who had led the light horse reconnaissance toward Princeton in 1776, lodged at the home of Judge Daniel Hunt in Maidenhead. At 6:00 p.m. Wayne wrote to Reed from Princeton that he would be safe for the night where he was, at Daniel Hunt's, and Wayne would see him in the morning.[31]

Two strangers came into Princeton the night of January 6. John Mason carried an offer from General Henry Clinton designed to encourage the mutineers to desert the cause. The proposal stated, "they are now offered to be taken under the protection of the British government to have their rights restored, a free pardon for all former offenses, and that pay due to them from Congress faithfully paid to them, without any expectation of military service, except it may be voluntary, upon laying down their arms and returning to their allegiance."[32] James Ogden guided Mason to Princeton.

They went straight to Nassau Hall, where Mason asked the sentry to direct him to the officer commanding the mutineers. He was sent up to Sergeant John Williams's room. Williams had been captured at Princeton by the British four years earlier on January 1, 1777. He had turned coat and enlisted in the 2nd Battalion of DeLancey's Loyalist Brigade in New York and spent about nineteen months in British service before deserting on July 24, 1778. Back with the Americans, Williams had been court-martialed in 1780, found guilty, and sentenced to death. However, Washington had pardoned him due to his youth and previous good character. Now, when Mason presented Williams with the lead-encased document from General Clinton, he opened it, read it, and asked where it came from. When told it was from Clinton, Williams placed Mason and Ogden under arrest and took them to the Committee of Sergeants, who quickly agreed to turn them over to General Wayne. Another currier from Clinton got to Princeton during the night but dropped his copy of the lead-encased message in front of the door to the house where the Committee of Sergeants met. Then he disappeared.

January 7 (Sunday)

General Wayne was awakened at about 4:00 a.m. on Sunday morning and shown Clinton's letter and the two men who brought it. The mutineers wanted nothing to do with them. Wayne wanted to get the two spies out of Princeton as soon as possible and persuaded the sergeants to hand them over to Joseph Reed.[33] Wayne sent them under escort down the road toward Trenton. That morning, Joseph Reed, General James Porter, and the Philadelphia Light Horse were traveling from Trenton toward Maidenhead to be closer to the mutineers. The two parties met on the road, and the spies were taken over by the Light Horse and Reed's party. When Reed reached Maidenhead, he interrogated the spies at Judge Daniel Hunt's house. General Wayne, with Colonels Butler, Moylan, and Stewart, left Princeton and arrived at Maidenhead before noon.[34]

Joseph Reed wrote to Wayne that he wanted to get the mutineers to march to Trenton "as soon as circumstances will admit." One reason he gave was that the provisions in Princeton were "nearly exhausted, and the men have hitherto behaved so well to the inhabitants, that it would be a pity to drive the troops to the necessity of distressing them, when at this place [Trenton] they may be otherwise supplied." However, John Butler wrote to Governor Livingston that sufficient supplies of beef did not exist at Trenton, and he implored Livingston to arrange speedily for beef and pork to be sent there.[35] Trenton was also more convenient than Princeton to receive the clothing promised to the soldiers from Philadelphia that would be shipped up the Delaware River. The mutineers would also be nearer to Congress, and it would be proper, and show respect for their government, for them to come to President Reed rather than insist he go to them.

Reed expressed his desire to be fair and resolve things "on every reasonable point; and when any doubt arises, the construction to be in favor of the soldier." He felt "the proposals made by them on the 4th instant seem to form a reasonable ground of accommodation." However, some points might require adjustments. Referring to a letter from their clerk, Sergeant Bouzar, Reed wanted the sergeants to be informed why Reed was asking the mutineers to come to Trenton, and that it should not be judged as any sort of threat to them. Reed stated, "though I must lament the unfortunate occasion, I shall with great pleasure hearken to well-founded complaints, and concur in any reasonable plan to accommodate matters to general satisfaction."[36]

In a letter to his Executive Council, Reed reported how the Pennsylvania soldiers had rejected the offers from General Clinton to join his army. Because of this, Reed had decided to meet with the soldiers, feeling confident he would be safe.[37] The Committee of Congress at Trenton agreed to stay there until it received further communications from Reed as to how they could aid in the situation.[38]

January 8 (Monday)

January 8 was clear and cold.[39] When Reed set out from Maidenhead on the 7th, a sergeant and four men had come to claim the two spies, Mason and Ogden. Colonel Butler and General Wayne had promised that the spies would be turned back over to them, so Reed felt compelled to do so. Some of Reed's officers felt that this changed things and he should not go to Princeton. However, Reed thought he should live up to his agreement to go. So, he set out and got to Princeton at 3:00 p.m. The posted guards turned out on their arrival and saluted them. Reed reported, "Near the college I found the whole line under arms, and the artillery ready to discharge [a salute]; but this was prevented lest the country should be alarmed. We passed in the front, the sergeants having the places of their officers respectively, and saluting. I did not think it prudent to refuse them the usual attention, though much against my inclination." Reed became concerned when, "Soon after I dismounted, a number of the sergeants came, under a pretense of knowing when they should wait on us, but really, as we were informed, to ascertain my identity; for so amazingly suspicious were they, that nothing but some sergeants who had personal knowledge declaring their satisfaction, would convince a great number of the soldiery."[40]

After completing the ceremonies and fixing a time to meet, Reed did what he could to get intelligence from the local people of Princeton. Shortly, Sergeant Williams and several others brought in Mason and Ogden, whom they "had paraded through the lines." General Wayne and others "strongly urged them to execute them by their own authority" or that the committee of sergeants would request Wayne "to sign the warrant" for their execution. Reed was not pleased that Sergeant Williams was against this and instead wanted to release both men with "a taunting message, to Sir Harry Clinton." Reed then proposed to do neither, but to keep them under "close guard till we should consider farther."

A great debate took place among the sergeants after the prisoners were taken away. They were "much divided in sentiment; some proposing one thing, and some another," and ultimately, Reed's advice prevailed. The sergeants met with Reed in the evening and presented him with their concerns. A lengthy discussion followed during which Reed found that "some of the sergeants spoke with a degree of intelligence and good sense that really surprised me, and stated some real hardships they have suffered, which I fear have too much foundation. I cannot but think some undue methods have been taken to engage many in the service." Reed concluded from this "that all those whose times were expired, and who had not freely entered again, knowing the duration of the service, should be discharged."

However, it would not be easy to determine just what incentives or understandings about the length of service had been used in each man's enlistment. The discussion continued through the evening and revealed to Reed that their complaints about enlistments were aimed mostly at their officers and they were looking to Congress and the Pennsylvania State government "for redress and help." Reed wrote out a plan that he believed should be implemented, which if refused, would reveal a lack of sincerity in their protests, and they might have to be dealt with more harshly. He wanted his plan to be printed and distributed among the troops because he had "reason to think the sergeants do not always communicate freely." He was especially concerned about Sergeant Williams, whom Reed felt was "either very ignorant and illiterate, or was drunk yesterday, as he showed no talents to conduct such an enterprise." If the men rejected his plan and began to move east toward British lines, he would get between them with whatever force he could muster, mostly New Jersey militia.

Reed ordered the sergeants to march their men to Trenton in the morning, where procedures would continue. He hoped the commissaries and quartermaster there were prepared and quarters could be provided for "at least 1500 men, though I will endeavor to detach 1000 at least to Bordentown and Burlington." He expected they would receive their officers, but he was quite concerned about the officers because "they appear so deeply to resent the conduct of the troops to them personally." Relations between the officers and men were still extremely tense. Reed continued to be very concerned about bringing things to a peaceful and satisfactory conclusion because he found so many men "so ignorant and capricious" and there were too many "wicked rascals."[41]

The mutineers had first offered Reed a proposition that amounted to "discharging every man who is or should be tired of the service, let the terms of enlistment have been what they would. This I peremptorily refused, but offered to discharge all those who had been detained beyond the time of their enlistment, or have been compelled or trepanned into a new engagement." As negotiations continued, he rejected their proposal that the mutineers should appoint commissioners to participate in the settlements and "directed them to march to-morrow morning to Trenton." Reed did not know how things would proceed since he could see that "the sergeants have as much difference of opinion as the men, though they know it is their interest to keep together and not be disorderly." He tried to be moderate and to listen honestly to their complaints, finding that some of the sergeants were "sensible fellows, and reason very speciously." However, he believed that Sergeant Williams, "their nominal leader, is certainly a very poor creature or very fond of liquor." Reed continued trying to get the sergeants to turn the two spies back over to him.[42]

Because of Reed's order to march to Trenton, Wayne, "being determined to bring matters to a speedy issue at every consequence & risk," sent for the sergeants at 4:30 p.m. and "insisted upon their marching from this place towards Trent-town in the morning, or that we would leave them to act as they pleased, & to abide the bad effects of their own folly. In consequence of which they had come to a resolution of moving in the morning" and bringing the two spies.[43]

Auditors brought in to meet with mutineers to resolve back pay and other monetary issues began to set up shop in Trenton. Some New Jersey militia units continued to scout to determine British intentions. Others remained in a position to engage any British troops coming over from Staten Island or to engage the mutineers if negotiations broke down and things got ugly. The mutineers mingled amicably with the residents of Princeton and sought to reassure them that the struggle was not with them. The Pennsylvania troops insisted that all they wanted was justice and that they would join with the militia to repel any British incursion. They also rescinded their threat to destroy the countryside if the militia made an attempt to quell the mutiny before it was amicably resolved.

At 2:30 p.m., Reed wrote to the Committee of Congress from Maidenhead that he had received "no direct accounts from Princeton this morning; but, from the straggling soldiers and indirect intelligence I understand that my proposal has been generally acceptable" with a few issues still to negotiate. He understood that, if ordered, they were to go to Trenton the next morning. He also learned that a letter similar to the one brought by the two spies had been dropped before the door where the sergeants held their meetings, and it was delivered to General Wayne. The mutineers keep the two spies "in close prison, but have not settled their fate." He had sent out three light horsemen toward Perth Amboy to gather intelligence on any British movements because the weather would be favorable for actions.[44]

Writing to the Committee of Congress at 7:00 p.m., Reed stated that he had ordered the mutineers to give up the spies and march to Trenton the next day. He added, "If they do neither, we must, however disagreeable, use force; for which the country must be prepared by showing that terms of a reasonable kind have been offered and refused." General Wayne had promised to leave Princeton that evening, as his service in staying with the mutineers "is no longer of any benefit." Reed was not sure Wayne would be allowed to leave because "they certainly take countenance and spirit from having him among them."[45]

Reed and the sergeants had reached an agreement; a committee would review the enlistment of each soldier and discharge those eligible. Also, the men would receive proper uniforms as well as warrants for their back-pay that Pennsylvania would honor as soon as it could raise the money.

January 9 (Tuesday)

On the morning of January 9, the mutineers began an orderly march down the Post Road through Maidenhead to Trenton to meet with the auditors. Due to the cold weather, the bad roads, and horses in poor condition pulling heavy wagons, the mutineers did not arrive at Trenton until 2:00 p.m. This removed Princeton from involvement in this affair. Over the next few weeks, the individual issues of enlistment terms, pay, clothing, and the like were gradually resolved, but the successful resolution of this mutiny would not solve all grievances within units of the Continental Army.[46]

A New Citizen Committee

Colonists had formed committees early in the revolution to help redress their grievances, and people now created committees to help the State Legislature and Continental Congress deal with the persisting problems. The editor of the *New Jersey Gazette* received a letter from Middlesex County dated January 1, 1781, the same day as the Pennsylvania Line mutiny, giving an account of a society recently organized there, the purpose of which was to overcome these problems and help strengthen civil government by defeating the designs of traitors. The group called itself The Society of Whigs of the County of Middlesex, and they had sent the letter to the newspaper in the hope of inspiring other counties to form similar committees that could all work together, much as the committees of correspondence had done earlier.

The letter laid out four functions this Society would pursue, with "the public good, and the establishment of the liberty and independence of America" as its only goal. The committee members would seek out and bring to prosecution anyone who did not obey the laws of the new government and especially anyone trading with the enemy. They would support the execution of laws and assist in getting out the militia and supplies of the State in actions against the enemy. They would recommend any new laws they believed "to be for the interest of this commonwealth in particular, and of the continent in general." Finally, they would seek ways to relieve and compensate those men suffering in captivity or "by their generous exertions in behalf of their country." Their primary attention, though, "shall be principally directed to the sufferers of our own county." They divided the county into three districts, each with its own society that would send seven delegates to a county meeting as voting members. Other people could attend but not vote. The Society President was Rev. Azel Roe of Woodbridge, Vice President Rev. Samuel S. Smith of Princeton, and Secretary Colonel Jonathan Deare of Princeton.[47]

Death of Richard Stockton

The death of Richard Stockton on February 28 brought great sadness to the community. For many years after, Annis wrote anniversary elegies and odes in his honor.[48] His obituary statement in the *Pennsylvania Packe*t commented that "The ability, dignity and integrity with which this gentleman discharged the duties of the several important offices to which he was called by the voice of his country, are well known." To those who knew him, "he was peculiarly engaging. His manners were easy, and his conversation was at all times embellished with the marks of education, taste, and knowledge of the world." He had fought for several years against cancer that began on his lip, spread to his throat, and ultimately killed him. His funeral took place in Nassau Hall, where Rev. Samuel Stanhope Smith preached the sermon. Afterward, he was buried in the Stony Brook Friends burial ground.[49]

A questionable inventory of Morven was made, theoretically by Annis. In addition to the many items of furniture and personal belongings in each room, his farm animals and equipment were also listed. He may have had nine milch cows, fourteen young cattle, twenty sheep, and fifteen hogs. His seven horses included two old sorrel horses, two brown carriage horses, one small bay mare, one small black mare, and one small bay horse. For the horses to pull, he had one plow, one harrow, one wagon, one sled, one pleasure sleigh, one coach, and one chariot. This was not a complete inventory of his total estate and omitted several valuable items, such as properties he owned, as well as the people he owned as slaves.[50]

Militia

Militia morale was low after several years of frequent call-outs taking men away from their regular employment, and officers became increasingly hard-pressed to get their men to turn out for service. On February 20, Colonel William Scudder wrote Livingston from Princeton about his concerns involving the militia. He enclosed a return of the men from his regiment who had served in the State and Continental service the past year, apologizing for its late submission and attributed the delay to "my long severe illness." He noted that illness had prevented him from turning out himself, and "had I been able to attend to the business myself, I should have had more men in the field."

Scudder also wanted to inform Livingston about problems in receiving his orders and wrote, "It may not be amiss to inform your Excellency how I come by your orders." For example, the first message of January 7, picked up by a boy at William Mountier's "dram shop" and brought to Scudder's Mill "some time after it was wrote." A second message of the same date "was found at Hyers Tavern seven days after the date of it." This made it very difficult to obey Livingston's orders effectively and promptly. In addition to these problems, Scudder reported, "we had a good guard out last month and hope we shall not fail this" month. However, both his officers and men felt "themselves sensibly injured by being obliged to do the duty of other counties, whose inhabitants are but a day or two march farther from the lines than they." In addition to the perceived unfair duty, there was also the issue of low pay. If a man chose to hire a substitute instead of turning out at a difficult time for him, the cost was very high. In conclusion, Scudder told Livingston, "I could wish to assure the men, that those near the lines would be some way considered for their extra services."[51]

Militiamen continued to be called out to take care of prisoners. On April 14, Continental artillery Captain Thomas Proctor wrote to Captain Moore in Princeton that he had taken up a deserter from his regiment "and am quite at a loss for a guard to take him to Trenton gaol." Proctor's regiment was at Newtown, Pennsylvania, and Proctor told Moore, "I am now sentinel over him myself at Mr. Burgen's tavern & beg to be relieved." He hoped Moore could supply a couple of his local militiamen to take the deserter from the Princeton tavern "to Trenton gaol, as he has three times deserted & three times taken the bounty allowed by the State from different officers."[52]

Militiamen did not always behave properly when called out on active duty and became subject to court-martial. On March 23, a court-martial convened at New Brunswick, and Ensign Morford of the 3rd Battalion of Middlesex County was tried for "parading in arms with the men belonging to Capt. Perine's company, and marching from their post in mutiny." The court found him guilty and ordered him "cashiered and rendered incapable of serving in the militia as an officer during the war." He could, of course, still serve as a militia private.

On March 15, a court-martial convened at Jacob Hyer's Hudibras. Lieutenant Charles Fisher, of Colonel William Scudder's regiment, was charged with disobeying the orders of his Colonel by refusing to march with a regiment detachment to Morristown in June 1780. The court found him "guilty of unofficerlike behavior, and adjudged to be fined in the sum of five pounds lawful money, or the exchange thereof in continental money, to be recovered and applied as directed by the militia law." The court tried Ensign Lewis Baremore for refusing to turn out in January at the time of the revolt of the Pennsylvania line. He was found guilty of "unofficerlike behavior, and adjudged to be cashiered and reduced to the ranks." Lieutenant David Gilliland, of Colonel Scudder's regiment, was tried for disobedience of orders, in not turning out in February 1779 and October 1780. In his case, though, the court found that he had sufficient reasons for not marching and acquitted him. Livingston approved all the verdicts and sentences.[53]

Supply Department

Obtaining ammunition for the New Jersey troops continued to be a constant concern throughout the war. Persistent shortages often meant appealing to the Continental Army for assistance, and on June 1, Livingston wrote to Washington on behalf of the Legislature asking for some. He stated that there was no lead at Philadelphia to purchase and the Legislature had even sent a person to Boston to try to procure some, including from British ammunition left behind when they evacuated Boston in 1776. Even if successful, getting supplies from Boston would take time and "necessarily keep us too long without that essential article."[54]

A very busy Elias Woodruff had to tell Governor Livingston on September 4 that he could not submit a requested return of the ammunition he had on hand but would attempt to prepare one by September 16 and send it to him.[55]

On September 20, Livingston urged the Assembly to continue its efforts to procure ammunition because he believed "that as soon as the enemy at the post [New York] shall learn the fate of Lord Cornwallis, they will make an excursion to desolate and ravage New Jersey. The procuring a proper supply of ammunition is therefore so essentially necessary that I cannot ascertain a doubt of the Legislature's taking the most effectual & expeditious way to procure it."[56]

Woodruff finally submitted a report on September 25, showing the military stores received between April 27, 1779, and September 25, 1781. These included powder, lead, ball, flints, cannonballs, boxed grapeshot tubes, portfires, staffs, slow matches, linstocks, beige, and tin that had been delivered by Princeton merchant John Denton, Purchaser of Military Stores for New Jersey, and Samuel Hodgdon, Commissary of Military Stores in Philadelphia. It also reflected deliveries Woodruff had made to various officers of New Jersey regiments. Continually frustrated and probably exhausted, Woodruff resigned that day.[57]

On September 27, the Assembly appointed James Hamilton of Princeton to replace Woodruff as Commissary and authorized him to take custody of the military stores in Woodruff's possession belonging to the State.[58] In line with efforts to reduce complaints about the supply departments, he was given a salary and received no commission or percentage on transactions. For Hamilton's first trip to Philadelphia, Livingston wrote to Elias Boudinot from Princeton on September 29. It introduced Hamilton, who carried the message, and requested Boudinot's assistance and influence in helping him, since he did not know Philadelphia, to deliver the Legislature's application for ammunition to the Board of War.[59] The trip proved to be harrowing when three thieves attacked Hamilton, and he narrowly escaped with his life. For many such trips afterward, Princeton resident Andrew McMackin, nicknamed "the Governor," accompanied him.[60]

The College

When the college trustees met at Princeton on May 30, an immediate order of business was to choose a trustee to replace the deceased Richard Stockton. They chose Joseph Reed, President of the State of Pennsylvania. Since previous agreements on salary for Witherspoon had not been clear as to the type of money to be paid, the trustees agreed that he receive gold and silver, and not depreciated paper money. He should also receive back-pay to cover the previous two years. They tried again to get the General Assembly to reduce the number of trustees required for a quorum. The trustees also reminded the Legislature that they had paid large amounts of money to repair the damages to Nassau Hall inflicted by the British. Repaired areas had been re-damaged and new damages inflicted on the building by American troops, especially the militia that had passed through the town and used the building for quarters.

The trustees asked the Legislature to establish a penalty that "may be laid on any civil or military officer who shall hereafter quarter or suffer to be quartered any troops in the said building and its appurtenances or to grant your petitioners such other remedy as in your wisdom you shall think fit." The trustees appointed Witherspoon, Spencer, and Woodhull to be a committee to superintend the repairs and added Professor Samuel Stanhope Smith to the committee. Witherspoon offered to personally back any loans necessary for the repair of Nassau Hall.[61]

On July 7, student Peter Elmendorf from Kingston, New York, wrote his first letter from Nassau Hall to his mother. Elmendorf may have enrolled in the college as early as November 1780 but had probably been living in a private home in the village while repairs to Nassau Hall progressed. A room was ready for him by July 7, and he commented on it, saying, "I am well pleased, the place agrees admirably with my disposition, my room tho' not yet finished, is decent, clean, and nobly situated, we have the finest prospect that ever could be desired, in short we have everything comfortable in life." When he wrote again on July 27, he expressed the need to purchase "a broad cloth for a winters dressing coat." He wanted to fit in socially, and such a coat was "very necessary here as all the students in general wear them."[62] Elmendorf was settling in very successfully.

At the September meeting, the trustees approved seniors for bachelor's degrees, including Joseph Clark, the young man who had served in the local militia after the college closed on November 30, 1776. The repair committee reported it had "not been able to effect much in repairing the college, thro a failure of the remittances that were ordered at the last session of the board." In consequence, they ordered that all students entering the college would pay one guinea, "which, together with the rents of the chambers, shall be appropriated by the treasurer as a fund to discharge the expense of such repairs as shall be judged to be indispensably necessary in the college."

Acting on the need for a new college steward "to accommodate the students, under the regulations that existed before the war," the trustees elected Jonathan Baldwin to return again to that office with the understanding that he would provide each student with meals at the value of ten shillings per week. Just where Baldwin had been living in town the past couple of years and what activities he had been doing besides his work for the war are not known. He did not appear on the February 1780 tax list. Concerning education, the trustees approved the proposal by professors William Churchill Houston and Samuel Stanhope Smith that the college confer degrees in theology and law.[63]

The annual grammar school public examination and exercises took place on September 24 and 25, followed by commencement on September 26. The commencement exercises began as usual with the procession from the president's house to Nassau Hall. The usual series of orations preceded the awarding of six bachelor's degrees, seven master's degrees, and honorary master's degrees to Major General Nathanael Greene, Chief Justice of the State David Brearley, and several others. President Witherspoon's talk preceded the valedictory address on "the advantages which the United States of America enjoy above other republics which have arisen in the world, for framing wisely items of civil policy."[64]

Several days after commencement, Witherspoon published a letter in the paper describing the improvements being made to Nassau Hall and the degree to which college life was getting back to normal. He noted that "the seminary notwithstanding its late desolation by the enemy, and by the confusion of the times, is now filling fast." Therefore, the trustees "were of opinion, that the whole former system might be re-established, and took every necessary measure for that purpose." He declared that a "considerable part of the college is already repaired" and other repairs will be completed without delay.

This would eventually allow all undergraduates to lodge in Nassau Hall as formerly. In the meantime, those who might still live outside of it, with permission, were expected to follow the same rules as if they lived on campus. Students taking meals on campus were to pay ten shillings per week to the steward. Students not dining at Nassau Hall were still to pay one shilling and sixpence per week to the steward for "keeping the college and rooms in order." Regarding the cost to attend the college, new students paid a one-guinea entrance fee, six pounds per year tuition, and two pounds per year for chamber rent. Payment were to be made in advance for six months. Tuition for the grammar school was the same as for the college, but the young students were not required to live in the building. If residing locally, they could live at home, and if at a distance, they might stay with someone arranged by their parents. Things were getting back to normal and the college community hoped they would be completely normal soon.[65]

Elmendorf wrote another letter home on November 30, indicating he had returned to school from the fall vacation. He was not happy about the new policy of paying for tuition and board in advance. His primary complaint, though, was about the food provided by the college steward. Peter whined, "I often repent that I saw his face; after having paid him 24 pounds and then to live in the way we do is the most provoking thing I ever met with." Describing this food in more detail, he stated, "We eat rye bread—half dough and as black as it possibly can be, old oniony butter and sometimes dry bread, and thick coffee for breakfast, a little milk or cyder and bread, and sometimes meagre chocolate for supper, very indifferent dinners, such as lean, tough, boiled fresh beef with dry potatoes! And if this deserves to be called diet for mean ravenous people let it be so styled, and not a table kept for collegians!"[66] His mother had to guess whether things were really that bad or whether he was just a young man who liked to complain.

The Legislature finally did approve a smaller quorum for trustee meetings on November 2.[67]

Community Events

The Quakers continued their usual activities as they dealt with the war and social issues. In May, the Monthly Meeting approved the Stony Brook Preparatory Meeting request to build a house on its land for a schoolmaster's home. Most members were making efforts to "support love and unity amongst us," and some made persistent efforts "to discourage backbiting and evil reports and to end difference." Members generally made efforts to bring up their children and new members "in plainness of speech and apparel and to reading the Holy Scriptures but the customs of the world is too prevalent with some respecting speech and apparel."

All members except one had refrained from importing, buying, or holding slaves. Members who continued to own slaves were treating them well but too much neglected their education. In December, the meeting appointed Robert White to a committee formed to work on the manumission of the few remaining enslaved persons owned by Friends and also to see that those freed individuals received full justice and encouragement to follow Quaker beliefs, as well as school learning.[68] Occasional advertisements for the sale of slaves in the broader community appeared, including in January, when Dr. Thomas Wiggins advertised "a likely Negro wench, about 17 years of age" for sale.[69]

Enslaved people continued to resist their subjugation by running away, and this led to suspicion falling on any black person unknown to a community. In December, a black man was arrested by local Constable John Totten as a runaway, or at least a possible runaway. The man "called himself" Henry Heywood and "says [he] is a freeman." He was not known in the neighborhood because he had been in Virginia when the British surrendered at Yorktown and "came away with the Continental troops." From the constable's ad, dated Princeton, December 25, 1781, it is unclear whether Heywood was with the British army in some capacity. He was described physically in the ad, like other runaways and suspected runaways, and it was noted that, "he seems to understand housework best, and is very handy at that." The constable at least had enough doubt to say that "if" his owner were to for him, pay the charges, and take him away, the case would be settled. However, the owner only had six weeks to act. In the meantime, Heywood was to remain jailed. If no owner showed up, he "will be discharged according to law."[70] Throughout the advertisement, the wording indicates the belief that Heywood was a runaway. Typically, confirmed runaways not claimed by their owner by the time stated were sold by the constable. Just how this case ended is not known.

Property sales and rentals continued at their usual pace. In late January, Thomas Watson of Bordentown advertised a small farm for sale near Princeton, where John Bowne lived. He also announced for sale a lot of land by Worth's Mill on Stony Brook, containing a large stone dwelling house that would make a good store, and one had been kept there for many years.[71] Another farm, containing 140 acres of land with 30 being good meadow, was for sale in December. Situated on the Stony Brook and the Mill Stone about 1 1/2 miles from Princeton, it had a solid 2-story frame building with a brick front, containing 4 rooms on a floor. The property also had a kitchen, a large barn with stables, and other outbuildings. Its 2 apple orchards contained 150 trees each. The 60-acre woodlot was located about 1½ miles away. Matthew Clarke, living at Stony Brook Bridge, could be contacted for the terms of sale, as could Colonel William Scudder, who lived near the farm.[72] These men lived at opposite ends of town but must have had strong connections. In March, Scudder again advertised that he would be renting out Castle Howard located 1 mile from Princeton and 2 from Kingston.[73]

In July, Daniel Manning published a notice that he had for sale at his house, within 2 1/2 miles of Princeton and two of Rocky Hill, an 80-gallon still, which he would sell cheaply, but only for hard money. He had decided to leave the distilling business, proposing to set up a brewery instead.[74]

Busy merchant John Denton advertised items for sale at his store in the lane opposite the college. Just a few of them included Bohea Tea, gun powder, silks and satins, salt, and black pepper. Also, he had almanacs for the year 1782, available in large or small quantities at the printer's price. More substantial items included one large yoke of oxen in good order. He also offered to pay cash for clean linen rags and old brass and copper. This was a common practice for merchants who were helping the cause by obtaining rags for paper manufacture, and brass and copper could be recycled in many ways.[75]

Like any town, the Princeton area had its quota of dishonest men. In February, Constable John Totten at Princeton placed a notice in the paper offering a reward for an escaped prisoner of Windsor Township, one Jacob Maple, convicted of larceny and sentenced to a whipping. Maple had escaped while preparations were being made for the whipping. He was not a transient and appears on tax records for Middlesex County, along with several other men with the same last name.[76]

On the morning of the annual July 4 celebrations, "the ladies discovered their taste in ornamenting the houses with greens and flowers." At noon, the principal gentlemen of the town met at Mr. Beekman's tavern, at the Sign of the College, where they joined Governor Livingston. After a "few good draughts of good punch, they repaired to a tree in front of Mr. Beekman's house, from the top of which a union flag was displayed." The inhabitants gathered with the field piece belonging to the town and thirteen rounds were fired in honor of the States. Before each firing, a sentence expressing the wishes of the people upon the occasion was read. For example, round number ten came after hearing, "If there are British officers who treat a traitor as he deserves let their enemies esteem them; but perpetual infamy on the wretches who are not ashamed to consult with, or to serve under BENEDICT ARNOLD!!!"

At the conclusion, the crowd dismissed with three cheers. Many gentlemen enjoyed an elegant dinner at Mr. Bergen's and drank many patriotic toasts. In the evening, students of the college paraded along with the town militia in the presence of the Governor and his guests. Each corps fired thirteen rounds and gave three cheers, before every man returned home peaceably, "happy in the memory of this great revolution," even though this was several months before the events at Yorktown.[77]

The New Jersey Medical Society planned to meet at Princeton at Beekman's tavern on October 3, but it was rescheduled for the first Tuesday of November at Princeton. Due to the war, the Society had ceased to meet, and the members wanted to reconstitute it. Trenton's Dr. Isaac Smith led this effort.[78]

Colonel George Morgan continued developing the old Baldwin farm at Prospect. On January 29, Morgan purchased 500 flat rails and 500 round rails, with requests to his supplier for a few hundred more of each kind. They were to be good sound timber of white oak, black oak, and chestnut, and 11 feet long. He also ordered 125 white oak posts and stakes.[79] In May, he paid men for carting oats and wheat, threshing oats, and planting corn. He paid Andrew Johnson for 465 square rails, 1,045 flat rails, 250 posts, and 11 bushels of wheat; John Clark for mason work; and Robert White for making 100 hooks for his smokehouse and a large trammel for the kitchen. Late in the year, he paid Samuel Heath for hauling 420 rails the past April and for 300 white oak posts 6½ feet long, 100 white oak posts 5 feet long, 1,200 rails all broad and 11 feet long. Finally, Morgan paid John Mollison for wintering his sorrel horse and stabling and providing hay for his black horse. While he had some positive experiences with neighbor Isaac Anderson, in July Anderson borrowed his wagon and horses without permission, and a horse ended up lame. Anderson also took a bag and lost it, and borrowed a set of plow clevises that he did not return.[80]

Troops to Yorktown and Their Return

Throughout the war, Washington had kept at least part of his army where he could launch a significant attack to force the British out of New York City. He obsessively wanted to retake New York. Now, although Washington tried to convince the British forces occupying the city that he was preparing to attack them, he took advantage of changing conditions in the south and sent his American and French forces to Virginia. When the American and French armies passed through Princeton in late August, people in New Jersey could be forgiven if they felt abandoned by the Continental Army and worried that the British might attempt operations in their State during its absence.

In 1776, Washington had been pursued through New Jersey and then crossed the Delaware River for relative safety in Pennsylvania, and the British troops had ravaged the middle part of the State, including Princeton. Now, Washington's army had again left the State and crossed the Delaware River on its way to Virginia. As reported in the Loyalist *New York Gazette*, when those troops passed through a town in New Jersey, people tended to ask, "What is to be our fate now! In the winter we were told we should be in New York in the spring...we should certainly walk the streets of that place in September; and now instead of attacking that city, supported by a powerful French Navy, our whole army is leaving us to the mercy of our enemies."[81] People in Princeton must have felt that way during the several days it took for the two armies to pass through town. On August 29, Washington and Rochambeau dined at Morven.[82]

The French came through town first, and Rochambeau lodged at a tavern while his men camped out. The armies camped at Princeton on August 31 and September 1, in fields across the Post Road from Morven near the Barracks and extending across today's Mercer Street to land that is now part of the

Princeton Theological Seminary. By the night of August 31, the French were at Trenton, and Washington was at and about Princeton with his Continentals.[83]

Continental Army doctor James Thacher recorded in his journal that, "In passing through Princeton, but little time was allowed me to visit the college. This once celebrated seminary is now destitute of students, and the business of education is entirely suspended in consequence of the constant bustle and vicissitudes of war. The little village of Princeton is beautifully situated, and the college edifice is of stone, four stories high, and lighted by twenty-five windows in front, in each story. It has suffered considerable injury in being occupied alternately by the soldiers of the two contending armies."[84] Thacher's account contained several descriptive inaccuracies and certainly did not depict the return to normalcy that Witherspoon would advertise in his article a month later.

The people of Princeton provided some supplies and services for the troops. Matthew Clarke received pay for two days of service for a two-horse team transporting stores for the Jersey Brigade. When soldiers returned north in December, Aaron Longstreet loaned a horse for three days for use by an express rider. He also supplied two cords of wood for a detachment of troops and two loads of straw to the 1st New Jersey Regiment on December 6.[85]

When word that Cornwallis had surrendered to Washington at Yorktown reached Princeton, people understandably became very joyous. On October 23, at 12:00 p.m., the gentlemen of the town and vicinity met at Beekman's tavern and "enjoyed the occasion awhile over some good punch and wine." They adjourned to the green in front of the inn where the militia cannon was stationed, and after an address by a college professor, it fired thirteen rounds. A public dinner followed, and thirteen toasts made in celebration. Town leaders even invited several strangers just passing through town to join in. The crowd broke up with decency at 6:00 p.m. and during the evening illuminated the village, and thirteen rounds from the militia concluded the "rejoicings of the day."[86] Annis Stockton "dashed off a letter" to her brother Elias. Although things had been emotionally sad after Richard's death, and she had seldom felt joy, this exciting news was so good that she had to say something and told him, "Pardon this fragment but when the fit is on me I must jingle." She enclosed a stanza of poetry in praise of Washington.[87]

Some weeks later, the troops began passing back through town on their way north. Dr. Thacher notes on December 7 that some returning forces crossed the Hudson at King's Ferry, having recently passed through Philadelphia, Trenton, Princeton, Bound Brook, and Morristown. Although joyous in many ways, it had not been a comfortable march. He noted, "On account of the inclemency of the season we have suffered exceedingly from cold, wet and fatigue, during our long march. But we return in triumph to rejoin our respective regiments, and enjoy a constant interchange of congratulations with our friends, on the glorious and brilliant success of our expedition which closes the campaign."[88]

About the same time Thacher wrote those words, the *Pennsylvania Packet* published an address from the citizens of Annapolis to General Washington stating that "the successes at Trenton and Princeton, laid the cornerstone of our freedom and independence, and that the capture of earl Cornwallis and his army has completed the edifice, and secured the temple of liberty to us and our posterity."[89] There was a real sense that the war had succeeded and a real hope that life could get back to normal. Of course the normal would include something new in terms of what sort of government would be created. Hopefully, things would be decided soon.

Chapter 11

1782

After the defeat of Lord Cornwallis at Yorktown, fears of large-scale military activity subsided, although the civil war in New Jersey between Patriots and Loyalists continued. Concerns turned to when a peace treaty would be written and finalized. By the end of the year there would be a preliminary treaty. In the meantime, the militia and Continental Army still had to exist, and some men had to serve while others helped keep them supplied with their necessities.

Military Activities

Militia duties were reduced but did not entirely cease, due to the civil war as well as the lingering war for independence. The less-intense military activity led to additional problems within the militia itself. Several local officers served on a court-martial board on January 28, held at New Brunswick. Major Thomas Egberts served as president of the court, and Captain James Moore and Lieutenant James Hamilton served on the board. Ensign Jacob Merceroll pled not guilty to charges that he had behaved in a un-officer-like manner during an enemy incursion toward New Brunswick, by turning out late, unarmed, and not making any exertion to alarm the country or collect his company to oppose the enemy. The court found him guilty and sentenced him to be cashiered from his rank and reduced to serving as a private.[1]

The Continental Army continued to need medical help, and upon the recommendation of Dr. Benjamin Rush, Ebenezer Stockton, son of Major Robert Stockton, was commissioned surgeon for a New Hampshire regiment.[2]

College Restoration

Peter Elmendorf, now a senior, who had written the blistering letter about food the previous November, wrote again on January 19 and confessed that in the previous letter he had expressed "some sentiments which are now not altogether just." Things got even better in June when Elmendorf received permission to take his meals outside the college and wrote to his mother, "I have changed my board and find the difference to be very great with respect to diet and politeness."[3]

Ashbel Green entered the college on May 9, wearing a coat for which he had paid $1,000 in Continental currency—depreciation at that time being more than forty to one. He found Nassau Hall still not completely repaired. While still visibly damaged, a room at the east end of the cellar had been fixed up for use by the grammar school, and opposite to it, another room had been partially repaired for use as the dining room. The students in the Cliosophic Society had restored their hall on the top story. On the two main floors just above the cellar, enough rooms had been fixed to be habitable and decent to accommodate the forty or so students. However, some rooms still lay wasted, displaying "a desolation of soiled walls, gaping windows, broken partitions, fallen ceilings, and heaps of plaster and filth." Notably, Green observed "the whole building still exhibited the effects of General Washington's artillery" volleys fired over five years previously.[4]

With the September trustee meeting and the annual commencement approaching, Witherspoon sent a note to Governor Livingston on September 22 requesting that Council members attend commencement. He pointed out that it would not only support the college trustees but would be an inspiration to public service for the students.[5] On September 24, the grammar school students demonstrated their improvement in Greek and Latin for the faculty and other gentlemen. Several students from the highest class were formally admitted as freshmen in the college, and competition in extemporaneous speaking in Latin took place in the afternoon. The usual orations occurred that evening.[6]

When the trustees met on September 25, they elected a new trustee to replace Rev. James Caldwell, killed at the Battle of Springfield in June 1780. Steward Jonathan Baldwin asked the board for a salary of 13 shillings 6 pence per week. However, the trustees could not agree to his request. They considered him dismissed from office and began the search for a successor.[7] Commencement was held that afternoon, and among the young men awarded the Bachelor of Arts degree was Elmendorf. During the afternoon orations, after all his earlier complaining, he addressed "a very polite and splendid assembly" on "the nature of happiness." His cousin Conrad Elmendorf took part in a debate on the question of whether, in a confederation like that of America, the large or the small states were more favorable to union, population, and improvement in the arts. This question would be a significant one during the efforts to write a constitution a few years later.[8]

In early October, Witherspoon announced the re-establishment of the pre-war regulations of the college and that they would be strictly enforced. Every student was to lodge at the college and only board out with special permission. Tuition and board were to be paid six months in advance without exception. Students not arriving on the first day of a session might were in danger of losing their room and being assigned another. Students were not allowed to keep horses, except by special permission. Various fees were listed that were to be paid in advance to Elias Woodruff, "who is elected steward" once again to replace Baldwin. Parents were advised to "put the expenses of their children under the direction of some person of prudence in the college or the town, to prevent them from running to that extravagance that will be injurious both to the interest of their parents, and to the reputation of the institution."[9]

Community Events

The presence of a market house appears for the first time in newspapers this year, and it may have been a new addition to the village. It was no doubt located somewhere on the main road through town.[10] A public auction was announced for September 26 at the market house in Princeton, beginning at 1:00 p.m., when a valuable collection of divinity books, several classics, and some modern authors could be purchased for cash only.[11]

Concerns among the Quaker community focused on the continuing efforts to have Friends marry Friends in a proper Quaker ceremony, counseling members who missed meetings or who imbibed in spirituous liquors, and the persistent concern over drowsiness during meetings. Even with the war winding down, there was still concern about men participating in military service.[12]

In January Matthew Clarke's farm advertised for sale the previous December had not yet been sold.[13] Late in the year, in December, a house and lot in Princeton came up for sale. The lot had one acre of mowing ground, about thirty apple trees, a stable, and a well of good water near the door, and the property adjoined lots owned by Rev. Witherspoon and Colonel Hyer. Anyone seeking more information could see Ephraim Manning, near Princeton, or Elias Woodruff, Steward of the College.[14]

Jacob Bergen announced he had moved to Philadelphia and intended to keep a tavern at the Bunch of Grapes between Arch and Market streets. His Princeton tavern was now kept by Asher West of Shrewsbury.[15] Marshal James McCombs held a sale there on May 4 to dispose of items captured at sea by privateer Captain Adam Hyler and ordered to be sold. These included "a number of muskets, one swivel gun, one blunderbuss, several barrels of gunpowder, a valuable chest of medicine that cost 120£ in New York, two cases surgeons instruments, one cask raisins, some bohea tea, a quantity of wearing apparel, among which are a great number of mens shoes." Not all items were sold, and a subsequent sale followed at John Cape's tavern in Trenton on May 11.[16]

Taverns were always popular for meetings, and the New Jersey Medical Society met on May 1 at Christopher Beekman's Sign of the College and on November 5 at Jacob Hyer's Hudibras.[17] Sheriff John Conway of Middlesex County announced that courts of Oyer and Terminer and General Gaol Delivery for the County would be held at Princeton on June 11—no doubt at one of the taverns.[18]

Businessmen who advertised included resigned clothier Enos Kelsey, who "advertised he had for sale at his store in Princeton "an assortment of European and West India goods, which he engages to dispose of on the lowest terms for cash." However, because of the current economic problems, he added, "as the times wholly forbid his booking goods as heretofore, it will be taken as a mark of kindness, should his good customers forbear asking trust from him in future."[19]

Also, in December, goldsmith Daniel Van Voorhis announced he had opened shop in Princeton, a small distance to the eastward of the college. He made and sold at a better price than similar goods in Philadelphia. Van Voorhis gave a very long list of items, including urns, coffeepots, teapots, sugar dishes, tankards, candlesticks, milk pots, soup ladles, tablespoons, teaspoons, sugar tongs, shoe and knee buckles, scissors, and buttons. He also gave high prices for old gold and silver.[20]

Sales of enslaved persons and the breaking up of enslaved families continued. In December, Samuel Minor of Windsor offered for sale a twenty-six-year-old "negro wench," an eight-year-old boy, and a two-year-old girl. They could be purchased together or separately, as best suited the purchasers.[21] Enslaved persons still demonstrated their resistance to that condition by running away.

Horses stolen this year included a black horse taken out of Samuel Worth's pasture at Stony Brook on September 26. Worth believed the thief had gone toward New York, because "a negro was seen riding in haste that way the night of the theft, on a horse which bore his description."[22] Other men desiring independence also stole horses at times. James Rock, living in Princeton, offered ten dollars reward for a horse stolen in September, supposedly by an Irish deserter of the British Army named Daniel Daley.[23]

Merchants and craftsmen needed skilled labor. In addition to buying the time of indentured servants and the lives of enslaved persons, they sometimes hired labor. In just one example, Anthony Joline of Princeton advertised for a nailer, who was a master of the business and willing to instruct several boys. An interested single man of good character would "meet with great encouragement and employ, for a considerable time."[24]

In pursuance to the Legislative Act of December 20, 1781, regarding damages inflicted by either the British or American armies, inhabitants of Middlesex County wishing to make a claim for restitution could meet with appraisers Benjamin Manning, Joseph Olden, and Nathaniel Hunt at one of several places and dates, including Princeton from October 14 to 19. Claims must include inventories of the damaged, plundered, burned, or destroyed, property and state the general date of destruction and at whose hands.[25]

Colonel Morgan undertook some building projects and paid Joseph Horner for forty thousand high quality bricks and Noah Morford for carting timber, stone, and lath for his building. The projects included building a lengthy addition to his house and building a smokehouse, carriage house, and poultry house. All were constructed of stone. He continued hiring labor as needed, including for digging more ditches across a field south from his house. He also continued contracting with craftsmen such as Noah Morford for saddlery work and James Finley for weaving.[26]

Supply Department

Hard-pressed Commissary of Military Stores James Hamilton wrote to Governor Livingston from Princeton on May 18 that he could not give an account of the state military stores on hand until the following Tuesday. The greatest part of the cartridges he had were unbundled, and he had men at work filling and bundling them. Since he last drew money from the treasury, he had purchased 718 pounds of powder and 838 pounds of lead. About half of it was now on hand. He enclosed an account of the ammunition and military stores in the magazine at Princeton on September 5, 1781. It recorded about 1,000 pounds of powder and no lead, 268 cannon shot, 83 filled canisters, 800 blocks, 151 sheets of tin, 19 tubes, 12 port fires, two dozen match ropes, 109 flannel bags, 5 match sticks, 20 yards of flannel, 887 flints, 900 sacks, 3 bullet molds, 6 store boxes, 1 pair of nippers.[27] Several days later, on May

24, the Assembly authorized Hamilton to draw up to £1,000 for the use of his department.[28] Hamilton engaged in many transactions for which the Assembly paid him, including on November 30, when it authorized a payment of £13.12.5. The same day it authorized payment to Hamilton's predecessor, Elias Woodruff, of £184.12.3 to settle his account.[29] Other Princeton-area men also received payments, such as on June 22, when the Assembly directed the Treasurer to pay James McCombs, late Clothier of the State, £200.[30]

Hamilton was thirty-three years old and, despite his busy commissary duties, he decided to marry. On August 6, he married twenty-two-year-old Sarah Anderson of Princeton in a ceremony at Rocky Hill officiated by Rev. Witherspoon. Sarah noted that, at the time of the wedding and for a time afterward, her husband had "numerous wagons loaded with military stores at his own residence for the use of the military at the different depots in the State."[31]

Trade with the Enemy

Trade with the enemy continued to be a significant problem after hostilities ceased. In July, several trials took place at Princeton concerning goods seized from people trading with the enemy going to and from New York.[32] The inhabitants of Princeton and the surrounding area met that month at the market house to discuss a plan of association to prevent trade and intercourse with the enemy.

The group appointed Jonathan Deare to be chairman and then agreed "to detect and bring to justice all who shall be in any way concerned in this traffick, and encourage and strengthen the hands of all civil and military officers, by every justifiable means, to punish and suppress it." To this end they pledged to "give every assistance to those who are vested with authority, to detect and punish all suspicious persons traveling without the legal passports, or carrying goods, or going through the country in any manner contrary to the intention of the laws, or the interest of the State." They would stop all interactions with people known or suspected to be trading with the enemy and fight any opposition to their endeavors that insinuated it was "not highly honorable and praiseworthy." They would cease the purchase or use of British manufactured goods or goods that have come from behind British lines, except items "captured, condemned, and sold according to law." Finally, a committee was appointed "to present the association to the inhabitants for signing, and for the purpose of using the best means to have the same carried into execution." It would meet at Beekman's tavern on August 17 at 2:00 p.m. The committee consisted of Jacob Schenck, Jonathan

Deare, Colonel William Scudder, Thomas Stockton, David Olden, John Bergen, Captain William Covenhoven, Captain Jonathan Combs, George Bergen, Major Thomas Egberts, Captain James Moore, Doctor Thomas Wiggins, Rev. John Witherspoon, Jr., Enos Kelsey, James Hamilton, David Snowden, Daniel Slack, and Thomas Skillman, Jr.[33] This was another example of people organizing to help enforce laws.

Loyalists

Dealing with confiscated Loyalist property proved an involved undertaking. On May 21, the Assembly heard a petition from David Olden, one of the agents dealing with Loyalist real estate, setting forth several deficiencies in the act appointing him to his position that made it difficult to carry out his job.[34] Then, on June 19, the Assembly heard a petition from Robert Stockton and ordered it read with a bill entitled, "An Act to declare the Value of Debts due from Fugitives."[35] On November 2, the Assembly heard another David Olden petition on dealing with Loyalist estates.[36] Then, on November 6, his appeal was read along with a bill entitled, "An Act to Enable the Agents of the Respective Counties in this State to Proceed to the Sale of Certain Lands Therein Mentioned."[37] On December 3, the Legislature continued to debate the issues raised by David Olden and others regarding taking control of and leasing Loyalist properties. The Legislature ordered that the petition "be committed to the committee appointed on the 25th ultimo, to prepare and bring in a bill to amend the Act, entitled, 'An Act for taking charge of and leasing the real estates of the subjects of the King of Great Britain lying within this State.'"[38]

While still dealing with Loyalist estates, on August 15, David Olden announced himself as a candidate for sheriff of Middlesex County.[39]

The end of the year left open the final resolution of the war, although peace negotiations were in progress and preliminary peace treaty provisions had been drawn up on November 30. More and more, the Continental Congress and the New Jersey State government were looking to the future to determine how things would be arranged in peacetime. The military hospital was disbanded and the supply magazines were less needed, but questions remained about how to dismantle the army, and how public debts could be paid fairly and fiscal confidence restored in the government. Some of those issues would be debated in Princeton when the town temporarily became the seat of the Continental Congress the next summer.

Chapter 12

1783

The war for independence that divided the Princeton community had been disrupting peaceful life for about eight years, and people must have been wondering just when it would officially end, and what would come afterward when the thirteen states were no longer united in the common cause of fighting for independence. A British army continued to occupy New York, but with hostilities virtually ended, at least with British regulars, militia duty was significantly reduced. Washington's army was primarily at New Windsor above New York City, just waiting to be discharged. Soldiers still had complaints about their conditions and especially failing to receive their back pay. The Continental Congress would not ratify the peace treaty provisions until April 15, 1783, and the final peace treaty would not be signed until months later. Washington would issue the joyful orders that "all acts of hostility" should stop immediately on April 18, and General Sir Guy Carleton did the same for the British on the same day. Meanwhile, Princeton residents continued their regular interactions and business with each other. But, normal life would become complicated when the Continental Congress took up residence in Princeton beginning in late June.

With the cessation of hostilities, confidence in the future was strong for people like Colonel Morgan who, in April, planted a young apple orchard of three hundred trees, planted twenty feet apart, on ground too stony to plow. Scientific farmer that he was, Morgan noted in his journal—on the same page with the information about its planting—that the next year this orchard became threatened with total destruction by locusts.[1]

Quakers continued to suffer because of their religious convictions against participating in warfare. Stony Brook Quaker Benjamin Clarke served on a committee "to take notice and care of such of their members who may suffer by imprisonment or otherwise, in faithfully supporting our Christian testimony against war." He, along with Trenton's Stacy Potts, petitioned Governor Livingston and the Council at Burlington on behalf of Samuel Worth, Jr., who lived with his parents at Stony Brook, but was presently in jail for failing to pay a fine for "nonperformance of military services." If a man did not pay his fine, authorities could confiscate private property of that value. Young Samuel Worth had "no visible property whereon to levy." So, he was taken and delivered into the custody of the Middlesex County Sheriff and "kept prisoner at a considerable distance from his home upwards of eleven months." Because the legislature had not passed measures to resolve this type of situation, Clarke and Potts pointed out that Worth "must continue in this unhappy situation, or violate that invariable principle which we have steadily maintained ever since we were gathered to be a people. Wherefore we hope, the Governor and Council will take such measures for his relief, either in a judicial or legislative capacity, as the particular difficulties of his case may appear to the Governor & Council to require." The Privy Council pardoned Worth on June 17 after hearing the petition. After all, the fighting had been over for two months.[2]

The Continental Congress Comes to Princeton

The end of fighting did not mean an end to the political difficulties under the Articles of Confederation that kept the men in the Continental Army continually distressed about their lack of pay and other aspects of their relationship with Congress. Developing a system to dissolve the Continental Army without alienating the soldiers was a significant and challenging problem to solve. Would soldiers be furloughed without receiving full back pay, or would they continue in active service until fully paid?

On June 13, sergeants from troops stationed at the Philadelphia barracks wrote to Congress, describing the overwhelming hardships experienced by the soldiers fighting for the cause and declaring it was the duty of Congress to make sure the men were treated fairly as the army disbanded. They threateningly demanded that Congress reply to them positively by that night, or they would not be responsible for what might happen. Congress did not respond, but General St. Clair and Secretary at War Benjamin Lincoln went to the troops and allayed their fears. Members of Congress once again sought financial help from Robert Morris, but he was unable to come up with the money to pay the men. Efforts to resolve the issues were unsuccessful, and angry troops at other locations near Philadelphia threatened to march on Congress.[3]

On Saturday, June 21, a group of mutineers came to Philadelphia and surrounded Congress, causing the President of Congress, Elias Boudinot, to ask for assistance from local authorities. If support was not forthcoming, he said the Congress would remove to either Trenton or Princeton the following Thursday, "in order that further and more effectual measures may be taken for suppressing the present revolt, and maintaining the dignity and authority of the United States."[4] Whether the actions involved sprang strictly from concerns of the soldiers or were part of a political move in the struggle between those who favored a strong central government and those who supported strong State governments has been the subject of debate.[5]

Hearing that Congress might relocate to New Jersey, the inhabitants of Trenton and vicinity met on June 24 and "resolved unanimously that we would deem ourselves highly honored by the presence of Congress, and by an opportunity of testifying our zeal in support of their dignity and privileges, should they in their wisdom think proper to adjourn to or fix their residence in this State."[6]

The same day, Governor Livingston wrote to Boudinot, assuring him of the loyalty of the state. However, Boudinot had already decided on Princeton. He had many personal reasons for choosing Princeton. In the opinion of historian Varnum Collins, Boudinot's experiences in Congress drove him to want to "shield Congress from most of the distractions and various forms of political jobbery that were already hampering legislation." Philadelphia was the largest and most cosmopolitan city in the thirteen new states, with about six thousand houses and between thirty-five and forty thousand inhabitants, while Princeton was a war-torn village of only about seventy houses and several hundred residents. The two locations could not have been more different.[7]

Boudinot also knew Princeton very well. His father's silversmith shop served as the village post office for several years when Elias was a boy, and he must have played along today's Nassau Street. He married Hannah Stockton, sister of Richard Stockton, who married Elias's sister Annis. John Witherspoon had recently left Congress to restore the college to full life, and his reputation for common sense and willingness to assist made being near him very attractive. There were also five graduates of the college in Congress at the time. Boudinot also knew of the unwavering loyalty to the cause of the current citizens of Princeton.[8]

President Boudinot wrote to his brother Elisha on June 23 that, because of the mutiny and fear for the safety of Congress, "I mean to adjourn to Princeton if the inhabitants of Jersey will protect us." He expected to get to Princeton the next Saturday or Sunday but did not want this to be public knowledge. He ended with "I wish Jersey to show her readiness on this occasion as it may fix Congress as to their permanent residence."[9] Then, on June 24, Boudinot spoke with every Congressman he could find before issuing a broadside to be publicly posted in Philadelphia calling on Congress to meet at Princeton on June 26, in order "that further and more effectual measures may be taken for suppressing the present revolt, and maintaining the dignity and authority of the United States."[10]

Colonel Morgan wrote to Boudinot on June 25, offering "Congress the use of several buildings [at Prospect], on their own terms, during their stay at Princeton. One of them will afford a better room for them to meet in than they can be immediately accommodated with elsewhere—Any or every part of his farm & meadows shall also be at their command." He also "takes the Liberty to tender his utmost services, in every way he can be useful to Congress, during their residence in New Jersey."[11] Several days later, he expanded the offer to include the construction of any needed buildings on his farm and to purchase up to three hundred acres for them. He promised to provide the materials and workmen on "the shortest notice."[12]

About the same time, Colonels Joseph Phillips, Henry VanDike, and William Scudder of the three Hunterdon, Somerset, and Middlesex County militia regiments, respectively, whose soldiers' homes surrounded Princeton, pledged to Congress to "tender our services to Congress to protect them from all insolence and violence, and to march under proper command for this purpose whenever & wherever it may be necessary."[13]

Morgan also sought to find additional accommodations for Congressmen, and several local men made offers, including merchant and former army clothing purchaser Elias Woodruff and Anthony Joline. On July 1, Morgan reported to Boudinot that the town could accommodate Congress with sixty beds in the village and neighborhood, in addition to the buildings of Woodruff and Joline, opposite the college on the Post Road, with two huge rooms, "either of which would dine forty persons conveniently," in addition to six other good rooms, "some of them more than twenty feet square." They also had an excellent cellar, two "perfect kitchens," a back building for servants, stable, garden, and pasture. Another person offered to provide forty "covers" (meals) for Congress and to supply their liquids.[14]

Innkeeper John Cape also offered to provide meals or act as the steward for Congress. However, Congress turned down these offers, even though Cape had guaranteed to serve "fish crabs and lobsters at least three days in the week—The lobsters & crabs to be brought to Princeton alive."[15]

On June 26, the day Congress expected to arrive, the Princeton inhabitants asserted their loyalty, confidence, and welcome to Congress via

Colonel Morgan and Dr. Samuel Stanhope Smith with a resolution signed by twenty-eight male citizens.[16] Professor Smith also prepared an address to Congress in which he stated, while "convinced how few accommodations this small village possesses, in comparison with those which, for several years, Congress have enjoyed in a large & flourishing city, we wish to offer them every convenience that the college, in its present state, can afford." He offered rooms such as the library for Congress to use for various purposes. Probably in an attempt to get Congress to provide more reconstruction funds for the college, he noted, "and if, in the common shock of our country this institution hath suffered more than other places, both by friends & foes; from its readiness to assist the one, while the public was yet poor & unprovided with conveniencies for its troops; & from the peculiar & marked resentment of the other, as supposing it to be a nursery of rebellion, we doubt not but the candor of that most honorable body will readily excuse the marks of military fury which it still retains."[17]

Although the distance from Philadelphia was not great, delegates experienced various difficulties preventing their timely attendance. John Rutledge wrote to Jacob Read from Philadelphia the evening of, June 26: "I would have been at Princeton, before this will reach you, but, one of my feet is much swelled, & very painful—some people would call it a touch of the gout." Rutledge also doubted that enough members would arrive "or, whether they will stay at Princeton, above a few days, (for, it seemed to be the opinion of the members whom we saw at the President's on Tuesday, that Congress would return when a proper force was procured to suppress the revolt, & preserve the peace,) &, as traveling in such hot weather, is very disagreeable, I shall deter setting off, till I hear from you"—about whether a meeting was actually to take place and for how long at Princeton. He would then make the appropriate arrangements.[18]

John Montgomery did get to Princeton on time and found the people made every effort to receive the delegates well and provide comfortable lodgings, even with the very short notice due to the situation.[19] In a letter to Montgomery, Benjamin Rush told him, "Should Congress conclude finally to settle at Princeton, I shall cheerfully convey to them one half of a 20-acre lot in the heart of the town and 100 acres of woodland within two miles of the same." He went on to propose that Nassau Hall was so well suited for Congressional offices that "the wisest thing the trustees of it could do would be to sell it to the public. The revenue arising from the price of it would maintain two or three professors, while the boys might be boarded with more advantage to their morals and manners in private houses."[20] Witherspoon would no doubt strenuously object to such a move.

The public learned of the move to Princeton in the June 28 edition of Philadelphia's *Independent Gazetteer*, in a somewhat cynical notice reporting that "The honorable Congress of the United States of America having been for eight years past resolving and resolving, did, on Tuesday last, without their usual mature deliberation, hastily resolve to exchange their old sitting place for the more salubrious air of Princeton in the state of New Jersey, where they will enjoy the double satisfaction of the Reverend Doctor W__[itherspoon]'s lectures on politics and divinity." In general, the relocation was not greeted favorably, although people still criticized the actions of the mutineers.[21]

Montgomery wrote to Rush from Princeton on June 30, when Congress finally had a quorum of delegates, that in the evening they expected eleven hundred men commanded by General Robert Howe to arrive from headquarters that evening on their way to Philadelphia, to mop up the mutiny and guard Congress when it returned. He noted the kind treatment by the people of Princeton, who made every effort to make the delegates happy and comfortable. He felt there was "no inland situation preferable to this." He also asked to receive copies of Eleazer Oswald's *Independent Gazetteer*, and he would pay Oswald when he returned to Philadelphia.[22]

That same day, Secretary of Congress Charles Thomson wrote to his wife, Hannah, to fill her in on his arrival in Princeton. He had arrived at about 11:00 a.m., after setting out from Bristol a little after 3:00 a.m., and noted, "I had a fine air in my face but the sunbeams were excessively hot & scorching." He drove his carriage to Colonel Morgan's Prospect farmhouse, which he said was "just behind the college in a most elegant situation commanding an extensive and delightful prospect." His accommodations there included a downstairs parlor and a small room above it that was "clean, cool and pleasant." He found both Colonel George and Mary Morgan to be "easy, polite and agreeable," and the colonel enjoyed the life of a country gentleman on his "farm of two hundred acres of good land, and enjoys the benefit of an agreeable society." Thomson found Princeton to be a small town with most of the houses on the small side and built of wood, although there were also "a number of genteel houses around & in the neighborhood." Altogether, he praised Princeton because "with respect to situation, convenience & pleasure I do not know a more agreeable spot in America." Thomson reassured Hannah that his slave "Peter behaves well, his horses are just under my eye in Mr. Morgans stables & he lodges & diets with the family. My carriage is also safe under cover."[23]

Thomson was born in County Derry, Ulster, Ireland, in November 1729, so he was about fifty-five years old. As a young man, he was first a teacher and then became a merchant. He was a strong advocate for the opposition to

Parliament and then the cause of independence. A friend noted, "his natural temper was remarkably good and cheerful, and nothing delighted him more than free and social conversation with his friends." But, he was also a deep thinker and "possessed a great share of natural sagacity; he seemed to penetrate into the characters of men, and into their motives, with surprising facility; and he could, when provoked, or the occasion called for it, use a caustic severity in reproof, which was felt the more severely, as not inflicted willingly." Politically, "He was a true republican of the old school; he hated all the 'necessities' of royalty, and the pomp and trappings of aristocracy." He was also very religious, "attending more to the spirit than to the forms of religion, but his mind was fully imbued with the great truths of Christianity."[24]

Knowing that Congress required a quorum, as soon as he changed clothes, Thomson left Colonel Morgan's house and headed to Nassau Hall. Before leaving, he asked Morgan whether he was to take his meals "as well as lodge with him." Morgan invited Thomson "to dine with him as oft as was convenient & particularly that day," but Morgan believed the delegates planned to regularly dine together at a tavern, having appointed a commissary to make the arrangements. Delegates would only eat breakfast in their quarters. Thomson told Morgan he would be dining with the delegates, especially since "the hours of Congress would ill suit with rural economy." Before Thomson's arrival, Congressmen may have met informally before June 30, transacting no business, in Colonel Morgan's Prospect farmhouse.[25]

Upon reaching the college, Thomson reported, "I was conducted along an entry (which runs from one end to the other through the middle of the college) & was led up into the third story where a few members were assembled." However, unlike John Adams in 1774, he was not at all impressed while following the route his guide used. He began to have doubts because what he saw "had the effect of raising my mortification & disgust at the situation of Congress to the highest degree. For as I was led along the entry I passed by the chambers of the students, from whence in the sultry heat of the day issued warm streams from the beds, foul linen & dirty lodgings of the boys." Congress met in the library room, located on the second floor, north side, over the main entrance, and on formal occasions in the prayer hall. It was about thirty by twenty-four feet in size, opening onto the long hallway that ran east to west on each floor, and had been stripped by the British. Congressional Committees made use of unoccupied student rooms.[26]

Meeting his fellow delegates, Thomson found them "extremely out of humor and dissatisfied with their situation. They are quartered upon the inhabitants who have put themselves to great inconveniencies to receive them into their houses & furnish them with lodgings, but who are not in a situation to board them." It did not help that Thomson brought a letter from the President of Pennsylvania that "was dry and laconic and contained nothing that invited a return" to Philadelphia.[27]

After many conversations with fellow delegates, the one remaining topic was where to dine. President Boudinot's servant came in to tell Thomson that dinner was ready and several other delegates would join them. After dinner, Thomson talked with Boudinot and found him in favor of returning to Philadelphia. Boudinot felt that Princeton residents "had exerted themselves & put themselves to inconveniences to accommodate the members but it was a burden which they could not bear long."

However, life in Princeton could be quite pleasant for the delegates. President Boudinot settled in at Morven and later at Elias Woodruff's house opposite the college. He spent money lavishly on entertainment, and the bills from one merchant alone totaled up to $1,000 per month. His first order was for "a side of lamb and a gallon of wine, which were supplemented next day with two more gallons of wine, seventeen pounds of sugar, and a couple of three-shilling 'Juggs' and his steward forwarded to him fifty lemons and fifty limes."[28] Ashbel Green wrote letters home describing the passing of coaches and chaises on the street without stop and a "crying about of pineapples, lemons, and every luxurious article both foreign and domestic."

Delegates could visit local merchants for quality items. Enos Kelsey sold West Indian fancy goods and haberdashery, while John Harrison sold American and foreign cloths, silks, velvets, and calicos. Daniel Van Voorhis, a Philadelphia goldsmith, had opened a shop east of the college, where he offered the latest thing in silver knee and shoe buckles, gold beads and chains, punch strainers, and soup ladles. Monsieur D'Orssiere opened a dancing school that the college trustees forbade students to attend because it was held in a tavern.[29]

Expecting the arrival of the French Minister, the chevalier de La Luzerne, there was no place to accommodate him. Princeton was out of spare lodgings. Congress either needed to return to Philadelphia or find another more suitable location, but at the moment, this discussion would have to wait because the delegates "were not yet in temper, that they must have time to cool."

Not all delegates found comfortable accommodations in Princeton. James Madison wrote a lengthy letter to Thomas Jefferson in September and apologized that it might have been more interesting, but his "present situation required a great effort to accomplish as much as I have." The problem was that "I am obliged to write in a position that scarcely admits the use of any of my limbs, Mr. Jones & myself being lodged in a room not 10 feet square and without a single accommodation for writing."[30]

At its June 30 meeting, in addition to dealing with the mutiny that had caused it to come to Princeton, the immediate problems Congress faced were the payment and discharge of the men in the army, the final establishment of peace, the nature of a new army, and the selection of a permanent residence for the federal government. But, those issues were only the tip of the iceberg of matters demanding attention, which included dealing with foreign powers, establishing relations with Indian nations, and the inadequacies of the Articles of Confederation. Coping with the mutiny led to troop movements toward Philadelphia, some coming through Princeton, leading to the rumor that hundreds of men, with artillery, had been placed at Princeton to guard the Congress. The people of Princeton knew better, as the troops had kept moving toward Philadelphia.

The biggest problem in Princeton was maintaining a quorum in Congress, and with only seven states in attendance, the Congress put out the order on July 2 that absent States "be informed that it is indispensable they should without loss of time send forward a delegation to Congress."[31] The Articles of Confederation required a quorum of two delegates from seven States to be present for general business and from nine States when acting on critical matters. During the first six weeks at Princeton, at least seven times, there were not enough delegates to conduct an official meeting. During its first sessions, the Congress recognized with appreciation the support it felt from the citizens of Princeton, Trenton, and New Jersey in general. On July 4, President Boudinot wrote to Colonel Morgan that Congress accepted "the use of any of your buildings that may be indispensably necessary for public offices; and to express their high sense of your kind offers of service and attention to their accommodation and convenience."[32]

Congress met on July 4 and applauded the significant efforts of Princeton citizens, as well as dealing with financial issues and pay for the soldiers.[33] However, Benjamin Rush urged Congress to return to Philadelphia, insisting, "You have no time to lose. If you remain one week longer at Princeton feeding one another with ideas of insulted and wounded dignity (all stuff in a republic), you may lose Pennsylvania forever from your wise plans" to rectify the problems of Continental revenue. Rush argued, "You have not a single advocate in our city. An hundred ludicrous anecdotes are told of you every day." Rush expected to hear soon that Congress was highlighted in a ballad, no doubt a sarcastic and ribald one. So, he begged, "For heaven's sake! Forget and forgive. I honor your power, and I place all my hopes of the perpetuity of our happiness in the restoration of your influence and government over the United States."[34]

A very frustrated Charles Thomson had written Hannah on July 3 and told her, "it seems at least a month since I left you." The disruption of Congress was a big part of the seemingly slow passage of time, and he told her, "How can it be otherwise, while I see folly, weakness and passion marking the characters of those who ought to be distinguished by their wisdom and prudence." He believed it was impossible to stay in Princeton and get anything done, but it did not look like they would be leaving Princeton any time soon.

Celebrating July 4

Just four days after Congress began its session, Princeton planned to celebrate July 4 in typical fashion, eight years after the signing. Thomson commented on the upcoming celebration, noting that "lamps it is said are to be hung up on Mrs. Stockton's cherry trees." He told Hannah that he was invited to the dinner that evening at Morven hosted by President Boudinot. That led him to comment that "I have the honor of breakfasting at my lodging, of eating stinking fish & heavy half baked bread & drinking if I please abominable wine at a dirty tavern. On Monday indeed I got some pretty good porter, but on Tuesday the stock was exhausted, and yesterday I had the honor of drinking water to wash down some ill cooked victuals." But still, he could proclaim, "we are honorable gentlemen and we are out of Philadelphia."[35]

Writing to Hannah on the morning of July 4, Thomson told her that he wished he could have come to Philadelphia to celebrate the day with her, but he had a horse with a physical problem that he was afraid of hurting and that "conveyance by the stage is so inconvenient & disagreeable that I am quite discouraged from attempting it." He described Princeton as "a small scattered village, consisting of about 50 houses most of them low wooden buildings, several of them tumbling to pieces & some new & unfinished. There are five or six tolerable good brick houses or with brick fronts two stories high & there are several good farmhouses around."

He described the Stockton property that had so impressed John Adams in 1774 as being "large for a country house, it has four rooms on a floor commodious but not grand." Although there were remnants of gardens and walks on the property, after all the military occupation, "they are all a waste & only the traces of them left." This was currently where President Boudinot was staying because of his family connections. Opposite it was the house of Thomas Lawrence, where Alexander Hamilton lodged. Thomas FitzSimons was quartered at a farmhouse adjoining the Stockton lands further from the village on the road to Trenton. Theodoric Bland of Virginia found lodging in a "tolerable" house across from the college. The Maryland delegates were quartered about a mile from the village on the road to New Brunswick. "The rest are scattered up and down in the village."[36]

Thomson reported to Hannah on July 5 that the special morning of July 4 had not been ushered in with a joyous ringing of bells, but rather with the "jingle of the college bell, which being cracked exhibits exactly such a sound as a farmer makes with a frying pan when bees are swarming & he wants to settle them." A pole set in front of the college gate flew a flag "emblazoned with stars & stripes & with a motto, Virtue liberty & independence." Part of the ceremonies featured the first orator presentations by the Whig and Cliosophic societies. College senior Ashbel Green of the Whig society was chosen by lot to speak first and spoke on the subject of "the superiority of a republican government over any other form." His address was followed by one on Independence. Congressional delegates made up part of the audience, and the orators were invited by Boudinot to dine that evening with him and his other invited guests at Morven.[37]

During these morning events at the college, Annis Stockton was seeing to preparations at Morven, which Charles Thomson referred to as the "Palace." Thomson described a bower erected on the Morven green, under which the large company of guests would dine that evening. Thomson admitted to Hannah that he could not "boast of its columns, colonades or festoons nor of its triumphant arches or commodious apartments." Rather, it was more pedestrian and "composed of stakes stuck in the ground with forked tops, on which were laid rails & across these some poles to support the heavy branches lopt from the neighboring forest which served for a covering." A "grand arcade" was also erected in front of Morven for the fireworks display that evening, featuring fireworks brought up from Philadelphia.

While the sky had been clear in the morning, around 3:00 p.m. it became overcast, and at about 4:00 pm, just at the time scheduled for dinner, the skies opened, and rain came in a deluge. All those involved in setting things up had to move as much as they could into the house. Thomson had returned to his lodgings to wait out the storm but came back for dinner at about 6:00 p.m. He described the meal, stating, "The table was well furnished with hams & rounds of beef. But unfortunately the benches on which the company sat had felt the effects of the storm. However we had this comfort, that though our heads might be heated with wine, we would be cool at bottom." The crowd was further disappointed when it was found that the fireworks had not arrived from Philadelphia, and the oil lamps expected to be hung in the cherry trees did not appear.

In one last effort to make some celebratory noise, the militia cannon was dragged out from town. However, while being dragged, the pole was broken that mounted the sponge used to put out any sparks in the cannon barrel and prevent a misfire when loading. Thomson felt this eliminated the use of the cannon, but then, "happily there was an old bombardier present who undertook to fire without a sponge." After a rocket signal, "the cannon began to fire, but for want of a sponge they were ob[l]iged to fire so slow that it appeared to be minute guns fired on the death of some eminent commander" rather than a joyous occasion. The celebration ended after just a few additional rockets, and Thomson had to "confess I was very little entertained, and wished myself, a thousand times in Philadelphia with my dear Hannah."[38]

Congress Attempts to Work

During a heavy rain on July 6, Charles Thomson expressed to Hannah, "When I look back on the occurrences & transactions of a fortnight past I see few marks of wisdom, when I look forward I see a dark cloud and gloomy prospects for America. I confess I have great apprehensions for the union of the states, & begin to fear that America will experience internal convulsions, and that the fabric of her liberty will be stained with the blood of her sons. Those jarring principles which were kept down by common danger begin to operate. And pride & passion seem to occupy the seat of reason."

The only real achievement of Congress so far had been making cordial replies to the people of Trenton and Princeton for their invitations. However, he even questioned the motives of the residents that he felt were "evidently dictated by self-interest, and with a view to engage Congress to fix its residence among them & thereby promote their private emolument & not the public good." He predicted that Congress could not long remain at Princeton.[39]

Soon after their arrival in Princeton, Congressional delegates could feel the differing opinions in Philadelphia about their departure. However, if the residents of Philadelphia had mixed feelings about the benefits to them of Congress sitting in their city, it was also true that many Congressional delegates did not feel supported there by the local government, which had failed to protect them from the mutineers. Robert Morris entered in his diary on July 9 that if Congress "are ill accommodated at Princeton they will remove to Trenton or to some more convenient place" but "by no means return to this city." Congress was in no real hurry to return to Philadelphia, even though the accommodations in Princeton were not the most convenient.[40]

Hannah Thomson came to Princeton for a short visit in mid-July, and after she left, Governor Livingston's wife felt terrible that she had not visited Hannah.[41] Charles later sent Hannah a message for Mary Morgan, who must have then been in Philadelphia. He told Hannah, "Please to make my compliments to Mrs. Morgan & tell her all her family are well and that Miss Nancy does the honors of the table with a grace, which does great credit to herself and to the instructions she must have received from her Mamma. Miss Molly is cheerful as a bird and George finds a new play for every day. Master John as usual attends his book & horses. And the Colonel is as attentive as ever to his farm. In short you may tell her that they are all as happy as they can be without her company."[42] "Miss Nancy" was eleven-year-old Ann, "Miss Molly" was nine-year-old Mary, George was about three years old, and John about thirteen.

The weather continued hot and oppressive as Congress continued to debate whether to stay in Princeton or return to Philadelphia. Mary Morgan returned by stage from Philadelphia on July 24, when "the weather was so extremely hot that the passengers suffered greatly. Some of the horses dropped down & died & the rest came in excessively jaded. It was the same with the stages from Elizabethtown, which were obliged to leave the passengers on the road, some of whom walked into this town through the broiling sun & fresh horses were sent to bring in others. I think I never felt such a night and day as yesterday and the night before. Last evening a fine breeze sprung up which continues this morning and is very refreshing." However, the 25th was hot again, such that in the evening, "after dark we found it only tolerable, sitting in Col. Morgan's passage with both doors open" to get a cross breeze. The 26th was cool again.

The heat only exacerbated the divisions in Congress. Thomson wrote to Hannah that, "The common danger which has hitherto held these states together being now removed, I see local prejudices, passions and views already beginning to operate with all their force. And I confess I have my fears, that the predictions of our enemies will be found true, that on the removal of common danger our Confederacy & Union will be a rope of sand." While some kind of confederacy was needed for security, he questioned, "how many of the states will be comprehended in a Confederacy or how many confederacys there will be is yet uncertain."[43]

During the debates over the location for Congress in July, James Madison wrote to Thomas Jefferson that the people of Philadelphia would like Congress to return and conduct their business there until their place of permanent residence was determined. He was not sure how much their desires would be met even though "backed by the scanty accommodations of Princeton." He felt some factions wanted to keep Congress in Princeton until a final determination of a permanent location was made for their own purposes.[44]

Delegates continued to arrive in town, and on July 28, Samuel Huntington and his cousin Benjamin Huntington from Connecticut took up residence "in the stone house at the foot of the hill beyond Col. Morgan's cornfield." Richard Beresford from South Carolina took a "house below Jug town" with his wife. Thomson despaired, "Thus are the members dispersed among the neighboring farmhouses. How far they are in a situation to conduct public business their works will manifest, and if in their present situation they long preserve respect, I shall be greatly disappointed."[45] Alexander Hamilton came to Princeton on July 29 on his way to New York and represented New York for a very short time, making nine states in attendance so that the treaty with Sweden could be ratified. Then he left.[46]

Moving Congress back to Philadelphia was a persistent discussion, but Charles Thomson noted to Hannah on August 1 that typically, instead of making a decision, Congress held debates that went on—and on.[47]

Benjamin Rush could not help continuing to keep Boudinot informed about the low opinion people held of Congress and that "Strangers from Europe as well as every state in the Union condemn you. You are called the little Congress" or even "no Congress at all." Rush feared Pennsylvania might even leave the confederation. In consequence, "You have no time to lose. For God's sake, be wise, and let not those words dignity of Congress produce the same fatal effects upon our Union that Supremacy of Parliament has produced upon the British empire." He then noted that the "wrongs" committed by the mutinous soldiers and the lack of action by the local government were now past, and the only step remaining "wrong" was Congress's relocation to Princeton.[48]

Seeking the Help of George Washington

The question about what sort of army would be needed after the establishment of peace was becoming more urgent in July. General Washington's advice had been sought in May, and now it was believed that it would be very beneficial to have him come to Princeton to participate in the discussions.[49] Therefore, Boudinot wrote to Washington on July 31, informing him that Congress requested his attendance at Princeton to help deal with the situation that had brought Congress to Princeton. Boudinot closed with the comment that he looked forward to seeing both the General and Mrs. Washington. He also sent "the most affectionate wishes" for their health and happiness from Mrs. Boudinot and Miss Susan.[50] But, Washington felt that if he was only being called to help with the peace establishment, on which he had already given his views, and although Congress thought he would be more comfortable at Princeton, he would rather stay where he was until he could retire to private life at Mount Vernon. Congress had more in mind, and on August 7, resolved to have an equestrian statue of Washington in noble Roman attire be created to be placed at the permanent seat of government.[51] Washington ultimately decided to make the journey to Princeton.

The prospect of Washington coming to Princeton meant that suitable quarters for him needed to be found. Colonel Morgan again assisted and was able to secure an estate about four miles from town at Rocky Hill on the banks of the Millstone River and on the road leading to Morristown. This was "Rockingham," the property of the late Judge John Berrien that his widow, Margaret, offered to rent fully furnished to Colonel Morgan for Washington. This 320-acre property was good farmland with a good proportion of meadow and woodland. The house contained more than 20 rooms, including a very "conveniently contrived and genteelly finished" kitchen. A good variety of outbuildings in addition to a "very good barn and stables" occupied the land along with several orchards "containing the best grafted fruit in our country" that supplied apples, pears, plums, peaches, cherries, raspberries, and currants. There were also "several thousand very thrifty Red Cedar trees, a great number of which have been trimmed and properly cultivated." Very importantly, the property "abounds in springs of the best water."[52]

By the middle of August, President Boudinot was still looking for suitable lodgings and was very interested in the college president's house, but professor Samuel Stanhope Smith occupied it. Since President Witherspoon lived on his Tusculum estate, Boudinot thought he might rent him the college president's house for income. However, when the subject was mentioned to Smith, he received it like "a thunderclap" because no one had hinted at it, and he had no idea where he would go with this family. He had worked hard with others to help delegates find lodging, but now believed he might have to give up his own house.[53]

While Boudinot continued looking for accommodations, the Congress continued to debate where to "fix the place of their permanent residence" but again put off a decision until the first Monday in October.[54] Although definitive information on the peace treaty had not been confirmed, Boudinot informed Washington that Congress had received information from General Carleton that he had been ordered to evacuate his troops from New York without delay.[55]

Washington Comes to Princeton

After a short wait caused by "fatigued" horses and Martha Washington fighting a fever, Washington set out from Newburgh, New York, on August 18, leaving Henry Knox in command. He arrived on August 23, accompanied by twelve young (none older than twenty) New England troopers of Von Heer's Dragoons. They pitched their tents on the lawn around Rockingham, with Captain Bezaleel Howe placing his marquee directly in front of the house.[56]

Captain Howe served in the 1st New Hampshire Regiment as a lieutenant from November 8, 1776, until discharged September 17, 1783. Shortly after, he was promoted to Captain, and during much of 1783 commanded Washington's guard. His commission from Congress, awarded September 30, 1783, was signed at Princeton on October 4 by President Boudinot.[57]

Among his baggage, Washington had four boxes and three trunks full of his books and papers.[58] Congress learned of Washington's arrival on Monday the 25th, and Princeton residents held a public meeting that drew up an address to be sent immediately to Rocky Hill. In this address, residents of the town and vicinity and the college community congratulated him on the current promising state of affairs. It was especially noted that his presence at Princeton was appropriate because, "As the College of New Jersey devoted to the interests of religion & learning was among the first places in America that suffered by the ravages of the enemy[,] so happily this place & neighborhood was the scene of one of the most important & seasonable checks which they received in their progress. The surprise of the Hessians at Trenton & the subsequent victory at Princeton redounded much to the honor of the commander who planned & the handful of troops with him which executed the measures. Yet were they even of greater moment to the cause of America than they were brilliant as particular military exploits."[59] In his gracious reply, Washington also connected with the events at Princeton "The prosperous situation of our public affairs, the flourishing state of this place, and the revival of the seat of literature from the ravages of war, increase to the highest degree, the pleasure I feel in visiting (at the return of peace) the scene of our important military transactions, and in recollecting the period when the tide of adversity began to turn, and better fortune to smile upon us."[660]

About eleven o'clock on the morning of August 26, the General set out from Rockingham for Princeton accompanied by his escort of dragoon troopers and riding on a small, young favorite roan horse equipped with an "old crooked saddle with a short deep blue saddlecloth flowered, with buff cloth at the edge, buckskin seat, the cloth not below the skirts of the saddle at the sides; double skirts, crupper, surcingle, and breast strap... double bitted steal bridle, and plated stirrups." The four- to five-mile ride took about forty minutes, and in his pocket he carried his written response to the congratulatory address, sent in advance to him, which he would hear in Congress.[61]

He arrived at about noon in the excitement-filled village. Taverns could scarcely accommodate all the visitors in town, and more had come on the morning stages from Philadelphia and New Brunswick. Local farm families had come into town to mingle with the distinguished visitors. The college boys in their black gowns were gathered at the entrance to Nassau Hall, waiting to see the hero. Spectators filled the gallery of the prayer hall, while the floor was filled with seated delegates without head coverings. President Boudinot sat facing them, wearing his hat as a sign of his authority. When the prayer hall door swung open, two delegates from the committee on arrangements escorted Washington into the room and to a chair beside President Boudinot. On the wall hung the large gilt picture frame that had contained the full-length portrait of George II destroyed by the American cannonball as the Battle of Princeton came to an end on January 3, 1777. Once Washington was seated, Boudinot read the Congressional congratulatory message, and Washington read his reply.[62]

Writing to Edmund Randolph about the debate over Congress remaining in Princeton or returning to Philadelphia, James Madison noted that several places, including Annapolis, were encouraging Congress to make them the permanent seat. As a result, "during this contest among the rival seats, we are kept in the most awkward situation that can be imagined; and it is the more so as we every moment expect the Dutch Ambassador. We are crowded too much either to be comfortable ourselves or to be able to carry on the business with advantage. Mr. Jones & myself on our arrival were extremely put to it to get any quarters at all, and are at length put into one bed in a room not more than 10 feet square."[63]

A Young Artist Meets Washington

William Dunlap was a seventeen-year-old aspiring artist from Perth Amboy who came to Rocky Hill as the guest of John Van Horne, living a short walk from Rockingham, while Congress was at Princeton and Washington at Rockingham. Dunlap wrote that one day, "before I left Princeton for Rocky Hill, I saw, for the first time, the man of whom all men spoke—whom all wished to see." This sighting "was accidental. It was a picture. No painter could have grouped a company of military horsemen better, or selected a background better suited for effect." This exciting encounter occurred:

> As I walked on the road leading from Princeton to Trenton, alone, for I ever loved solitary rambles, [and] ascending a hill [there] suddenly appeared a brilliant troop of cavaliers, mounting and gaining the summit in my front. The clear autumnal sky behind them equally relieved the dark blue uniforms, the buff facings, and glittering military appendages. All were gallantly mounted—all were tall and graceful, but one towered above the rest, and I doubted not an instant that I saw the beloved hero. I lifted my hat

> as I saw that his eye was turned to me, and instantly every hat was raised and every eye was fixed on me. They passed on, and I turned and gazed as at a passing vision. I had seen him. Although all my life used to the 'pride, pomp and circumstance of glorious war'—to the gay and gallant Englishman, the tartan'd Scot, and the embroidered German of every military grade, I still think the old blue and buff of Washington and his aids, their cocked hats worn sidelong, with the union cockade, their whole equipment as seen at that moment, was the most martial of anything I ever saw.[64]

While staying with the Van Horne's, Dunlap writes, Washington "frequently called, when returning from his ride, and passed an hour with Mrs. Van Horne and the ladies of the family, or with the farmer, if at home. I was of course introduced to him." Dunlap discovered that the widespread belief that Washington never laughed was mistaken. Dunlap felt that Washington "had from early youth been conversant with public men and employed in public affairs—in affairs of life and death." Despite that, "He was not an austere man either in appearance or manners, but was unaffectedly dignified and habitually polite. But I remember, during my opportunity of observing his deportment, two instances of unrestrained laughter." One was in reaction to an anecdote from a member of Congress dining with him, while the second occurred at the Van Horne's house.

> Mr. John Van Horne was a man of uncommon size and strength and bulky withal. His hospitable board required, that day, as it often did, a roasting pig in addition to the many other substantial dishes which a succession of guests, civil and military, put in requisition. A black boy had been ordered to catch the young porker, and was in full but unavailing chase, when the master and myself arrived from a walk. "Pooh! You awkward cur," said the good-natured yeoman, as he directed Cato or Plato (for all the slaves were heathen philosophers in those days) to exert his limbs—but all in vain—the pig did not choose to be cooked. "Stand away," said Van Horne, and throwing off his coat and hat he undertook the chase, determined to run down the pig. His guests and his negroes stood laughing at his exertions and the pig's manifold escapes. Shouts and laughter at length proclaimed the success of the chasseur, and while he held the pig up in triumph, the big drops coursing each other from forehead to chin, over his mahogany face, glowing with the effect of exercise, amidst the squealing of the victim, the stentorian voice of Van Horne was heard, "I'll show ye how to run down a pig!" and, as he spoke, he looked up in the face of Washington, who, with his suite, had trotted their horses into the courtyard unheard amidst the din of the chase and the shouts of triumphant success. The ludicrous expression of surprise at being so caught, with his

George Washington
Pastel on paper by William Dunlap ca1783.
(US. Senate Collection)

attempts to speak to his heroic visitor, while the pig redoubled his efforts to escape by kicking and squeaking, produced as hearty a burst of laughter from the dignified Washington as any that shook the sides of the most vulgar spectator of the scene.[65]

During his time at Rockingham, Washington complimented Dunlap's portraits of the Van Hornes. Dunlap "was delighted by the approbation of General Washington—doubtless the mere wish to encourage youth. My friend Van Horne requested him to sit to me and he complied. This was a triumphant moment for a boy of seventeen," but also "one of anxiety, fear and trembling." Dunlap did pastel crayon sketch portraits of General and Mrs. Washington and painted a full-length one of the General in oil. Overall, Dunlap recalled, "I was quite at home in every respect at headquarters; to breakfast and dine day after day with the General and Mrs. Washington, and members of Congress, and noticed as the young painter, was delicious."[666]

The Peace Treaty and Continuing Problems

Just over two months after the delegates moved to Princeton, on September 3, the American and British negotiators signed the definitive peace treaty in Paris, but the news would not reach Princeton until the end of October. By mid-September, Washington had seen enough of Congress to have severe doubts about its effectiveness while continuing at Princeton. He was especially concerned about the peacetime army that would replace the Continental Army and had recently given his opinions, but it appeared to him that there would not be enough delegates present to discuss and act on such an important topic while Congress continued at Princeton. He described the problem: "the want of accommodation, added to a disinclination in the Southern Delegates to be further removed (than they formerly were) from the centre of the empire, and an aversion in the others to give up, what they conceive to be a point gained, by the late retreat to this place; keeps matters in an awkward situation; to the very great interruption of national concerns."

In the matter of choosing a permanent location for Congress, he believed, "seven States it seems (by the Articles of Confederation) must agree before any place can be fixed on for the seat of the Federal Government; and seven States it is said, never will agree. Consequently as Congress came here, here they are to remain to the dissatisfaction of the majority." Little business can be done "having none of the public offices about them, nor no places to accommodate them if they were brought up; and the members from this, or some other causes, are eternally absent."[67] Congress also needed to work on western land policies, such as those that had led Colonel Morgan to resign and come to Princeton hoping to see to the education of the three Delaware boys.

During August and September, the subject of whether or not to return to Philadelphia kept being put off because October 1 had previously been set as the date to discuss and determine the permanent home for Congress. In general, Charles Thomson made frequent comments to Hannah about the work of Congress, with phrases such as, "Another day is spent in ill humor and fruitless debates." On September 17, it was, "Another day is passed in disputations which though they did not wound the feelings of humanity as those of the day before, yet excited no less indignation, being founded on ignorance as well as malice." He ended a long letter on the 18th after describing a tempestuous debate in detail: "I am indeed heartily weary of this scene and if it continues much longer, I am inclined to think I shall wish to withdraw from it. Still however I entertain a fond hope that the same kind providence which has conducted us so far in our journey will open a way for the future happiness and prosperity of the United States."[68]

Congressional delegate Benjamin Huntington of Connecticut was still finding life in Princeton a bit challenging. He wrote to his wife, Anne, on September 8 that they expected the arrival soon of the Dutch minister. He felt "This must be a wonderful great affair, and what Congress can do with this Great Personage in Princeton is more than humane wisdom can devise for there are not buildings sufficient to house more Dons nor indeed as many as are already here."

He noted that some delegates found it necessary to go to Philadelphia "once or twice a fortnight to breath in polite air. The country so badly agrees with those sublime & delicate constitutions that it is to be feared that many of them will contract a rusticity that can never be wholly purged off." He missed city life and the luxuries it provided. However, "The ladies make less complaint than the gentlemen and the gentlemen who have their ladies here seem in some degree contented."

Huntington could not help commenting that "A new fashion is among the ladies here which is the same as at Philadelphia. The Roll is much less than formerly and is raised to a peak on their forehead frowzled & powdered and they wear mens beaver hats with a large tye of gauze like a sash or mourning wead about the crown & decorated with feathers & plumes on the top which makes a very daring appearance. The brim of the hat is tapered before about as low as their eyes and is a kind of riding hat, they walk abroad and sit in Church in the same. Some have them in the same figure made of paper and covered with silk with deep crevices as a beaver hat but as this is much out of the line of business I was sent here to do I have not been very particular on the subject." In terms of ladies clothing, "I might also mention the waistcoat and long sleeves much like the riding habits our ladies wore twenty five years ago but as they differ some from them & having no right to be very much in observation upon the ladies I am not able to say much on the subject."[69]

Some of the college students had harassed or negatively influenced the Indian boys sponsored by Colonel Morgan. Thomas Killbuck was put out to work on the farm of "Mr. Lukins of Bucks Co.," where he learned some farming and blacksmithing. But, he became addicted to liquor and lying, and his services to Lukins had little value. By 1783 he was very homesick and requested through Colonel Morgan to leave and return home. He would be sent home in 1784, intending to become a blacksmith among his people. John Killbuck was very studious and advanced rapidly, studying geography and mathematics, hoping to become a merchant in his own country. While generally showing good common sense, he fell in love and entered into a secret marriage contract with a Morgan-serving maid, and she became pregnant. Morgan discovered this in September. John was willing to legalize the marriage but also wanted to continue his studies. After some negotiation with Congress, John and his family stayed together, under the guidance of Morgan, who saw to John's continuing education.[70]

College Commencement

The college trustees met on September 24, commencement day, and approved awarding a bachelor's degree to twenty-two-year-old Captain Nathaniel Lawrence, originally from Long Island, whose education had been interrupted by the war. Lawrence had entered the college in May 1776 when not quite fifteen years old. He left when Witherspoon closed the college in November, and on June 1, 1777, he became a second lieutenant in a North Carolina regiment at age 15. Lawrence became a British prisoner at the surrender of Fort LaFayette below West Point on June 1, 1779, until March 28, 1781, when he was exchanged. In the confusion of the times, Lawrence went through several efforts to rejoin the army and was back in Princeton by late February 1783, but whether he had returned to his studies is not clear. Shortly after graduation, he began to study law and was admitted to the New York bar in 1786.[71]

As a way for the trustees to "give some testimony of their high respect for the character of his excellency general Washington, who has so auspiciously conducted the armies of America," they formed a committee, including Witherspoon, to request Washington "to sit for his picture to be taken by Mr. Charles Wilson Peale of Philadelphia—And, ordered that his portrait, when finished be placed in the hall of the college in the room of the picture of the late king of Great Britain which was torn away by a ball from the American artillery in the Battle of Princeton."[72] For his part, Washington had donated fifty guineas to the trustees "as a testimony of his respect for the college."

William Churchill Houston resigned from the college because he had entered "into another profession incompatible with the discharge of his duty in the college." He moved to Trenton, where he established his law practice.

The dancing school established by D'Orssiere some months before had become an object of concern to the college. The trustees discussed it and, "It being represented, that permitting the students to attend a dancing school in the town is useless to them in point of manners, they being generally past that period of youth in which the manners are formed, & it being represented that their attendance in such school involves them immediately, or by consequence in considerable expenses, to the injury & ill report of the college, & it being held in a tavern, & often late at night, circumstances very unfriendly to the order of good government of the institution—it was unanimously resolved, that from henceforth the students shall not be permitted to attend a dancing school, during the sessions of the college, under any pretense whatever."[73]

The college held its commencement exercises at the Presbyterian Church near Nassau Hall. The damage caused by its use as a barracks had not yet been completely restored. Ashbel Green, class of 1783, described the commencement:

> The church in Princeton had been repaired during the summer which preceded the commencement at which I received my bachelor's degree. An extended stage, running the length of the pulpit side of the church, had been erected; and as the president of congress was a trustee of the college, and the president of the college had recently been a distinguished member of congress, and that body itself had been accommodated in the college edifice, an adjournment to attend commencement seemed to be demanded by courtesy, and was readily agreed on. We accordingly had on the stage, with the trustees and the graduating class, the whole of the congress, the ministers of France and Holland, and commander-in-chief of the American army. The valedictory oration had been assigned to me, and it concluded with an address to General Washington. I need not tell you, that both in preparing and delivering it, put forth all my powers. The General colored as I addressed him, for his modesty was among the qualities which so highly distinguished him. The next day, as he was going to attend on a committee of congress, he met me in one of the long entries of the college edifice, stopped and took me by the hand, and complimented me on my address, in language which I should lack his modesty if I repeated it, even to you. After walking and conversing with me for a few minutes, he requested me to present his best wishes for their success in life to my classmates, and then went to the committee room of congress.[74]

Several graduates had seen service in the army, including Ashbel Green, valedictorian, and Nathaniel Lawrence. Washington attended in his blue and buff, having ridden in from Rocky Hill. Congressional delegates included James Madison and many others who had served in the war in various capacities. On the platform sat seven signers of the Declaration of Independence, nine signers of the Articles of Confederation, eleven future signers of the Constitution, two future Presidents—Washington and Madison—and members of the New Jersey branch of the Society of the Cincinnati, founded the previous May at Newburgh, New York.

Final Months of Congressional Work in Princeton

In October, the debate over a permanent residence for Congress continued. In his cramped quarters, James Madison jotted notes for and against Princeton as a temporary seat of Congress. Positives included its closeness to Philadelphia, the inconvenience of removing Congress from it, the popularity of Congress throughout the State, and "the risque in case of removal from Princeton of returning under the commercial and corrupt influence of Philadelphia." However, the town was unfit for transacting the public business. Perhaps most importantly, its "deficiency of accommodation, exposing the attending members to the danger of indignities and extortions, discouraging perhaps the fittest men from undertaking the service, and amounting to a prohibition of such as had families from which they would not part."[75] It seems neither Princeton nor Philadelphia suited Congress well.

On October 1, Boudinot undertook some personal business with General Carleton in New York. He requested that Carleton look into finding and returning items plundered from his brother-in-law, Richard Stockton, by British troops stationed at Princeton. These included "his title deeds—Bonds Acct Books, and other papers therewith, personal property to the amount four or five thousand pounds."[76]

General Nathanael Greene came through Princeton on October 7 on his way home to Rhode Island. At his command in the south, he had furloughed the soldiers and ceased making any Continental expenditures. In a letter to Boudinot, he noted it had been "going on nine years since I have had an opportunity to visit my family or friends or pay the least attention to my private fortune." He already had Washington's permission to go home, and he was now asking for the consent of Congress. However, he could not yet return home, spent some time in Philadelphia, and was back in Princeton on November 1 when he again wrote to Boudinot, this time about finding a way to save and organize his papers relating to the southern operations.[77] Leaving the army was proving complicated.

Washington wrote to the Marquis de Chastellux on October 12 that "Having the appearance, and indeed the enjoyment of peace, without a final declaration of it, I, who am only waiting for the ceremonials, or till the British forces shall have taken leave of New York, am placed in an awkward and disagreeable situation, it being my anxious desire to quit the walks of public life, and under the shadow of my own vine and my own fig tree to seek those enjoyments and that relaxation, which a mind, that has been constantly upon the stretch for more than eight years, stands so much in need of. I have fixed the epoch to the arrival of the definitive treaty, or to the evacuation of my country by our newly acquired friends."[78]

At that time, Charles Thomson wrote to Hannah that the debate over even a temporary home for Congress was still the subject of "fruitless debates." This was because "The unaccommodating spirit of some and the jealousy nay I may say the deep rooted hatred which others bear to the city of Philadelphia were displayed in the strongest colors."[79] Several days later he wrote, "I begin to be afraid we shall be tied down for the winter to this uncomfortable village, notwithstanding eight states have resolved 'that for the more convenient transaction of the business of the United States and accommodation of Congress it is expedient for them to adjourn from their present residence.'" This had been resolved on October 10, and it was now the 16th. However, he also pointed out to Hannah that "yesterday for the first time since their removal from Philadelphia they seriously entered upon the business of the Continent and finished a very important matter relative to Indian Affairs." Had Colonel Morgan been in the meeting, he would not have been happy with the policies adopted.[80]

Peter Van Berckel, the Minister Plenipotentiary from the Netherlands, landed at Philadelphia in October after an uncomfortable sea voyage and was dismayed to find Congress no longer there. He was angered that no arrangement had been made for a residence or place to keep his horses. He also felt insulted by Boudinot's steward, who suggested that he should not remain in Philadelphia but proceed to Princeton and Congress. When he arrived in Princeton, he was openly not pleased, although Congress made every effort to honor him, and John Witherspoon put him up at Tusculum.

The next day, October 31, Robert Morris and General Benjamin Lincoln rode out to Tusculum and told Van Berckel that Congress would receive him in town. Van Berckel left Tusculum in his private coach and, just before reaching Nassau Hall, saw a horseman come dashing along the Post Road from the east and stop at the gate to the campus. The rider was Colonel Mathias

Ogden of the 1st New Jersey Regiment, who had just returned the previous day from England bearing the news that the final peace treaty between Great Britain and the United States had been signed. So, an especially joyous group welcomed Van Berckel. He was ushered by Morris and Lincoln into the chamber, where members of Congress sat arranged by state, with Boudinot sitting facing them and wearing his hat. A chair was placed for Van Berckel in front of Boudinot, and the very formal and dignified ceremony of greetings, with translations, was completed in style.[81]

On October 25, Benjamin Harrison wrote to the Virginia delegates that "we are all anxious to know where Congress means to fix its permanent residence, reports say it is to be in the woods near Princeton or on the Delaware a little below Trenton. I think it impossible that either can be true." Such a move would have completely alienated the south and the idea arose that it should be in the central state of Maryland.[82]

John Paul Jones sought to discuss issues regarding prizes taken at sea in European waters and dealing with France and Denmark about them. He wrote to Boudinot on October 18, "I propose to visit Princeton about the middle of next week, and shall then have the honor to give such further explanation as may be necessary."[83] He did come to Princeton, and on November 1, Congress resolved to recommend to the Minister Plenipotentiary of the United States at the Court of Versailles to help Jones deal with the issues and seek "payment and satisfaction to the officers and crews for all prizes taken in Europe under his command, and to which they are in anywise entitled."[84]

In early November, Washington welcomed Thomas Paine, whom he had invited to visit in September, when a case of scarlet fever had delayed Paine. Washington felt that Paine's visit might "remind Congress of your past services to this country." At the time, Paine was having difficulties with delegates to Congress and in finding a home. Washington signed his invitation, "by one who entertains a lively sense of the importance of your works." On a Sunday during his visit, Paine and Washington drove to church, and Paine asked to stop at a friend's house, where he left his heavy overcoat with the friend's servant. He then walked to the church and joined Washington. When he went back after the service to get his coat, he found that the friend's servant had run off with it, along with some of his master's silver plate. Washington chuckled and amusingly reminded Paine that "it was necessary to watch as well as pray." He later gave Paine one of his own coats.

During Paine's visit, Washington suggested a scientific experiment after being told by local people that the creek running near the bottom of Rocky Hill could be set on fire. Paine learned that in the opinion of the local people "on disturbing the bottom of the river, some bituminous matter arose to the surface, which took fire when the light was put to it." However, Paine "supposed that a quantity of inflammable air was let loose, which ascended through the water and took fire above the surface." At Washington's suggestion, a small boat was found along with several soldiers to guide it with poles. According to Paine, "General Washington placed himself at one end of the scow and I at the other. Each of us had a roll of cartridge paper, which we lighted and held over the water about two or three inches from the surface when the soldiers began disturbing the bottom of the river with the poles." This caused air bubbles to rise fast, "and I saw the fire take from General Washington's light and descend from thence to the surface of the water." This provided evidence that the river was set on fire by inflammable air rising out of the mud.[85]

On November 4, Congress adjourned at Princeton, agreeing to meet at Annapolis on the 26th. Thomas Jefferson, again a delegate from Virginia, attended and took his seat for that one day.[86]

Washington traveled to West Point before heading home to Virginia and, on November 9, wrote to Captain Bezaleel Howe at Rockingham with instructions regarding the removal of his papers and other items to Mount Vernon. The six baggage wagons got to Philadelphia on the evening of November 11 and left there the next day.[87]

With the end of hostilities, Loyalists who had fled to New York looked for ways to evacuate before or when the British army did. Also, several runaway enslaved men from Princeton awaited ships to transport them from New York. John Longstreet, age forty-five, was a former slave who ran off in 1776 from his owner, Derrick Longstreet. He was now free, had a certificate of freedom issued by General Musgrave, and was currently working in the Wagon Master General's Department of the British army. He was cleared on November 19 to depart for Port Mouton, Nova Scotia, on the ship *Nesbitt*.[88] Peter Stogdon (Stockton), age twenty-three, had run off in about 1780 from his owner, Robert Stockton. He was now free and had a certificate of freedom issued by General Birch. He was cleared on July 8 to leave for the St. John River, New Brunswick, Canada, on the ship *Ann*, shipmaster John Clark.[89]

Witherspoon and the college trustees continued their efforts to obtain funds from the State Legislature for the restoration of the college. A memorial signed by Witherspoon was read to the Assembly on November 21, "setting forth the great damages the college has sustained during the war, not only by the buildings being laid waste, and the destruction of the library and apparatus, but by the almost total annihilation of its funds." The Assembly agreed to draw up a bill "to appropriate such fines or amercements as may be assessed and levied in the several courts in the respective counties in this State, for two years, to the benefit of the College of New Jersey."[90]

As Washington made his way from New York to Virginia in early December, he must have passed through Princeton about December 6. Charles Willson Peale was in Philadelphia between December 8 and 13 and sent Washington a note on December 9 requesting him to sit for a portrait at a convenient time. This portrait had been commissioned by the trustees of the College of New Jersey to replace the damaged portrait of King George II that had been destroyed at the Battle of Princeton. Washington did sit, and the painting was presented to the college at commencement in 1784. It still hangs in Nassau Hall to this day.[91] The background depicts the closing moments of the Battle of Princeton. Nassau Hall and the steward's house appear in the distance as they appeared from the south in 1777. The British retreat toward Nassau Hall behind a red flag, while the Americans push them, marked by a blue flag and a blue-uniformed officer waving a sword. A white flag carried by a horseman appears halfway between Nassau Hall and the combatants. The mortally wounded Mercer lies in the foreground at Washington's feet.[92]

By December, the war was officially over, and the residents of Princeton now had to face the complications to life that came with the efforts of their new country to devise a political system amidst all the diversity among the thirteen states that threatened to tear them apart if some compromises could not be made by all. There was still the remaining animosity between those who had supported the war for independence and those who wanted to remain loyal to England. Loyalists dealt with this in different ways. Some, like Richard Cochran, ended their days back in Great Britain or other British territories, while others, like Dr. Absalom Bainbridge and Mary, remained in America under the now-independent government, and their children grew to adulthood as citizens of the new country. Their son William, born in Princeton just a few months before the John Adams party passed through in 1774, became the American naval hero Commodore William Bainbridge in the War of 1812. William and Charity Millette returned to Princeton and resumed life in the new country and continued to be active in the Presbyterian Church.

As 1783 came to a close, the people of Princeton could look back on ten years of complex changes to their lives. A Revolution had changed many ideas, and the war for independence had been won, setting up the hope for a new government that would provide more freedoms than the British government they had left. One of the most significant battles of that war had been fought on their land, an action that saved the Revolution from early defeat and allowed it to take on new life and achieve ultimate victory. The town had also served the cause as a supply magazine for the Continental Army and the State militia, a military hospital for the Continental Army, and a center of government for the independent State of New Jersey and, toward the end, for the Continental Congress.

A number of the leaders in the Revolutionary movement had strong ties to Princeton, including John Witherspoon, Richard Stockton, Elias Boudinot, Jonathan Dickinson Sergeant, William Churchill Houston, and others. Other Princetonians whose names are not as well-remembered sacrificed much to help support the cause, including Jonathan Baldwin, Enos Kelsey, Elias Woodruff, David Olden, James Moore, Jonathan Deare, Jacob Hyer, George Morgan, and many others. All Princetonians had their lives intimately influenced by the Revolution and war, including women, such as Annis Stockton, Mary Morgan, and Sarah Clarke, and enslaved persons, such as Prime, Susannah, and so many others. Princeton experienced the Revolution and the war as a diverse community trying to deal with events that were outside their control but frequently interrupted their lives. In many ways, they were like us today, and understanding their struggles in the eighteenth century can help us understand our struggles today. Their stories, and their names, are well worth remembering.

Citation Abbreviations

Microform identifications - r – roll, i – image, p - page, f – frame

AA – Force, American Archives

AO12 - Great Britain, Exchequer and Audit Department. *American Loyalist Claims.* Series 1, 1776-1831, AO 12 [microform] Exchequer and Audit Department

AO13 - Great Britain, Audit Office. *American Loyalist Claims.* Series 2, 1780-1835, AO 13 [microform] Exchequer and Audit Department

BPMP – Selig, Harris and Catts. Battle of Princeton Mapping Project.

GWPLOC – George Washington Papers at the Library of Congress, 1741-1799, available on line at memory.loc.gov

JCC – Journals of the Continental Congress

NJSA – New Jersey State Archives

PA Archives – Pennsylvania Archives

PCC – Papers of the Continental Congress

PF - Pension application file

PMH&B - Pennsylvania Magazine of History & Biography

QMR - U.S., Quaker Meeting Records, 1681-1935

General Assembly - Votes and Proceedings of the General Assembly

Legislative-Council - Journal of the Proceedings of the Legislative-Council

Joint Meeting - Minutes and Proceedings of the Council and General Assembly of the State of New Jersey in Joint Meeting

Source Notes

Introduction

1 Gigantino, *Livingston's Revolution*, 36–37; Greiff, Gibbons, and Menzies, *Princeton Architecture*, 3.
2 Several other lines were drawn in the decades after the Keith Line, but even today the boundaries of towns and counties reflect the Keith Line influence.
3 Joseph Worth married Sarah Giles, making him brother-in-law to both William Olden and Benjamin Clarke. Benjamin Clarke left England due to the persecution of Quakers and arrived in Perth Amboy, East Jersey, in 1683. His son Benjamin married Ann Giles, the sister of William Olden's wife, and then inherited his father's vast estate late in 1689. William Olden married Elisabeth Giles, daughter of James Giles of Bound Brook, and they had eight children. For an overview of early settlement in the Princeton area, see: Hageman, *Princeton and Its Institutions*, I: 19–56, and Greiff, Gibbons, and Menzies, *Princeton Architecture*, 3–9.
4 Although by tradition Stony Brook received its name from early settler Richard Stockton, who named it after a stream he knew where the family had lived on Long Island, the name appears on a map drawn in 1685, several years before Stockton arrived. It is more likely that the stream received its name because of its appearance. Greiff, Gibbons, and Menzies, *Princeton Architecture*, fig. 3.
5 Woodward and Hageman, *Mercer and Burlington*, 600.
6 Collins, *Princeton Past and Present*, xi; Hageman, *Princeton and Its Institutions*, I: 12.
7 *QMR*, New Jersey, Burlington, Chesterfield Monthly Meeting, Women's Minutes, 1766–1771, 28; Men's Minutes, 1738–1786, 415; Chesterfield Monthly Meeting Minutes, 1756–1786, 201.
8 *QMR,* Chesterfield Monthly Meeting, Minutes, 1688–1809, 358; Women's Minutes, 1772–1786, January 7, 1773; 1772 Chesterfield Monthly Meeting, Men's Minutes, 1738–1786, 459.
9 *QMR*, New Jersey, Burlington, Chesterfield Monthly Meeting, Minutes, 1688–1809, page 366, microform frame 376.
10 *QMR* , New Jersey, Burlington, Chesterfield Monthly Meeting, Men's Minutes, 1738–1786, Frames 239–48.
11 Jamison, *Religion in New Jersey*, 13–14.
12 Pomfret, *Colonial New Jersey*, 231.
13 Ibid., 206–207.
14 Gigantino, *Ragged Road to Abolition*, 18.
15 Pomfret, *Colonial New Jersey*, 213–14.
16 Witherspoon, "A Description of the State of New Jersey," *Works of John Witherspoon*, IX: 199–212.
17 Jamison, *Religion in New Jersey*, 42.
18 Witherspoon, "A Description of the State of New Jersey," *Works of John Witherspoon*, IX: 199–212.
19 Pomfret, *Colonial New Jersey*, 195–96.
20 Ibid., 201.
21 Proclamation money was coin valued according to a proclamation issued by Queen Anne on 18 June 1704. It remained in effect until 1775. The 17½ pennyweight Spanish dollar was rated at six shillings in all the colonies.
22 *College of New Jersey Trustees Minutes.*
23 Information on settling the transaction is found in the minutes of the college trustees through the period of the Revolution. Collins, *Princeton Past and Present*, 26.

24 Jamison, *Religion in New Jersey*, 57–58.
25 Pomfret, *Colonial New Jersey*, 193–94, 268.
26 Cutler and Cutler, *Life, Journals, and Correspondence*, I: 245.

Chapter 1

1 Collins, *Princeton Past and Present*, 32. The term Boston Tea Party was first used in 1826. See J. L. Bell's *Boston 1775* Blogspot of December 22, 2010, for the story of its introduction, http://boston1775.blogspot.com/2010/12/man-who-named-boston-tea-party.html.
2 Charles C. Beatty to Enoch Green, January 31, 1774; Leitch, *A Princeton Companion*, 74; *Newport Mercury*, February 28, 1774, 2.
3 *College of New Jersey Trustees Minutes*, 203–07.
4 *Pennsylvania Gazette*, February 16, 1774, 3.
5 See Ferling, *Leap in the Dark*, chapter 1 and especially pages 14–16, for more on this. Also, Ferling, *Almost a Miracle*, 26–29.
6 *PCCS*, 1–3. *Votes and Proceedings of the General Assembly of the Colony of New Jersey*, February 8, 1774, 122–23.
7 *College of New Jersey Trustees Minutes*, 203–07.
8 *College of New Jersey Trustees Minutes*; Helen Hamilton Stockton, "Woodruffs and the Woodruff House, Now 68 and 70 Nassau Street" (1939), Historical Society of Princeton, File 470 typewritten.
9 College of New Jersey Trustees Minutes. Charles Candee Baldwin, The Baldwin Genealogy, from 1500 to 1881, Cleveland: 1881, 320. The Sergeant and Baldwin families both came to Princeton from Newark, where they were prominent. McLachlan, Princetonians, I: 131. Jonathan Baldwin lived until November 28, 1816, when he died at Newark, age 85, and Sarah until May 29, 1804, age 68.
10 William Smith, Nassau Hall, to Philip Fithian, February 28, 1773. Fithian, *Journal and Letters*, 34.
11 *New York Gazette, and Weekly Mercury*, August 10, 1772, Supplement 1.
12 Gigantino, *William Livingston's Revolution*, 42.
13 McLachlan, *Princetonians*, I: 133.
14 For the Middlesex meeting, see: *PCCS*, 15–17. For the Somerset meeting, see: *Pennsylvania Journal*, July 20, 1774, 5.
15 *PCCS*, 25–27; see pages 28–30 for communications to and from Boston on the relief effort from New Jersey. See also Gerlach, *New Jersey in the American Revolution*, 76–78, for the Resolves of the New Brunswick Convention; *Pennsylvania Packet*, July 25, 1774, 5.
16 Gigantino, *William Livingston's Revolution*, 49, 53.
17 Collins, *Princeton Past and Present*, xiv–xv.
18 *Pennsylvania Gazette*, February 3, 1773, 3; *The Pennsylvania Packet*, February 1, 1773, 3.
19 *Pennsylvania Chronicle*, November 15, 1773, 384.
20 *New York Gazette, or Weekly Post-Boy*, Monday, June 27, 1768, 4. His damage claim for December 1776 when the British occupied Princeton shows the extent of his endeavors and well as a bit about his lifestyle. *NJSA*, Legislative Series, Inventories of Damages by the British and Americans in New Jersey, 1776–1782.
21 Advertised throughout the year, for example in the *New York Gazette*, January 3, 1774, 2, and December 5, 1774, Supplement 2.
22 Harrison, *Princetonians*, II: 513–14.
23 Deane, *Correspondence of Silas Deane*, 164–65.
24 Cutler, *Life, Journals, and Correspondence*, I: 245. See also *The Works of John Witherspoon*, VIII: 326, for a very similar description by longtime resident John Witherspoon.
25 William Smith, Nassau Hall, to Philip Fithian, July 27, 1773; Fithian, *Philip Vickers Fithian Journal and Letters*, I: 38–39.

26 Young William later became a Commodore in the U.S. Navy and hero in the war of 1812. The house is now known as Bainbridge House because William was born there.
27 William Whitehead sold his house and three-acre lot in Princeton on May 2 at public vendue. Catalpa trees lining Nassau Street are mentioned by Moreau de St. Mery in 1794, and they seem to be mature then. Just when they were planted is not known, but it seems likely it was after 1774. Any trees on the road then would likely have been cut down for firewood by the British occupation forces in 1776. *Moreau de St. Mery's American Journey [1793–1798]*, 106.
28 For additional information on Hick and his sufferings as a Loyalist, see *AO* 13, piece 061, 233–34. He had further troubles at Amboy, was arrested and imprisoned at Trenton until he had paid a heavy bail, sought protection in New York where his wife died, and took passage for England but died during the voyage, leaving four children, three boys and a girl, the oldest age seventeen, to survive in England. *Pennsylvania Packet*, March 7, 1774, Supplement 2; *Pennsylvania Gazette*, January 26, 1774, 1; March 23, 1774, Supplement 2; *New York Gazette*, December 12, 1774, Supplement 2; Notice of Whitehead taking over appeared in *Pennsylvania Packet*, May 2, 1774, 4.
29 *Thomas Patterson, Account book: Princeton, New Jersey, 1774–1776*, August 18, 1774, page 1. Princeton University Special Collections, C0199 no. 825q.
30 *McClean House, National Register of Historic Places Inventory—Nomination Form*, Charles W. Snell, Survey Historian, February 8, 1971, 2.
31 Bill and Edge, *A House Called Morven*, 24–25.
32 32 *Votes and Proceedings of the General Assembly of the Colony of New Jersey, Session Beginning at Burlington, November 10, 1773*, March 2, 1774, 187.
33 Greiff, Gibbons, and Menzies, *Princeton Architecture*, 25–27; Greiff and Gunning, *Morven: Memory, Myth, and Reality*, 48–51. The Greiff and Gunning book is the most reliable and up-to-date account of Morven and its occupants. They give a detailed account of why an exact knowledge of what Morven looked like at the time of the Revolution is not possible. They also correct a number of inaccuracies found in earlier works on the subject, such as Bill and Edge, *A House Called Morven*.
34 Hageman, *Princeton and Its Institutions*, I: 81–82; Bill and Edge, *A House Called Morven*, 3, 5, 13; Greiff and Gunning, *Morven: Memory, Myth, and Reality*, 40.
35 Butterfield, "Morven: A Colonial Outpost of Sensibility," 3–4; Mulford, *Only for the Eye*, 18; Bill and Edge, *A House Called Morven*, 31.
36 Richard Stockton, Princeton, to Robert Ogden, September 13, 1765; Gerlach, *New Jersey in the American Revolution*, 12–13; Mulford, *Only for the Eye*, 19.
37 Bill and Edge, *A House Called Morven*, 25.
38 *Maine Memory Network of the Maine Historical Society* #102184, Richard Stockton, Morven, September 21, 1774, to Elisha Lawrence, https://www.mainememory.net/search?keywords=102184.
39 Cutler, *Life, Journals, and Correspondence*, I: 245.
40 Based on the plan of Gov. Belcher—the only contemporary plan in existence. Collins, *Princeton*, 332.
41 Collins, *President Witherspoon*, 83–86.
42 Glenn, *William Churchill Houston*, 1–20, 87–88; McLachlan, *Princetonians*, I: 643–45.
43 Rice, *Rittenhouse Orrery*, 38. A second Orrery was constructed for the College of Philadelphia over the next few months.
44 Green, *Life of John Witherspoon*, 258–59.
45 45 We can assume it was the college president's house and not Witherspoon's farm at Tusculum which he did not occupy full-time until 1779. National Register of Historic Places Inventory—Nomination Form, Charles W. Snell, Survey Historian, February 8, 1971, 2.
46 Pomfret, *Colonial New Jersey*, 267.

47 Gigantino, *William Livingston's Revolution*, 41, 47.
48 Witherspoon, "Thoughts on American Liberty," *The Works of John Witherspoon*, IX: 73–77. These thoughts were expressed in the several months leading up to the Continental Congress and were certainly expressed in his conversations with people like Adams.
49 Gigantino, *William Livingston's American Revolution*, 41.
50 Collins, *Princeton Past and Present*, 32; James Madison, Nassau Hall, to James Madison (his father), July 23, 1770; Madison, *The Writings of James Madison*, I: 6.
51 Cohen and Gerlach, "Princeton in the Coming of the Revolution," 11.
52 Harrison, *Princetonians*, II: 440–42.
53 Schmidt, *Princeton and Rutgers*, 42–43.
54 Letter from John Adams to Abigail Adams, August 28, 1774 [electronic edition]; *Adams Family Papers: An Electronic Archive*, Massachusetts Historical Society, http://www.masshist.org/digitaladams/.
55 Green, *Life of John Witherspoon*, 144–45.
56 Cutler, *Life, Journals, and Correspondence*, I: 236.
57 Hatfield, "Jonathan Dickinson Sergeant," 441.
58 John Adams diary 21, August 15–September 3, 1774, Massachusetts Historical Society, *Adams Family Papers: An Electronic Archive*, https://www.masshist.org/digitaladams/archive/index, 27–31.
59 "A Description of the State of New Jersey," Witherspoon, *Works of John Witherspoon*, IX: 199–212.
60 Greiff, Gibbons, and Menzies, *Princeton Architecture*, 25.
61 Kalm, *Travels into North America*, 220–27.
62 *NJSA*, Tax Ratables and Probate records. Although the tax lists and estate inventories described things after 1777, there is no doubt the farms were very similar at the time of Revolution. Sheep were not taxed, but estate inventories list sheep.
63 *QMR*, New Jersey, Burlington, Chesterfield Monthly Meeting, Deeds of Trust, Certificates of Removal, Epistles, Acknowledgments.
64 Hageman, *Princeton and Its Institutions*, I: 205. The family is often spelled Mellet, Millet, Millett, or another variation. William Millette was a French-Canadian Loyalist who returned to Canada during the war but came back afterward and contributed to repairing the Presbyterian Church. Creesy, "The Battle of Princeton," 18.
65 *A0* 12, A013, 69–76.
66 *Pennsylvania Journal*, September 7, 1774, 3.
67 Harrison, *Princetonians*, II: 442–45. He went south to Virginia and qualified to practice law in 1783. He made a good marriage in 1788 in North Carolina and became the largest slave owner in his county.
68 *College of New Jersey Trustees Minutes*, 207–11.
69 *New York Gazette and Weekly Mercury*, October 24, 1774, 1.
70 Collins, *Princeton*, 75; letter to the editor by Causidicus dated November 24, 1772, in the *New York Gazette*, December 7, 1772, 1; letter to the editor by A Friend to Impartiality, dated Lancaster, October 19, 1772, in the *Pennsylvania Chronicle*, October 31, 1772, 165; Cohen and Gerlach. "Princeton in the Coming of the American Revolution," 9.
71 Cohen and Gerlach, "Princeton in the Coming of the American Revolution," 10.
72 *Thomas Patterson, Account Book: Princeton, New Jersey, 1774–1776*, September 30, 1774, 35. Princeton University Special Collections, C0199 no. 825q.
73 John Williams Sanders, advertisement for Constant, *New York Gazette*, November 7, 1774, 2. Sanders appears on tax lists in 1778, but not later. He did not own land or personal property for which he was taxed.
74 *New York Gazette*, December 26, 1774, 4.
75 *Thomas Patterson, Account Book: Princeton, New Jersey, 1774–1776*, Princeton University Special Collections, C0199 no. 825q. Woodruff did not have a son named Amos

76 *New York Journal*, October 27, 1774, 3.
77 Bamberg, "Bristol Yamma and John Quamine in Rhode Island," 2–31. See also Joseph Yannielli, "Princeton and Slavery, African Americans on Campus, 1746–1876," https://slavery.princeton.edu/stories/african-americans-on-campus-1746-1876.
78 Stockton, "An Expedient," 228–29.
79 *Thomas Patterson, Account Book: Princeton, New Jersey, December 16, 1774*, 72, Princeton University Special Collections, C0199 no. 825q.
80 Jemima Condict, *Jemima Condict, Her Book: Being a Transcript of the Diary of an Essex County Maid During the Revolutionary War* (Newark: The Carteret Book Club, 1930).
81 Cohen and Gerlach, "Princeton in the Coming of the Revolution," 10.

Chapter 2

1 Pomfret, *Colonial New Jersey*, 191.
2 *PCCS*, 56–62. J. W. Sanders is often given as T. W. Sanders. The author believes this is the John Williams Sanders mentioned later.
3 Ibid., 42–44.
4 Gigantino, *William Livingston's Revolution*, 49.
5 Pomfret, *Colonial New Jersey*, 225.
6 *PCCS*, 103, 109.
7 Deane, *Correspondence of Silas Deane*, 226–27; see also Force, *AA*, II: 517, for the New York paper of May 9.
8 *PCCS*, 169.
9 Mulford, *Only for the Eye*, 20.
10 *PCCS*, 114–15.
11 Ibid., 170, 175. William Paterson had grown up in Princeton, graduated from the college, and studied law with Richard Stockton. He later became governor of New Jersey in 1790.
12 Gigantino, *William Livingston's Revolution*, 51–53, 55–57.
13 *PCCS*, 179–81, 183.
14 Ibid., 162–63.
15 Stryker Rodda, New Jersey Rateables, Middlesex County, 125.
16 For a fuller discussion of this, see Ferling, *Almost a Miracle*, 69–71.
17 *PCCS*, 184–85.
18 Ibid., 185–87.
19 Ibid., 192–94.
20 *New York Journal*, August 31, 1775, 2.
21 *PCCS*, 195–96. This is a rare reference to any kind of uniform for militia units.
22 *PCCS*, 196–97, 321–23.
23 *PCCS*, 208–10; *JCC*, October 9, 1775, III: 285–86; Berg, *Encyclopedia of Continental Army Units*, 81–82; Ferling, *Almost a Miracle*, 107; Wright, *Continental Army*, 76.
24 *Dunlap's Pennsylvania Packet*, Monday, October 30, 1775, 3.
25 *PCCS*, 233–35, 245–46.
26 *JCC*, III: 376.
27 Ibid., III: 416.
28 Kidder, *A People Harassed and Exhausted*, 72.
29 For a complete discussion of this, see Brendan McConville, *These Daring Disturbers of the Public Peace: The Struggle for Property and Power in Early New Jersey* (Philadelphia: University of Pennsylvania Press, 1999).
30 Cohen and Gerlach, "Princeton in the Coming of the Revolution," 10.
31 *PCCS*, 179–81, 183.
32 Ibid., 187–92.

33 James Moore, *NARA M804 PF* W1060.
34 *QMR*, New Jersey, Burlington, Chesterfield Monthly Meeting, Men's Minutes, 1738–1786, frame 253.
35 *QMR*, 1681–1935, New Jersey, Burlington, Chesterfield Monthly Meeting, Men's Minutes, 1738–1786, frame 254–55.
36 *QMR*, 1681–1935, New Jersey, Burlington, Chesterfield Monthly Meeting, Men's Minutes, 1738–1786, frame 256–58.
37 *New York Gazette*, February 6, 1775, 4; O'Connor, *William Paterson: Lawyer and Statesman*, 34.
38 O'Connor, *William Paterson: Lawyer and Statesman*, 293 n45, quoting Haskett, "William Paterson, Counsellor at Law," Ph.D. thesis, Princeton University, 1951, 82n.
39 *Pennsylvania Journal*, March 29, 1775, 4.
40 *Pennsylvania Packet*, August 8, 1774, Supplement 2.
41 Cohen and Gerlach, "Princeton in the Coming of the Revolution," 12.
42 Hatfield, "Jonathan Dickinson Sergeant," 441.
43 The children were Julia, b. 1759 (16); Mary and Susan (Sukey and Polly), twins b. 1761 (13); John Richard (Dicky), b. 1764 (11); Lucius Horatio (Horace), b. 1768 (7); and Abigail, b. 1773 (2). All born when Annis was between 23 and 37.
44 Rush, *Dearest Julia*, xiii–xvi; Fried, *Rush*, 129–37.
45 *Pennsylvania Packet*, November 13, 1775.
46 *New England Chronicle*, December 14, 1775, 4.
47 Bamberg, "Bristol Yamma and John Quamine in Rhode Island," 2–31. See also Yannielli, "Princeton & Slavery, African Americans on Campus, 1746–1876."
48 *College of New Jersey Trustees Minutes*, 212–14.
49 Cohen and Gerlach, "Princeton in the Coming of the Revolution," 10.
50 *New York Gazette*, October 9, 1775, 3.
51 Gigantino, *William Livingston's Revolution*, 58–60.

Chapter 3

1 Alexander McDonald, George Gillespie, J. W. Sanders to Jonathan Dickinson Sergeant, delegate in Continental Congress, March 12, 1776, *PCC*, Letters Addressed to Congress, 1775–89, r99 i78 p20.
2 John Witherspoon, Philadelphia, to David Witherspoon, March 17, 1777; Smith, *Letters of Delegates*, VI: 455–57. Stryker-Rodda, New Jersey Rateables, 1778–1780, Somerset County, 112.
3 Richard Cochran file, *AO* 13, 013, 69–76.
4 *New York Gazette*, March 4, 1776, 4. Witherspoon signed the newspaper report.
5 *QMR*, 1681–1935, frame 270–71.
6 Carleton, *British Headquarters Papers*, Book of Negroes 10427 (139): MG23 B1, Microform: M-369, Item Number: 1528.
7 *PCC*, New Jersey State Papers, 1775–88, r82, i68 p39. Signed Samuel Tucker, President.
8 *PCCS*, 576. He is mentioned on August 21, 1776.
9 Graydon, *Memoires of His Own Times*, 136–38; John Hancock, Philadelphia, to the Commissioners to Canada, May 24, 1776; Smith, *Letters of Delegates to Congress*, IV: 66. Which innkeeper he stayed with is not known, but it very likely could have been Jacob Hyer.
10 Bill and Edge, *A House Called Morven*, 35.
11 Collins, *Narrative*, 24–26.
12 Rush, *Dearest Julia*, xv.
13 *Proceedings of the Committee of Safety*, 327–28.
14 *Pennsylvania Gazette*, March 13, 1776, 4.

15 Jonathan Dickinson Sergeant, Princeton, to John Adams, April 6, 1776; Smith, *Letters of Delegates to Congress*, III: 495–96.
16 "A Friend to Government by Assembly," *Pennsylvania Evening Post*, April 4, 1776, 169–70.
17 This had been done on April 6. Instructions came on November 9, 1775. See *PA Archives*, 8th ser. VIII: 7352–53, 7513; Force, *AA*, 4th ser. V:434–35.
18 Jonathan Dickinson Sergeant, Princeton, to John Adams, April 11, 1776; Smith, *Letters of Delegates to Congress*, III: 507–09.
19 19 See Marine Committee to Esek Hopkins, April 23, 1776; Smith, *Letters of Delegates to Congress*, III: 576–77. He was on the committee that wrote this letter and was a signer.
20 *Pennsylvania Packet*, May 13, 1776, 1, 4.
21 Witherspoon, *The Writings of John Witherspoon*, VI: 202–16.
22 Cohen and Gerlach, "Princeton in the Coming of the Revolution," 10; Green, *Life of John Witherspoon*, 149–50. Witherspoon, *The Works of John Witherspoon*, V: 202–16.
23 Jonathan Dickinson Sergeant, Princeton, to John Adams, May 20, 1776; Smith, *Letters of Delegates to Congress*, IV: 45–46.
24 See *Dunlap's Pennsylvania Packet, or the General Advertiser*, May 27, 1776.
25 "Expense Account of Journey to and from Philadelphia, 21 May–12 June 1776," *Founders Online, National Archives*, https://founders.archives.gov/documents/Washington/03-04-02-0298. [Original source: "The Papers of George Washington," *Revolutionary War Series*, vol. 4, "1 April 1776–15 June 1776," ed. Philander D. Chase (Charlottesville: University Press of Virginia, 1991), 363–68.]
26 *PCCS*, 445–46, 455–58.
27 Jonathan Dickinson Sergeant, Burlington, to John Adams, June 15, 1776; Smith, *Letters of Delegates to Congress*, IV: 224.
28 Sergeant to Samuel Adams, June 24, 1776; *Samuel Adams Papers, 1635–1826*. [microform]. See also Abraham Clark to Elias Dayton, July 4, 1776, note.
29 *PCCS*, 524.
30 Sergeant to Samuel Adams, June 24, 1776; *Samuel Adams Papers, 1635–1826*. [microform].
31 Collins, *President Witherspoon*, 86.
32 Green, *Life of John Witherspoon*, 160–61.
33 Ibid., 159.
34 McLachlan, *Princetonians*, I: 439.
35 Ibid., III: 231.
36 Collins, *Princeton*, 78; Collins, *President Witherspoon*, 90. By tradition, senior William Richardson Davie formed and led this group, but it cannot be proven, and several factors make it doubtful.
37 John Pintard, *PF* R8265; Harrison, *Princetonians*, III: 91. After some other duties, he was named assistant to his uncle Louis Pintard, deputy commissary general of prisoners in New York.
38 *College of New Jersey Trustees Minutes*, 214–15; Collins, *President Witherspoon*, 88.
39 Harrison, *Princetonians*, III: 121–22.
40 *Pennsylvania Journal*, October 23, 1776, 3.
41 *PCCS*, 395.
42 Ibid., 457–58.
43 Green, *Life of John Witherspoon*, 61.
44 Epstein, *The Loyal Son*, 256–67.
45 Harrison, *Princetonians*, III: 119.
46 For more on the five-month levies and how they affected the New Jersey militia structure and commitments, see Kidder, *A People Harassed and Exhausted*, chapters 4–9 *passim*.
47 Pomfret, *Colonial New Jersey*, 267.
48 John Adams to Hezekiah Niles, February 13, 1818; *Founders Online, National Archives*, accessed August 6, 2019, https://founders.archives.gov/documents/Adams/99-02-02-6854.

49 Extract of a letter from Princeton, *Pennsylvania Packet*, July 15, 1776, 3; Collins, *Princeton*, 77.
50 Carpenter Wharton, Trenton, to John Hancock, July 15, 1776, *PCC*, i78 v23 p298 r104.
51 *PCCS*, 559–61.
52 *JCC*, Wednesday, August 14, 1776, V: 653.
53 *PCCS*, 541–42.
54 Collins, *Narrative*, 6; *NJSA*, MSS 167.
55 *Pennsylvania Gazette*, July 17, 1776, 3.
56 *JCC*, Wednesday, January 17, 1776, IV: 62. Stainforth was punished as a Loyalist later in the war.
57 Ibbetson Hamar, Kingsberry near Trenton, to John Hancock, July 9, 1776; *PCC*, Miscellaneous Letters to Congress, 1775–89, r96, i78, p63.
58 Richard W. Stockton, *AO*13, 112A, 259–65.
59 *PCCS*, 538, 544.
60 Creesy, "The Battle of Princeton," 18. *Second Report of the Bureau of Archives*, Toronto, 1905. Alexander Fraser, "United Empire Loyalists: Enquiry into the Losses and Services in...," Part 1, Ontario Department of Public Records and Archives, Joseph Stockton, *AO*13, 112, 272.
61 Green, *Life of John Witherspoon*, 258–59.
62 John Witherspoon, Philadelphia, to David Witherspoon, July 29, 1776, Smith, *Letters of Delegates to Congress*, IV: 566–67. David Witherspoon (1760–1801) became lieutenant of a company of Hampden-Sydney student volunteers in 1777 and in 1780 secretary to Samuel Huntington, then president of Congress. Collins, *President Witherspoon*, I: 25n.19, 193n.37.
63 John Witherspoon, Philadelphia, to David Witherspoon, August 26, 1776; Smith, *Letters of Delegates to Congress*, V: 68–69. The Pennsylvania Associators were the volunteer State troops of Pennsylvania. Pennsylvania did not have a militia law and the Associators filled that gap. For more on the Associators, see Joseph Seymour, *The Pennsylvania Associators, 1747–1777* (Yardley: Westholme, 2012).
64 *QMR*, frame 271–72.
65 Collins, *Narrative*, 51; Harrison, *Princetonians*, III: 82.
66 Stryker Rodda, New Jersey Rateables Somerset County Western Precinct, 111. Hageman, *Princeton and Its Institutions*, I: 96.
67 *General Assembly* (session beginning August 27, 1776), 2. On October 2 the pay for the Sergeant at Arms was set at three shillings per diem and four shillings per diem for the Doorkeeper; Ibid., 32. Hamilton was spelled Hambleton in the record, and he was probably a member of the Hamilton family of Somerset County. The name is variously spelled as Hammelton and Hamelton in the tax records.
68 *Joint Meeting*, 3–5. Bill and Edge, *A House called Morven*, 38.
69 *General Assembly* (session beginning August 27, 1776), 9–10; *Legislative Council* (session beginning August 27, 1776), 9–10.
70 *Joint Meeting*, 7, 8.
71 *General Assembly* (session beginning August 27, 1776), 40.
72 Ibid., 28–29. See also p. 4—October 8—for their authorization to be paid six pounds for bringing the money from Philadelphia. *Journal of Council*, 27.
73 Richard Stockton, Saratoga, to Abraham Clark, October 28, 1776; Smith, *Letters of Delegates to Congress*, V: 415–16.
74 Harrison, *Princetonians*, II: 126–27.
75 John Witherspoon, Princeton, to Horatio Gates, October 30, 1776; Smith, *Letters of Delegates to Congress*, V: 419–20.
76 *JCC*, Friday, November 8, 1776, V: 934.
77 John Witherspoon, Princeton, to Benjamin Rush, November 17, 1776; Smith, *Letters of Delegates to Congress*, V: 511. For more on the growing criticism of Dr. Morgan, resulting

in his abrupt dismissal as director general and physician in chief of the Continental Army on January 9, 1777, see John Hancock to John Morgan and William Shippen, December 1, 1776; and Samuel Adams to John Adams, January 9, 1777.

78 Collins, *President Witherspoon*, 87–88.

79 John Witherspoon, Princeton, to Richard Stockton, November 21, 1776; Smith, *Letters of Delegates to Congress*, V: 527–28. The medicine is in *PCC*, M247 [Miscellaneous] Letters Addressed to Congress, 1775–89, item 78, 23:323.

80 George Ross, Princeton, to James Wilson, November 28, 1776; Smith, *Letters of Delegates to Congress*, V: 547; *JCC*, November 27, 1776, VI: 973, 986, *JCC*, January 18, 1777, VII: 48.

81 Collins, *President Witherspoon*, 88–89; Collins, *Princeton*, 78.

82 John Witherspoon, Princeton, to William Livingston, November 29, 1776; *Livingston Papers, Microform*, Reel 3: 659-660.sxq.

83 Glenn, *William Churchill Houston*, 22–23; Harrison, *Princetonians*, II: 317; Creesy, "The Battle of Princeton," 18.

84 Harrison, *Princetonians*, III: 140–44 (Barber), 170–71 (Hackett); Hackett became a 2nd Lieutenant the following January, 184–88 (Hoops), 303 (Stockton), 285–86 (Woodruff), 6 (Armstrong).

85 Bill and Edge, *A House Called Morven*, 39-40.

86 See *AO*12, vol. 14; *AO*13, bundle 61. Some accounts say she entertained British officers, but the British did not come into the area until after her husband's death.

87 This proclamation was printed widely and multiple times. For examples, see *New York Gazette and Weekly Mercury*, January 27, 1777, 1; December 9, December 16, December 23, December 30, 1776; and January 6, 1777.

88 *Joint Meeting*, 12.

Chapter 4

1 Hall, *History of the First Presbyterian Church in Trenton*, 161.

2 John Witherspoon, to David Witherspoon, January 8, 1777, and February 2, 1777; Smith, *Letters of Delegates to Congress*, VI: 63, 269. Graham did not return to school. Hawkins had a younger brother, Joseph, also at the college, and what he did is unknown. Perhaps he also went with the Witherspoons and his brother.

3 Miller, *Life of Samuel Miller*, 147–48; Dwyer, *The Day Is Ours*, 89–90; John Witherspoon, to David Witherspoon, February 12, 1777; Smith, *Letters of Delegates to Congress*, VI: 269n1.

4 Cresswell, *Journal*, 163–64.

5 Lefkowitz, *The Long Retreat*, 100–103.

6 Stryker, *Trenton and Princeton*, 15.

7 Glenn, *William Churchill Houston*, 23.

8 George Washington, Trenton, to President of Congress, December 5, 1776; Fitzpatrick, *Writings of Washington*, VI: 331.

9 McMichael, "Diary," 139.

10 *General Assembly* (session beginning August 27, 1776), 52.

11 Richard Stockton to New Jersey Assembly, December 2, 1776; Smith, *Letters of Delegates to Congress*, V: 465n.

12 McBurney, "Was Richard Stockton a Hero?" An extract of an anonymous letter dated Philadelphia, December 30, 1776, published in the *Connecticut Journal*, New Haven, CT, January 30, 1777, 2. A shorter version of the letter appeared in the *Massachusetts Spy*, January 30, 1777, 2.

13 Bill and Edge, *A House Called Morven*, 40; *New Jersey Gazette*, July 8, 1778, 3. A Monmouth County grand jury later indicted Van Mater for informing the enemy about Stockton and Covenhoven.

14 Glenn, *William Churchill Houston*, 23. The Drake family lived in Hopewell, and two men with the name John were active in the Revolution. One was a lieutenant in the Hunterdon Militia and owned a 180-acre farm, and the other was a blacksmith. In 1780, Jacob Johnson owned a 180-acre farm in Amwell, according to the New Jersey tax records for Amwell Township.

15 Collins, *A Brief Narrative*, 3–4, 10.

16 Robert Treat Paine, Philadelphia, to David Cobb, December 6, 1776; Smith, *Letters of Delegates to Congress*, V: 580–82

17 Collins, *A Brief Narrative*, 3.

18 William Ellery, Philadelphia, to Nicholas Cooke, December 10, 1776; Smith, *Letters of Delegates to Congress*, V: 591–92; McMichael, "Diary," 139.

19 *Inventories of Damages*, James Finley Damage Claim; Thomas Robenson Damage Claim.

20 Ewald, *Diary of the American War*, 27; Glyn, "Ensign Glyn's Journal."

21 Collins, *A Brief Narrative*, 3; Creesy, "The Battle of Princeton," 18.

22 Richard Cochran, *AO*13, 013, 69–76.

23 Collins, *A Brief Narrative*, 3, 28.

24 Ibid., 14.

25 McLachlan, *Princetonians*, I: 374. Quoting letter of West Hyde.

26 Richard Cochran, *AO*13, 013, 69–76.

27 *Inventories of Damages*, Somerset County, page 270, dated October 21, 1782. Jonathan Baldwin attested to the accuracy of the claim before Joseph Olden.

28 *Inventories of Damages*, Somerset County sworn before Joseph Olden, October 22, 1782, attested to by Jonathan Baldwin.

29 Collins, *A Brief Narrative*, 8.

30 Ibid.; Headquarters Trenton Tuesday 10 December 1776, *Order Book: 17th Regiment of Foot, Oct. 11–Dec 28, 1776.*

31 Collins, *A Brief Narrative*, 4.

32 Robert Stockton Inventory; James McCombs inventory; Captain James Moore Inventory, *Inventories of Damages by the British and Americans in New Jersey, 1776–1782*.

33 Collins, *A Brief Narrative*, 8.

34 Ibid., 12.

35 *Inventories of Damages*, Jonathan Deare Damage Claim.

36 *Inventories of Damages*, Joseph Olden Damage Claim.

37 *Inventories of Damages*, Aaron Longstreet, Jr., Damage Claim.

38 *Inventories of Damages*, Matthew Clarke Damage Claim.

39 *Inventories of Damages*, Thomas Stockton Damage Claim.

40 *Inventories of Damages*, William Worth Damage Claim.

41 Collins, *A Brief Narrative*, 24, 10.

42 Ibid., 12–13.

43 *Inventories of Damages*, Thomas Olden Damage Claim.

44 Collins, *A Brief Narrative*, 16.

45 John Witherspoon to David Witherspoon, February 12, 1777; Smith, *Letters of Delegates to Congress*, VI: 269.

46 Collins, *A Brief Narrative*, 10–11, 13–14.

47 Ibid., 39.

48 Ibid., 14–15. See Kidder, *A People Harassed and Exhausted*, 193–96, for some examples in the vicinity of Pennington in Hopewell Township.

49 *Orderly Books: Sir William Howe, September 26, 1776–June 2, 1777*; Collins, *A Brief Narrative*, 21–22.

50 McBurney, "The Battle of Bennett's Island."

51 Ege, *Pioneers of Old Hopewell*, 31–35; *Minutes of the Council of Safety of the State of New Jersey*, 147, 159; *NJSA*, mss SZSAF001, 27.

52 Colonel Donop, Bordentown, to General Leslie, December 16, 1776; Stryker, *Trenton and Princeton*, 318.

53 Glenn, *William Churchill Houston*, 24. See Kidder, *A People Harassed and Exhausted*, chapter 10, for more on how militia units fragmented and combined in makeshift ways.

54 Grant to Donop, December 17, 1776; *Donop papers, Morristown National Historic Park*; Stryker, *Trenton and Princeton*, 52.

55 Fischer, *Washington's Crossing*, 188.

56 tryker, *Trenton and Princeton*, 52.

57 Robert Morris, Philadelphia, to Silas Deane, December 20, 1776, Smith, *Letters of Delegates to Congress*, V: 620–28.

58 Stryker, *Trenton and Princeton*, 108.

59 Fischer, *Washington's Crossing*, 196; General Leslie, Princeton, to Colonel Rall, December 21, 1776, 1:00 a.m.; Stryker, *Trenton and Princeton*, 339.

60 Fischer, *Washington's Crossing*, 198; Colonel Rall, Trenton, to Colonel Donop, December 20, 1776; Stryker, *Trenton and Princeton*, 329.

61 Stryker, *Trenton and Princeton*, 100.

62 Colonel Rall, Trenton, to Colonel Donop, December 21, 1776; Stryker, *Trenton and Princeton*, 231.

63 Rall to Donop, Trenton, December 22, 1776; Stryker, *Trenton and Princeton*, 70.

64 General Grant to Colonel Donop, December 23, 1776; Stryker, *Trenton and Princeton*, 70.

65 Stryker, *Trenton and Princeton*, 116.

66 Glenn, *William Churchill Houston*, 24–25.

67 Stryker, *Trenton and Princeton*, 234.

68 Glenn, *William Churchill Houston*, 24–25.

69 Collins, *A Brief Narrative*, 29; Glyn, "Ensign Glyn's Journal."

70 Collins, *A Brief Narrative*, 30–31. How he did that is not known, but he could have known of a nearby small group of militia who could have gotten the men to Washington across the Delaware River.

71 General Leslie, Princeton, to Colonel Donop, December 27, 1776, 4:00 p.m., Stryker, *Trenton and Princeton*, 424.

72 Stryker, *Trenton and Princeton*, 236–37. For more depth on General Howe's changing information and thinking after the defeat at Trenton and how his New Jersey troops should have been redeployed in consequence, see the Grant Papers for letters from Howe and others to and from Grant.

73 Colonel Donop, Princeton, to General Grant, December 29, 1776; Striker, *Trenton and Princeton*, 246–47.

74 Stryker, *Trenton and Princeton*, 238–39.

75 Ibid., 239.

76 Ewald, *Diary of the American War*, 44.

77 Reed, *Life and Correspondence*, I: 282–83, Wilkinson, *Memoirs*, I: 133–34; Collins, *A Brief Narrative*, 30; Reed, "Reed's Narrative, 1776–77," 399–400; Young, "Young's Journal," 261.

78 Colonel John Cadwalader, Crosswix, to George Washington, December 31, 1776, *GWPLOC*.

79 Bradley, Catts, and Selig, *"Cheer Up My Boys the Day Is Ours…,"* 91–92.

80 Ewald, *Diary of the American War*, 45.

81 Robertson, *Robertson's Diary*, 118; see also Ewald, *Diary of the American War*, 45, 48, and "Reed's Narrative, 1776–77," 397–98.

82 Benjamin Rush, Crosswicks, to Richard Henry Lee, December 30, 1776; Smith, *Letters of Delegates to Congress*, V: 705–06. For Congress's response to this request, see the resolution of January 3, 1777, concerning the treatment of Richard Stockton. *JCC*, 7:12–13.

83 For additional information on this subject, see John Witherspoon to David Witherspoon, March 17, 1777, Smith, *Letters of Delegates to Congress*, VI: 456 n1.

84 Ewald, *Diary of the American War*, 45.

85 *Inventories of Damages*, William Scudder Damage Claim, page 7.
86 Collins, *A Brief Narrative*, 5–7.
87 Ewald, *Diary of the American War*, 44.

Chapter 5

1 Collins, *A Brief Narrative*, 31.
2 Ewald, *Diary of the American War*, 48; Stryker, *Trenton and Princeton*, 247. Ewald describesthe troops under Grant as two British light infantry regiments and the 4th Hessian grenadier battalion of Major Kohler, while Ensign Glyn lists them as The British grenadiers and 1st Battalion of Guards.
3 Glyn, "Ensign Glyn's Journal."
4 Collins, *A Brief Narrative*, 20–21, 24; Thomas Olden *PF* S23828.
5 Glenn, *William Churchill Houston*, 25.
6 Thomas Olden *PF* S23828.
7 Ewald, *Diary of the American War*, 48; Stryker, *Trenton and Princeton*, 247.
8 Collins, *A Brief Narrative*, 31
9 Ewald, *Diary of the American War*, 48.
10 Stryker, *Trenton and Princeton*, 248.
11 Glenn, *William Churchill Houston*, 25.
12 Collins, *A Brief Narrative*, 17–18.
13 Collins, *A Brief Narrative*, 32.
14 For more information on this group, see "Notes on the Composition of the Crown Forces Transfers and Recruits on 3 January 1777" in Appendix III of *BPMP* and "Operations of the Army under Lt. G. Clinton (Beginning on 12 February 1776)." David Library of the American Revolution, Sol Feinstein Collection No. 132 (Card No. 409); *An Officer of the Army, The History of the Civil War in America,* I: 245–52; George Inman's "Narrative of the American Revolution." PMH&B 7 no. 3 (1883), 237–48; "Letters written during the American War of Independence. By the Late Capt. W. Hale, 45th Regt." in Col. H. C. Wylly, ed., *1913 Regimental Annual. The Sherwood Foresters. Nottinghamshire and Derbyshire Regiment* (London, 1913), 16.
15 Thomas Olden *PF* S23828.
16 Wilkinson, *Memoir*, 141; Smith, *Princeton*, 19–20.
17 Rodney, *Diary of Captain Thomas Rodney*, 33; William McCracken *PF* R6665.
18 Rodney, *Diary of Captain Thomas Rodney*, 33; *BPMP*, 42–48, Appendix IV. Tilton was afterwards a lieutenant colonel. Different sources give somewhat different compositions for the divisions, but the objectives of each are consistent.
19 "A little before we got in sight of the enemy, our whole army halted. The captain sent me a sergeant with a bucket full of powder and rum, every man must drink a half gill. He came to me to know if I had drank any, I told him no: drink some, said he, I have, so I took a little." "The Good Soldier White," 78.
20 Selig, Harris, and Catts, *BPMP*, 45.
21 Apollos Morris, aide-de-camp to Washington; *BPMP*, 50. No attribution as to the document; Armstrong: "As the day broke upon us, we discovered troops apparently on the march on the road from Princeton to Trenton...the Brigade [Sullivan's] was accordingly halted until Gen. Washington joined it." Wilkinson, *Memoirs*, I: 142; "We discerned the enemy, by the reflection of their arms against the rising sun ascending the hill in the wood near Cochran's." Cochran's Hill referred to land of Princeton Loyalist Richard Cochran. Cochran's Hill was also known as Millett's Hill, after William Millette, a French-Canadian Tory living near Worth's Mill who returned to Canada during the war.
22 (Root) Sergeant R__, "The Battle of Princeton," 516–18; Nathaniel Root *PF* S18574.

23 An Officer of the Army, *The History of the Civil War in America,* I: 245–52; Selig, Harris, and Catts, *PBMP*, 54.
24 An Officer of the Army, *The History of the Civil War in America,* I: 245–52, 248.
25 Ibid., I: 245–52.
26 Collins, *A Brief Narrative*, 17–18.
27 Morris, "Major Morris's Account of the Affair at Trenton, 1776." MS Sparks 53 (Miscellaneous papers relating to the Revolution, 1752–1779). Item 4, pp. 11–19. Harvard University Library, Cambridge, *BPMP*, Appendix 1, item 90; BPMP, 62.
28 Dexter, *The Literary Diary of Ezra Stiles*, II: 118–20.
29 *BPMP*, 56.
30 Fischer, *Washington's Crossing*, 330.
31 Ibid.
32 Ibid., 329; They went straight across what is today known as the D'Ambrisi Property. Bradley, Catts, and Selig, *"Cheer Up My Boys the Day Is Ours...,"* 22–24.
33 Collins, *A Brief Narrative*, 32–33, 36–37.
34 [Hood], "Engagements at Trenton and Princeton, January 2 and 3, 1777," 265.
35 Glenn, *William Churchill Houston*, 25.
36 Morris, "Major Morris's Account of the Affair at Trenton, 1776." MS Sparks 53 (Miscellaneous papers relating to the Revolution, 1752–1779). Item 4, pp. 11–19. Harvard University Library, Cambridge, *BPMP*, Appendix 1, item 90; *BPMP*, 62; Rodney, *Diary of Captain Thomas Rodney*, 34.
37 John Armstrong, undated "Memorandum of Gen. H. Mercer's...services and character" by Lieutenant John Armstrong, to Hugh Mercer Jr., in Fredericksburg, Virginia. Enclosed in a letter to William B. Reed of Philadelphia, dated September 13, 1839; Collections of Princeton Battlefield State Park, Clarke House. *BPMP*, Appendix I: Primary Sources: Continental Army, item 7.
38 Root, "The Battle of Princeton," 515–16.
39 McMichael, "Diary of Lieutenant James McMichael," 203.
40 *NARA M804, PF* S5501 Jacob Hefflebower.
41 Root, "The Battle of Princeton," 515–16.
42 John Belsches to the Earl of Leven, May 21, 1777; Hale, "Letters Written During the American War of Independence."
43 Curry, ed., "Martin Hunter's Journal," 20. *BPMP*, Appendix II: British sources, item 14.
44 Gilchrist, "The Tragedy of Captain William Leslie & Dr. Benjamin Rush," 25–30. The article gives further source notes and explains the deep relationship between Benjamin Rush and the Leslie family. Several days after the death, Rush came across Leslie's body and saw to it that it was interred with full military honors, with the approval of Washington; "Lt. Armstrong's Account of the Engagement of the 3rd January," GD 26/9/513/5, National Archives of Scotland. *BPMP*, Appendix II, Primary sources, British, Item 3.
45 Rodney, *Diary of Captain Thomas Rodney*, 34.
46 Chilton, "Diary of John Chilton," 283.
47 *NARA M804, PF* S9006 Cary McClelland.
48 Lossing, *Pictorial Field Book*, II: 29 n3; Custis, *Recollections of Washington*, 180–81.
49 Hale, "Letters Written During the American War of Independence." Nathanael Greene to Catherine Greene, January 20, 1777, Showman, *Papers of General Nathanael Greene,* II: 6–7. Waterman, *With Sword and Lancet*, 155–56.
50 Skeen, *John Armstrong, Jr., 1758–1843: A Biography*, 3. After the battle he accompanied Mercer's troops to Morristown. He had lost his job as aide-de-camp with Mercer's death, but soon became aide to General Gates in the northern army.
51 Chilton, "Diary of John Chilton," 283.
52 Collins, *A Brief Narrative*, 43–44; Benjamin Rush to R. H. Lee, January 14, 1777, in *Memoir of R. H. Lee*, II, 165; Affidavit of Lieutenant Yeates in *PCC*, 53: 47. Affidavit is dated

January 9, 1777, at Princeton and says he was of Col. Read's Regiment of Virginia and attested by Benjamin Rush.

53 *NARA M804, PF* S42758 Jonathan Grant.

54 Young, "Journal of Sergeant William Young," 265–66. They were probably British mistaken for Hessians.

55 Chastellux, *Travels*, I: 443–44; Chastellux, on his travels through America in 1780, relates stopping at a tavern in New York State where he conversed with the cousin and neighbor of the tavern-keeper he calls "Mr. Makingston," who described the wound and its cure at Princeton. Probably, McKinstry extended his service, as a number of his men did, just days before the battle. Private David Hunt wrote in his pension application that he enlisted in the "company of Capt McKinstry" in January 1776 (in Colonel Patterson's Regiment of the Massachusetts line, the 15th Continental Regiment), was at both Trenton and Princeton, and was discharged at Morristown in February 1777. *NARA M804, PF* David Hunt W3421.

56 [Root], "The Battle of Princeton," 515–18.

57 Henry Knox, Morristown, to Lucy Knox, January 7, 1777; Drake, *Life and Correspondence of Henry Knox*, 38.

58 Hale, "Letters Written during the American War of Independence."

59 Rodney, *Diary of Captain Thomas Rodney*, 32; "Capt. Henry with the other three companies of Philadelphia light Infantry brought up the rear."

60 "An Account of the Battle of Princeton," *Pennsylvania Evening Post*, January 16, 1777. Also in Stryker, *Trenton and Princeton*, 446–48. See the letter from an officer of distinction in General Washington's Army, dated Pluckemin, Jan. 5, 1777. Cadwalader is identified as the writer in Smith, *Battle of Princeton*, 38.

61 Sellers, "Charles Willson Peale: Artist-Soldier," 280.

62 *NARA M804, PF* W10367 Zebulon Applegate.

63 Haven, *Thirty Days in New Jersey*, 44–47.

64 Gratz, "Thomas Rodney," 8–9.

65 John Belsches to the Earl of Leven, Edinburgh, May 21, 1777; National Archives of Scotland, General Deposit 26/9/513/8, transcription online at https://www.17th.com/the-241st-anniversary-of-the-battle-of-princeton-surgeon-wardrops-account/. Transcribed by Dr. Will Tatum.

66 "An Account of the Battle of Princeton," *Pennsylvania Evening Post*, January 16, 1777. Also in Stryker, *Trenton and Princeton*, 446–48. See the letter from an officer of distinction in General Washington's Army, dated Pluckemin, Jan. 5, 1777. Cadwalader is identified as the writer in Smith, *Battle of Princeton*, 38.

67 Collins, *A Brief Narrative*, 16.

68 Dexter, *The Literary Diary of Ezra Stiles*, II: 138–39.

69 Williams, *Biography of Revolutionary Heroes*, 198–99.

70 Dexter, *Literary Diary of Ezra Stiles*, 120, 138–39.

71 Williams, *Biography of Revolutionary Heroes*, 198–99.

72 [Root], "The Battle of Princeton," 515–16.

73 Keen, "Descendants of Joran Kyn," 350.

74 "Major Morris's Account of the Affair at Trenton, 1776." MS Sparks 53 (Miscellaneous papers relating to the Revolution, 1752–1779). Item 4, pp. 11–19. Harvard University Library, Cambridge, *BPMP*, Appendix 1: item 90.

75 James Read of Philadelphia to his wife from Morristown. *PMH&B*, XVI, 465–66. He was granted leave from the naval service to join a company of Philadelphia Associators as a junior officer.

76 Collins, *A Brief Narrative*, 33.

77 Rodney, *Diary of Captain Thomas Rodney*, 136.

78 [Hall], *The History of the Civil War in America*, I: 251.

79 John Belsches to the Earl of Leven, Edinburgh, May 21, 1777, National Archives of Scotland, General Deposit 26/9/513/8, transcription online at https://www.17th.com/the-241st-anniversary-of-the-battle-of-princeton-surgeon-wardrops-account/. Transcribed by Dr. Will Tatum. McPherson recovered over several months during his captivity, was eventually exchanged, and sailed home to Edinburgh. He was promoted to full captain on January 4 and retired in 1778, just a few years before his death.

80 *Pennsylvania Packet*, January 22, 1777, 2.

81 Collins, *A Brief Narrative*, 33, 37–38.

82 Ibid., 34; Creesy, "The Battle of Princeton," 18; Fraser, *United Empire Loyalists: Enquiry into the Losses and Services*, I: 111.

83 Inman, "George Inman's Narrative of the American Revolution," 240.

84 *BPMP*, Appendix IV. This is a detailed analysis of the controversy surrounding this incident. *NARA M804, PF* S40389 Jacob Saylor—see the deposition of Henry Harberger. See also Bradley, Catts, and Selig, *"Cheer Up My Boys the Day Is Ours... ,"* 36–40.

85 "Major Morris's Account of the Affair at Trenton, 1776." MS Sparks 53 (Miscellaneous papers relating to the Revolution, 1752–1779). Item 4, pp. 11–19. Harvard University Library, Cambridge, *BPMP*, Appendix I: item 90.

86 Beale, Robert: "An Account of the Services of Major Robert Beale of Westmoreland in the War of the Revolution, as Written by Himself." Mss 5:1 B3657:1 Virginia Historical Society, Richmond. *BPMP*, Appendix I: item 9.

87 Sullivan, "The Battle of Princeton," 55: "The 40th Regiment formed in the College Yard."

88 Wilkinson, *Memoirs*, I: 144. This is at least claimed in Smith, *The St. Clair Papers*, I: 36–42, who prefaces this section with "In his own brief narrative, St. Clair says... ." It is not known which narrative Smith refers to, but this description is not in St. Clair, *A Narrative of the Manner in Which the Campaign against the Indians, in the Year One Thousand Seven Hundred and Ninety-One, Was Conducted*, 242–43. "Major Morris's Account of the Affair at Trenton, 1776." MS Sparks 53 (Miscellaneous papers relating to the Revolution), 1752–1779. Item 4, pp. 11–19. Harvard University Library, Cambridge, *BPMP*, Appendix I: item 90.

89 "We have a number of officers prisoners. I am just called on to command the infantry at the funeral of Capt. Leslie a British-officer, killed at Princeton. We bury him with military honors. On the field I saw lying another Captain of the name of Mostyn said to be the next heir to an estate of twenty-five thousand pounds per annum in England." Extract of a letter from a gentleman in the army to his friend in this city, dated Pluckemin, January 5, 1777; *Pennsylvania Evening Post*, January 7, 1777. On the identity of the prisoners, see the letter by Donop to Sir William Howe, January 6, 1777 in *BPMP*, Appendix II: Item 6.

90 Haven, *Thirty Days in New Jersey*, 44–47.

91 James Hamilton *NARA M804, PF* W793. He says he was later in charge of the sick at Nassau Hall when it was the hospital in Princeton. Hageman, *Princeton and Its Institutions*, I: 213.

92 Chastellux, *Travels*, I: 167.

93 Collins, *Princeton*, 80; Green, *Life of Ashbel Green*, 136–37.

94 Collins, *President Witherspoon*, 95.

95 [Root], "The Battle of Princeton," 518. Wertenbaker, *Princeton, 1746–1896*, 60. Citing *College of New Jersey Trustees Minutes*, I: 236. Minutes for September 24, 1783 (Accessed online May 3, 2017, at Princeton University Digital Library, http://pudl.princeton.edu/objects/7w62f826z.) The Trustees resolved to request Washington to sit for a portrait by Charles Willson Peale "And ordered that his portrait, when finished be placed in the hall of the college in the room of the picture of the late King of Great Britain which was torn away by a ball from the American artillery in the Battle of Princeton." Some sources suggest Alexander Hamilton was involved in the cannon fire on Nassau Hall. There is a common tradition that the cannonball decapitated King George II in the portrait, but that cannot be verified.

96 Hageman, *History of Princeton and its Institutions*, I: 138.
97 Glenn, *William Churchill Houston*, 25.
98 Sellers, "Charles Willson Peale, Artist-Soldier," 272; Lord Stirling wrote from Newtown on January 4: "Gen'l Washington's army passed thro' Prince Town about nine o'clock A.M. and the Enemy's army arrived there about 2 o'clock P.M. from Trenton"; Hazard, *PA Archives*, V: 157; "Memorandum of Occurrences attending the Armies of the United States...," Manuscript of Samuel Massey, Captain 7th Co. Philadelphia militia, 4th Battalion in 1777—The Property of Louis C. Massey, great grandson. John Reed Collection, Record Group 10, Valley Forge NHP, *BPMP*, Appendix I, item 81; "about Sun rise an Attack began at Princeton which lasted about 2 Hours."
99 He lived with his family in Flatbush, Long Island. In 1778 he was appointed surgeon for the 3rd New Jersey Volunteers but apparently did not get too involved in action. His New Jersey property was confiscated and sold. He later presented damage claims to the British for both material losses and loss of income. He did receive compensation, and returned to Flatbush and continued his profession. In 1790 he was living in New York City when the first U.S. Census was taken, which recorded him as head a household of eleven people, including three slaves. He died in New York in 1807. McLachlan, *Princetonians*, I: 374–75.
100 Richard Cochran, *AO*13, 013, 69–76.
101 Ibbetson Hamar *AO*12, vol. 14, *AO*13, bundle 61. He refused to renounce his loyalty to the British government, and the State government confiscated his property. He and his wife removed to England.
102 Collins, *Princeton*, 34.
103 While he was not apprehended at the time, the incident surfaced again in spring of 1778 but Crane was apparently never punished. Washington ordered him to Philadelphia on January 7 to "prepare fix'd ammunition of all kinds" for artillery, but on January 15, General Knox informed him that he was no longer an artillery officer, with no reason given. George Washington, Valley Forge, to George Clinton, April 24, 1778; *GWP UVA*, XIV: 611–12; Richard Kip Pompton, to Alexander Hamilton, April 15, 1778; *George Clinton Papers*, III: 173; George Clinton to George Washington, May 8, 1778; *GWPLOC*; George Washington to Robert Morris, George Clymer, and George Walton, Morristown, January 7, 1777; Fitzpatrick, *Writings of Washington*, VI: 474; *Henry Knox Papers*, microform, reel 3, frame 116.
104 Smith, *Battle of Princeton*, 28, citing Joseph White.
105 Davis, *History of Buck's County*, 125–26.
106 Muster Roll, Light Infantry Company of Dover; Delaware Public Archives Commission, *Delaware Archives: Revolutionary War in Three Volumes* (Wilmington: Chas. L. Story Company Press, 1919), III: 1243. This was apparently made when the company left Morristown in mid-January, 1777, and contains information from December 14, 1776.
107 Collins, *A Brief Narrative*, 38–39.
108 Ibid., 38; actual numbers are hard to know precisely.
109 Ibid., 36–37.
110 Ibid., 42.
111 *NARA M804 PF* S13381; Ensign John Hendy, Northhampton County Militia. His company was "attached to a Battalion under the Command of Major Benjamin Van Campen which Battalion was annexed to the Brigade under the Command of Gen. Mifflin." Several people are said to have helped carry Mercer. Major John Armstrong, his aide, says he was ordered by Mercer to rejoin the army. Harrison, *Princetonians*, III: 6. See Carl Edward Skeen, *John Armstrong, Jr., 1758–1843: A Biography* (Syracuse, NY: Syracuse University Press, 1981).
112 Collins, *A Brief Narrative*, 38; actual numbers are hard to know precisely.
113 Root, "The Battle of Princeton," 517–18.

114 Collins, *A Brief Narrative*, 36–37. Also, an August 20, 1913, letter to W. H. Olden at Princeton discusses which house she may have been in and describes the wound as a cannon ball severing her foot. *Olden Collection*, Princeton Historical Society.

115 Smith, *Battle of Princeton*, 28, citing Apollos Morris.

116 Ibid, 28, citing Thomas Rodney, 36–37.

117 Williams, *Life of Stephen Olney*, 199. Rodney wrote that "As soon as the enemy's main army heard our cannon at Princeton (and not 'til then) they discovered our maneuver and pushed after us with all speed and we had not been above an hour in possession of the town before the enemy's light horse and advanced parties attacked our party at the bridge but our people by a very heavy fire kept the pass until our whole army left the town."

118 William McCracken *NARA M804 PF* R6665; Sergeant Thomas Sullivan of the 49th Regiment of Foot wrote that "When we came to the river that is near Princetown, a party of the Rebels were formed on one side of the bridge, and another party cutting it down. The 5th. Batallion, which marched in front of the Brigade with two 6 pounders, engaged them from the opposite side; and in a few minutes drove them from the bridge, which they had cut down, and retreated into the woods." Sullivan, "The Battle of Princeton," 56. See also the letter by Washington to Congress of January 5, 1777: "The rear of the Enemy's army laying at Maidenhead (not more than five or Six Miles from Princeton) were up with us before our pursuit was over, but as I had the precaution to destroy the Bridge over Stony Brooke (about half a Mile from the Field of Action) they were so long retarded there, as to give us time to move of in good order for this place." Watching from his farmstead along the road, Robert Lawrence recorded that "as soon as the battle was over [Washington] ordered some of his men to be placed near the Bridge over Stoney brook on the Main Road to hinder the Regulars passing over and to pull up the bridge which was scarcely done when the Regulars appeared which caused a Second firing about three quarters of an hour apart from the first." Collins, *A Brief Narrative*, 35.

119 George Espy *NARA M804 PF* S23621; Egle, "The Constitutional Convention of 1776," 445.

120 Collins, *A Brief Narrative*, 35–36.

121 Williams, *Biography of Revolutionary Heroes*, 199–200.

122 Rodney, *Diary of Captain Thomas Rodney*, 37.

123 Glyn, "Ensign Glyn's Journal."

124 Collins, *A Brief Narrative*, 35, and Glyn, 39.

125 Extract of a letter from Col. Jesse Root, in the Provincial service, dated January 8, 1777; \ *The North British Intelligencer; or, Constitutional Miscellany*, Volume V (Edinburgh: Churnside and Wilson, 1777), 52; *Freeman's Journal*, Portsmouth, NH, January 21, 1777, 3.

126 Thomas Olden, *NARA M804 PF* S23828. Curiously, Olden does not comment about being in a battle on his neighbors' farms or of stopping by his house after the battle.

127 Haven, *Thirty Days in New Jersey Ninety Years Ago*, 44–47. "Moulder's guns were saved and taken into camp at Morristown, when Moulder was called before a Court for disobedience of orders in risking the loss of his men. On receipt of the order to appear before Court, the Company formed and marched in silence to headquarters, where after a formal reprimand Moulder received his sword, and the boys after three hearty cheers, struck up 'Yankee Doodle,' and returned to their quarters in high glee."

128 "George Washington to John Hancock, 5 January 1777," *The Papers of George Washington, Revolutionary War Series*, VII: 519–30; Collins, *A Brief Narrative*, 34.

129 Collins, *A Brief Narrative*, 34–35.

130 Magee, "Major John Polhemus," 289. Also, Ryan, *Salute to Courage*, 38–39; Polhemus *NARA M804 PF* S40271; he does not mention Trenton or Princeton.

131 John Cheston, *NARA M804 PF* W906.

132 Robertson, *Archibald Robertson: His Diaries and Sketches in America: 1762–1780*, 119–20.
133 Johann Ewald, *Diary of the American War*, 49–50; Sellers, "Charles Willson Peale, Artist-Soldier," 281.
134 Glyn, "Ensign Glyn's Journal."
135 Collins, *A Brief Narrative*, 17.
136 Thomas Dowdeswell to Rockingham, January 16, 1777, in Dowdeswell, "The Operations in New Jersey," 136. He was about twenty-two or twenty-three years old. He suffered from eye problems caused by exposure to the cold and damp and eventually lost his sight. He left America in April 1777 and retired from the army in June 1778 (Ibid.,133).
137 Collins, *A Brief Narrative*, 18–20.
138 bid., 37–38.
139 Ewald, *Diary of the American War*, 49–50.
140 Richard Henry Lee, *Memoir*, II: 164.
141 Collins, *A Brief Narrative*, 36–37.
142 Ensign Thomas Glyn, entry for January 3, "Ensign Glyn's Journal on the American Service."
143 Thomas Rodney to Caesar Rodney from Trenton, January 23, 1777; Gratz, "Thomas Rodney," 8.
144 Ewald, *Diary of the American War*, 49–50, 387 n145.
145 Tyler, "The Operations in New Jersey," 135.
146 Inman, "George Inman's Narrative of the American Revolution," 240.
147 Glyn, "Ensign Glyn's Journal."
148 Thomas Rodney, *Diary*, 37.
149 Curry, ed., "Martin Hunter's Journal: America 1774–1778," 20. *BPMP*, Appendix II: British sources, item 14.
150 Glenn, *William Churchill Houston*, 25.
151 Bradley, Catts, and Selig, *"Cheer Up My Boys the Day Is Ours…,"* 54.
152 Kemble, *Kemble's Journal*, 115.
153 Ida Agnes La Force, 1925; *Olden Papers*, Box 9, Folder 7. Historical Society of Princeton, New Jersey.
154 Sources variously give him as ensign, captain, or major. See Moon, *The Morris Family*, I: 380–81.
155 Jerry Carino, "A Slain Patriot, a Historic Letter and the Push to Preserve a NJ Battlefield," *Asbury Park Press*, June 19, 2017, online at http://www.app.com/story/news/history/2017/06/19/slain-patriot-historic-letter-and-push-preserve-nj-battlefield/408765001/. Thank you to Robert Selig for alerting me to this document
156 John Potts to Owen Biddle, field of Action, near Princeton, Sunday Evening, January 5, "Death of Major Anthony Morris, Jr., Described in a Letter Written on the Battle-Field, near Princeton, by Jonathan Potts, M.D.," *PMH&B* (1877) I: 175–80. Also in Ryan, *Salute to Courage*, 62. See Stryker, *Trenton and Princeton*, 455; R. H. Lee, *Memoir*, II: 165—Rush letter of January 14; *PCC* vol. 53 p. 47—affidavit of Dr. Rush on his case stating how he was wounded and then abused by the British, shot, bayonetted, and finally died.
157 Collins, *A Brief Narrative*, 39.
158 Ibid., 36.

Chapter 6

1 Collins, *Princeton*, 50–51.
2 Thomas Nelson to Thomas Jefferson, Baltimore, January 2, 1777; *Papers of Thomas Jefferson*, II: 3–4.
3 Rice, *The Rittenhouse Orrery*, 45.

4 Green, *Life of Ashbel Green*, 136–37; Collins, *President Witherspoon*, 96; Ebenezer Hazard diary excerpt in Gerlach, *New Jersey in the American Revolution*, 299.
5 Green, *Life of Ashbel Green*, 136–37; Ebenezer Hazard diary excerpt in Gerlach, *New Jersey in the American Revolution*, 299.
6 Benjamin Rush to R. H. Lee, January 7, 1777, in Rush, *Letters of Benjamin Rush*, I: 126.
7 Extracts of letters from Princeton and Philadelphia, January 7, 14, and 15; *Virginia Gazette*, Williamsburg, VA, January 31, 1777, 7. This letter is almost identical to portions of other letters by Rush.
8 Collins, *A Brief Narrative*, 40.
9 Ibid., 22–23, 28–29, 33.
10 Moon, *The Morris Family of Philadelphia*, I: 380, quoting diary of Margaret Morris entries of January 4 and 14.
11 Rogers and Lane, "Pennsylvania Pensioners of the Revolution," 263–71 *passim*; Obituary: *Pennsylvania Evening Post*, January 18, 1777, 27; James Grant Wilson and John Fiske, eds. *Appleton's-Cyclopaedia of American Biography* (New York: D. Appleton and Co., 1888) V: 513.
12 Jonathan Potts, camp near Princeton, to Owen Biddle, Sunday evening, January 5, 1777, in Duncan, *Medical Men in the American Revolution*, 188.
13 George Washington, Pluckamin, to Continental Congress, January 5, 1777; *GWPLOC*.
14 George Washington, Pluckemin, January 5, 1777, to Israel Putnam; Livingston, *Israel Putnam, Pioneer, Ranger, and Major General*, 337–38.
15 General Putnam, Bristol, to Council of Safety, January 5, 1777; Hazard, *Pennsylvania Archives*, V: 163.
16 *Benjamin VanKirk Medical Day Books*, original in collection of the Hopewell Museum, microfilm copy at *NJSA*.
17 Gillett, *Army Medical Department*, 72; Benjamin Rush, Princeton, to Richard Henry Lee, January 7, 1777; Rush, *Letters of Benjamin Rush*, I: 125–26.
18 Benjamin Rush, Princeton, to Richard Henry Lee, January 7, 1783; Rush, *Letters of Benjamin Rush*, I: 127–28. When a memorial plaque was placed on the Princeton Battlefield near the Thomas Clarke house in 1897, newspaper notices reported that blood stains were still visible on the floor of the room where he died. *Trenton Evening Times*, September 26, 1897, 1; *Princeton Press*, October 2, 1897. English, *General Hugh Mercer*, 103.
19 Rush noted of Leslie, "His body was thrown into his baggage wagon, and carried by the American army along with them. It was discovered at Pluckamin. In his pocket was found a letter from me, in which I had requested if the fortune of war should throw him into the hands of the American army, to show that letter to General Washington or General Lee, either of whom would, I expected, indulge him in a parole to visit Philadelphia, where I begged he would make my house his home." When the letter was discovered, General Mifflin ordered Leslie buried with the honors of war in the church yard at Pluckamin. In the summer of 1777, Rush visited the grave. At the end of the war he arranged for a stone giving his age, family, rank in the army and time and manner of his death and let some of his family members know. Capt. McPherson recovered in spite of his severe wound. Benjamin Rush, Princeton, to Richard Henry Lee, January 7, 1783; Rush, *Letters of Benjamin Rush*, I: 126.
20 George Washington, Morristown, to Continental Congress, January 7, 1777; *GWPLOC*.
21 Rush, *Autobiography of Benjamin Rush*, 128–30.
22 Gillett, *Army Medical Department*, 72; Benjamin Rush, Princeton, to Richard Henry Lee, January 7, 1777; Rush, *Letters of Benjamin Rush*, I: 125–26.
23 Benjamin Rush, Princeton, to Richard Henry Lee, January 14, 1777; Benjamin Rush to Julia Rush, Baltimore, January 24, 1777; Rush, *Letters of Benjamin Rush*, I: 127–29, 130–31; Rush, *Autobiography of Benjamin Rush*, 128–30.

24 Jacob Hefflebower *NARA M804 PF* S5501. Hefflebower says in his pension statement that he was taken to a hospital at Trenton. He must have been mistaken and meant to say Princeton. There are no other documents indicating men sent to Trenton and a number of documents about establishing a hospital at Princeton. This type of error is common in pension files.
25 Rogers and Lane, "Pennsylvania Pensioners of the Revolution," 469–70.
26 James English *NARA M804 PF* W97.
27 Harrison, *Princetonians*, II: 498–502.
28 Custis, *Recollections of Washington*, 183–84.
29 Dr. William Shippen, Jr., from General Hospital to Gen. Sullivan at Princeton, May 29, 1777; Hammond, *Letters and Papers of Major General John Sullivan Continental Army*, I: 346.
30 Gillett, *The Army Medical Department*, 1775–1818, 79–80.
31 Elias Boudinot, Camp at White Marsh, PA, to Commissioner of Prisoners in the British Army, November 12, 1777; Boyle, "Their Distress Is Almost Intolerable," 40.
32 Klepp, *Souls for Sale*, 192–93. For Buettner's complete journal and very colorful story, see *Narrative of Johann Carl Buettner in the American Revolution* (New York: Printed for C. F. Heartman, [1915]), available online at Hathi Trust Digital Library, https://catalog.hathitrust.org/Record/000364548.
33 Wickes, *History of Medicine in New Jersey*, 67–68.
34 Gillett, *The Army Medical Department, 1775–1818*, 79–80.
35 Harrison, *Princetonians*, III: 303; *NARA M246*, NJ Various Organizations, folder 91.
36 George Washington, to Nathanael Greene, November 25, 1777; Showman, *Greene Papers*, II: 217–18.
37 Gillett, *The Army Medical Department, 1775–1818*, 81.
38 *Pennsylvania Packet*, October 14, 1780, 2. The charge concerning Trenton was defended by Dr. Bodo Otto and Conrad Kotts the hospital Commissary at Trenton. *Pennsylvania Packet*, September 19, 1780, 4.
39 Benjamin Rush, Princetown, to Nathanael Greene, December 2, 1777; Rush, *Letters of Benjamin Rush*, I: 168–69.
40 Ibid., I: 169–70.
41 Benjamin Rush, Princetown, to William Duer, December 8, 1777; Rush, *Letters of Benjamin Rush*, I: 171–74.
42 Benjamin Rush, Princetown, to William Duer, December 13, 1777; Rush, *Letters of Benjamin Rush*, I: 175–76.
43 Gillett, *Army Medical Department, 1775–1818*, 81.
44 Benjamin Rush, Princetown, to George Washington, December 26, 1777; Rush, *Letters of Benjamin Rush*, I: 180–82.
45 William Livingston, Ringoes Tavern, Hunterdon County, to Henry Laurens, December 25, 1777; *Livingston Papers*, II: 144–47.
46 General Putnam, Bordentown, to Council of Safety, January 6, 1777; Hazard, *Pennsylvania Archives*, V: 168–69.
47 General Putnam, Trenton, to Council, January 7, 1777; Hazard, *Pennsylvania Archives*, V: 171.
48 George Washington to Lord Cornwallis, Morristown, January 8, 1777; *Papers of George Washington, Revolutionary War Series*, VIII: 13–14.
49 Livingston, *Israel Putnam*, 338–39.
50 Stryker, *Trenton and Princeton*, 274.
51 General Putnam, Crosswicks, to Council of Safety, January 9, 1777; Hazard, *Pennsylvania Archives*, V: 177.
52 George Washington, Morristown, to Joseph Reed, January 14, 1777; *Papers of George Washington, Revolutionary War Series*, VIII: 67–69.
53 Benjamin Rush, Philadelphia, to Richard Henry Lee, January 14, 1777; Rush, *Letters of Benjamin Rush*, I: 127–28.

54 George Washington, Morristown, to Joseph Reed, January 15, 1777; *Papers of George Washington, Revolutionary War Series*, VIII: 76–77.
55 Thomas Savadge, Philadelphia, to Council, January 18, 1777; Hazard, *Pennsylvania Archives*, V: 194.
56 Kemble, *The Kemble Papers*, 1: 395.
57 Samuel Tucker to John Hart, Speaker of the Assembly, January 20, 1777; *NJSA*, BAH Box 5-02, #113. For more on Tucker's loss and the State money, see Kidder, *Crossroads of the Revolution: Trenton, 1774–1783*, 136, 197–99.
58 General Putnam, Princeton, to Council of Safety, January 21, 1777; Hazard, *Pennsylvania Archives*, V: 196. For more on this battle and the Forage War, see Steven M. Richman, "The Battle of Millstone," *Journal of the American Revolution*, October 22, 2014, at https://allthingsliberty.com/2014/10/the-battle-of-millstone/.
59 Livingston, *Israel Putnam*, 340–41.
60 Washington's Proclamation of January 25, 1777; *Papers of George Washington, Revolutionary War Series*, VIII: 152–53, Smith, *Letters of Delegates*, 240–241n1, for letter of Abraham Clark, Baltimore, to John Hart, February 8, 1777. Washington to _, Morristown, February 14, 1777; Fitzpatrick, *Writings of Washington*, VII: 144; *JCC*, VII: 95, 165–66. Henry Waddell, Freehold, to William Livingston, April 11, 1777; *Livingston Papers*, I: 302.
61 Israel Putnam to Lord Stirling, Princeton, January 19, 1777; *PCC*, Letters from General Officers, 1775–89, r178, i159, p35.
62 Letter—War Office Baltimore, January 25, 1777; M247, *PCC*, Reports of the Board of War, v1, 1776–1777, p41, r157 i147, signed by Roger Sherman, Francis Lightfoot Lee, and Samuel Adams.
63 Collins, *President Witherspoon*, 93.
64 General Putnam, Princeton, to Council of Safety, January 31, 1777; Hazard, *Pennsylvania Archives*, V: 208–09.
65 *NJSA* New Jersey Council of Safety Records, Series SZSAF001, box 2, folder 6.
66 *Council of Safety Minutes*, 8.
67 Cutter, *Life of General Putnam*, 282.
68 William Livingston Proclamation, Haddonfield, February 5, 1777; *Livingston Papers*, I: 214–15.
69 General Putnam, Princeton, to Council, February 8, 1777; Hazard, *Pennsylvania Archives*, V: 215.
70 Daniel Putnam, Princeton, to General Putnam, February 8, 1777; Hazard, *Pennsylvania Archives*, V: 215–16.
71 Israel Putnam, Princeton, to William Livingston, February 10, 1777; *Livingston Papers*, I: 220–21.
72 William Livingston, Haddonfield, to Israel Putnam, February 13, 1777; *Livingston Papers*, I: 221–23.
73 Israel Putnam, Princeton, to William Livingston, February 18, 1777; *Livingston Papers*, I: 241–42. Fatigue duties would be non-military things like camp maintenance, constructing defenses, etc.
74 George Washington, Morristown, to William Livingston, February 22, 1777; *Livingston Papers*, I: 250.
75 Extract of a Letter from an Officer of Distinction, Dated Princetown, February 18, 1777; *Connecticut Journal*, New Haven, CT, March 12, 1777; *Virginia Gazette*, Williamsburg, VA, March 7, 1777; General Putnam, Princeton, to the Council, February 18, 1777; Hazard, *Pennsylvania Archives*, V: 230–31. Israel Putnam, Princeton, to William Livingston, February 18, 1777; *Livingston Papers*, I: 241–42. William Livingston, Haddonfield, to the Assembly, February 22, 1777; Ibid., 249.
76 General Putnam, Princeton, to Major Boggs, February 19, 1777; Hazard, *Pennsylvania Archives*, V: 232. For more on this episode in his life, see Christian M. McBurney, "The Battle of Bennett's Island." at https://allthingsliberty.com/2017/07/battle-bennetts-island-new-jersey-site-rediscovered.

77 General Washington, Morristown, to General Gates, March 10, 1777; *GWPLOC.*
78 General Putnam, Princeton, to General Gates, February 27, 1777; Hazard, *Pennsylvania Archives*, V: 247.
79 Cutter, *Life of General Putnam*, 285–86.
80 Thomas Proctor, Princeton, to Council of Safety, March 1, 1777; Hazard, *Pennsylvania Archives*, V: 249–250.
81 Cutter, *Life of General Putnam*, 286.
82 Harrison, *Princetonians*, II: 191–204.
83 Kemble, *The Kemble Papers*, 111.
84 William Livingston, Haddonfield, to John Witherspoon, May 29, 1777; *Livingston Papers*, I: 344.
85 *Pennsylvania Evening Post*, March 13, 1777, 140.
86 Israel Putnam, Princeton, to William Livingston, March 10, 1777; *Livingston Papers*, Microform. 4: 273–77.
87 *General Assembly* (Session beginning August 17, 1776), 106–07.
88 Israel Putnam to John Hancock, Princeton, March 17, 1777; *PCC*, Letters of General Officers, 1775–89, r178 i159 p38.
89 Israel Putnam to John Hancock, Princeton, April 5, 1777; M247, *PCC*, r178 i159 p47; The intelligence letter is dated April 5 and signed by Major William Scudder at Cranbury. It is page 55.
90 *PCC*, Letters from General Officers, 1775–89, r178, i159 p58; General Putnam, Princeton, to President of Congress, April 8, 1777; Hazard, *Pennsylvania Archives*, V: 300.
91 *Pennsylvania Gazette*, April 23, 1777, 4.
92 *Pennsylvania Evening Post*, April 26, 1777, 235.
93 William Livingston, Bordentown, to Major General Putnam, April 11, 1777; *Livingston Papers*, Microfrom, r4: 566–67. Captain Thomas Webb is a very interesting character who was also an active Methodist missionary and claims to have been a British spy who forwarded advance information on the December 25 crossing of the Delaware and attack on Trenton that the British ignored. The letter does not give his first name, but all things fit together to make this identification plausible.
94 Nathanael Greene, Baskenridge, to Catharine Greene, April 27, 1777; Showman, *The Papers of General Nathanael Greene*, II: 60.
95 Showman, *The Papers of General Nathanael Greene*, II: 62–63.
96 General Putnam to John Hancock, Princeton, April 29, 1777; *PCC M247*, Letters from General Officers, 1775–89, i159 p69 ro178.
97 Return of troops at Princeton on May 3, 10, 1777, under General Putnam; Hammond, *Letters and Papers of Major General John Sullivan Continental Army*, I: 335, 338.
98 William Livingston, Bordentown, to Thomas Wharton, Jr., May 1, 1777; *Livingston Papers*, I: 318–19.
99 Israel Putnam, Princeton, to William Livingston, April 26, 1777; *Livingston Papers*, Microform, r4:724–26.
100 Cutter, *Life of General Putnam*, 286.
101 Israel Putnam, Peekskill, to Jeremiah Wadsworth, Hartford, CT, May 22, 1777; *Israel Putnam Papers*, 1772–82 [microform].
102 Collins, *President Witherspoon*, 94.
103 Colonel John Hawkins Stone to General Sullivan, Kingston, May 19, 1777; Hammond, *Letters and Papers of Major General John Sullivan Continental Army*, I: 337. Stone was Colonel of the 1st Maryland Regiment, promoted February 18, 1777.
104 *Philip Schuyler Papers*, microform. See also *JCC*, 7: 367, and John Hancock to Washington, May 20, 1777.
105 Gen. Philip Schuyler to Gen. Israel Putnam, May 22, 1777; Hammond, *Letters and Papers of Major General John Sullivan Continental Army*, I: 341.

106 Graydon, *Memoirs of His Own Times*, 275–77.
107 Lewis Morris, Princeton, to Congress, May 29, 1777; Hazard, *Pennsylvania Archives*, V: 351.
108 Hammond, *Letters and Papers of Major General John Sullivan Continental Army*, I: 349.
109 Ibid., 354.
110 Gen. Benedict Arnold, Philadelphia, to Gen. Sullivan, Princeton, June 1, 1777; Hammond, *Letters and Papers of Major General John Sullivan Continental Army*, 355.
111 Anderson, *Personal Recollections*, 29–30.
112 *Norwich Packet*, Norwich, CT, July 7, 1777, 2; Benedict Arnold, Coryell's Ferry, to ___, June 15, 1777; Hazard, *Pennsylvania Archives*, Series 1, V: 367–68.
113 Anderson, *Personal Recollections*, 29–30.
114 Kemble, "Kemble's Journal," 120–22.
115 Benedict Arnold, Coryell's Ferry, to ___, June 15, 1777; Hazard, *Pennsylvania Archives*, Series 1, V: 367–68.
116 J. P. Eustace, Sourland Mountains, to Major General Mifflin, June 19, 1777; Hazard, *Pennsylvania Archives*, Series 1, V: 381.
117 Kemble, "Kemble's Journal," 120–22; Dexter, *The Literary Diary of Ezra Stiles*, 175–76.
118 General Israel Putnam, Peekskill, to Jeremiah Wadsworth, June 24, 1777; *Israel Putnam Papers, 1772-1782*, Microform.
119 Anderson, *Personal Recollections*, 29–30.
120 Thomas Olden *NARA M804 PF* S23828.
121 Glenn, *William Churchill Houston*, 25, 28.
122 Ibid., 26–28.
123 James Moore, *NARA M804 PF* W1060; Abraham Skillman, PF W992.
124 James Moore, *NARA M804 PF*1060; Stephen Morford, PF S1064. Moore had been recommended by Governor Livingston.
125 *NJSA* Mss 1489.
126 *Minutes of Council of Safety*, 14–15; Enos Kelsey, Princeton, to William Livingston, March 30, 1777; *Livingston Papers*, Microform, reel 4: 403.
127 *NJSA* Mss 1485; *NARA M804*; James Hamilton *PF* W793 gives May 1, 1777; *Minutes of Council of Safety*, 34, 68; James Moore *NARA M804 PF* W1060; James Stockton *PF* W2485.
128 *Minutes of Council of Safety*, 40; Stephen Morford *NARA M804 PF* S1064.
129 Abraham Skillman PF W992. See also General Arnold, Coryell's Ferry, to General Mifflin, June 15, 1777, in Stiles, *Literary Diary*, II: 176.
130 *NJSA* Mss 1497, 1498 (two versions). Pay role of Captain James Moore company of 2nd Battalion of Somerset commanded by Governor Livingston at Princeton from August 26 to September 3, 1777. Some served 4 days and others 8: Captain James Moore 8, Ensign James Hamilton 4, Sergeant Elijah Leigh 8, Sergeant Isaac Cool 4, Corporal John Lake 4, Corporal William Heulse 4, William Gaa 8, Alexander Gaa 4, Andrew McKim 8, Thomas Norris 8, Ephraim Yates 4, David Cool 4. William Downy 4, Matthew Buzzy 8, Thomas Skelton 8, James Davis 4, Garret Schenck 8, John Chambers 4, John Conover 4, Anthony Conway 4, Nicklas, Voorhees 4, John Wilson 4, Licha Juel 8, Mathew Mount 4, Charles Fisher 8, Isack Updike 4, Thomas Skillman 8, Jacob Vandyke 8, Garret Lake 4, Peter Voorhees 4. A total of 24 privates.
131 *Joint Meeting*, 21.
132 *Minutes of the Council of Safety*, 146.
133 James Moore, *NARA M804 PF* W1060; James Hamilton PF 793; John Hulfish PF W2553; NJSA mss 1499; NARA M881, Compiled Service Records; NJSA MSS 1499 company pay roll—September 15 to October 9, 1777—25 days: James Moore, Captain James Hamilton, 1st Lieutenant Elijah Leigh—sergeant, Isaac Cook—sergeant, Robert McCullough—corporal, Abraham Updike—corporal, and privates David Cook, John Claymont, Richard Dunn, Samuel Forman, John Hulfish, John Johnson, Richard

Longstreet, Stephen Morford, Aaron Manley, Andrew McKim, Allen Rhodes, James Smith, Ethan Smith, Ebenezer Stockton, Powles Smith, James Tomlinson, Burgen Updyke, Peter Updyke, Robert Yates, and Ephraim Yates.

134 James Moore, *NARA M804 PF* W1060; James Hamilton, *PF* W793; Stephen Morford, *PF* S1064.

135 Harrison, *Princetonians*, II: 127.

136 *NJSA* Mss 1500, copy of Captain James Moore class list October 24, 1777. Individuals may also have cards in NARA M881 Compiled Service Records that reference this list.
Class 1: Isaac Coole, serg't. William McConky, Luke Reeves, Phenix Carter, Noah Morford, Peter Updyke, Cornelius Irwin, Henry Silvers, John Forman.
Class 2: William Minor, serg't. Thomas Wilson, Nathaniel Runyan, Walliam Savage, Peter Bowne, William Hyer, James Hoppy, Arthur Reeves, Henry Savage.
Class 3: James Finley, Job Runyan, Benjamin Hoppy, John Stevenson, John Hubbard, Rulief Updyke, James Rock, John Paxon, John Hamilton, Abraham Voorhees, Gideon Lyon, James Egbert.
Class 4: William Gaa, Richard Scott, Samuel Ruckman, Daniel Leigh, Harmon Morford, John Stevenson (weaver), Andrew Mershon, James Mounteer.
Class 5: Benjamin Updyke, serg't. Samuel Forman, Lemuel Scudder, Daniel Manning, Samuel Scott, John Dildine, Peter Mullison, Benjamin Skillman, David Vost.
Class 6: Daniel Heath, Abraham Updyke, Job Anderson, David Anderson, John Stockton, Jr., Cornelius Stevenson, Daniel Mickleson, Hendrick Waters, William Savage (William's son), Isaac Leigh, Richard Hunt.
Class 7: Samuel Skillman, serg't, Abraham Skillman, Allen Rhodes, Stephen Morford, Aaron Longstreet, Jacob Updyke, Zebulon (illegible), George Skillman, John McCombs, Jr.
Class 8: Andrew McMackin, Ethan Smith, Aaron Manley, John Stockton (mason), Christopher Stryker, John Johnson, Joseph Mottison, Wilson Burdine, John Weight, James Norris, Jared Saxton, John Packer, Peter Packer, John Daniels, John Scott, Azariah Compton, Jonathan Bowen, Amos Anderson, Benjamin Hunt, Oliver Hunt, Varnel Hunt.
Listed on the back of the roll: Conart Cone, Zebulon Leigh, Louis Morford, Isaac Updyke, Jr., Jesse Updyke, Thomas Miller, John Mottison, Charles Stuart, John Leonard, Archibald McCollom, Ephraim Yates, Thomas Yates, James Campbell, Joseph Gilmore, Aaron Gilkit, Isaiah Smith, John Leigh, David Vant, John Thompson, Luis Heath, Licha Higby, John Van Norden, Duke Brown, John Fraser, Jacob Templeton, James Grace, Peter Higby, John McCombs, Richard Scudder, Perry Rollins.

137 Thomas Olden PF S23828.

138 *New Jersey Gazette*, Burlington, NJ, December 24, 1777, 1.

139 *NJSA* Mss 1501, pay role of Moore's company of VanDike's battalion commanded by Governor Livingston, December 18–24, 1777. James Moore Captain, Robert McCullough sergeant, Isaac Cook sergeant, John Carman, John Connelly, Reuben Mullison, Nat Runyan, George Skillman, James Skillman, John Totten, Peter Updyke, Isaac Updyke, Rulief Updyke, and Doctor Wiggins.

140 Bill and Edge, *A House Called Morven*, 45.

141 "Receipts of Enos Kelsey," Princeton University Rare Books and Special Collections, Princeton Revolution Collection, Box 1, folder call number C0032.

142 *Pennsylvania Journal*, September 3, 1777, 4.

143 September 18, 1777; "Return of Stores received by Col. Charles Stewart Commissary General of Issues and his deputies in the Middle Department of the United States from Col. Joseph Trumbull his deputies & assistants, specifying the times of delivery, & posts, places or Magazines. Where the Stores were received with observations in the Quality of the stores where damaged." *PCC*, Letters and Papers Relative to the Quartermaster's Department, 1777–84, M247, r199, i192, pages 483-5.

144 *Minutes of the Council of Safety*, 146.
145 *Ibid.*, 156.
146 Stratford and Wilson, *Certificates and Receipts*, 183–84.
147 *Pennsylvania Evening Post*, March 25, 1777, 167.
148 *College of New Jersey Trustees Minutes*, 215–16.
149 *Pennsylvania Packet*, July 1, 1777, 1.
150 Collins, *Princeton*, 80; *Pennsylvania Evening Post*, July 12, 1777, 371.
151 Deposition of Joseph Scudder in James English, *NARA M804 PF* W97.
152 *CC*, VIII: 558; *PCC*, No. 41, VII, folio 6.
153 General Orders, July 25, 1777; *GWPLOC*.
154 *JCC*, VIII: 615–16.
155 See McBurney, "Was Richard Stockton a Hero?" for a well-researched and thoughtful essay on how Stockton can be remembered. See also J. L. Bell (http://boston1775.blogspot.com) for a series of short articles on the Stockton question with links to a number of sources.
156 James Webster Lt. Col. 33d Regt., Perth Amboy, to Col. Elisha Lawrence of the New Jersey Volunteers, December 29, 1776; *NJSA*, Dept. of Defense Manuscripts, Loyalist Mss. No. 192-L, quoted in McBurney, "Was Richard Stockton a Hero?"
157 Benjamin Rush to Richard Henry Lee, January 7, 1777; Rush, *Letters of Benjamin Rush*, 1:126; Elias Boudinot to Guy Carlton, October 2, 1783; Smith, *Letters of Delegates to Congress*, XXI: 10.
158 Edmund C. Burnett, *Letters of Members of the Continental Congress*, II: 243.
159 John Hancock to Robert Treat Paine, Baltimore, February 9, 1777; Smith, *Letters of Delegates to Congress*, VI: 247.
160 John Witherspoon to David Witherspoon, February 2, 1777; Smith, *Letters of Delegates to Congress*, VI: 268–69.
161 Fitzpatrick, *Writings of Washington*, VII: 92.
162 McLachlan, *Princetonians*, I: 439.
163 Jonathan Dickinson Sergeant, Baltimore, to John Hart, February 5, 1777; Smith, *Letters of Delegates to Congress*, VI: 223–24; *Joint Meeting*, 21.
164 John Witherspoon, Philadelphia, to David Witherspoon, March 17, 1777; Smith, *Letters of Delegates to Congress*, VI: 455–57.
165 Kasden, "The Manumission of Prime." "Receipt for Slave and Other Items—Mary Bainbridge," April 4, 1777; *MS775*, Manuscript Collection, Historical Society of Princeton (Princeton, NJ).
166 *QMR*, 1681–1935, New Jersey, Burlington, Chesterfield Monthly Meeting Minutes, 1774–96.
167 Ebenezer Hazard diary excerpt in Gerlach, *New Jersey in the American Revolution*, 299.
168 *Pennsylvania Journal*, June 18, 1777, 3.
169 *QMR* frame 280.
170 *General Assembly (Session beginning August 17, 1776)*, 188.
171 Ibid., 196–97; *Legislative Council (Session beginning August 17, 1776)*, 118–19.
172 *General Assembly (Session beginning August 17, 1776)*, 202–06.
173 *General Assembly (Session beginning October 28, 1777)*, 6.
174 *Minutes of the Council of Safety*, 158.
175 *General Assembly (Session beginning October 28, 1777)*, 28.
176 *Ibid.*, 44–45, 48.
177 *Minutes of the Council of Safety*, 8.
178 Ibid., 161, 162.
179 Ibid., 175.
180 Ibid., 176–77.
181 Creesy, "The Battle of Princeton," 18.
182 Hageman, *Princeton*, I: 211.

183 *Minutes of the Council of Safety*, 178; *NJSA* Mss 1490, Bounty Roll of the guard at Princetown under the command of Lt. Jacob G. Bergen, December 1777—12 men.
184 *Minutes of the Council of Safety*, 168.
185 See Fraser, *United Empire Loyalists: Enquiry into the Losses and Services*, 111; Joseph Stockton, *AO*13, 112, 272; Creesy, "The Battle of Princeton," 18.
186 *Pennsylvania Ledger*, January 10, 1778, 2.
187 Notice from Philadelphia, August 23, 1777; *Virginia Gazette*, Williamsburg, VA, September 12, 1777, 1.
188 Richard Cochran, *AO*13, 013, 69–76.
189 Collins, *A Brief Narrative*, 40.
190 Ibid., 41.

Chapter 7

1 *General Assembly (Session beginning October 28, 1777)*, 102, 103. The Assembly met until April 18, when it adjourned to meet again at Princeton on May 27; 116. The Joint Meeting met on April 18, 1778, at the house of Mr. Bergen in Princeton. *Joint Meeting*, 27.
2 Benjamin Rush, Princeton, to Jonathan Bayard Smith, April 20, 1778; Rush, *Letters of Benjamin Rush*, I: 211–14.
3 Boudinot, ed., *The Life, Public Services, Addresses and Letters of Elias Boudinot, LL.D.*, I: 131–32.
4 Dr. Nathaniel Scudder, no date, to Elias Boudinot; Boudinot, ed., *The Life, Public Services, Addresses and Letters of Elias Boudinot, LL.D.*, I: 174–75; *Royal Gazette*, New York, NY, June 17, 1778, 3; *New-Jersey Gazette*, June 17, 1778, 3.
5 *Council of Safety Minutes*, 257.
6 *New Jersey Gazette*, July 22, 1778, 1.
7 Collins, *A Brief Narrative*, 6.
8 Boudinot, ed., T*he Life, Public Services, Addresses and Letters of Elias Boudinot, LL.D.*, I: 136.
9 Ibid., 138.
10 James Kirby Martin, ed., *Ordinary Courage*, 79–80.
11 Lieutenant James Hamilton later stated that at the Battle of Monmouth he served under Colonel Lee, who commanded the reserve; when a messenger arrived he was not to be found. Lieutenant Hamilton gave the orders for a detailed corps, which marched under Captain Moore and Lieutenant Hamilton to the battle. This could not be true, as it runs counter to Captain Moore's statement, unless only part of the company stayed back with Moore and Hamilton took the rest of the company to Monmouth. James Hamilton *NARA M804 PF* W793.
12 *New Jersey Gazette*, July 22, 1778, 1.
13 *Livingston Papers Microform*, r6, f628; Stryker, *New Jersey Men in the Revolution*, 344.
14 *Joint Meeting*, 27. The Joint Meeting met again at Bergen's tavern on October 7.
15 *Council of Safety Minutes*, 223.
16 *NJSA* Mss 802, 805; Pay roll of militia detachment of Col Jacob Hyer's battalion commanded by Lieut. Joseph Schenck as guards for prisoners from Princeton to Morristown, April 11, 1778—4 days.
The privates were: Thomas Olden, Luke Covenhoven, John Totton, Samuel Minor, William Gaa, and William Noris. Both versions of the document were signed by Jonathan Baldwin. *Council of Safety Minutes*, for September 24, p283, says it was agreed that there be paid to Lieu' Joseph Schenk the sum of £5. 7. for guarding, with an officer & six privates, a number of prisoners from Princeton, to Morristown in the month of April last. June 19, *Council of Safety Minutes*, 257. Agreed to pay Captain Samuel Stout, "for the amount of a Bounty Roll, of a detachment of Colonel Hyer's Battalion of Middlesex Militia, who were sent as a guard with prisoners from

Princeton to Head Quarters the sum of £12. 9. 8. That there be paid to Capt. Stout for the amount of a Pay Roll, for the same detachment and for the same Duty, the sum of £17.15.2."

17 *NJSA* Mss 1502; Pay roll of Moore's company Col Van Dyke battalion serving as guard at Princeton and guarding prisoners at Head Quarters from May 24 to June 4, 1778: Capt. James Moore, Isaac Cook sergeant, John Britton, Henry Cook, Benjamin Cull, John Dildine, William Groom, William Heulse, James Horlan, Daniel Harper, John Hulfish, Josiah Harnet, John Lewis, Reuben Mullison, Stephen Morford, Thomas Morris, Thomas Olden, Job Runyon, Nat Runyan, Lemuel Scudder, Thomas Skillman, George Skillman, Samuel Skillman, Abraham Slayback, William Slayback, James Smith, Isaac Updyke, Thomas Wilson, and William Gaa. In his *PF* S23828, Thomas Olden states that about May 10 he went out to guard New Brunswick, to prevent it being burned by the enemy coming out from Staten Island, and continued there until July 10. Whether he was wrong about the timing or it happened while out with Captain Moore is not clear. He continued there until July 10. Whether he was wrong about the timing or it happened while out with Captain Moore is not clear.

18 *Council of Safety Minutes, 251.*

19 *NJSA* Mss 826; Jacob Hyer, Princetown, to Gov. Livingston, June 15, 1778. Also in *Livingston Papers*, Microform, 7: 605. His resignation was accepted on October 2.

20 *NJSA* Mss 1503a; roll of Moore's company as a guard at Princeton and guarding prisoners to Philadelphia and Morristown from 19 June to 3 July 1778—signed July 4: James Moore captain, Isaac Cook sergeant, Stephen Morford sergeant, John Britton, John Dildine, William Gaa, Andrew McKim, Aaron Manley, Reuben Mullison, William Minor, Benjamin Mtichell, Thomas Norris, John Tottin, Luke Reeves, Job Runyan, Lemuel Scudder, Thomas Skillman, Samuel Skillman, Ethan Smith, Abraham Skillman, Burgen Updyke, Peter Updyke, Abraham Updyke, and William Hoyer. The three prisoners were Josiah Grey, John Jones, and George Robinson. *Council of Safety Minutes*, 261. June 21—*Council of Safety Minutes*, 262—Agreed that "M Bach be discharged from his parole, & sent under guard to Morristown Gaol, together with Josiah Grey, John Jones, & George Robinson, & that Captain Moore see this order carried into effect."

21 James Moore *NARA M804 PF* W1060. *NJSA* Mss 1503; roll of Moore company, June 28, 1778, made at Princeton July 4, 1778: James Moore Captain, Stephan Morford Sergeant, Isaac Cook sergeant, John Britton, John Dildine, William Gaa, William Hyer, Andrew McKim, Aaron Manley, Reuben Mullison, William Minor, Benjamin Mitchell, Thomas Norris, Luke Reeves, Job Runyan, Lemuel Scudder, Samuel Skillman, Abraham Skillman, Thomas Skillman, Ethan Smith, John Totten, Bergen Updyke, Abraham Updyke, Peter Updyke, and William Kerr.

22 *Council of Safety Minutes*, 266.

23 *NJSA* Mss 1504—Moore company, October 7, 1778—served September 25 to October 7, 1778: James Moore capt., James Stockton Lt., Robert McCullough sergeant, William Hyer sergeant, Isaac Cool sergeant, John Britton, John Dildine, Daniel Leigh, Stephan Morford, Andrew McKim, Daniel Manning, Benjamin Mitchell, David Mullison, Abraham Skillman, Samuel Skillman, Ethan Smith, George Skillman, Silas Waters, and Luke Reeves.

24 *Royal American Gazette*, New York, NY, August 25, 1778, 3.

25 William Livingston, Princeton, to George Washington, December 14, 1778; *Livingston Papers*, II: 511; *New Jersey Gazette*, December 9, 1778, 3.

26 *Council of Safety Minutes*, 267.

27 John Hulfish *NARA M804 PF* W2553.

28 Elias Boudinot, Camp at Valley Forge, to Henry Hugh Fergusson, January 8, 1778; Boyle, "Their Distress Is Almost Intolerable," 77

29 Benjamin Rush, Princetown, to George Washington, February 25, 1778; Rush, *Letters of Benjamin Rush*, I: 200–204.

30 Benjamin Rush, Princetown, to Congressional delegate Daniel Roberdeau, March 9, 1778; Rush, *Letters of Benjamin Rush*, I: 204–07.
31 *Pennsylvania Ledger*, March 25, 1778, 3.
32 Gillett, *Army Medical Department: 1775–1818*, 91.
33 Ibid., 99.
34 Joseph Scudder deposition in James English *NARA M804 PF* W97.
35 Gillett, *Army Medical Department, 1775–1818*, 110
36 Joseph Scudder deposition in James English *NARA M804 PF* W97.
37 Deposition of Lewis Johnstone in James English, *PF* W97.
38 Deposition of Ann Conover (sister of James English), *PF* W97.
39 *Council of Safety Minutes*, 286.
40 Livingston, *Livingston Papers*, II: 245n.
41 Tench Tilghman, Trenton, to George Washington, February 19, 1778; *GWPLOC*.
42 William Livingston, Trenton, to George Washington, March 2, 1778; *Livingston Papers*, II: 243.
43 For more details on the structure of these departments, see Livingston's report of March 5, 1778; *PCC*, New Jersey State Papers, 1775–88, M247, r82, i68, p340–42; and *NJSA* Mss 7269, p9. Also *Livingston Papers*, II: 244–45.
44 William Livingston, Trenton, to Henry Laurens, March 5, 1778; *Livingston Papers*, II: 246.
45 William Livingston, Trenton, to Henry Laurens, March 17, 1778; *Livingston Papers*, II: 257–59; *JCC*, X: 284–85.
46 Carp, *To Starve the Army at Pleasure*, 102.
47 *Council of Safety Minutes*, 214.
48 Ibid., 222. Colonel Sullivan had previously been ordered to purchase powder. Ibid., 212–13.
49 William Livingston, Trenton, to Nathaniel Scudder, March 20, 1778; *Livingston Papers*, II: 265. The word "corruption" is conjectured from his use of it in similar phrasing.
50 *General Assembly (Session beginning October 28, 1777)*, 90. March 25, 1778 (134), June 6, 1778 (140), June 11, 1778 (199, 202), October 8, 1778—message from Council concurring.
51 McLachlan, *Princetonians*, I: 133; William Livingston, Princeton, to George Washington, May 29, 1778; *Livingston Papers*, II: 356.
52 *Council of Safety Minutes*, 239–40, 244, 247, 255; *General Assembly (Session beginning October 28, 1777)*, 139.
53 *General Assembly (Session beginning October 28, 1777)*, 158–60.
54 *New Jersey Gazette*, August 12, 1778, 3.
55 William Livingston, Princeton, to the New Jersey Delegates, July 3, 1778; *Livingston Papers*, II: 379.
56 *Legislative-Council (Session beginning October 28, 1777)*, 27, 54, 74; *General Assembly (Session beginning October 28, 1777)*, 140.
57 *Council of Safety Minutes*, 272.
58 *General Assembly (Session beginning October 28, 1777)*, 201–02.
59 *New Jersey Gazette*, October 28, 1778, 2.
60 Ibid., 3, and November 11, 1778, 4.
61 *NJSA* Mss 1505; Pay roll of Moore's company contingent serving as a guard for clothes from Princetown to Elizabethtown, November 26–30, 1778. James Moore Capt, Abraham Updyke sergeant, Stephan Morford , Arthur Reeves, Benjamin Mitchell, Abraham Skillman, and George Skillman.
62 *General Assembly (Session beginning October 27, 1778)*, 45, 49.
63 Ibid., 60–61.
64 David Olden purchases as Commissioner for clothing in Stratford and Wilson; *Certificates and Receipts*, 184–92,

65 Livingston, Elizabethtown, to Caleb Camp, Speaker of the General Assembly, December 26, 1778; *Livingston Papers*, II: 523–24.
66 *College of New Jersey Trustees Minutes*, 217–18. The Assembly had heard a petition on March 17 from Dr. Witherspoon asking for the boys to be exempt, but it did not go far. *General Assembly (Session beginning October 27, 1778)*, 81–82.
67 *New Jersey Gazette*, April 23, 1778, 3.
68 Ibid., October 21, 1778, 2.
69 Ibid., June 3, 1778, 3.
70 Ibid., August 26, 1778, 3.
71 Ibid., December 31, 1778, 4.
72 Ibid., November 25, 1778, 1.
73 Ibid., September 9, 1778, 3.
74 Ibid., November 11, 1778, 1.
75 Ibid., December 16, 1778, 4.
76 Ibid., August 4, 1778, 1.
77 *QMR*, 4th day of 6th month 1778, frame 289; 3rd day of 8th month 1778, frame 290.
78 *Council of Safety Minutes*, 270.
79 *New Jersey Gazette*, October 7, 1778, 2.
80 Benjamin Rush, Philadelphia, to Julia Rush, August 24, 1778; Rush, *Letters of Benjamin Rush*, I: 211–16.
81 Mulford, *Only for the Eye*, 22.
82 Richard Stockton, Philadelphia, to Annis Stockton, December 9, 1778; Bill and Edge, *A House Called Morven*, 48–49.
83 Notice from the Commissioners for the County of Somerset, Jacob Bergen and Hendrick Wilson, August 8, 1778; *New Jersey Gazette*, August 12, 1778, 4.
84 *New Jersey Gazette*, December 31, 1778, 3.
85 "Two Guineas Reward," *The Royal Gazette*, August 22, 1778, 3.
86 Giles R. Wright, "Prime: Another Resident of Bainbridge House," *Princeton History* 10 (1991): 60–70; Izzy Kasdin, "The Manumission of Prime." After the war, Prime had great difficulties in having his freedom recognized and had to go to court to win his ultimate freedom. William Churchill Houston was one man who helped him in that case. For a complete discussion of Prime's efforts and digital copies of primary sources, see Kasdin.
87 *Pennsylvania Packet*, July 14, 1778, 4.

Chapter 8

1 William Livingston, Princeton, to Elisha Boudinot, May 8, 1779; *Livingston Papers*, III: 83–84.
2 James Moore, *NARA M804 PF* W1060.
3 *New Jersey Gazette*, March 31, 1779, 3.
4 John Hulfish, *NARA M804 PF* W2553.
5 Thomas Olden, *NARA M804 PF* S23828. No other record of this service has been found, so we have to take Olden at his word.
6 William Livingston, Trenton, to John Neilson, June 7, 1779; *Livingston Papers*, III: 108. William Livingston, Trenton, to William Scudder, June 7, 1779; *Livingston Papers*, Microform, r9: 735. William Livingston, Middlebrook, to William Scudder, June 23, 1779; *Livingston Papers*, III: 120–21.
7 William Livingston, Trenton, to William Scudder, June 8, 1779; *Livingston Papers*, III: 109. William Livingston, Raritan, to William Scudder, June 26, 1779; Ibid., 126.
8 *Pennsylvania Packet*, June 12, 1779, 3.
9 Ibid., April 20, 1779, 4. Notice signed by Rev. James Caldwell, Clerk.

10 Collins, *President Witherspoon*, 103.
11 *College of New Jersey Trustees Minutes*, 219–21. See also Collins, *President Witherspoon*, 101.
12 *New Jersey Gazette*, May 5, 1779, 3.
13 Collins, *President Witherspoon*, 104; *College of New Jersey Trustees Minutes*, 221–24.
14 *New Jersey Gazette*, October 13, 1779, 1.
15 Harrison, *Princetonians*, III: 440–42. However, he appears in Middlesex County on the 1778 tax returns and Somerset County in 1780. See Stryker-Rodda, "New Jersey Rateables, 1778–1780."
16 *New Jersey Gazette*, October 13, 1779, 1.
17 Ibid.
18 Collins, *President Witherspoon*, 94.
19 *New Jersey Gazette*, December 16, 1778, 4.
20 Ibid., March 10, 1779, 4.
21 *General Assembly (Session beginning October 27, 1778)*, 147–49, 155–56. Council concurred and Jonathan Deare reported one of the concurrences to the Assembly.
22 Ibid., 79–80.
23 Ibid., 89.
24 Ibid., 111–13.
25 *General Assembly (Session beginning October 27, 1778)*, 100–102, 138, 142; *Legislative Council (Session beginning October 27, 1778)*, 27, 65, 72, 75; *Joint Meeting*, 31; *Livingston Papers*, III: 65.
26 Bond of Kelsey, Stockton, and Olden, June 15, 1779; *Livingston Papers*, Microform, r9: 788–89.
27 Stratford and Wilson, *Certificates and Receipts*, David Olden certificates.
28 *Assembly*, 147–49, 155–56. Council concurred and Jonathan Deare reported one of the concurrences to the Assembly.
29 *New Jersey Gazette*, July 28, 1779, 3.
30 *General Assembly (Session beginning October 27, 1778)*, 190–93.
31 *General Assembly (Session beginning October 26, 1779)*, 19–20, 46–48.
32 Ibid., 59, 61.
33 Ibid., 83–84, 93.
34 Ibid., 83, 100; *Legislative Council (Session beginning October 27, 1778)*, 41–42, 51.
35 Ibid., 162.
36 Ibid., 109.
37 *New Jersey Gazette*, September 8, 1779, 3.
38 Ibid., November 10, 1779, 4.
39 Ibid., October 27, 3.
40 Stratford and Wilson, *Certificates and Receipts*, certificates issued at Princeton by Robert Stockton, Q.M. 1779–80, 204–06.
41 William Livingston, Raritan, to Jeremiah Wadsworth, October 15, 1779; *Livingston Papers*, III: 181–82. Wadsworth replied that the removal was proper. Jeremiah Wadsworth, Murderers Creek, to William Livingston, October 21, 1779; *Livingston Papers*, II: 182. The Congressional resolution of July 9, 1779, was very similar to the resolution of February 9, 1778 and is found in *JCC*, XIV, 812–13.
42 William Livingston, Princeton, to Samuel Huntington, October 29, 1779; *Livingston Papers*, III: 186–88. William Livingston, Princeton, to Robert Stockton, October 12, 1779; *Livingston Papers*, Microfrom, r10:392. In his letter to Stockton, Livingston reiterated that he was not fired for cause, but merely because the job was no longer needed.
43 Ibid.
44 *QMR*, January meeting, frame 297–98; followed up in June, frame 303.
45 Ibid., frame 306.

46 *QMR*, 1681–1935, New Jersey, Burlington, Chesterfield Monthly Meeting Minutes, 1774–1796. The Chesterfield Monthly Meeting Minutes, 1774–1796, contain a collection of manumission papers.
47 *New Jersey Gazette*, March 3, 1779, 4.
48 Ibid., April 7, 1779, 4.
49 Ibid., April 21, 1779, 3.
50 Ibid., September 8, 1779, 4,
51 *Pennsylvania Packet*, July 31, 1779, 4; *Morgan Account Book*, 1779. George Morgan Collection: 1759–1806, C1394, Box 1, Folder 4, Princeton University Library, Special Collections, Manuscripts Division.
52 *New Jersey Gazette*, August 18, 1779, 3.
53 Morgan's Account book for Princeton begins on April 3, 1779, when he paid Josiah Skelton $200 for sundry articles needed for his farm. The next item is April 19, 1779, when he paid Easter Mollison $17 for a young sow he killed on his farm belonging to her son Reuben Mollison. *Morgan Account Book*, 1779. George Morgan Collection: 1759–1806, C1394, Box 1, Folder 4, Princeton University Library, Special Collections, Manuscripts Division.
54 Savelle, *George Morgan, Colony Builder*, 182. See *Pennsylvania Packet*, Tuesday, April 6, 1779, for announcement of meeting of The Proprietors of Indiana at the Indian Queen tavern in Philadelphia, signed by George Morgan, Secretary and Treasurer of the Land Office, and, *Pennsylvania Packet*, Tuesday, March 30, 1779, 4, for notice of his land sales including Indiana tracts.
55 Savelle, *George Morgan, Colony Builder*, 182, 160–61; Schaff, *Wampum Belts and Peace Trees*, 201.
56 Savelle, *George Morgan, Colony Builder*, 185.
57 Ibid., 186.
58 Woodward and Craven, *Princetonians*, IV: 416–17. Hutchins was class of 1789.
59 Morgan Account Book May 21, 1779; George Morgan Collection: 1759–1806, C1394, Box 1, Folder 4, Princeton University Library, Special Collections, Manuscripts Division; Hageman, *Princeton*, I: 212.
60 Thacher, *A Military Journal*, 195. Thacher described them as they appeared for the meeting with Washington at Middlebrook.
61 Savelle, *George Morgan, Colony Builder*, 160–61; Schaff, *Wampum Belts and Peace Trees*, 201.
62 Collins, "Indian Wards at Princeton," 101–02; *Morgan Account Book.*
63 George Morgan, Princeton, to Nathanael Greene, May 2, 1779; Showman, *Greene Papers*, III: 445.
64 Speech to the Delaware Chiefs, May 12, 1779, Middlebrook; Fitzpatrick, *Writings of Washington*, XV: 53–56.
65 Washington to Morgan, Middlebrook, May 21, 1779; *GWPLOC*.
66 Savelle, *George Morgan, Colony Builder*, 166, 201; *JCC*, XIV: 669.
67 *Jonathan Baldwin Damage Claim*.
68 Savelle, *George Morgan, Colony Builder*, 185; George Morgan Receipt Book, May 8, May 15, and May 18, 1779; Princeton University Special Collections; Col. George Morgan Journal, page 6, Princeton University Special Collections. C1394, Box 1, Folder 5, Princeton University Library, Special Collections, Manuscripts Division.
69 *Morgan Account Book*, June and July 1779. George Morgan Collection: 1759–1806, C1394, Box 1, Folder 4, Princeton University Library, Special Collections, Manuscripts Division.
70 This included 45 yards of linen, 3½ yards of Jane [jean], another 40 yards of linen, and weaving 4 yards of linen.
71 *Morgan Account Book*, 1779, George Morgan Collection: 1759–1806, C1394, Box 1, Folder 4, Princeton University Library, Special Collections, Manuscripts Division.
72 Benjamin Rush, Philadelphia, to Colonel Morgan, November 8, 1779; Rush, *Letters of Benjamin Rush*, I: 245–46.

73 William Livingston, Mount Holly, to Jacob Bergen, November 19, 1779; *Livingston Papers*, III: 224.
74 William Livingston, Mount Holly, to John Witherspoon, December 15, 1779; *Livingston Papers*, III: 268–69.
75 William Livingston, Princeton, to John Witherspoon, December 31, 1779; *Livingston Papers*, Microform, 10: 933.
76 William Livingston, Brunswick, to John Witherspoon, January 29, 1780; *Livingston Papers*, III: 293–94.
77 Ferling, *Almost a Miracle*, 399–400.
78 *New Jersey Gazette*, February 10, 1779, 3; February 24, 1779, 3; March 3, 1779, supplement 1; Wednesday, March 10, 1779, 4; March 31, 1779, 3; September 1, 1779, 3.
79 Richard Cochran, *AO 12*, 013, 69–76.

Chapter 9

1 John Witherspoon, Tusculum near Princeton, to a friend in Scotland, March 20, 1780; Green, *Life of John Witherspoon*, 173–75.
2 Thomas Olden *NARA M804 PF* S23828; Extract of a letter from New Barbados, Bergen County, dated May 30, 1780; *Pennsylvania Packet*, June 17, 1780, 2.
3 Jonathan Baldwin, Princeton, to William Livingston, June 8, 1780; *Livingston Papers*, Microform, r12: 206.
4 James Moore *NARA M804 PF* W1060; Stephen Morford *PF* S1064; NJSA Mss 1507, Moore's Company, 2nd Regt, Somerset Militia in active service stationed at Springfield, June 8–15, 1780: James Moore capt, James Hamilton ensign, Robert McCullough sergeant, Isaac Cool serg, Burgen Updike serg, David Maxwell serg, John Britton, Peter Bowne, Mathias Buzzy, Elliot Creasey, David Cool, William Downey, Neil Forman, Samuel Forman—deserted, James Higgins, David Hamilton, Samuel Heath, James Heath, Daniel Leigh, Joseph Lancaster, William McConkey, Noah Morford, William Minor, John Mullison, James McCombs, Stephen Morford, Andrew McMackin, Aaron Manley, Joseph Mattison, John Nickleson, William Parr, John Paxon, Luke Reeves, Nathaniel Runyan, Job Runyan, Samuel Ruckman, Allen Rhodes, Thomas Robinson, John Robinson, Samuel Skillman, Samuel Scott, Richard Scott, Abraham Skillman, Christopher Stryker, George Skillman, Samuel Stout—deserted, William Savage—deserted, Isaac Updike, Thomas Wilson, Hendrick Waters, Samuel Wood, Silas Waters—deserted, Richard Vandoozer—deserted, Wilson Burdine. See also: NARA M881, Compiled Service Records for individuals. Allen Rhodes served as a wagoner for the company.
5 James Moore, *NARA M804 PF* W1060.
6 Ibid.; Stephen Morford, *NARA M804 PF* S1064.
7 William Livingston, Trenton, to Thomas Egbert, November 28, 1780; *Livingston Papers*, IV: 102, 102n1.
8 William Scudder, New Market, to William Livingston, November 27, 1780; *Livingston Papers*, Microform, r13: 651.
9 *Pennsylvania Packet*, March 23, 1780, 1.
10 *College of New Jersey Trustees Minutes*, 223–24.
11 *Pennsylvania Journal*, October 25, 1780, 1.
12 Collins, *Princeton*, 81.
13 Stratford and Wilson, *Certificates and Receipts*, Certificates Issued at Princeton by Robert Stockton, Q. M., 1779–80, 204–06.
14 William Livingston, Trenton, to General Assembly, March 7, 1780; *Livingston Papers*, III: 317–18.
15 *General Assembly (Session beginning October 26, 1779)*, 172–73.
16 *General Assembly (Session beginning October 26, 1779)*, 188, 193.

17 Ibid., 205, 208.
18 Ibid., 294–95.
19 *General Assembly (Session begun October 24, 1780)*, 14.
20 *General Assembly (Session beginning October 26, 1779)*, 177–78.
21 Ibid., 180.
22 Ibid., 190, 201.
23 Ibid., 211.
24 Ibid., 251–52.
25 Ibid., 291.
26 Ibid., 297.
27 William Livingston, Morristown, to Azariah Dunham, 17 April 1780; *Livingston Papers*, III: 352–53.
28 Nathanael Greene, Camp Preakness, to William Livingston, July 20, 1780; *Livingston Papers*, IV: 15.
29 For an example, see Abraham Clark to Mrs. Furman, July 11, 1780; *NJSA*, Department of Education, New Jersey State Library, BAH, box 4-1a, Revolutionary War Documents, #95.
30 Mary Dagworthy to General Washington, July 17, 1780; *GWPLOC*. George Washington to Mary Dagworthy, August 6, 1780; *GWPLOC*.
31 Ferling, *Almost a Miracle*, 406; Mary Dagworthy to General Washington, December 29, 1780; *GWPLOC*. For more on this whole story see Conner Runyon, "Offering of the Ladies: Esther Reed's Sentiments, Washington's Objections," *Journal of the American Revolution*, July 12, 2017, at allthingsliberty.com, and Catherine Hudak, "The Ladies of Trenton: Women's Political and Public Activism in Revolutionary NJ," *New Jersey Studies: An Interdisciplinary Journal*, Summer 2015, 39.
32 Info on her broadside.
33 Morgan Account Book, 1780. George Morgan Collection: 1759–1806, C1394, Box 1, Folder 4. Princeton University Library, Special Collections, Manuscripts Division.
34 Col. George Morgan Journal, George Morgan Collection: 1759–1806, C1394, Box 1, Folder 5. Princeton University Library, Special Collections, Manuscripts Division.
35 *New Jersey Gazette*, March 29, 1780, 4.
36 *Ibid.*, May 17, 1780, 3.
37 *Ibid.*, July 5, 1780, 4.
38 *Pennsylvania Packet*, August 22, 1780, 3.
39 *QMR*, frame 312, 320, 324–25.
40 William Livingston, Brunswick, to John Witherspoon, January 29, 1780; *Livingston Papers*, III: 293–94.
41 *Pennsylvania Gazette*, July 19, 1780, 4.
42 *New Jersey Gazette*, March 29, 1780, 4.
43 Ibid., February 2, 1780, 4; February 9, 1780, 3.
44 Ibid., April 12, 1780, 4.
45 Ibid., July 5, 1780, 3.
46 Ibid., October 4, 1780, 4.
47 *Pennsylvania Packet*, May 30, 1780. Over the following month Morgan reprinted his ad at least four times in two different newspapers: *Pennsylvania Packet*, May 30, June 20, 1780; *Pennsylvania Gazette*, May 31, June 7, June 28, 1780. For Rev. Smith's ad for stolen horse, see *New Jersey Gazette*, June 14, 1780, 4.
48 *British Headquarters Papers* (Carleton Papers or American Manuscripts). Book of Negroes: 10427 (58): MG23 B1, Microform: M-369, Item Number: 2387.
49 *New Jersey Gazette*, November 15, 1780; November 22, 1780, 4.
50 Ibid., November 29, 1780, 3.
51 Chastellux, *Travels in North America*, 160, 162–64.
52 *New Jersey Gazette*, July 12, 1780, 3.

Chapter 10

1 Ferling, *Almost a Miracle*, 468–71.
2 Linn and Egle, eds., "Diary of the Revolt, 659.
3 Nagy, *Rebellion in the Ranks*, 82.
4 Lovell to John Adams, January 2, 1781; Smith, *Letters of Delegates to Congress*, XVI: 537.
5 Linn and Egle, eds., "Diary of the Revolt," 659.
6 Stile, *Major General Wayne*, 243.
7 Major Moore to General Wayne, Pennytown, January 5, 1781, 3:00 p.m.; Stile, *Major General Wayne*, 254–55; Nagy, *Rebellion in the Ranks*, 93.
8 *JCC*, XXIX: 20.
9 *Livingston Papers*, Microform, r14, i038; *Minutes of the Governor's Privy Council, January 3, 1781*, 192.
10 John Fiddler, *NARA M804 PF* S2552; William Doris, *NARA M804 PF* W916; Henry Simmons, *NARA M804 PF* S4838—deposition of Isaac Dunn; David Golden *NARA M804 PF* W7553. When a company was "classed," the men were divided into a stated number of groups, called classes. Things could be arranged so that members of families were in different classes or near neighbors were in different classes. By calling out classes instead of the whole company, it would place less burden on families and neighbors to pick up the work of those called out. It also meant, however, that men would often serve under different officers than they were accustomed, and this no doubt diminished the ability of the militia to serve effectively.
11 Israel Hunt PF S1024—deposition of Oliver Hunt; *NJSA* Auditor's Book B, 465, shows Captain Phil Phillips serving under Colonel Joseph Phillips at Princeton in January 1781.
12 Samuel Smith, Princeton, to William Livingston January 3, 1781; *Livingston Papers*, Microform, r14, 33–35.
13 Robert Stockton, to William Livingston, January 3, 1781; *Livingston Papers*, Microform, r14: 39.
14 See Stratford and Wilson, Certificates and Receipts, quartermaster certificates: Page 166, James Moore per Gershom Moore, February 16, 1782, for the service of three horse employed by the troops of the Pennsylvania Line four days in January 1781, L1.10; Page 138, Thomas Olden, July 8, 1782, received L1.8.1 for three-quarters a cord of wood delivered the soldiers of the Pennsylvania Line in January 1781; Page 139, John Johnson July 17, 1782, Received certificate no. 8169 for L1.16 for three cords wood furnished the Pennsylvania Line in January 1781; Page 88, John Johnson, July 17, 1782, 4 & 72/90 dollars for three cords wood furnished the Pennsylvania Line in January 1781 No 8169; Page 139, Joseph Olden, July 25, 1782, received certificate no. 8174 for L3.15 for five cords wood for the Pennsylvania Line at the time of the revolt in January 1781; Page 89, Joseph Olden, Esq., July 25, 1782, 10 dollars, for five cords wood made use of by soldiers of the Pennsylvania Line at the time of revolt in January 1781 No. 8174.
15 Nagy, *Rebellion in the Ranks*, 87–88.
16 Major Moore to General Wayne, Pennytown, January 5, 1781, 3:00 p.m.; Stile, *Major General Wayne*, 254–55; Nagy, *Rebellion in the Ranks*, 93.
17 St. Clair to the President of Pennsylvania, Trenton, January 4, 1781; Linn and Egle, eds., "Diary of the Revolt," 664–65.
18 Linn and Egle, eds., "Diary of the Revolt," 660–61. St. Clair to the President of Pennsylvania, Trenton, January 4, 1781; Ibid., 664–65. For the list of propositions of the mutineers, see Linn and Egle, eds., 661.
19 Linn and Egle, eds. "Diary of the Revolt," 663; Nagy, *Rebellion in the Ranks*, 95.

20 Linn and Egle, eds. "Diary of the Revolt," 664; Nagy, *Rebellion in the Ranks*, 96. In a January 4, 1781 letter from Princeton, Moylan asked Reed to let him know whether he should stay in Princeton or rejoin his regiment.
21 Information for Gen. Wayne, Elizabethtown, January 4, 1781, 5:00 a.m.; Linn and Egle, eds. "Diary of the Revolt," 665–66.
22 Linn and Egle, eds., "Diary of the Revolt," 666; Major Moore to General Wayne, Pennytown, January 5, 1781, 3:00 p.m.; Stile, *Major General Wayne*, 254–55; Nagy, *Rebellion in the Ranks*, 93.
23 General St. Clair to General Washington, Morristown, January 7, 1781; *The St. Clair Papers*, I: 532–34.
24 See Kidder, *A People Harassed and Exhausted*, 348–51.
25 *NJSA* Mss 1506—Pay roll for Capt. James Moore's Company of militia of Col. Vandike's of Somerset County. James Moore capt., Joseph Mattison sergeant, Wilson Burdine, Allen Rhodes, Than Smith, and William Minor.
26 Diary of Capt. Joseph McClellan of the 9th Pennsylvania; Linn and Egle, eds., "Diary of the Revolt," 670. Reed to Wayne, January 6, 1781, 11:30 p.m.; Ibid., 675.
27 Reed to Committee of Congress, Trenton, 3:00 p.m., January 6, 1781; Linn and Egle, eds.,"Diary of the Revolt," 670–71. Reed to Wayne, 11:30 p.m.; Ibid., 674–75.
28 Sergeants to President Reed, Princeton, January 6, 1781; Linn and Egle, eds.,"Diary of the Revolt," 671.
29 Sergeants to Wayne, January 6, 1781, and Wayne's reply; Linn and Egle, eds.,"Diary of the Revolt," 671–72.
30 Reed to General Wayne, Trenton, past 11:00 p.m.; Linn and Egle, eds.,"Diary of the Revolt," 673–75. Committee of Congress to President Reed, Bristol, January 6, 1781; Ibid., 675.
31 Wayne to Reed, Princeton, January 6, 1781; Linn and Egle, eds., "Diary of the Revolt," 672–73.
32 Propositions sent by General Clinton, January 7, 1781; Linn and Egle, eds.,"Diary of the Revolt," 68.
33 Nagy, *Rebellion in the Ranks*, 127–28.
34 Ibid., 130–32.
35 *Livingston Papers*, Microform, r14, i065.
36 President Reed to General Wayne, Trenton, January 7; Reed, *Life and Correspondence of Joseph Reed*, II: 323–24; also President Reed to Wayne (not sent because Wayne arrived) at D. Hunt's in Maidenhead, January 7, 1781.
37 Joseph Reed to the Executive Council, Daniel Hunt's, four miles from Princeton (Maidenhead), January 7, 1781; Reed, *Life and Correspondence*, I: 326.
38 Linn and Egle, eds., "Diary of the Revolt," 679.
39 McClellan Diary; Linn and Egle, eds., "Diary of the Revolt," 682.
40 President Reed to the Committee of Congress, Hunt's, Maidenhead, January 8; Reed, *Life and Correspondence*, I: 327–28.
41 Ibid., 329–30.
42 Reed to Committee of Congress, Maidenhead, January 8, 1781; Linn and Egle, eds., "Diary of the Revolt," 682–83.
43 General Wayne to President Reed, Princeton, January 8, 1781, 7:00 p.m.; Stile, *Major General Wayne*, 254–55; Linn and Egle, eds., "Diary of the Revolt," 683.
44 Reed to Committee of Congress, Hunt's, Maidenhead, January 8, 1781, 2:30 p.m.; Linn and Egle, eds., "Diary of the Revolt," XI: 653–54. The two spies were eventually hung on January 11. See Nagy, *Rebellion in the Ranks*, 150–52.
45 Reed to Committee of Congress, Maidenhead, January 8, 1781, 7:00 p.m.; Linn and Egle, eds., "Diary of the Revolt," XI: 654–55.
46 For a detailed account of the mutiny, see Nagy, *Rebellion in the Ranks*, chapters 5–11.
47 Letter to the editor from Middlesex, January 1, 1781; *New Jersey Gazette*, January 17, 1781, 1.

48 Mulford, *Only for the Eye*, 22.
49 *Pennsylvania Packet*, March 10, 1781, 2.
50 Historical Society of Princeton Collections, Stockton Papers, item 658. See Greiff and Gunning, *Morven: Memory, Myth & Reality*, 52, 74n107, for more about the difficulties with this document.
51 William Scudder, Princeton, to William Livingston, February 20, 1781; *Livingston Papers*, Microform, r14: 465–46.
52 Document to Captain James Moore, April 14, 1781—"Thos Proctor, Capt 4th Battn Artillery"—in James Moore, PF W1060.
53 *New Jersey Gazette*, March 28, 1781; *Livingston Papers*, IV: 162–63.
54 William Livingston, Princeton, to George Washington, June 1, 1781; *Livingston Papers*, IV: 212.
55 Elias Woodruff, Princeton, to William Livingston, September 4, 1781; *Livingston Papers*, Microform, 15: 695.
56 William Livingston at Princeton to the Assembly, September 20, 1781; *Livingston Papers*, IV: 300.
57 *NJSA*, Book B of Auditors Accounts, 222–24.
58 *Legislative-Council (Session beginning October 24, 1780)*, 39; *General Assembly (Session beginning October 24, 1780)*, 12; James Hamilton, PF W793.
59 William Livingston, Princeton, to Elias Boudinot, September 29, 1781; *Livingston Papers*, IV: 305–36.
60 James Hamilton, PF W793; *NJSA*, Book B Auditors accounts, 225.
61 *College of New Jersey Trustees Minutes*, 225–27; Collins, *President Witherspoon*, 113.
62 Harrison, *Princetonians*, III: 360–61.
63 *College of New Jersey Trustees Minutes*, 227–30.
64 *Pennsylvania Packet*, October 9, 1781, 3.
65 Witherspoon notice, dated September 28, in *New Jersey Gazette*, October 10, 1781, 1.
66 Harrison, *Princetonians*, III: 361.
67 *College of New Jersey Trustees Minutes*, 231–35.
68 *QMR*, frame 325, 331, 332, 333, 336, 339.
69 *New Jersey Gazette*, January 10, 1781, 4.
70 *Pennsylvania Journal*, January 30, 1782, 4. Source from Gigantino, etc.
71 *New Jersey Gazette*, February 7, 1781, 4.
72 *Pennsylvania Gazette*, December 26, 1781, 3.
73 *New Jersey Gazette*, March 21, 1781, 4.
74 Ibid., August 1, 1781, 4.
75 Ibid., November 28, 1781, 4.
76 Ibid., February 7, 1781, 3.
77 Ibid., July 11, 1781, 3.
78 Ibid., September 19, 1781, 4; October 31, 1781, 4.
79 George Morgan Account Book inside front cover, George Morgan Collection: 1759–1806, C1394, box 1, Folder 4, Princeton University Special Collections.
80 Morgan Receipt Book, 1781, 1782.
81 *New York Gazette*, September 3, 1781, 3.
82 Bill and Edge, *A House Called Morven*, 53.
83 *Moreau de St. Mery's American Journey*, 106.
84 Thacher, *A Military Journal*, 325.
85 Stratford and Wilson, *Certificates and Receipts*, 138, 89.
86 *New Jersey Gazette*, October 31, 1781, 3.
87 Bill and Edge, A *House Called Morven*, 53.
88 Thacher, *A Military Journal*, 363.
89 *Pennsylvania Packet*, December 6, 1781, 3.

Chapter 11

1 Proceedings of general court martial at New Brunswick January 28, 1782, for trial of Ensign Jacob Merceroll, *NJSA* Mss 851.
2 He served until November 1783, when he returned home and practiced medicine in Princeton at the Bainbridge house. Harrison, *Princetonians*, III: 303.
3 Harrison, *Princetonians*, III: 362. See this article for more about his life before and after college at Princeton.
4 Ashbel Green's address to the Alumni Association in 1840, quoted in Maclean, *History of the College of New Jersey*, 331; Green, *Life of Ashbel Green*, 137–38: Green, *Life of John Witherspoon*, 171; Collins, *Princeton*, 82; Collins, *President Witherspoon*, 96.
5 John Witherspoon, Princeton, to Governor Livingston, September 22, 1782; *Livingston Papers*, Microform, 17: 930.
6 *New Jersey Gazette*, October 9, 1782, 1.
7 *College of New Jersey Trustees Minutes*, 231–35.
8 *New Jersey Gazette*, October 9, 1782, 1. The newspaper report on the event did not indicate whether the Council members attended.
9 Ibid., October 23, 1782, 4; for another version, see *Pennsylvania Packet*, October 5, 1782, 2.
10 Notice dated Princeton, July 31, 1782; *Pennsylvania Evening Post*, August 23, 1782, 120.
11 *New Jersey Gazette*, September 18, 1782, 4.
12 *QMR*, frame 340, 342, 343, 346.
13 *New Jersey Gazette*, January 16, 1782, 4.
14 Ibid., December 18, 1782, 4.
15 Ibid., February 27, 1782, 4; *Pennsylvania Packet*, June 25, 1782, 902.
16 *New Jersey Gazette*, May 1, 1782, 3; May 8, 1782, 3.
17 Ibid., May 1, 1782, 1; October 23, 1782, 4.
18 Ibid., June 5, 1782, 4.
19 Ibid., December 11, 1782, 3.
20 Ibid., December 11, 1782, 4.
21 Ibid., December 4, 1782, 4.
22 Ibid., October 23, 1782, 4.
23 *Pennsylvania Packet*, September 10, 1782, 4.
24 *New Jersey Gazette*, December 25, 1782, 3.
25 Ibid., September 11, 1782, 4.
26 Morgan Journal; Morgan Receipt Book, 1782.
27 *Livingston Papers*, Microform, 17: 008–009.
28 *General Assembly (Session beginning October 22, 1782)*, 11.
29 Ibid., 41–42.
30 Ibid., 46.
31 James Hamilton *NARA M804 PF* W793. On November 18, the Assembly resolved to pay the expenses for conveying ammunition from Princeton to Sussex County in April and June 1782, and on December 21, to pay Charles Allen for conveying ammunition from Princeton to Cumberland in March and August 1782. Assembly, Session begun at Trenton on the 22d Day of October, 31, 71.
32 *Pennsylvania Packet*, July 27, 1782, 3.
33 Notice dated Princeton, July 31; *Pennsylvania Evening Post*, August 23, 1782, 120.
34 *General Assembly (Session beginning October 22, 1782)*, 8. Second Reading on May 29. 19.
35 Ibid., 38.
36 Ibid., 18.
37 Ibid., 20.
38 Ibid., 45.
39 *New Jersey Gazette*, October 2, 1782, 4.

Chapter 12

1 Morgan Receipt Book, 1783; Morgan Journal.
2 *Livingston Papers*, V: 21–22; *NJSA*, Privy Council Minutes, 244.
3 Collins, *Congress at Princeton 1783*, 10–13. See Collins, 13–27, for the story of the mutiny.
4 *JCC*, XXIV: 410.
5 For details on the mutiny and the politics involved, see Kenneth R. Bowling, "New Light on the Philadelphia Mutiny of 1783: Federal-State Confrontation at the Close of the War for Independence," *PMH&B*, Vol. 101, No. 4 (October 1977), 419–50.
6 John Cox, Vice President of NJ State Council; *PCC*, r60, i46; Locating the Seat of Government, 83–84.
7 Collins, *Congress at Princeton 1783*, 37. John K. Alexander, "The Philadelphia Numbers Game: An Analysis of Philadelphia's Eighteenth-Century Population," *PMHB*, XCVIII (1974), 314–24.
8 Collins, *Congress at Princeton 1783*, 37–38.
9 Boudinot, *Elias Boudinot, LL.D.*, I: 336–37.
10 Collins, *Congress at Princeton 1783*, 28–29.
11 *PCC*, r60, i46, p67.
12 *PCC*, Locating the Seat of Government, r60 i46 p63.
13 *PCC*, Locating the Seat of Government, r60, i46, p51–52. It is marked as read July 23, 1783, in Congress.
14 *PCC*, Locating the Seat of Government, r60 i46 p63.
15 Collins, *Congress at Princeton 1783*, 48–51.
16 *PCC*, roll 60, item 46, p75–76. See also *Pennsylvania Packet*, July 17, 1783, and *Virginia Gazette*, July 26, 1783.
17 *PCC*, Locating the Seat of Government, r60, i46, p71.
18 Smith, *Letters of Delegates to Congress*, XX: 371.
19 John Montgomery, Princeton, to Benjamin Rush, June 27, 1783; Smith, *Letters of Delegates to Congress*, 373.
20 Benjamin Rush, Philadelphia, to John Montgomery, June 27, 1783; Rush, *Letters of Benjamin Rush*, I: 301–02.
21 *Independent Gazetteer* (Philadelphia), June 28, 1783, 2.
22 John Montgomery, Princeton, to Benjamin Rush, June 30, 1783; Smith, *Letters of Delegates to Congress*, XX: 381.
23 Charles Thomson, Princeton, to Hannah Thomson, June 30, 1783; Smith, *Letters of Delegates to Congress*, XX: 386–87.
24 Sheridan and Murrin, *Congress at Princeton*, xxiv.
25 Charles Thomson, Princeton, to Hannah Thomson, June 30, 1783; Smith, *Letters of Delegates to Congress*, XX: 387 n4.
26 Green, *Life of Ashbel Green*, 142.
27 Charles Thomson, Princeton, to Hannah Thomson, June 30, 1783; Smith, *Letters of Delegates to Congress*, XX: 383–87.
28 Bill, *House Called Morven*, 55. Citing ledger of Thomas Stockton.
29 D'Orssiere ad, *New Jersey Gazette*, February 19, 1783, 4; Harrison ad, ibid., February 19, 1783, 1; Van Voorhis ad, ibid., March 5, 1783, 1.
30 James Madison, Princeton, to Thomas Jefferson, September 20, 1783; *Writings of James Madison*, II: 22.
31 *JCC*, XXIV: 422–25.
32 Smith, *Letters of Delegates to Congress*, XX: 396; *PCC*, i16, f208, i46, f67–70; Collins, *Congress at Princeton*, 43–44.

33 *JCC*, XXIV: 425–26.
34 Benjamin Rush, Philadelphia, to John Montgomery, July 4, 1783; Rush, *Letters of Benjamin Rush*, I: 304–05.
35 Charles Thomson, Princeton, to Hannah Thomson, July 3, 1783; Sheridan and Murrin, eds., *Congress at Princeton*, 14.
36 Charles Thomson, Princeton, to Hannah Thomson, July 4, 1783; Sheridan and Murrin, eds., *Congress at Princeton*, 16–18.
37 Green, *Life of Ashbel Green*, 142–43.
38 Charles Thomson, Princeton, to Hannah Thomson, July 5, 1783; Smith, *Letters of Delegates to Congress*, XXV: 748–50. This letter was a late addition to this collection so it does not appear in proper sequence, but rather toward the end of the last volume.
39 Charles Thomson, Princeton, to Hannah Thomson, July 6, 1783; Sheridan and Murrin, eds., *Congress at Princeton*, 19–20.
40 Collins, *Continental Congress at Princeton*, 86, citing Morris's Diary, July 9, 1783 in Robert Morris, *Diary and Letter Books*, Library of Congress, Washington, DC.
41 Charles Thomson, Princeton, to Hannah Thomson, July 22, 1783; Sheridan and Murrin, eds., *Congress at Princeton*, 22.
42 Charles Thomson, Princeton, to Hannah Thomson, July 23, 1783, Sheridan and Murrin, eds., *Congress at Princeton*, 25–26.
43 Charles Thomson, Princeton, to Hannah Thomson, July 25, 1783, Sheridan and Murrin, eds., *Congress at Princeton*, 28–29; July 26, 1783, 31–33.
44 James Madison, Philadelphia, to Thomas Jefferson, July 17, 1783; *Jefferson Papers*, VI: 318–19.
45 Charles Thomson, Princeton, to Hannah Thomson, Princeton, July 29, 1783; Sheridan and Murrin, eds., *Congress at Princeton*, 33–35.
46 Charles Thomson, Princeton, to Hannah Thomson, July 30, 1783; Sheridan and Murrin, eds., *Congress at Princeton*, 36–37.
47 Charles Thomson, Princeton, to Hannah Thomson, August 1, 1783; Sheridan and Murrin, eds., *Congress at Princeton*, 39–42.
48 Rush, *Letters of Benjamin Rush*, I: 307–08.
49 Collins, *Congress in Princeton 1783*, 94.
50 Boudinot, *Elias Boudinot*, I: 346–47.
51 *JCC*, XXIV: 494–95.
52 *Rivington's Royal Gazette*, July 5, 1783, sale advertisement. See also *Pennsylvania Packet*, October 14, 1783, which notes Washington was occupying the property. Also mentioned in Boudinot to Washington from Princeton, August 12, 1783; Boudinot, *Elias Boudinot*, I: 349.
53 Charles Thomson to Hannah Thomson, August 19, 1783; Sheridan and Murrin, eds., *Congress at Princeton*, 42–44.
54 Boudinot to Franklin, August 15, 1783; Boudinot, *Elias Boudinot*, 353.
55 Boudinot to Washington, August 21, 1783; Boudinot, *Elias Boudinot*, 357.
56 Washington to Boudinot, August 14, 1783; Boudinot, *Elias Boudinot*, 351; see Dunlap, *History of the Arts of Design*, 300.
57 Bezaleel Howe, *NARA M804 PF* R5286; supporting statement for Thomas Bunting, *PF* W834.
58 Collins, *Congress at Princeton*, 102.
59 Ibid., 104.
60 Ibid., 106.
61 Note of Nathaniel Lawrence, Attorney General of New York, dated September 28, 1783; *Itinerary of General Washington, 1783*, 416.
62 Collins, *Congress at Princeton*, 107–08.
63 James Madison, Princeton, to Edmund Randolph, August 30, 1783; *Writings of James Madison*, II: 11–13.

64 Dunlap, *A History of the Rise and Progress of The Arts of Design*, 297–98.
65 Ibid., 298–99.
66 Ibid., 298–300.
67 George Washington, Rocky Hill, to Governor George Clinton, September 11, 1783; *GWPLOC*.
68 Charles Thomson to Hannah Thomson, September 17 and 18, 1783; Sheridan and Murrin, eds., *Congress at Princeton*, 56–57, 58–61.
69 Benjamin Huntington, Princeton, to Anne Huntington, September 8, 1783; Smith, *Letters of Delegates to Congress*, XX: 625–26.
70 Collins, "Indian Wards at Princeton," 103. Savelle, *George Morgan, Colony Builder*, 197.
71 Harrison, *Princetonians*, III: 425–29.
72 *The College of New Jersey Trustees Minutes* for September 29, 1784 (p. 245), state that the painting had been executed, and it was ordered that it be hung in the college hall. The board also resolved on October 22, 1783 (p. 240–41), to obtain a portrait of former royal governor Belcher to replace one destroyed "during the late war." It was to be hung where the destroyed one had been "as a testimony of the gratitude of the board for the eminent services formerly rendered by his Excellency to this institution."
73 *The College of New Jersey Trustees Minutes*, 235–39.
74 Green, *Life of Ashbel Green*, 143–44. *The Pennsylvania Gazette* for October 8, 1783, contained the commencement program.
75 Notes by Madison, October 1783; *Jefferson Papers*, VI: 362–63.
76 Boudinot, *Elias Boudinot*, I: 397–98.
77 Nathanael Greene, Princeton, to Elias Boudinot, November 1, 1783; *Papers of Nathaniel Greene*, XIII: 137, 167–68.
78 Fitzpatrick, *Writings of Washington*, XXVII: 188–90.
79 Charles Thomson to Hannah Thomson, October 13, 1783; Sheridan and Murrin, eds., *Congress at Princeton*, 62.
80 Charles Thomson to Hannah Thomson, October 16, 1783; Sheridan and Murrin, eds., *Congress at Princeton*, 70.
81 V. Lansing Collins, "The History of Old North," *Princeton Alumni Weekly*, vol. 7, No. 10, December 1, 1906, 168–72, 170–71.
82 Benjamin Harrison, Princeton, to the Virginia Delegates, October 25, 1783; *Jefferson Papers*, VI: 345.
83 John Paul Jones, Philadelphia, to President of Congress, October 18, 1783; *The Diplomatic Correspondence of the United States of America*, Washington, DC: 1837, III: 663–64.
84 *JCC*, XXV: 787–88.
85 Hawke, David, *Paine*, 1974, 141–42.
86 *JCC*, XXII: 807, 803.
87 Hiltzheimer, Jacob. *Extracts from the Diary of Jacob Hiltzheimer of Philadelphia, 1765–1798*. Jacob Coxe Parsons, ed., Philadelphia, 1893, 59.
88 *British Headquarters Papers* (Carleton Papers or American Manuscripts). Book of Negroes: 10427 (139): MG23 B1, Microform: M-369, Item Number: 1528.
89 *British Headquarters Papers* (Carleton Papers or American Manuscripts). Book of Negroes: 10427 (58): MG23 B1, Microform: M-369, Item Number: 2387.
90 An amercement referred to fines also and gave a broader meaning to them. *Votes and Proceedings of the Eighth General Assembly of the State of New Jersey, at a Session begun at Trenton on the 28th Day of October, 1783, and continued by Adjournments, being the first sitting of the Eight Assembly* (Trenton: Isaac Collins, 1784), 29, 32.
91 Miller, *Selected Papers of Charles Willson Peale*, I: 402.
92 Collins, *Princeton Past and Present*, 34.

Bibliography

Manuscripts (original, digital, and microform)

Adams, Samuel. *Samuel Adams Papers, 1635–1826* [microform]. New York Public Library Manuscripts Division. Wilmington, DE: Scholarly Resources, 1964–71.

Carleton, Sir Guy. *British Headquarters (Sir Guy Carleton) Papers, 1777–1783* [microform]. Washington, DC: Microfilming Service, Recordak Corp., 1957.

College of New Jersey Trustees Minutes. AC120 Collections of the Seeley G. Mudd Manuscript Library, Princeton, NJ. Online at: https://webspace.princeton.edu/users/mudd/Digitization/AC120/AC120_c0003.pdf and https://webspace.princeton.edu/users/mudd/Digitization/AC120/AC120_c0004.pdf

Glyn, Thomas. "Ensign Glyn's Journal on the American Service with the Detachment of 1,000 Men of the Guards commanded by Brigadier General Mathew in 1776." In Varnum Lansing Collins, *Revolutionary War Papers, 1913–1932*. Manuscript Department, Princeton University Library, Princeton, NJ. Call number C0199 no. 380.

Governor's Privy Council Minutes, 1777–1845 (manuscript and microform), *NJSA*.

Grant, James. *James Grant of Ballindalloch Papers, 1740–1819 (bulk 1760–1780)*. Microfilm produced from originals in the National Archives of Scotland. Edinburgh: National Archives of Scotland, 2003.

Great Britain, *Audit Office. American Loyalist Claims. Series 1, 1776–1831, AO 12* [microform]. Exchequer and Audit Department.

Great Britain, *Audit Office. American Loyalist Claims. Series 2, 1780–1835, AO 13* [microform]. Exchequer and Audit Department.

Inventories of Damages by the British and Americans in New Jersey, 1776–1782 [microform]. Trenton: New Jersey Bureau of Archives and History, 1976. Reel 2: *British Damages—Bergen, Burlington, Middlesex & Somerset Counties.*

Knox, Henry. *The Papers of Henry Knox, 1719–1825* [microform]. Owned by the New England Historic Genealogical Society and deposited in the Massachusetts Historical Society. Boston: [The Massachusetts Historical Society?], 1960.

Livingston, William. *The Papers of William Livingston* [microform]. Ann Arbor, MI: University Microfilms, 1986.

NARA M246. Muster rolls, payrolls, strength returns, and other miscellaneous personnel, pay, and supply records of American Army units, 1775–83. 138 microfilm reels; 35 mm. Washington, DC: National Archives and Records Service, General Service Administration, 1980. [Also online at Fold3.com]

NARA M804. Revolutionary War pension and bounty-land-warrant application files [microform]. Washington, DC: National Archives and Records Service, General Services Administration, 1974. 2670 microfilm reels; 35 mm. [Also online at Fold3.com]

NARA M881. Compiled service records of soldiers who served in the American Army during the Revolutionary War. Washington, DC: National Archives and Records Service, General Services Administration, 1976. [Also online at Fold3.com]

New Jersey Adjutant General's office. *Index to Revolutionary War Manuscripts: New Jersey Service Abstracts [cards], ca. 1776–1783.* [microform]. 9 reels; 16 mm. Alphabetical index to New Jerseyans who served on the American side of the conflict. Abstracts information and cites references to the State Archives' manuscript records.

New Jersey Adjutant General's Office. *Revolutionary War Manuscripts, New Jersey: numbers 1–10811* [microform]. 30 reels; 35 mm. Individual items are noted in the source notes as RevWarMss ___.

U.S., Quaker Meeting Records, 1681–1935 [database on-line] Provo, UT: Ancestry.com Operations, Inc., 2014. Original data: Swarthmore, Quaker Meeting Records. Friends Historical Library, Swarthmore College, Swarthmore, PA. (*QMR*)

Washington, George. *George Washington Papers. Library of Congress.* (*GWPLOC*)

New Jersey Government Documents

Journal of the Proceedings of the Legislative-Council of the State of New Jersey. Burlington, NJ, then Trenton, NJ: Isaac Collins, 1777–84.

Minutes of the Council of Safety of the State of New Jersey. Jersey City, NJ: J. H. Lyon, 1872.

Minutes and Proceedings of the Council and General Assembly of the State of New Jersey in Joint Meeting, from August 30, 1776 to May, 1780. Trenton, NJ: Isaac Collins, 1780.

Minutes of the Provincial Council and Council of Safety of the State of New Jersey. Trenton, NJ: Naar, Day & Naar, 1879. (*PCCS*)

Votes and Proceedings of the General Assembly of the Colony of New Jersey. At a Session began at Burlington, Wednesday, November 10, 1773. Burlington, NJ: Isaac Collins, 1774.

Votes and Proceedings of the General Assembly of the State of New Jersey. Burlington, NJ, then Trenton, NJ: Isaac Collins, 1777–84.

Manuscript Collections—Published

Delaware Archives: Revolutionary War in Three Volumes. Wilmington, DE: Chas. L. Story Company Press, 1919.

Force, Peter, comp. *American Archives.* Fourth and Fifth Series. 9 vols. Washington, DC: 1904–37.

Fraser, Alexander. *United Empire Loyalists: Enquiry into the Losses and Services in Consequence of Their Loyalty: Evidence in the Canadian Claims. Second Report of the Bureau of Archives for the Province of Ontario.* Baltimore: Genealogical Publishing Company, 1994.

Hazard, Samuel. *Pennsylvania Archives.* Series 1. Philadelphia: J. Severns, 1852–56.

Jefferson, Thomas. *The Papers of Thomas Jefferson.* Edited by Julian P. Boyd. Princeton, NJ: Princeton University Press, 1950-.

Kemble, Stephen. *The Kemble Papers, 1773–1789.* New York: New York Historical Society, 1884–85.

Livingston, William. *The Papers of William Livingston.* Edited by Carl E. Prince. Trenton: New Jersey Historical Commission, c. 1979–c. 1988.

Madison, James. *The Writings of James Madison. Volume 1: Correspondence 1769–1783.* Edited by Gaillard Hunt. New York: G. P. Putnam's Sons, 1900.

Paine, Robert Treat. *The Papers of Robert Treat Paine.* Volume III: 1774–77. Boston: Massachusetts Historical Society, 2006.

Putnam, Israel. *Israel Putnam Papers, 1772–1782.* Microfilm of originals in the Connecticut Historical Society. Hartford, CT: New England Archives Center, 1992. 1 reel.

Reed, Joseph. *Papers of Joseph Reed: 1757–1795, 1824–1842* [microform]. Filmed from material held by the New York Historical Society.

Smith, Paul H., ed. *Letters of Delegates to Congress, 1774–1789.* Washington, DC: Library of Congress, 1976–85.

Smith, William Henry. *The St. Clair Papers: The Life and Public Services of Arthur St. Clair.* 1881. Reprint, Freeport, NY: Books for Libraries Press, 1970.

Washington, George. *The Papers of George Washington.* Revolutionary War Series. Edited by Philander D. Chase. Charlottesville, VA: University Press of Virginia, 1985–97.

_________. *The Writings of George Washington: From the Original Manuscript Sources, 1745–1799.* Edited by John C. Fitzpatrick. Washington, DC: Government Printing Office, 1931–44.

Witherspoon, John. *The Works of John Witherspoon.* Edinburgh: Ogle & Aikman, 1804–05.

Diaries, Correspondence, Journals, and Memoirs—Published

Adams, John. *Diary and Autobiography of John Adams.* Edited by L. H. Butterfield. Cambridge, MA: Belknap Press of Harvard University Press, 1962.

Anderson, Enoch. *Personal Recollections of Captain Enoch Anderson, an Officer of the Delaware Regiments in the Revolutionary War.* Wilmington, DE: Historical Society of Delaware, 1896.

Avery, Rev. David. "Battle of Princeton—From the Diary of the Rev. David Avery." *The American Monthly Magazine,* XIX (July–December 1901), Washington, DC: National Society, D.A.R., 1901, 260–62.

Baker, William S. "Itinerary of General Washington from June 15, 1775, to December 23, 1783." *The Pennsylvania Magazine of History and Biography,* 15, no. 4 (1891), 394–428.

Boudinot, J. J., ed. *The Life, Public Services, Addresses and Letters of Elias Boudinot, LL.D. President of the Continental Congress.* Boston: Houghton, Mifflin and Company, 1896.

Boyle, Joseph Lee. "Their Distress Is Almost Intolerable." In *The Elias Boudinot Letterbook, 1777–1778.* Bowie, MD: Heritage Books, 2002.

Chastellux, Francois Jean. *Travels in North America, in the Years 1780, 1781, and 1782.* Translated by Howard C. Rice, Jr. Chapel Hill: University of North Carolina Press, 1963.

Chilton, John. *Diary of John Chilton, 3rd VA Regiment.* Virginia Historical Society Mss10: no. 106. Diary, 1777 January 3–September 8. Also published as "The Old Virginia Line in the Middle States during the American Revolution. The Diary of Captain John Chilton, 3d Virginia Regt." *Tyler's Quarterly Magazine* XII (1931), 283–89.

Clinton, George. *Public Papers of George Clinton, First Governor of New York, 1777–1795—1801–1804.* Edited by Hugh Hastings. Albany: The State of New York, 1899–1914.

Collins, Varnum Lansing, ed. *A Brief Narrative of the Ravages of the British and Hessians at Princeton in 1776–77: A Contemporary Account of the Battles of Trenton and Princeton.* Princeton, NJ: Princeton University Library, 1906.

Cresswell, Nicholas. *The Journal of Nicholas Cresswell, 1774–1777.* 1924. Reprint, Port Washington, NY: Kennikat Press, 1968.

Custis, George Washington Parke. *Recollections and Private Memoirs of Washington.* New York: Derby & Jackson, 1860.

Cutler, William Parker, and Julia Perkins Cutler. *The Life, Journals, and Correspondence of Rev. Manasseh Cutler, LL.D.* Cincinnati, OH: Robert Clarke & Co., 1888.

Deane, Silas. *Correspondence of Silas Deane, Delegate to the First and Second Congress at Philadelphia, 1774–1776.* Hartford: Connecticut Historical Society, 1870.

Dowdeswell, Thomas. "The Operations in New Jersey: An English Officer Describes the Events of December 1776." Edited by J. E. Tyler. *Proceedings of the New Jersey Historical Society* 70 (1952), 133–36.

Ewald, Johann. *Diary of the American War: A Hessian Journal.* Edited and translated by Joseph P. Tustin. New Haven, CT: Yale University Press, c. 1979.

Fithian, Philip Vickers. *Philip Vickers Fithian, Journal and Letters, 1767–1774.* Edited by John Rogers Williams. Princeton, NJ: The University Library, 1900.

Graydon, Alexander. *Memoirs of His Own Times: With Reminiscences of the Men and Events of the Revolution.* Edited by John Stockton Littell. Philadelphia: Lindsay & Blakiston, 1846.

Greene, Nathanael. *The Papers of General Nathanael Greene.* Edited by Richard K. Showman. Chapel Hill: University of North Carolina Press, 1976.

Greenwood, John. *The Wartime Services of John Greenwood: A Young Patriot in the American Revolution, 1775–1783.* Edited by Isaac J. Greenwood. Tyrone, PA: Westvaco, 1981.

Hale, Capt. W. "Letters Written during the American War of Independence. By the late Capt. W. Hale, 45th Regt." In *1913 Regimental Annual. The Sherwood Foresters. Nottinghamshire and Derbyshire Regiment,* edited by Col. H. C. Wylly, 9–59. London: 1913.

[Hall, Capt. William C.]. *An Officer of the Army, The History of the Civil War in America.* Vol. 1. London: 1780. The "Officer" was Capt. William C. Hall of the 28th Regt. of Foot.

[Hood]. "Engagements at Trenton and Princeton, January 2 and 3, 1777." *The Pennsylvania Magazine of History and Biography* 10, no. 3 (Oct. 1886), 263.

How, David. *Diary of David How, a Private in Colonel Paul Dudley Sargent's Regiment of the Massachusetts Line, in the Army of the American Revolution.* Morrisania, NY: 1865.

Howe, William. *The Narrative of Lieut. Gen. Sir William Howe, in a Committee of the House of Commons, on the 29th of April, 1779, Relative to His Conduct, During His Late Command of the King's Troops in North America.* 3rd ed. London: H. Baldwin, 1781.

Hunter, Martin. "Martin Hunter's Journal: America, 1774–1778." Edited by Lawrence H. Curry. *The Valley Forge Journal* IV, no. 1 (June 1988), 20.

Inman, George. "George Inman's Narrative of the American Revolution." *The Pennsylvania Magazine of History and Biography* VII (1883), 237–48.

Kalm, Peter. *Travels into North America*. Translated by John Reinhold Forster. London: 1770.

Kemble, Stephen. "Kemble's Journal." *Collections of the New York Historical Society for the Year 1883*. New York: New York Historical Society, 1884.

Lee, Richard Henry. *Memoir of the Life of Richard Henry Lee, and His Correspondence with the Most Distinguished Men in America and Europe*. Philadelphia: H. C. Carey and I. Lea, 1825.

Linn, John Blair and William H. Egle, eds. "Diary of the Revolt in the Pennsylvania Line." *Pennsylvania Archives*. Ser. 2, XI: 659–762. Harrisburg: 1880.

Martin, Joseph Plumb. *Ordinary Courage: The Revolutionary War Adventures of Joseph Plumb Martin*. Edited by James Kirby Martin. Chichester, West Sussex, UK: Wiley-Blackwell, 2013.

McCarty, Thomas. "The Revolutionary War Journal of Sergeant Thomas McCarty." Edited by Jared C. Lobdell. *Proceedings of The New Jersey Historical Society* 82, no. 1 (January, 1964), 29–46.

McMichael, James. "Diary of Lieutenant James McMichael, of the Pennsylvania Line, 1776–1778." *Pennsylvania Magazine of History and Biography* 16 (1892), 129–59. Also *Pennsylvania Archives*. 2nd series, XIV, 195–218.

Miller, Lillian B., ed. *The Selected Papers of Charles Willson Peale and His Family*. New Haven: Yale University Press, c. 1983.

Moreau de Saint-Méry, M. L. E. (Médéric Louis Elie). *Moreau de St. Méry's American Journey (1793–1798)*. Edited and translated by Kenneth Roberts and Anna M. Roberts. Garden City, NY: Doubleday & Company, 1947.

Peale, Charles Willson. "The Artist-Soldier: A Chapter of the Revolution—Journal by Charles Wilson Peale." Edited by Rembrandt Peale. *The Crayon* III (1856), 37–40.

Powell, William S. "A Connecticut Soldier Under Washington: Elisha Bostwick's Memoirs of the First Years of the Revolution." *The William and Mary Quarterl*. 3rd Series, VI (Jan. 1949), 94–107.

Reed, Joseph. "General Joseph Reed's Narrative of the Movements of the American Army in the Neighborhood of Trenton in the Winter of 1776–77." *The Pennsylvania Magazine of History and Biography* VIII (1884), 391–402.

Reed, William B. *Life and Correspondence of Joseph Reed*. Philadelphia: Lindsay and Blakiston, 1847.

Robertson, Archibald. *Archibald Robertson: His Diaries and Sketches in America, 1762–1780*. Edited by Harry Miller Lydenberg. New York: The New York Public Library, 1930.

Rodney, Caesar. *Letters to and from Caesar Rodney, 1756–1784*. Edited by George Herbert Ryden. New York: DaCapo Press, 1970.

Rodney, Thomas. *Diary of Captain Thomas Rodney, 1776–1777*. Introduction by Caesar A. Rodney. Wilmington: The Historical Society of Delaware, 1888.

[Root, Nathaniel] Sergeant R---. "The Battle of Princeton." From *The Phoenix* of March 24, 1832, published at Wellsborough, PA. Also in *The Pennsylvania Magazine of History and Biography* XX (1896): 515–18.

Rush, Benjamin. *The Autobiography of Benjamin Rush: His Travels through Life Together with His Commonplace Book for 1789–1813*. Edited by George W. Corner. Westport, CT: Greenwood Press, 1970.

_____. *Letters of Benjamin Rush*. Edited by L. H. Butterfield. Philadelphia: American Philosophical Society, 1951.

_____. *My Dearest Julia: The Love Letters of Dr. Benjamin Rush to Julia Stockton*. New York: N. Watson Academic Publications, 1979.

____. *The Selected Writings of Benjamin Rush*. Edited by Dagobert D. Runes. New York: Philosophical Library, 1947.

Serle, Ambrose. *The American Journal of Ambrose Serle*. Edited by Edward H. Tatum, Jr. New York: New York Times, c. 1969.

Sheridan, Eugene R., and John M. Murrin, eds. *Congress at Princeton: Being the Letters of Charles Thomson to Hannah Thomson June–October 1783*. Princeton, NJ: Princeton University Library, 1985.

Smith, Sergeant John. "Sergeant John Smith's Diary of 1776." Edited by Louise Rau. *The Mississippi Valley Historical Review* 20, no. 2 (Sept., 1933), 247–70. Original pages are digitized online at http://www.americanantiquarian.org/.

Stiles, Ezra. *The Literary Diary of Ezra Stile*. Edited by Franklin Bowditch Dexter. New York: 1901.

Sullivan, John. *Letters and Papers of Major General John Sullivan Continental Army*. Edited by Otis. G. Hammond. Concord: The New Hampshire Historical Society, 1930.

Sullivan, Thomas. "The Battle of Princeton." *Pennsylvania Magazine of History and Biography*, XXXII, no. 1 (January 1908), 54–57.

____. *From Redcoat to Rebel: The Thomas Sullivan Journal*. Edited by Joseph Lee Boyle. Bowie, MD: Heritage Books, 1997.

Thacher, Dr. James. *A Military Journal During the American Revolutionary War, from 1775 to 1783*. Boston: Richardson and Lord, 1823.

Tyler, J. E. "The Operations in New Jersey. An English Officer Describes the Events of December, 1776." *Proceedings of the New Jersey Historical Society* (April 1952), 133–36.
White. Joseph. "The Good Soldier White." *American Heritage* VII no. 4 (June 1956), 73–79,

Wilkinson, General James. *Memoirs of My Own Times*. Philadelphia: Abraham Small, 1816.

Young, William. "Journal of Sergeant William Young Written during the Jersey Campaign of the Winter of 1776–77." *Pennsylvania Magazine of History and Biography*, VIII (1884), 255–78.

Secondary Sources

Baldwin, Charles Candee. *The Baldwin Genealogy, from 1500 to 1881*. Cleveland, OH: 1881.

Bamberg, Cherry Fletcher. "Bristol Yamma and John Quamine in Rhode Island." *Rhode Island History* 73, no. 1 (winter/spring 2015), 2–31.

Berg, Fred Anderson. *Encyclopedia of Continental Army Units: Battalions, Regiments, and Independent Corps.* Harrisburg, PA: Stackpole Books, 1972.

Bill, Alfred Hoyt, and Walter E. Edge. *A House Called Morven: Its Role in American History, 1701–1954.* Princeton, NJ: Princeton University Press, 1954.

Bowler, R. Arthur. *Logistics and the Failure of the British Army in America: 1775–1783.* Princeton, NJ: Princeton University Press, 1975.

Bradley, Kevin, Wade P. Catts, and Robert Selig. *"Cheer Up My Boys the Day Is Ours...": Field Survey, Preparation of Maps, and Preparation of Local and National Landmark/National Register Historic District Applications for the D'Ambrisi Property, Princeton, New Jersey* (Draft). West Chester, PA: Commonwealth Heritage Group, 2017.

Butterfield, L. H. "Morven: A Colonial Outpost of Sensibility. With Some Hitherto Unpublished Poems by Annis Boudinot Stockton." *The Princeton University Library Chronicle*, VI, no. 1 (November 1944), 1–16.

Carp, E. Wayne. *To Starve the Army at Pleasure: Continental Army Administration and American Political Culture, 1775–1783.* Chapel Hill: University of North Carolina Press, 1984.

Cohen, Sheldon S. and Larry R. Gerlach. "Princeton in the Coming of the American Revolution." *Princeton Alumni Weekly* 76, no. 7 (November 10, 1975), 6–13.

Collins, Varnum Lansing. *The Continental Congress at Princeton.* Princeton, NJ: Princeton University Library, 1908.

_____. "Indian Wards at Princeton." *Princeton University Bulletin*, XIII (1901), 101–06.

_____. *Princeton.* New York: Oxford University Press, 1914.

_____. *Princeton Past and Present.* Princeton, NJ: Princeton University Press, 1945.

_____. *President Witherspoon.* New York: Arno Press & The New York Times, 1969.

Creesy, Virginia Kays. "The Battle of Princeton: An Encounter in a Farmer's field 200 Years Ago Changed the Course of the Revolution," *Princeton Alumni Weekly* 77 (Dec. 6, 1976), 12–20.

Cutter, William. *The Life of Israel Putnam: Major-General in the Army of the American Revolution.* New York: G. F. Cooledge, 1848.

Davis, William W. H. *History of Bucks County, Pennsylvania.* New York: Lewis, 1905.

Duncan, Lewis Casper. *Medical Men in the American Revolution, 1775–1783.* New York: A. M. Kelley, 1970.

Dunlap, William. *A History of the Rise and Progress of the Arts of Design in the United States.* Boston: C. E. Goodspeed & Co., 1918.

Dwyer, William M. *The Day Is Ours! November 1776–January 1777: An Inside View of the Battles of Trenton and Princeton.* New York: Viking Press, 1983.

Ege, Ralph. *Pioneers of Old Hopewell: With Sketches of Her Revolutionary Heroes.* Hopewell, NJ: Race & Savage, 1908.

Egle, William H. "The Constitutional Convention of 1776: Biographical Sketches of Its Members." *The Pennsylvania Magazine of History and Biography* III (1879), 438-446.

English, Frederick. *General Hugh Mercer: Forgotten Hero of the American Revolution*. New York: Vantage Press, 1975.

Epstein, Daniel Mark. *The Loyal Son: The War in Ben Franklin's House*. New York: Ballantine Books, 2017.

Ferling, John. *Almost a Miracle: The American Victory in the War of Independence*. New York: Oxford University Press, 2007.

_____. *A Leap in the Dark: The Struggle to Create the American Republic*. New York: Oxford University Press, 2004.

Fischer, David Hackett. *Washington's Crossing*. Oxford, UK: Oxford University Press, 2004.

Fried, Stephen. *Rush: Revolution, Madness, and the Visionary Doctor Who Became a Founding Father*. New York: Crown, 2018.

Gerlach, Larry R. *New Jersey in the American Revolution, 1763–1783: A Documentary History*. Trenton: New Jersey Historical Commission, 1975.

Gigantino, James J. *The Ragged Road to Abolition: Slavery and Freedom in New Jersey, 1775–1865*. Philadelphia: University of Pennsylvania Press, 2015.

_____. *William Livingston's American Revolution*. Philadelphia: University of Pennsylvania Press, 2018.

Gilchrist, Marianne McLeod. "The Tragedy of Captain William Leslie and Dr. Benjamin Rush." *The Loyalist Gazette* XXXVII (1999), 25–30.

Gillett, Mary C. *The Army Medical Department, 1775–1818*. Washington, DC: Center of Military History United States Army, 2004.

Glenn, Thomas Allen. *William Churchill Houston, 1746–1788*. Norristown, PA: 1903.

Gratz, Simon. "Thomas Rodney." *The Pennsylvania Magazine of History and Biography*, XLIII (1919), 1–23.

Green, Ashbel. *The Life of Ashbel Green, V.D.M.* Edited by Joseph H. Jones. New York: Robert Carter and Brothers, 1849.

Green, Ashbel. *The Life of the Revd John Witherspoon, D.D., LL.D.* Princeton, NJ: Princeton University Press, 1973.

Greiff, Constance M., Mary W. Gibbons, and Elizabeth G. C. Menzies. *Princeton Architecture: A Pictorial History of Town and Campus*. Princeton, NJ: Princeton University Press, 1967.

Greiff, Constance M., and Wanda S. Gunning. *Morven: Memory, Myth, and Reality*. Princeton, NJ: Historic Morven, Inc., 2004.

Gruber, Ira D. *The Howe Brothers and the American Revolution*. New York: Atheneum, c. 1972.

Hageman, John Frelinghuysen. *History of Princeton and Its Institutions*. Philadelphia: J. B. Lippincott & Co., 1879.

Hall, John. *History of the First Presbyterian Church in Trenton from the First Settlement of the Town*. Trenton, NJ: MacCrellish & Quigley, 1912.

Harrison, Richard A. *Princetonians, 1769–1775: A Biographical Dictionary*. Vol. II. Princeton, NJ: Princeton University Press, 1981.

Harrison, Richard A. *Princetonians, 1776–1783: A Biographical Dictionary*. Vol. III. Princeton, NJ: Princeton University Press, 1981.

Hatfield, Edwin F. "Jonathan Dickinson Sergeant." *The Pennsylvania Magazine of History and Biography*, II (1878), 438–42.

Haven, Charles Chauncy. *Thirty Days in New Jersey Ninety Years Ago: An Essay Revealing New Facts in Connection with Washington and His Army in 1776 and 1777*. Trenton: 1867.

Jamison, Wallace N. *Religion in New Jersey: A Brief History*. Princeton, NJ: Van Nostrand, 1964.

Kasden, Izzy. "The Manumission of Prime." *Princeton & Slavery Project* at https://slavery.princeton.edu/stories/the-manumission-of-prime

Keen, Gregory B. "The Descendants of Joran Kyn, the Founder of Upland." *The Pennsylvania Magazine of History and Biography* IV (1880), 343–60.

Kidder, Larry. *A People Harassed and Exhausted: The Story of a New Jersey Militia Regiment in the American Revolution*. 2013.

Kidder, William L. *Crossroads of the Revolution: Trenton, 1774–1783*. Lawrence Township, NJ: The Knox Press, 2017.

_____. *Ten Crucial Days: Washington's Vision for Victory Unfolds*. Lawrence Township, NJ: The Knox Press, 2019.

Klepp, Susan E., Farley Grubb, and Anne Pfaelzer de Ortiz, eds. *Souls for Sale: Two German Redemptioners Come to Revolutionary America: The Life Stories of John Frederick Whitehead and Johann Carl Büttner*. University Park: Pennsylvania State University Press, c. 2006.

Lefkowitz, Arthur S. *The Long Retreat: The Calamitous American Defense of New Jersey, 1776*. New Brunswick, NJ: Rutgers University Press, 1998.

Leitch, Alexander. *A Princeton Companion*. Princeton, NJ: Princeton University Press, 1978.

Livingston, William Farrand. *Israel Putnam: Pioneer, Ranger, and Major General, 1718–1790*. New York: G. P. Putnam's Sons, 1901.

Lossing, B. J. *Pictorial Field Book of the Revolution*. New York: Harper & Bros., 1860.

Ludlum, David M. "The Weather of Independence." *Weatherwise* 51, VI (Nov/Dec. 1998): 38–44.

Lundin, Leonard. *Cockpit of the Revolution: The War for Independence in New Jersey*. New York: Octagon Books, 1972 [reprint of 1940 edition].

Maclean, John. *History of the College of New Jersey: From Its Origin in 1746 to the Commencement of 1854*. Philadelphia: J. B. Lippincott, 1877.

Magee, Fannie S. "Major John Polhemus." *American Monthly Magazine* IX (July–Dec. 1896).

McBurney, Christian M. "The Battle of Bennett's Island: the New Jersey Site Rediscovered." *Journal of the American Revolution* (July 10, 2017) at allthingsliberty.com.

_____. "Was Richard Stockton a Hero?" *Journal of the American Revolution* (July 18, 2016) at allthingsliberty.com.

McLachlan, James. *Princetonians, 1748–1768: A Biographical Dictionary*. Vol. I. Princeton, NJ: Princeton University Press, 1977.

Moon, Robert C. *The Morris Family of Philadelphia: Descendants of Anthony Morris, 1654–1721.* Philadelphia: Robert C. Moon, 1898.

Mulford, Carla, ed. *Only for the Eye of a Friend: The Poems of Annis Boudinot Stockton.* Charlottesville: University of Virginia Press, 1995.

Nagy, John A. *Rebellion in the Ranks: Mutinies of the American Revolution.* Yardley, PA: Westholme, 2008.

O'Connor, John E. *William Paterson: Lawyer and Statesman, 1745–1806.* New Brunswick, NJ: Rutgers University Press, 1979.

Pomfret, John E. *Colonial New Jersey: A History.* New York: Charles Scribner's Sons, 1973.

Rice, Howard C. *The Rittenhouse Orrery: Princeton's Eighteenth-Century Planetarium, 1767–1954.* Princeton, NJ: Princeton University Library, 1954.

Rogers, Mrs. Harry and Mrs. A. H. Lane. "Pennsylvania Pensioners of the Revolution." *The Pennsylvania Magazine of History and Biography* XLII (1918), 259–77.

Ryan, Dennis P., ed. *A Salute to Courage: The American Revolution as Seen Through Wartime Writings of Officers of the Continental Army and Navy.* New York: Columbia University Press, 1979.

Savelle, Max. *George Morgan, Colony Builder.* New York: Columbia University Press, 1932.

Schmidt, George P. *Princeton and Rutgers: The Two Colonial Colleges of New Jersey.* Princeton, NJ: D. Van Nostrand Company, Inc., 1964.

Selig, Robert A., Matthew Harris, and Wade P. Catts. *Battle of Princeton Mapping Project: Report of Military Terrain Analysis and Battle Narrative, Princeton, New Jersey.* West Chester, PA: John Milner Associates, 2010.

Sellers, Horace Wells. "Charles Willson Peale, Artist-Soldier." *The Pennsylvania Magazine of History and Biography* XXXVIII (1914), 257–86.

Smith, Samuel Stelle. *The Battle of Princeton.* 1967. Reprint, Yardley, PA: Westholme, 2009.

Stille, Charles J. *Major-General Anthony Wayne and the Pennsylvania Line in the Continental Army.* Port Washington, NY: Kennikat Press, 1968.

Stockton, Richard. "An Expedient for the Settlement of the American Disputes Humbly Submitted to the Consideration of His Majesty's Ministers by an American." *The Historical Magazine*, ser. 2, vol. 4 no. 5 (November 1868), 228–29.

Stone, Edwin M. *The Life and Recollections of John Howland: Late President of the Rhode Island Historical Society.* Providence, RI: George H. Whitney, 1857.

Stratford, Dorothy Agans, and Thomas B. Wilson. *Certificates and Receipts of Revolutionary New Jersey.* Lambertville, NJ: Hunterdon House, 1996.

Stryker, William S. *The Battles of Trenton and Princeton.* Boston: Houghton, Mifflin, and Company, 1898.

Stryker-Rodda, Kenn. "New Jersey Rateables, 1778–1780, Middlesex County, Windsor Township, June 1778 and February 1780." *The Genealogical Magazine of New Jersey* 51, no. 3 (September 1976), 124–33.

Stryker-Rodda, Kenn. "New Jersey Rateables, 1778-1780, Somerset County, Western Precinct, May 1779 and May 1780." *The Genealogical Magazine of New Jersey* 53, no. 3 (September 1978), 108–16.

Waterman, Joseph M. *With Sword and Lancet: The Life of General Hugh Mercer*. Richmond, VA: Garrett and Massie, 1941.

Wertenbaker, Thomas J. "The College of New Jersey and the Presbyterian Church" *The Journal of Presbyterian History* 76, no. 1 (spring 1998), 31–35.

_____. *Princeton, 1746–1896*. Princeton, NJ: Princeton University Press, 1946.

Wickes, Stephen. *History of Medicine in New Jersey*. Newark, DE: M. R. Dennis, 1879.

Widmer, Kemble. *The Christmas Campaign: The Ten Days of Trenton and Princeton*. Trenton: New Jersey Historical Commission, 1975.

Williams, Catherine R. *Biography of Revolutionary Heroes: Containing the Life of Brigadier Gen. William Barton, and Also, of Captain Stephen Olney*. Providence, RI: Mrs. Catherine Williams, 1839.

Woodward, E. M., and John Frelinghuysen Hageman. *History of Burlington and Mercer Counties, New Jersey: With Biographical Sketches of Many of Their Pioneers and Prominent Men*. Philadelphia: Everts & Peck, 1883.

Woodward, Ruth L., and Wesley Frank Craven. *Princetonians, 1784–1790: A Biographical Dictionary*. Vol. IV. Princeton, NJ: Princeton University Press, 1991.

Wright, Giles R., "Prime: Another Resident of Bainbridge House." *Princeton History* 10 (1991), 60–70.

Wright, Robert K., Jr. *The Continental Army*. Washington, DC: Center of Military History, U.S. Army: 1983.

Yannielli, Joseph, "Princeton and Slavery: African Americans on Campus, 1746–1876," at https://slavery.princeton.edu/stories/african-americans-on-campus-1746-1876

D

I

J

K

N

Note on the Author

William L. Kidder, universally known as Larry, was born in California and raised in California, Indiana, New York, and New Jersey. He received his bachelor's and master's degrees from Allegheny College in Meadville, Pennsylvania.

Larry is a retired high school history teacher who taught for forty years in both public and private schools. He considers teaching to be both his vocation and avocation. During his 32 years of teaching at The Hun School of Princeton he enjoyed designing courses that gave his students the opportunity to develop the thinking, research, and writing skills that result from "doing history" and not just learning facts for a test.

Larry served four years of active duty in the US Navy and was assigned to the US Navy Research and Development Unit, Vietnam and then the destroyer USS Brownson (DD868) homeported in Newport, Rhode Island. In the 1980s he was the lead researcher and writer for the creation of the Admiral Arleigh Burke National Destroyermen's Museum aboard the destroyer museum ship USS Joseph P. Kennedy, Jr. (DD850) at Battleship Cove in Fall River, Massachusetts.

For over thirty years, Larry has been a volunteer at the Howell Living History Farm, part of the Mercer County Park System, in Hopewell, New Jersey. For varying lengths of time he has volunteered as an historian, interpreter, webmaster, and draft horse teamster. This interest led to the writing of his first book that tells the story of the local schoolhouse that is now part of the Howell Living History Farm and is also a case study of a rural school in central New Jersey from the early 19th to the mid-20th century.

Active in historical societies in Ewing, Hopewell, and Lawrence townships, Larry has given a number of talks on local history to a variety of civic groups. He is also a volunteer for the Crossroads of the American Revolution National Heritage Area, coordinating its Meet Your Revolutionary Neighbors project. He is a member of the board of the Princeton Battlefield Society and has developed tours of the Princeton Battlefield for both adults and children. He is a member of the board of TheTenCrucialDays.org, an organization dedicated to promoting the historic sites associated with the Ten Crucial Days and educating the public about them. He is an avid member of the Association for Living History, Farm, and Agricultural Museums (ALHFAM), the Washington's Crossing Roundtable of the American Revolution, and the New Jersey Living History Advisory Council.

He can be contacted by email at larrykidder@gmail.com and his website is at wlkidderhistorian.com.

Relive the "Ten Crucial Days" of the American Revolution

Visit these historic sites:

Washington Crossing Historic Park

This Pennsylvania state park and National Historic Landmark is where General George Washington's army began its epic crossing of the Delaware River the night of December 25-26, 1776, the beginning of the Ten Crucial Days which may have saved our nation's quest for independence when the American Revolution appeared all but lost. The park offers a visitor center and more than 500 acres of American history, natural beauty, and family fun.

Washington Crossing State Park

This New Jersey state park lies opposite its Pennsylvania sister and is part of the same National Historic Landmark. It is the site where Washington's army landed and began its march to attack the Hessian brigade occupying Trenton. This 3,500-acre park is also well known for its trails and wildlife habitat.

Old Barracks Museum

This museum in Trenton dates back to 1758, when it was built to house British soldiers during the French and Indian War. It helps visitors understand the two battles at Trenton on December 26, 1776 and January 2, 1777. Its history as a military quarters to a widow's home and from a brothel to a museum offers visitors a fascinating look at the history of the area.

Princeton Battlefield

This New Jersey state park is where the Battle of Princeton was fought on January 3, 1777 - the capstone event of the "Ten Crucial Days" that altered the course of the war. The 1772 Thomas Clarke House witnessed the battle and served as sanctuary for the wounded General Hugh Mercer, who died there nine days later. The house contains period furniture and Revolutionary War exhibits.

Learn more about these historic sites at:

www.tencrucialdays.org

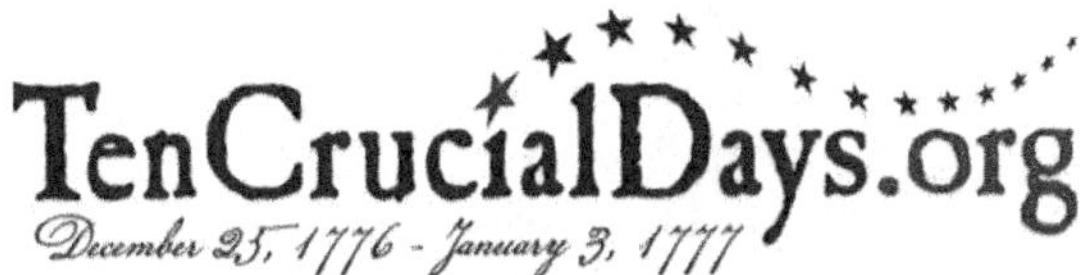

KnoxPress.com